Fashions of the Early Twenties

Fashions of the Early Twenties

The 1921 Philipsborn's Catalog

Philipsborn's

Dover Publications, Inc.
Mineola, New York

Copyright

Copyright © 1996 by Dover Publications, Inc.
All rights reserved under Pan American and International Copyright Conventions.

Published in Canada by General Publishing Company, Ltd., 30 Lesmill Road, Don Mills, Toronto, Ontario.
Published in the United Kingdom by Constable and Company, Ltd., 3 The Lanchesters, 162-164 Fulham Palace Road, London W6 9ER.

Bibliographical Note

Fashions of the Early Twenties: The 1921 Philipsborn's Catalog, first published by Dover Publications, Inc., in 1996, is a republication of *Philipsborn's Style and Shopping Guide, Vol. 39, No. 3, January 1921,* originally published by Philipsborn's, Chicago in 1921. One copy each of the order form and fitting instructions has been omitted and the following pages renumbered. With the exception of the illustrations reproduced in color on the covers of the present edition, illustrations appearing in color in the original are here reproduced in black and white. A new Publisher's Note has been written specially for the Dover Edition.

Library of Congress Cataloging-in-Publication Data

Fashions of the early twenties : the 1921 Philipsborn's catalog / Philipsborn's.
    p.   cm.
  Originally published: Philipsborn's style and shopping guide, vol. 39, no. 3, January 1921.
   ISBN 0-486-29385-8 (pbk.)
   1. Clothing and dress—Catalogs. 2. Philipsborn's (Department store)—Catalogs. I. Philipsborn's (Department store)
TT555.F33 1996
381'.45687'029477311—dc20
                                   96-27377
                                      CIP

Manufactured in the United States of America
Dover Publications, Inc., 31 East 2nd Street, Mineola, N.Y. 11501

Publisher's Note

In 1921, the 31-year-old company Philipsborn's in Chicago billed itself as "the fastest growing mail order house in America." It offered yard goods, men's and boy's clothing, children's wear and hats and shoes for the entire family, but, in this catalog at least, concentrated on moderately priced women's clothes. While style is not ignored—Philipsborn recruited popular ballroom, stage and film star Irene Castle to "design" a line of clothing for them—the emphasis is on value. The company had prepaid delivery charges, touted their low prices in much of the copy and offered a number of manufacturer's closeouts. In fact, the company guaranteed that their prices were "lower than the prices asked for the same goods anywhere else in the United States."

The clothes shown in the catalog are for day wear, although many of them are quite dressy, being embellished with beads or embroidery. For more casual wear, several pages are devoted to house dresses. Although the clothes are not generally described as being for specific functions, a few garments are listed as being suitable for mourning (pages 20 and 48). These are available in black, of course, but two of them are also available in gray for "second mourning," a concept that already seemed old-fashioned and was soon to disappear forever.

The 1920s saw an acceleration of the fashion changes begun in the teens. By the second decade of the century, the elegant Edwardian look, with its extreme "S-curve" stance, was being replaced with a freer, looser silhouette, with less restricting corsets, lower necklines and higher hemlines. The labor shortages of the war years saw women entering the work force at unprecedented rates, women who needed even less restrictive and more practical clothing. After the war, women were unwilling to give up this new freedom and a "defeminization" of the fashion silhouette took place as women bobbed their hair and flattened their figures in their efforts to prove their equality with men.

The tubular look that would define the decade's silhouette is already apparent in this catalog, although hemlines are still hovering below the calf. Although, in fact, the belts on most garments are at the natural waist, the prevalence of tunics, overblouses and free-hanging panels, together with the easy fit of the garments, give a hint of the long-waisted look to come.

Necklines are open, either round or square, with a very occasional "V." Many—in fact, the majority—of dresses feature a matching or contrasting "vestee," cut straight across and worn under a tuxedo collar or other type of collar. Sleeves have a smooth cap and are either tightly or somewhat more loosely fitted, with no fullness apparent. Many styles have kimono sleeves, cut in one with the bodice. Most garments are available in more than one color, with navy, often with contrasting trim, far and away the most commonly mentioned color.

Women's suits generally feature a long (below the hip) jacket, often loosely belted, with long slim sleeves and a slim skirt. Embroidery and braid were popular trimming choices.

In coats, wrap styles with large cape collars seem most popular. Although many coats appear somewhat top-heavy, being wider at the shoulders than at the hem, straight and flared styles are also shown. Two different lengths were popular—full length (the same length as dresses) and a new three-quarter sport length. Waterproof raincoats, in styles not too far removed from the still popular trench coat, are also shown.

Philipsborn's offered a wide variety of hats "direct from the boulevards of Paris," from wide-brimmed hats trimmed with feathers or flowers, to straight-brimmed sailor hats, to hats with turned-back brims. The close-fitting, bell-shaped cloche, so closely identified with the decade, has not yet made an appearance.

The pump was the most popular dress shoe, usually shown with straps, a slightly pointed toe and a Louis or a Cuban heel. Several examples of the "Egyptian anklet tie pump" can be seen. Black was the most common color for shoes, but by no means the only choice. Brown and gray were also popular, and, as befitting a spring/summer catalog, several pages are devoted to white shoes. Oxfords, dress and work boots and heavy service shoes are also offered, as are shoes for children and men.

In addition to corsets, corset covers, petticoats and camisoles, more modern undergarments such as breast confiners, envelope chemises (a combination of chemise and knickers) and step-in drawers are shown. White was no longer the only color choice for undergarments. Pink had replaced it in popularity, and on pages 195–197, a selection of vividly colored petticoats is offered. Japanese kimonos and pajamas for women are featured prominently. Also featured is a page (page 208) devoted to "sanitary products." Both cotton and silk hose are offered in black and a surprisingly wide variety of colors including white, brown, navy and gray.

Despite its emphasis on women's clothing, Philipsborn's did not neglect the rest of the family, featuring a full, if less extensive, line of clothing for children, young girls, boys and men.

The Philipsborn's catalog was not directed to the wealthy and fashionable, but to the style-conscious, and, more importantly, the price-conscious middle class. It offers a firsthand look at what the majority of Americans were actually wearing at the beginning of the 1920s.

Mary Carolyn Waldrep, Editor

Spring & Summer

1921

America's Best Styles   America's Lowest Prices

PHILIPSBORN'S

Chicago   Illinois

Irene Castle - Designer and Sponsor for
PHILIPSBORN'S
Styles in the greatest Triumph of her career

HAT
3K5202
$4.98

HAT
3K5201
$3.98

8K13300 *Fashionable CASTLE-designed blouse dress of chiffon taffeta silk.* Blouse has contrasting embroidery both front and back. Knife-plaited skirt. Tasseled sash belt. Very rich and dressy. COLORS: Tan with brown or navy blue with copenhagen blue embroidery. SIZES: 32 to 44 bust, 38 to 40 skirt length. PRICE, PREPAID to your home, **$15.98**

8K13301 For misses and small women. SIZES: 32 to 38 bust. PRICE, PREPAID to your home, **$15.98**

8K13302 *An exclusive IRENE CASTLE design in a charming new tricotine dress.* Front of blouse embroidery,—long hip effect. Ruching as shown. Novelty chain belt. Group of box plaits down front and back of skirt. COLOR: Navy blue. SIZES: 32 to 44 bust. Skirt length 38 to 40. PRICE, PREPAID to your home, **$18.98**

8K13303 For misses and small women. SIZES: 32 to 38 bust. PRICE, PREPAID to your home, **$18.98**

3K5201 *Colorful wool embroidery makes this hat extremely effective.* It has a beautiful caterpillar straw brim combined with a taffeta crown. Wool embroidery across front. Silk grosgrain ribbon. COLORS: Copenhagen blue with sand brim; navy blue crown with burnt orange brim; black crown with peacock blue brim; or all black. PRICE, PREPAID to your home, **$3.98**

3K5202 *A charming dress hat—very new of line and distinctly low priced.* Developed in Georgette crepe and Batavia cloth. Trimmed with fine quality satin and velvet applique flowers and silk grosgrain ribbon. All wool embroidery at front of crown. Very dressy. COLORS: American beauty red as illustrated or black, white or navy blue. PRICE PREPAID, to your home, **$4.98**

8K13302
ALL WOOL
TRICOTINE
$18.98
WORTH
$22.50

8K13300
CHIFFON
TAFFETA
SILK
$15.98
WORTH
$20.00

Be sure to state size
and color

"PHILIPSBORN'S" Style and Shopping Guide
Vol. 39, No. 3. January, 1921.

PHILIPSBORN'S

THE GREATEST POWER IN THE WORLD

The Power of Public Opinion—which is YOUR opinion
multiplied by millions—has made PHILIPSBORN'S

THE FASTEST GROWING MAIL ORDER HOUSE IN AMERICA

The one big thing behind this marvelous record is the big, broad PHILIPSBORN POLICY of giving you not only more in style, more in service but actually more in savings than you can get anywhere else.

PHILIPSBORN'S Set Aside Half a Million Dollars a Year to Carry Out This Policy of

Giving More In Savings, for the Prepaying of Delivery Charges Alone!

We don't ask you to send us 4c extra for a waist, whether it is made of light voile or heavy satin; 8c for a dress, whether it is made of heavy wool material or light weight silk georgette; 14c extra for a suit, whether it is made with a long or short coat, whether the material is heavy or light weight; 15c extra for a coat, whether it is a short jacket or a long coat, etc., etc. You pay only the Catalog price—NOT A PENNY MORE.

ONE PRICE TO ALL—PHILIPSBORN'S POLICY

Is sweeping the Country. That is one of the big things — that has influenced public opinion for PHILIPSBORN'S — that has enabled us to add one million new customers during the last year — a record which speaks for itself particularly when the general unsettled economic conditions of the last six months of 1920 are taken into consideration.

LAST MINUTE PRICES on EVERYTHING

Probably this book will reach you a few weeks later than our usual Spring edition—it was purposely delayed to take advantage of the markets "very-last-minute" price reduction. We know our low prices will amaze you. *We guarantee that they are lower than the prices asked for the same goods anywhere else in the United States. We stand back of this statement to the very letter.* If at any time you can buy the same quality elsewhere for less money we will immediately make good the difference. We make this statement without fear because we know that, if you will compare PHILIPSBORN'S prices with those in any catalog or retail store you will readily understand the cause of our remarkable growth. Our Policy Calls for small Profits and Large Turnover so don't be afraid to order on account of our low prices. Remember!—Everything is backed by the PHILIPSBORN GUARANTEE which means that you must be 100% satisfied, and if you are not your money will be refunded instantly. We particularly call your attention to PAGES 250 to 255 DEVOTED TO OUR NEW "GOODS-BY-THE-YARD" DEPARTMENT. The values speak for themselves. Put this department to the test!

A THING or TWO to REMEMBER

Be sure to state catalog number!
Be sure to state Color and Size!
Be sure to send your remittance by express or postal money order and avoid, if possible, sending cash or stamps!

We do ship orders C. O. D. when so requested, but we caution you of the extra shipping and collection charges. If the order blanks in back of the book are not sufficient, write for additional ones!

Irene Castle's exclusive designs are featured on many pages throughout this catalog.
Turn to the Index, Page 274, for a complete list. Loan your catalog to your friends and neighbors.

If you receive more than one catalog, please write us, giving us the correct name and initials of the head of the family.

It is our aim to have one PHILIPSBORN Catalog in every home in America.

The joy of Spring was Irene Castle's Inspiration for this design

8K13304 *All that is lovely and captivating in style is reflected in this latest creation from the hands of Irene Castle, our famous style expert.*

Through a special arrangement with Irene Castle, PHILIPS-BORN'S can now offer their customers the services of this master designer, at a price that is actually less than you would pay for ordinary styles elsewhere. For this beautiful dress Irene Castle used **taffeta silk** of excellent weight, and combined it with an ecru lace panel and vestee. The design is a clever adaptation of the Redingote style now so much favored by fashionable women. The especially new note is seen in the kimono style sleeve finished with turnover cuffs and terminating at the elbow. The skirt portion opens over the lace in panel fashion and is smartly sloped away at the sides to reveal the lace and taffeta silk underdress. The vestee of lace shows the same rich pattern as the skirt panel and is finished with a wide taffeta silk fold. A narrow velvet ribbon girdle provides the newest of waistline finishes. Light waist lining. One of the dressiest and most charming of models at a big price saving. COLOR: Navy blue with ecru lace or brown with ecru lace. SIZES: 32 to 44 bust. Skirt length 38 to 40. Skirt width (underdress) 52 inches.

PRICE, PREPAID to your home, **$16.98**

8K13305 Same style for misses and small women. SIZES: 32 to 38 bust. Skirt length 32 to 38. Skirt width (underdress) 52 inches.

PRICE, PREPAID to your home, **$16.98**

HOW TO ORDER

In ordering Women's and Misses' Dresses, state bust measure, size of waistband, and front length of skirt. For larger size than 44 bust, refer to Our Styles for Stout Women.

TAFFETA
SILK
8K13304
8K13305
$16.98

PHILIPSBORN'S

'P's & 'Q's are 'Price' & 'Quality'

Here are Two Examples

HOW TO ORDER

In ordering dresses for women and misses, be sure to state bust measure, size of waistband, and front length of skirt. IT IS IMPORTANT TO GIVE ALL THREE MEASUREMENTS. Also, do not order a larger size than is catalogued, but for these refer to our stout sizes. See index, page 274.

8K13306 *Every one who has seen this beautiful dress has been most enthusiastic in its praise, declaring that it is the most stunning model offered this season.*

All in all it is a triumph of design to which the excellent quality **taffeta silk** of which it is made lends itself beautifully. The new cut-work embroidery which will be used on the season's high-priced models contributes a rich and handsome trimming. Contrasting broadcloth outlined with tinsel threads is appliqued in lavish design at both front and back. The dress is designed in over-dress fashion with front panel and side sections, giving the fashionable extended hipline so much favored. Elbow length sleeves. All-around belt. Fastening at shoulder and underarm. COLORS: Navy blue with henna or brown with tan. SIZES: 32 to 44 bust. Front length of skirt 38 to 40.
PRICE, PREPAID to your home, **$18.98**

8K13307 For misses and small women. SIZES: 32 to 38 bust. Front length of skirt 32 to 38.
PRICE, PREPAID to your home, **$18.98**

8K13308 *Here is a new dress that will be greatly admired for its unusual and artistic style, an exclusive PHILIPSBORN'S model quoted at a special cut price.*

Taffeta silk of rich, lustrous quality combines with **Georgette crepe** to fashion this most attractive of models. Contrasting bugle beads are used to embroider the smartly shaped overblouse. Sash ties at sides. Georgette sleeves finished with flare cuffs. Plaited Georgette side panels. Self-material button trimming. COLORS: Navy blue or all black. SIZES: 32 to 44 bust. Front length of skirt 38 to 40.
PRICE, PREPAID to your home, **$12.78**

8K13309 Same style for misses and small women. SIZES: 32 to 38 bust. Front length of skirt 32 to 38.
PRICE, PREPAID to your home. **$12.78**

Be sure to state COLOR and SIZE when ordering

SILK TAFFETA
AND GEORGETTE
8K13308
8K13309
$12.78

TAFFETA SILK
8K13306
8K13307
$18.98

CHICAGO, ILL.

For Index See Page 274 and Remember PHILIPSBORN'S Prepay All Transportation Charges. There Are No Express or Mailing Charges for You to Pay.

5

3 Generations of PHILIPSBORN Shoppers - 31 years of Service

Descriptions for Page 7

8K13312 *Stunning new color combinations distinguish this rich* **taffeta silk dress.**

Gold tinsel embroidery appears in lavish design on the gathered overskirt and sleeves. Contrasting plaited Georgette is used for the smart, wedge-shaped vestee, the round collar and cuffs. Sash belt. Ribbon tie. Seco silk lining. COLORS: Navy blue and brick, or brown and tan. SIZES: 32 to 44 bust. Length 38 to 40 inches.
PRICE, PREPAID to your home, **$18.98**

8K13313 For misses and small women. SIZES: 32 to 38 bust. Length 32 to 38 inches.
PRICE, PREPAID to your home, **$18.98**

8K13314 *Altogether new and distinctive is the design of this PHILIPSBORN'S dress.*

Developed in a rich quality of **silk crepe de chine.** Close set rows of self-cording form a deep border at the bottom of the tunic, the deep bell cuffs, and Tuxedo collar cord trimmed to match. Lace vestee with contrasting silk braid. Wide, crushed girdle with flower ornament. Seco silk lining. COLORS: Taupe grey, navy blue, or black. SIZES: 32 to 44 bust. Length 38 to 40 inches.
PRICE, PREPAID to your home, **$16.98**

8K13315 For misses and small women. SIZES: 32 to 38 bust. Length 32 to 38 inches.
PRICE, PREPAID to your home, **$16.98**

8K13316 *This handsome* **silk Georgette** *dress is indeed a real bargain at our price.*

You can pay $5.00 and $10.00 more in the shops and not get one bit better style or material. Elaborately trimmed with iridescent beads on long overskirt and blouse. Ruffle-trimmed three-quarter length sleeves. Seco silk lining. Extremely dressy. COLORS: Navy blue or Taupe. SIZES: 32 to 44 bust. Length 38 to 40 inches.
PRICE, PREPAID to your home, **$14.78**

8K13317 For misses and small women. SIZES: 32 to 38 bust. Length 32 to 38 inches.
PRICE, PREPAID to your home, **$14.78**

IMPORTANT!
Be sure to state COLOR and SIZE when ordering

8K13310 *Certainly, for dressy wear, there is nothing more elegant than* **silk Georgette.**

The beautiful dress pictured at the left adds to its fascination with elaborate bead embroidery, which appears in garland-like strands on both the skirt and blouse. Wide three-quarter length sleeves. Silk lining. A dress that is never out of season, as it can be worn both summer and winter. COLORS: Navy blue, French blue, pearl grey, or flesh. SIZES: 32 to 44 bust. Length 38 to 40 inches.
PRICE, PREPAID to your home, **$16.98**

8K13311 For misses and small women. SIZES: 32 to 38 bust. Length 32 to 38 inches.
PRICE, PREPAID to your home, **$16.98**

A YEAR AGO, DRESSES OF THIS CHARACTER WOULD HAVE SOLD FOR $30.00.

OUR SPECIAL PRICE

$16.98

SILK GEORGETTE
8K13310
8K13311

6

PHILIPSBORN'S

GOLD EMBR'D
SILK TAFFETA
8K13312
8K13313
$18.98

SILK CREPE
DE CHINE
8K13314
8K13315
$16.98

SILK
GEORGETTE
8K13316
8K13317
$14.78

For Descriptions See Page 6

For a Complete List of Irene Castle's Exclusive Designs,
See the Index, Page 274

8K13318 *Beauty of line and material sets this beautiful dress of* **taffeta silk** *apart from ordinary styles.*
Draped bodice and five straps all embroidered in gold tinsel. Net collar and cuffs. Skirt width 52 inches. COLORS: Reseda green and gold or navy blue with gold. SIZES: 32 to 44 bust; skirt lengths 38 to 40 inches. PRICE, PREPAID. **$16.98**

8K13319 For misses and small women. SIZES: 32 to 38 bust; 32 to 38 inches skirt lengths. PRICE, PREPAID. **$16.98**

8K13320 *A most amazing value in a very rich looking* **silk Georgette crepe** *dress with the new eyelet embroidery as pictured.*
Fashioned with wide paneled waist both front and back and long gathered tunic. Wide satin sash. Skirt width 52 inches. COLORS: Navy blue with contrasting embroidery, or pearl grey with contrasting embroidery. SIZES: 32 to 44 bust; 38 to 40 inches skirt lengths. PRICE, PREPAID. **$19.98**

8K13321 For misses and small women. SIZES: 32 to 38 bust; skirt lengths 32 to 38 inches. PRICE, PREPAID, **$19.98**

Descriptions for Page 9

8K13322 *Think of it! This beautiful* **taffeta silk** *dress at a price you'd pay for the simplest sort of a model elsewhere.*
Contrasting rosette effect embroidery. Plaited side sections. Embroidered net collar. Novelty buckled belt. COLORS: Taupe with rose embroidery; navy blue with rose; or black with rose. SIZES: 32 to 44 bust. Skirt lengths 38 to 40 inches.
PRICE, PREPAID to your home. **$14.98**

8K13323 For misses and small women. SIZES: 32 to 38 bust. Skirt lengths 32 to 38 inches. PRICE, PREPAID, **$14.98**

8K13324 *For all around wear, certainly nothing equals this* **all wool serge** *dress which can be worn every day as well as Sundays.*
Brilliant color embroidery decorates the wide sleeves and the accordion plaited front panels of skirt. Satin girdle. Skirt width 68 inches. COLORS: Navy blue with contrasting color embroidery. SIZES: 32 to 44 bust. Skirt lengths 38 to 40 inches.
PRICE, PREPAID to your home. **$18.98**

8K13325 For misses and small women. SIZES: 32 to 38 bust. Skirt lengths 32 to 38 inches. PRICE, PREPAID, **$18.98**

8K13326 *The low price which we quote on this beautiful* **silk crepe de chine** *dress is in itself tempting to economical women.*
Embroidered waist and plaited tunic. Narrow tie sash. Width of drop skirt 53 inches. COLORS: Tan with brown embroidery; navy blue with black embroidery; or all black. SIZES: 32 to 44 bust. Skirt lengths 38 to 40 inches. PRICE, PREPAID, **$13.98**

8K13327 For misses and small women. SIZES: 32 to 38 bust. Skirt lengths 32 to 38 inches. PRICE, PREPAID, **$13.98**

8K13328 *Right up to the minute is this truly individual dress of fine quality* **taffeta silk** *with the new metal eyelet embroidery.*
Long over-dress designed in six panels. Buckled belt. Skirt width 47 inches. COLORS: Navy blue with red satin and red eyelets, or brown with red satin and red eyelets. SIZES: 32 to 44 bust. Skirt lengths 38 to 40 inches.
PRICE, PREPAID to your home, **$16.98**

8K13329 For misses and small women. SIZES: 32 to 38 bust. Skirt lengths 32 to 38. PRICE, PREPAID, **$16.98**

SILK
GEORGETTE
8K13320
8K13321
$19.98

RESEDA
TAFFETA SILK
8K13318
8K13319
$16.98

8

PHILIPSBORN'S Prepay All Transportation Charges. Remember, There Are No Express or Mailing Charges for You to Pay

PHILIPSBORN'S

TAFFETA
SILK
8K13328
8K13329
$16.98

SILK CREPE
DE CHINE
8K13326
8K13327
$13.98

ALL WOOL
SERGE
8K13324
8K13325
$18.98

For Descriptions See Page 8

TAFFETA
SILK
8K13322
8K13323
$14.98

TAFFETA SILK

For Descriptions
See Page 11

ALL WOOL SERGE
8K13332
8K13333
$8.48

8K13334
8K13335
$11.88

SILK
POPLIN
8K13330
8K13331
$6.88

The Style of the Minute at an unheard-of price!....

Descriptions for Page 10

8K13330 *A wonderful saving on a dressy* **all-silk poplin** *dress, trimmed with contrasting wool embroidery.*
Surplice waist with sash. Contrasting trimming. Georgette sleeves. Very new and becoming. COLORS: Hunter's green or plum with gold embroidery, or navy blue with **gold** embroidery. SIZES: 32 to 44 bust. Skirt length 38 to 40 inches.
PRICE, PREPAID to your home, **$6.88**
8K13331 Same style for misses and small women. SIZES: 32 to 38 bust. Skirt length 32 to 38 inches.
PRICE, PREPAID to your home, **$6.88**

8K13332 *There is nothing more satisfactory than a good* **all wool serge** *dress such as the model we present herewith.*
At our money-saving price this model has no equal. Silk braid and silk stitching provide an elaborate trimming as pictured. Narrow sash belt. COLOR: Navy blue with black embroidery. SIZES: 32 to 44 bust. Skirt length 38 to 40 inches.
PRICE, PREPAID to your home, **$8.48**
8K13333 Same style for misses and small women. SIZES: 32 to 38 bust. Skirt length 32 to 38 inches.
PRICE, PREPAID to your home, **$8.48**

8K13334 **Taffeta silk** *of rich, lustrous beauty fashions this very stylish dress, for which the price is only* **$11.88**
Contrasting wool embroidery with gold tinsel threads furnishes the newest of trimmings for the draped blouse and sash ends. COLORS: Pearl grey or navy blue. SIZES: 32 to 44 bust. Skirt length 38 to 40 inches.
PRICE, PREPAID to your home, **$11.88**
8K13335 Same style for misses and small women. SIZES: 32 to 38 bust. Skirt length 32 to 38 inches.
PRICE, PREPAID to your home, **$11.88**

IMPORTANT!
Be sure to always state COLOR *and* SIZE *when ordering*

8K13336 *This handsome* **taffeta silk** *dress is a recent importation from Paris, on which we name, as ever, a very low price.*
Clever style is displayed in the knife-plaited apron tunic, the double scalloped collar and cuffs, the dainty ruffled organdie vestee and new style half sleeves. Picoted sash belt. Ribbon drawstrings at sleeves. COLORS: Navy blue or Copenhagen blue. SIZES: 32 to 44 bust. Skirt length 38 to 40 ins.
PRICE, PREPAID to your home, **$17.77**
8K13337 Same style for misses and small women. SIZES: 32 to 38 bust. Skirt length 32 to 38 inches.
PRICE, PREPAID to your home, **$17.77**

TAFFETA
SILK
8K13336
8K13337
$17.77

8K13340 *This wonderful selling event presents to every woman in the country saving opportunities that are truly astonishing.*

Even at a dollar or two more this beautiful **Georgette crepe** dress would be a good purchase but at the low price we name it becomes one of the greatest dress values of the year. Fashion's demand for bead trimming is provided in the bead ornaments which trim the front of blouse and the short tunic. Elbow length sleeves. Tuck trimming as shown. Sash belt. Seco silk lining throughout. Very rich and dressy. COLORS: Navy blue or taupe. SIZES: 32 to 44 bust. Skirt length 38 to 40. Skirt width 60 inches.
PRICE, PREPAID to your home, **$12.98**

8K13341 For misses and small women. SIZES: 32 to 38 bust. Skirt length 32 to 38. Skirt width 60 inches.
PRICE, PREPAID to your home, **$12.98**

SILK GEORGETTE
8K13340
8K13341
$12.98

IMPORTANT!
Be sure to state SIZE and COLOR desired when ordering.

8K13338 *Past season's records have been eclipsed by this remarkable offer.*

Here is a style in a **taffeta silk** dress that you will not run across everywhere and every day. Lace collar and vestee. Contrasting embroidery on the gathered overskirt and sash ends. COLORS: Navy blue or pearl grey. SIZES: 32 to 44 bust. Skirt length 38 to 40. Skirt width (underdress) 60 inches.
PRICE, PREPAID to your home, **$13.98**

8K13339 For misses and small women. SIZES: 32 to 38 bust. Skirt length 32 to 38. Skirt width (underdress) 60 inches.
PRICE, PREPAID to your home, **$13.98**

8K13342 *You are sure of three things when you shop at PHILIPSBORN'S—style, quality and lowest price.*

In this handsome new dress of **taffeta silk** you have all three of these factors combined to a high degree. Very new style is displayed in the novel embroidery designs which ornament both tunic and waist, and which combine self-tone and contrasting colors in very lovely effects. New style upstanding collar. Surplice vestee. Sash belt. Elbow length sleeves. A remarkable money-saving offer. COLORS: Navy blue or brown. SIZES: 32 to 44 bust. Skirt length 38 to 40. Skirt width (underdress) 53 inches.
PRICE, PREPAID to your home, **$17.98**

8K13343 Same style for misses and small women. SIZES: 32 to 38 bust. Skirt length 32 to 38. Skirt width (underdress) 53 inches.
PRICE, PREPAID to your home, **$17.98**

TAFFETA SILK
8K13342
8K13343

Special! $17.98 Prepaid

TAFFETA SILK
8K13338
8K13339
$13.98
WORTH $16.00

12   IRENE CASTLE, the World's Famous Style Authority, Now Designs Clothes for PHILIPSBORN'S Customers

PHILIPSBORN'S

8K13348 *Look where you will you will not find a prettier or dressier model than this dress of rich* **taffeta silk.**

There is no need to wait for end-of-the-season sales when you can get such wonderful values here and now. Note the stunning effect given by the contrasting and self-tone embroidery which adorns both skirt and waist. 3-4 length sleeves. Draped waist portion. COLORS: Navy blue or black. SIZES: 32 to 44 bust. Skirt length 38 to 40.

PRICE, PREPAID to your home, **$8.48**

8K13349 For misses and small women. SIZES: 32 to 38 bust. Skirt length 32 to 38.

PRICE, PREPAID to your home, **$8.48**

TAFFETA SILK
8K13348
8K13349
$8.48

8K13346 *The season's favorite suit dress is this distinctive* **all wool jersey** *model.*
Self-tone embroidery of novel design ornaments the coat blouse as pictured. Narrow self-material sash belt. Very stylish for general wear COLORS: Navy blue or taupe brown. SIZES: 32 to 44 bust. Skirt length 38 to 40.
PRICE, PREPAID to your home, **$11.98**

8K13347 For misses and small women. SIZES: 32 to 38 bust. Skirt length 32 to 38.
PRICE, PREPAID to your home, **$11.98**

8K13344 *The splendid saving offered you in this beautiful dress is but another proof that we have forced prices down.*
The lines as you can see from the illustration conform to the season's new silhouette, and the excellent quality of **taffeta silk** which we have used in making the model, stamp it as a noteworthy offering indeed. Designed in long-waisted effect, the skirt is made very distinctive with self headings at either side. Contrasting embroidery decorates the front as shown. Elbow length Georgette sleeves add to the dainty effect. COLORS: Navy blue with henna embroidery or Copenhagen blue with rose. SIZES: 32 to 44 bust. Skirt length 38 to 40.
PRICE, PREPAID to your home, **$10.98**

8K13345 For misses and small women. SIZES: 32 to 38 bust. Skirt length 32 to 38 inches.
PRICE, PREPAID to your home, **$10.98**

ALL WOOL JERSEY
8K13346
8K13347

Special!
$11.98
Prepaid

TAFFETA SILK
8K13344
8K13345
$10.98

CHICAGO, ILL.

For Index See Page 274 and Remember PHILIPSBORN'S Prepay All Transportation Charges. There Are No Express or Mailing Charges for You to Pay

13

Specially Designed PHILIPSBORN'S Stout Dresses · Sizes 37 to 53 ·

8K13350 *Here is a dress whose beauty, style, and quality cannot be over-emphasized. It is specially designed to solve the "clothes" problem of the stout woman, and is offered at a price that defies competition.*

Made in the very fashionable suit effect of excellent quality **taffeta silk**. This model features the long waisted lines which are so generally becoming to full-formed figures. Both front and back of the waist portion are designed in panel style and ornamented at the front with fancy silk braid and gold tinsel embroidery. Tunic sections mounted at the hip line are laid in knife plaits with a wide box plait at the center. A shawl collar of self-material extends slightly below the waistline in newest fashion, opening over a contrasting tucked Georgette vestee. Sash belt with tassel finish. Light waist lining. COLORS: Black, taupe, or navy blue. SIZES: 37 to 53 bust. Front length of skirt 38 to 44.
PRICE, PREPAID to your home, **$18.98**

8K13351 *Without question one of the richest and dressiest models ever designed for the stout woman is this Georgette crepe dress. It is especially designed to give grace and becomingness to well-developed figures.*

Here is a charming example of the latest modes, fashioned of **silk Georgette crepe** and enhanced with self-tone and contrasting embroidery on the overskirt and blouse. The lines of the blouse are very new and becoming—cut away at the sides in overblouse fashion, becomingly draped at the sides, and joining sash ties at the back. Wide sleeves of self-material have picoted edges turned back in novel cuff effect and button trimmed. Drop skirt of Georgette. Light silk lining in blouse portion. Invisible fastening at the shoulder and underarm seams. A model that offers you latest style and wonderful materials at a big price. COLORS: Navy blue, taupe, or all black. SIZES: 37 to 53 bust. Front length of skirt 38 to 44. **$20.98**
PRICE, PREPAID to your home,

IMPORTANT!

Before sending your order, be sure of two things — *first*, have you mentioned the color you desire, and *second*; have you mentioned the size? *Be sure to send us this information, for without it we cannot fill your order.*

SILK GEORGETTE
8K13351

TAFFETA SILK
8K13350

$20.98

$18.98

SILK
GEORGETTE
AND TAFFETA
8K13354
$19.98

MOHAIR
8K13353
$12.98

SATIN
MESSALINE
8K13352
$16.98

8K13354 *Unquestionably one of the smartest and most becoming dresses for stout women in our entire line.*

This beautiful dress combines two of the season's favorite materials—**taffeta silk and Georgette crepe.** It is designed in long-waisted effect—a style that is especially becoming to full figures. Contrasting silk floss embroidery trims the front and back of model alike. The long overskirt mounted at the hip line is of Georgette crepe with a wide trimming fold of taffeta silk Small revers and round collar. Stylish wide sleeves with wide flarecuffs, novelty button trimming. COLORS: Navy blue with green embroidery; grey with Copenhagen blue embroidery; or all black. SIZES: 37 to 53 bust. Skirt-length **38 to 43** Skirt width (underdress) 64 inches.
PRICE, PREPAID
to your home, **$19.98**

8K13353 *The stout woman who buys at PHILIPSBORN'S can always be stylishly gowned, and still not pay high prices.*

This fashionable dress combines every feature that a woman requires in a dress—distinctive style, splendidly durable material, and moderate price. It is fashioned of a good quality **mohair,** a fabric that will withstand the hard wear which the stout woman usually gives her clothes. The season's vogue for tunic effects is carried out in the skirt, which opens in panel effect at the front. The waist portion is made with a vestee panel to correspond. Small self-covered buttons trim the model as pictured. Will give splendid service. COLORS: Navy blue or black. SIZES: 37 to 53 bust. Skirt length 38 to 43. Skirt width (underdress) 68 inches.
PRICE, PREPAID
to your home, **$12.98**

8K13352 *The lines of the smartest new modes have been adapted in this dress to the requirements of the stout woman.*

This is not merely a large-size model but a model that we have specially designed to be becoming to the full-formed woman. The material—a rich quality **satin messaline**—shows to wonderful advantage the beaded Georgette vestee in harmonizing color. Slenderizing lines are formed by the Tuxedo collar of self-material continuing into trimming straps on the tunic. Groups of self-covered buttons as shown. New style sleeves are close-fitting at the wrist. Side front fastening. Light waist lining. Dressy and extremely becoming. COLORS: Navy blue, taupe or black. SIZES: 37 to 53 bust. Skirt length 38 to 43. Skirt width (underdress) 60 inches.

PRICE, PREPAID to your home, **$16.98**

ALL
WOOL
SERGE
8K13357
$10.98

TAFFETA
SILK
8K13356
$13.98

SILK
POPLIN
8K13355
$10.98

8K13357 *Never out of season is the serge dress.
This smart model for the stout woman is offered
at a price that positively cannot be duplicated.*

It is made of **all wool serge** and is designed on very
becoming lines. The new style *stole* collar of self-
material extending below the waistline is finished with
silk braid trimming. Silk braid trimmed vestee and
cuffs. Unequaled for service. A big bargain at our
special cut price. COLORS: Navy blue or black.
SIZES: 37 to 53 bust. Front length of skirt 38 to 43.
PRICE, PREPAID
to your home,   **$10.98**

*Be sure to state COLOR and SIZE
when ordering*

8K13356 *You of stout figure will make no
mistake if you choose this dress of good quality
taffeta silk.*

At our low price it presents a wonderful bargain opportunity that no woman who needs a dressy new
frock of this type should overlook. Contrasting
silk embroidery gives a striking note of color on both
blouse and overskirt. Self-material vestee finished
with button trimming. Fashionably narrow sash
belt. Lawn lining in blouse. Drop skirt of taffeta
silk. A dress that offers you wonderful style at a
moderate price. COLORS: Navy blue with tan
embroidery or all black. SIZES: 37 to 53 bust.
Front length of skirt 38 to 43.
PRICE, PREPAID to your home,   **$13.98**

8K13355 *The suit dress, so becoming to full
figures is here shown in one of the season's
most charming styles.*

It is made of good quality **silk poplin** and is priced
at the lowest figure yet quoted on material of equal
quality. Contrasting silk embroidery in conventional scroll design ornaments the vestee and tunic
sections. Sash belt. Tuxedo collar to bottom of
tunic. Button trimming. Here is a dress that
offers you 100% value in service and satisfaction.
It is dressy enough for best yet not too elaborate for
general wear. COLORS: Navy blue, plum or taupe.
SIZES: 37 to 53 bust. Front length of skirt 38 to
43.
PRICE, PREPAID to your home,   **$10.98**

Be sure to state SIZE and COLOR.

Irene Castle designed this charming frock for Y-O-U · We put a · price on it! that challenges Competition!

$6.98

HOW TO ORDER

'ECONOMY IS KING'!! IN 1921

Buy this Great Bargain

$5.48

DRESSES OF THIS CHARACTER A YEAR AGO WOULD HAVE SOLD FOR

$10.00

EMBR'D VOILE
8K13368
8K13369
$5.48

8K13368 *"Where did you get that pretty dress?"* your friends will exclaim when they see this new model. It is one of summer's daintiest models, and is as effective in style as any high-priced model that you could choose.

The beauty of the material charms at once—it is an **embroidered dotted voile** which is much sought after by women of fashion this season. It shows to perfection every detail of the smart design. Especially new are the semi-attached side panels which are turned under in smartest fashion at the knees. Daintiness is added in the organdie vestee, collar and cuffs. Lace insertion and scalloped tucking are smart details of the vestee. Crushed self-material girdle. Elbow length sleeves. Waist portion partly lined Invisible fastening at side front. Here is a dress that embodies the smartest style features of the season, and we think you will agree with us when you see it. If you have ever seen a prettier style or a better value for the money, we want to know it. Or if you can duplicate this model at a lesser price elsewhere, let us know and we will gladly refund the difference. COLORS: Navy blue and white, Copenhagen blue and white or black and white. SIZES: 32 to 44 bust. Skirt length 38 to 40 inches.
PRICE, PREPAID to your home, **$5.48**

8K13369 Same style for misses' and small women. SIZES: 32 to 38 bust. Skirt length 32 to 38 inches.
PRICE, PREPAID to your home, **$5.48**

HOW TO ORDER

In ordering dresses, state bust measure, size of waistband, and front length of skirt. IT IS IMPORTANT TO GIVE ALL THREE MEASUREMENTS.
If a larger size than 42 bust measure is required, order from our stout sizes.

Be sure to state COLOR and SIZE desired when ordering

"A Thing or Two to Remember" and Some Other Interesting Facts to Be Found on Page 3

PHILIPSBORN'S

Let Experience be your GUIDE!

Read what "Others" say

8K13370 *Convincing proof that prices are lower at PHILIPSBORN'S is afforded you in this flowered voile dress.*

It has all the style and chic of a high-priced model, yet it is only $5.98. Note the stylish eyelet embroidered batiste trimming, the cross-over coatee-effect blouse and wide sash for its becoming lines. COLORS: Navy blue and white, rose and white; or lavender and white. SIZES: 32 to 44 bust. Skirt length 38 to 40. Skirt width 70 inches.
PRICE, PREPAID to your home, **$5.98**
8K13371 For misses and small women. SIZES: 32 to 38 bust. Skirt length 32 to 38. Skirt width 70 inches.
PRICE, PREPAID to your home, **$5.98**

8K13372 *Here is a particularly smart example of the smock dress so much favored this year.*

The material is **cotton ramie**, a darker color being used for the full plaited skirt which is mounted to a light underwaist. The stylish smock has embroidery designs to match skirt color. COLORS: White and Copenhagen blue or white with rose. SIZES: 32 to 44 bust. Skirt length 38 to 40. Skirt width 70 inches.
PRICE, PREPAID to your home, **$4.68**
8K13373 For misses and small women. SIZES: 32 to 38 bust. Skirt length 32 to 38. Skirt width 70 inches.
PRICE, PREPAID to your home, **$4.68**

RAMIE
8K13372
8K13373 } **$4.68**

FLOWERED VOILE
8K13370
8K13371 } **$5.98**

Descriptions for Page 21

8K13378 *Only Irene Castle could design so simple a dress and yet have it so thoroughly charming and distinctive.*

Organdie in a choice of several delicate colors makes this Castle model. An unusual design is carried out in the deep bordered tunic, with plaited frills as shown. Wool hand embroidery on girdle. New style Quaker collar. Elbow sleeves. COLORS: Light blue or maize. SIZES: 32 to 44 bust. Skirt length 38 to 40 inches.
PRICE, PREPAID to your home, **$7.98**

8K13379 Same style for misses and small women. SIZES: 32 to 38 bust. Skirt length 32 to 38 inches.
PRICE, PREPAID to your home, **$7.98**

8K13380 *Still another very smart and becoming creation of Irene Castle's is this* **novelty checked voile** *dress.*

Plaited frills in color to match the dark ground of the material contrast charmingly on the apron tunic. Wide girdle with sash at back and turnback cuffs of contrasting voile to match frills. Dainty Venise lace collar. COLORS: Navy blue and white or rose and white. SIZES: 32 to 44 bust. Skirt length 38 to 40 inches.
PRICE, PREPAID to your home, **$6.98**

8K13381 Same style for misses and small women. SIZES: 32 to 38 bust. Skirt length 32 to 38 inches.
PRICE, PREPAID to your home, **$6.98**

8K13382 *Summer's daintiest dress is this pretty* **organdie** *model designed for you by Irene Castle, our style expert.*

Dotted organdie makes the wide inset through the skirt, the stole collar which extends below the waistline, and the turnback cuffs. Tucking trims both skirt and vestee as shown. Val. lace edges collar and cuffs. Wide self-material sash. A wonderful value. COLORS: Flesh, light blue or lavender. SIZES: 32 to 44 bust. Skirt length 38 to 40 inches.
PRICE, PREPAID to your home, **$4.98**

8K13383 Same style for misses' and small women. SIZES: 32 to 38 bust. Skirt length 32 to 38 inches.
PRICE, PREPAID to your home, **$4.98**

HOW TO ORDER

In ordering women's dresses, give bust measure, size of waistband, and front length of skirt. IT IS IMPORTANT TO GIVE ALL THREE MEASUREMENTS. Also, do not order a larger size than is cataloged, for these see pages 14, 15, 16, 25, 26 and 27.

IMPORTANT!
Be sure to state SIZE and COLOR desired when ordering

VOILE

VOILE

8K13376 *A general utility dress for the woman in mourning is provided in this* **voile** *model in a choice of three colors.*

New and distinctive style is shown in the hand-embroidered side panels which are attached to the side seam. Hand embroidered Tuxedo collar. Vestee with Val. lace and tucking. Sash belt. Suitable for first and second mourning. COLORS: All black or light grey. SIZES 32 to 44 bust. Skirt length 38 to 40 inches. PRICE, PREPAID to your home, **$6.98**

8K13377 Same style for misses and small women. SIZES: 32 to 38 bust. Skirt length 32 to 38 inches.
PRICE, PREP'D to your home, **$6.98**

8K13374 *A smart and becoming* **voile** *dress, furnished in proper colors for first and second mourning.*

The skirt features four tunic-effect panels, two long panels at the front and back. Plaited frills provide a very dressy trimming on both skirt and waist exactly as pictured. Waist has front and back over panel. COLORS: All black, light grey or white. SIZES: 32 to 44 bust. Skirt length 38 to 40 inches. PRICE, PREPAID to your home, **$7.98**

8K13375 Same style for misses and small women. SIZES: 32 to 38 bust. Skirt length 32 to 38 inches.
PRICE, PREP'D to your home, **$7.98**

8K13376
8K13377
$6.98

8K13374
8K13375
$7.98

Remember, There Are No Extra Charges for Express or Mailing When You Shop Here. We Prepay All Transportation Charges

PHILIPSBORN'S

FIGURED
VOILE
8K13380
8K13381
$6.98

ORGANDIE
8K13382
8K13383
$4.98

*You have
my Guarantee
for Style! and
PHILIPSBORN'S
Guarantee for Price!
and Satisfaction!
And Remember,
Everything Prepaid!*

Irene Castle

ORGANDIE
8K13378
8K13379
$7.98

*For Descriptions
See Page 20*

8K13388 *Style and big value in this* **printed voile** *dress.* Skirt trimmed with wide fold. Contrasting plaited voile frills add dressiness. Sash belt. Large collar. COLORS: Blue and white; rose and white; or lavender and white. SIZES: 32 to 44 bust. Front length of skirt 38 to 40.
PRICE, PREPAID to your home, **$3.48**

8K13389 For misses and small women. SIZES: 32 to 38 bust. Front length of skirt 32 to 38.
PRICE, PREPAID to your home, **$3.48**

8K13384 *Women on the look-out for bargains will appreciate this remarkable offering in a stylish new wash dress.*
Embroidered voile of attractive pattern makes the model. It is designed on very becoming lines with long-waisted over-panels at the front and back. Contrasting silk ribbon lacings join the panels at the sides. Gathered skirt of embroidery flouncing with tucking. Tucked elbow length sleeves. Extremely dressy. COLOR: All white. SIZES: 32 to 44 bust. Front length of skirt 38 to 40.
PRICE, PREPAID to your home, **$6.48**

8K13385 For misses and small women. SIZES: 32 to 38 bust. Front length of skirt 32 to 38.
PRICE, PREPAID to your home, **$6.48**

8K13386 *An amazing bargain in a smart gingham dress quoted at a low price that has not been equaled in many years.*
Great individuality of design is a prominent feature of this dress. Fashioned in long-waisted effect with a wide bias fold at the hip line. The new style stole collar extends below the waistline and forms novel straps for the all-around sash belt. Embroidered organdie cuffs and vestee trimming. Button groups as shown. COLORS: Blue or pink plaid. SIZES: 32 to 44 bust. Front length of skirt 38 to 40.
PRICE, PREPAID to your home, **$3.88**

8K13387 For misses and small women. SIZES: 32 to 38 bust. Front length of skirt 32 to 38.
PRICE, PREPAID to your home, **$3.88**

VOILE
8K13388
8K13389
$3.48

EMB'D VOILE
8K13384
8K13385
$6.48

GINGHAM
8K13386
8K13387
$3.88

Prepaid to your Door!

All Merchandise in This Catalogue is Covered by Our Broad Guarantee. See Page 3

PHILIPSBORN'S

8K13394 *Undeniably one of our most attractive and becoming styles in this good quality* **linene** *dress.*

The smart design features a skirt with four swinging panels, two at the front and two at the back. Contrasting silk braid embroidery. COLORS: Copenhagen blue with white embroidery or tan with white. SIZES: 32 to 44 bust. Skirt length 38 to 40.

PRICE, PREPAID to your home, **$4.98**

8K13395 For misses and small women. SIZES: 32 to 38 bust. Skirt length 32 to 38.
PRICE, PREPAID to your home, **$4.98**

IMPORTANT!
Be sure to state COLOR and SIZE desired when ordering

8K13392 *Dressy and fascinating style is displayed in this new style smock dress.*

Designed in two-piece effect with plain **voile** skirt with groups of graduated tucks. The **waist is an effective combination of all-over embroidered voile** and plain voile. Cord girdle matches color in embroidery. Button trimming and fastening at side front. A remarkable value. COLORS: White and blue or all white. SIZES: 32 to 44 bust. Skirt length 38 to 40.
PRICE, PREPAID to your home, **$4.48**

8K13393 For misses and small women. SIZES: 32 to 38 bust. Skirt length 32 to 38.
PRICE, PREPAID to your home, **$4.48**

8K13390 *A charming example of the smock dresses so much in favor with women and misses.*

This two-piece **linene** model has a straight gathered skirt and slip-over smock blouse. Contrasting embroidery stitching and floral designs give charming style to the smock exactly as pictured. ¾ length sleeves. Sash belt. Opening at shoulders. COLORS: Rose, copenhagen blue, or tan. SIZES: 32 to 44 bust. Skirt length 38 to 40.
PRICE, PREPAID to your home, **$2.98**

8K13391 For misses and small women. SIZES: 32 to 38 bust. Skirt length 32 to 38.
PRICE, PREPAID to your home, **$2.98**

LINENE
8K13390
8K13391
$2.98
WORTH
$3.50

VOILE
EMBR'D
8K13392
8K13393
$4.48

LINENE
8K13394
8K13395
$4.98

Summer Dresses Very Low Priced!

Popular Dresses & Popular Prices

8K13398 *Designed on modified Redingote lines, this dress will make a charming addition to your summer wardrobe.*

It is made of good quality **linene**, and is one of the most serviceable dresses ever offered at our special cut price. Contrasting hand embroidery provides just the right trimming touch on the waist and tunic. Smartly shaped collar finished with ball drops. ¾ length sleeves. An extraordinary offering in ever respect. COLORS: Copenhagen blue or tan. SIZES: 32 to 44 bust. Skirt length 38 to 40. Skirt width 53 inches.
PRICE, PREPAID to your home, **$3.98**

8K13399 For misses and small women. SIZES: 32 to 38 bust. Skirt length 32 to 38.
PRICE, PREPAID to your home, **$3.98**

GINGHAM
8K13396
8K13397
$2.86

WORTH
~~$3.75~~

VOILE
8K13400
8K13401
$2.98

WORTH
~~$4.00~~

8K13400 *For warm days what could be more attractive than this dress in the fashionable combination of plain and printed voile.*

Plain voile is used for the wide, attractive collar and the swinging side panels, which are an especially new feature. Contrasting piping of self-material edges collar, cuffs and panels, three rows of piping trimming the panels as pictured. The wide self-material sash provides a youthful finishing touch. Sleeves are ¾ length. Invisible fastening at side front. If you like the style of this dress, don't look any further for it cannot be duplicated elsewhere at the very low price that we ask. COLORS: Blue and white; lavender and white; or rose and white. SIZES: 32 to 44 bust. Skirt length 38 to 40. Skirt width 54 inches.
PRICE, PREPAID to your home, **$2.98**

8K13401 Same style for misses and small women. SIZES: 32 to 38 bust. Skirt length 32 to 38.
PRICE, PREPAID to your home, **$2.98**

LINENE
8K13398
8K13399
$3.98

8K13396 *Here is one of the prettiest and most practical summer dresses that you could select, and the price is only $2.86.*

The model is fashioned of **plaid gingham** of very artistic design and colors, and the style is most becoming with its height-giving paneled skirt and vestee. Contrasting material is used for the Lucile collar, cuffs and sash belt, plaited frills adding a pretty finish on the collar and cuffs. Large patch pockets emphasize the smart lines of the skirt. Button trimming as shown. Pretty enough for any informal wear and a decided bargain at our low price. COLORS: Blue and white plaid; or pink and white plaid. SIZES: 32 to 44 bust. Skirt length 38 to 40. Skirt width 62 inches.
PRICE, PREPAID to your home, **$2.86**

8K13397 Same style for misses and small women. SIZES: 32 to 38 bust. Skirt length 32 to 38.
PRICE, PREPAID to your home, **$2.86**

PHILIPSBORN'S

Stout Sizes 37 to 53 Big Values

VOILE
8K13404
$7.98

GINGHAM
8K13402
$3.98

VOILE
8K13403
$6.50
WORTH **$8.00**

8K13404 *A new and distinctive dress that will delight the woman of large figure is here shown.*

Designed on the fashionable Redingote lines, it is one of the most becoming styles that the stout woman can select. The material is good quality voile, handsomely embroidered on the four loose panels of the skirt, the long-waisted vestee, and ¾ length sleeves. Full length shawl collar. Round, hemstitched neck. Velvet girdle with sash ends. COLORS: Lavender, taupe, or black. SIZES: 37 to 53 bust. Skirt length 38 to 43. Skirt width 66 inches.
PRICE, PREPAID to your home, **$7.98**

8K13402 *Smart and becoming style for the stout woman in a checked gingham dress.*

Usually gingham of this quality commands high prices but owing to a very fortunate purchase we are able to set a very low price of only $3.98. Designed with soft plaits from the front and back yoke, and loosely held at the waistline with a sash belt. Rep trimming. Fancy stitching. COLORS: Blue and white or black and white. SIZES: 37 to 53 bust. Skirt length 38 to 43. Skirt width 72 inches.
PRICE, PREPAID to your home, **$3.98**

8K13403 *The stout woman will find unusually becoming lines in this dress.*

It is a clever adaptation of the much-favored Redingote, and is developed in **fancy figured printed voile.** Wide panels open over the straight-line skirt, and there is a narrow sash belt of contrasting grosgrain ribbon defining the waistline. Embroidered organdie forms the square collar, vestee, and cuffs. ¾ sleeves. A dressy model of excellent style and value. COLORS: Blue and white, black and white or lavender and white. SIZES: 37 to 53 bust. Skirt length 38 to 43. Skirt width 58 inches.
PRICE, PREPAID to your home, **$6.50**

Descriptions for Page 27

8K13408 *One of summer's most fascinating styles is shown in this dainty and becoming dress.*

It is an effective **combination of flowered and plain organdie** Four swinging panels edged with plaited frills. Large surplice collar, and cuffs with frill trimming. A style usually offered only in high-priced garments. COLORS: Lavender, pink or light blue. SIZES: 32 to 44 bust. Skirt length 38 to 40. Skirt width 56 inches.

PRICE, PREPAID to your home, **$6.88**

8K13409 For misses and small women. SIZES: 32 to 38 bust. Skirt length 32 to 38.

PRICE, PREPAID to your home, **$6.88**

8K13410 *The effect of this pretty dress is altogether charming as the picture shows.*

Embroidered voile contrasts with plain voile to produce one of the season's prettiest models. Plaited side panels depend from hip sections as shown. Round neck finished with opening velvet bow and buttons. COLORS: Rose, copenhagen blue, or tan. SIZES: 32 to 44 bust. Skirt length 38 to 40. Skirt width 56 inches.

PRICE, PREPAID to your home, **$5.98**

8K13411 For misses and small women. SIZES: 32 to 38 bust. Skirt length 32 to 38.

PRICE, PREPAID to your home, **$5.98**

8K13412 *The style features of an expensive 1921 model have been reproduced in this pretty dress.*

Fancy figured voile forms a charming contrast with plain voile in making the model. Latest style is seen in the large becoming cross-over collar. Plaited frills ornament both overskirt and waist as pictured. Ribbon sash and voile rosettes. COLORS: Copenhagen blue and tan; or navy blue and tan. SIZES: 32 to 44 bust. Skirt length 38 to 40. Skirt width 56 inches.

PRICE, PREPAID to your home, **$6.88**

8K13413 For misses and small women. SIZES: 32 to 38 bust. Skirt length 32 to 38.

PRICE, PREPAID to your home, **$6.88**

How to Order Dresses for Women and Misses

State bust measure, size of waistband and front length of skirt. IT IS IMPORTANT TO STATE ALL THREE OF THESE MEASUREMENTS, as without this information we cannot fill your order promptly.

LINENE
8K13406
$5.98

Dresses of Unusual Charm That Will Improve Your Figure

DOTTED VOILE
8K13405
$4.88

8K13406 *The Redingote is a style that is very fashionable this season, and is particularly becoming to stout women.*

Our designers have used good quality **linene** for this smart model, and have achieved the much-desired Redingote effect with embroidered panels at either side of the skirt. There is a square collar of self-material and wide folds extending to the waistline. The vestee is of organdie, tucked and lace trimmed. All-around self-material belt. COLORS: Copenhagen blue, white or tan. SIZES: 37 to 53 bust. Skirt lengths 38 to 43. Skirt width 64 inches.

PRICE, PREPAID to your home, **$5.98**

8K13405 *The stout woman who shops here will find her needs charmingly anticipated in the most becoming styles.*

Here is a dress developed in **printed voile** and from the picture you can easily judge its pleasing attractiveness. Filet lace forms the collar and affords a becoming touch of white. Tucked organdie vestee. Crochet pendants at either side of fronts. Hemstitched organdie bands trim the ¾-length kimono sleeves. COLORS: Black and white or navy blue and white. SIZES: 37 to 53 bust. Skirt length 38 to 43. Skirt width 66 inches.

PRICE, PREPAID to your home, **$4.88**

ORGANDIE
8K13408
8K13409
$6.88

FRENCH
VOILE
8K13412
8K13413
$6.88

VOILE
8K13410
8K13411
$5.98

For Descriptions See Page 26

PHILIPSBORN'S "Everdainty" Undergarments Are Especially Designed for You Who Delight in
Dainty Lingerie of New Style and High Quality. Pages 216 to 241

ALL
WOOL
SERGE
8K13420
$8.98

FANCY
VOILE
8K13421
$5.98

TAFFETA
SILK
8K13419
$9.98

SILK POPLIN
8K13418
$6.48

*For Descriptions
See Page 29*

*PHILIPSBORN'S Millinery. Becoming Hats for Every Age and Every Face.
Prices Notably Low. Refer to Pages 139 to 156*   PHILIPSBORN'S

Youth-Beauty-Price!! Served in this unusual display of winsome frocks

for "Miss America" Frocks of rare distinction

Descriptions for Page 28

8K13418 *Becoming style for misses is this silk poplin dress, and at this low price a real bargain.*

At our special reduced price this pretty model is one of our greatest bargains. Over-blouse panel, embroidered in silk floss and beading. Georgette sleeves. Wide sash. COLORS: Plum, navy blue, or Copenhagen blue. SIZES: Bust 32 to 38. Skirt width 52 inches. Skirt length 32 to 38.
PRICE, PREPAID to your home, **$6.48**

8K13419 *Here is a misses' dress of quaint charm, specially priced. This is a wonderful value.*

Taffeta silk is the material used and the design shows the newest interpretation of the popular peasant blouse. Ribbon lacings at front of blouse, at sleeves, and patch pockets. Buckled belt. COLORS: Navy blue with red trimming. Copenhagen blue with red; or all black. SIZES: Bust 32 to 38. Skirt width 52 inches. Skirt length 32 to 38 inches.
PRICE, PREPAID to your home, **$9.98**

8K13420 *Misses' stylish all wool serge dress at a 25% reduction, now specially priced for only $8.98.*

Fashion's demand for plaited effects is supplied in the full knife-plaited skirt. Constrasting stitching in variegated colors give a trimming touch that is very girlish on the skirt and semi-fitted waist. COLOR: Navy blue. SIZES: Bust 32 to 38. Skirt width 68 inches. Skirt length 32 to 38.
PRICE, PREPAID to your home, **$8.98**

8K13421 *Fancy figured French voile fashions this charming misses' dress. Big value at our price of $5.98.*

The model is designed in long-waisted effect with a narrow ribbon sash at the normal waistline. New style apron tunic finished with self heading. Contrasting plaited frills at neck and sleeves. COLORS: Taupe and rose; navy blue and rose; or Copenhagen blue and tan. SIZES: Bust 32 to 38. Skirt lengths 32 to 38.
PRICE, PREPAID to your home, **$5.98**

HOW TO ORDER

Order Misses' dresses by exact measurements of bust, waistband, and front length of skirt. Do not order by age, and if a larger size than 38 bust is required, order from our women's dresses.

TAFFETA SILK
8K13422
$16.98
WORTH
$20.00

8K13422 *A fascinating style in a misses' dress offered at a very moderate cost.*

Weeks ago we searched Eastern markets for a **taffeta silk** dress to sell at $16.98, and this beautiful model is the result. Gilt metallic thread embroidery contributes an elaborate trimming for the long overskirt and the deep cape collar. Lace trimmed tucked net vestee. New style slashed ¾ sleeves. Jap silk waist lining. COLORS: Navy blue, brown, or black. SIZES: Bust 32 to 38, Skirt length 32 to 38. Width of underdress 48 inches.
PRICE, PREPAID to your home, **$16.98**

SILK
GEORGETTE
CREPE
8K13424
$16.98

TAFFETA
SILK
8K13423
$15.98

"Listen
Miss
America
My trip to
Havana was
the inspiration
for these frocks
They are 1921's
latest craze!"

Irene Castle

Descriptions for Page 31

8K13425 *Distinctive style and youthful smartness are portrayed in this* **taffeta silk dress.**

The accordion plaited skirt is a style feature that is particularly becoming to the miss. The simple lines of the blouse are made very effective with conventional embroidery designs, the smartly shaped yoke sections finished with tassel trimming. A dressy model of great charm. COLORS: Navy blue, copenhagen blue, or rose. SIZES: 32 to 38 bust. Skirt length 32 to 38. Skirt width 54 inches.

PRICE, PREPAID to your home, **$11.88**

8K13426 *Jersey dresses never seem to lose their popularity, and here is a very new model.*

Developed in all wool Jersey. Polka dot embroidery decorates the lower part of skirt. the back of collar, cuffs, and vestee. Self-material belt with novelty buckle. Long sleeves. One of the smartest and most practical dresses ever designed for misses. COLORS: Navy blue with red dots; peacock blue with tan dots; or tan with brown dots. SIZES: 32 to 38 bust. Skirt length 32 to 38. Skirt width 53 inches.

PRICE PREPAID to your home, **$9.98**

8K13427 *It would be hard to find a more attractive dress than this* **taffeta silk model** *for misses.*

We chose this model from among many hundreds as being the most exceptional value we could find at the price. Contrasting scroll design embroidery provides an elaborate trimming as pictured. Full side-plaited underskirt. ¾ length sleeves. Sash belt. A decided bargain at this price. COLORS: Navy blue with gold embroidery or tan with copenhagen blue embroidery. SIZES: 32 to 38 bust. Skirt length 32 to 38. Skirt width 48 inches.

PRICE, PREPAID to your home, **$10.98**

8K13428 *Among the season's new serge dresses this model for misses will take first place.*

We have selected this model in a **wool and cotton mixed serge** because the material is quite satisfactory for all around wear. The swinging panels with contrasting embroidery are very fashionable and especially becoming to youth. Embroidery at square neck and long sleeves. A tremendous bargain at $5.98. COLOR: Navy blue. SIZES: 32 to 38 bust. Skirt length 32 to 38. Skirt width 58 inches.

PRICE, PREPAID to your home, **$5.98**

8K13424 *A triumph of design is this original misses' dress, created for you by our master style expert, Irene Castle.*

For this model we have used an excellent quality **silk Georgette crepe.** The side draping of the skirt adds to the youthful air of the dress, while harmonizing embroidery forms an elaborate design on the front of blouse and skirt. ¾ length sleeves with picoted cuffs. Novelly designed girdle. COLORS: Navy blue, beige tan or Copenhagen blue. SIZES: 32 to 38 bust. Skirt length 32 to 38. Skirt width 60 inches.

PRICE, PREPAID to your home, **$16.98**

8K13423 *PHILIPSBORN'S style expert; Irene Castle, designed this winsome dress for the American miss.*

The material is an excellent weight **taffeta silk** which lends itself admirably to the graceful design. Newest style is displayed in the coatee-effect waist, which features an elaborate use of eyelet embroidered batiste for the collar, cuffs and vestee. A remarkable dress for the money. COLORS: Navy blue, reseda green or taupe brown. SIZES: 32 to 38 bust. Skirt length 32 to 38. Skirt width 52 inches.

PRICE, PREPAID to your home, **$15.98**

SERGE
8K13428
$5.98

TAFFETA
SILK
8K13425
$11.88

Last Minute
Modes-Priced
to the Hour!

CHICAGO, ILL.

ALL WOOL
JERSEY
8K13426
$9.98

WORTH
$12.00

For Descriptions
See Page 30

TAFFETA
SILK
8K13427
$10.98

WORTH
$12.50

See Page 274 for Index and Don't Forget When Ordering to
State the Color and Size Desired

"*I thought of* STYLE *I thought of* PRICE *I thought of* Y·O·U *When I sketched these two dainty Misses Frocks*"

Irene Castle

8K13433 *Specially designed to enhance the charms of misses is this* **two-color voile** *dress of splendid attractiveness.*

For this model Irene Castle uses a combination of two delicate colors, giving an effect that is indescriba ly dainty and becoming. The design features a light overdress over a 'darker under slip. The overdress is designed in two-tier effect with lace trimming, the long shawl collar continuing below the waistline as shown. Elbow length kimono sleeves. Self-material girdle. COLORS: ᵀink and white or light blue and white. SIZES: Bust 32 to 38. Skirt length 32 to 38.
PRICE, PREPAID to your home, **$4.98**

8K13434 *No one knows better than Irene Castle how to fashion clothes for the miss.*

This unusually appealing and effective dress pays high tribute to her ability as a designer. The material is a **printed organdie** in the polka dot pattern so very fashionab e this season. The wide, attractive fichu-like collar edged with contrasting plaited frills extends in coquettish fashion below the sash belt as pictured. Two rows of plaiting adorn the skirt in pocket effect. Elbow length sleeves with plaited frills. COLORS: Lavender and white; navy blue and white; or rose and white. SIZES: Pust 32 to 38. Skirt lenght 32 to 38.
PRICE, PREPAID to your home, **$4.98**

HOW TO ORDER

Order misses' dresses by exact measurements of bust, waistband, and front length of skirt. Do not order by age, and if a larger size than 38 bust is required, order from our women's dresses.

A YEAR AGO DRESSES OF THIS CHARACTER WOULD HAVE SOLD FOR $9.00

VOILE
8K13433
$4.98

ORGANDIE
8K13434
$4.98

For a Complete List of Irene Castle's Exclusive Designs, See the Index, Page 274

PHILIPSBORN'S

FANCY VOILE

8K13435
$3.68

LINENE
8K13436
$3.49

ORGANDIE
8K13437
$4.98

No Better Values ever offered

LINENE
8K13438
$2.98

WORTH **$3.50**

CHICAGO, ILL.

A New Department—"Goods by the Yard." You Cannot Equal These Values Anywhere. See Pages 250 to 255

33

8K13442 *The demand for gingham dresses continues, and no wonder when they are as pretty as this new model for misses.*

Assorted plaid gingham in artistic color combinations makes this model most effective and becoming. Stylish basque waist designed in one with sash extensions. Embroidered organdie forms the dainty collar and cuffs. Patch pockets with piping and button trimming. Invisible fastening at shoulder and underarm seams. Skirt sweep 62 inches. A model of unquestioned style and great durability. COLOR: Assorted blue or pink plaid. SIZES: Bust 32 to 38; skirt length 32 to 38.

PRICE, PREPAID to your home, **$2.98**

8K13441 *An appealing style for misses in this* **printed voile** *dress.*

The material comes in pretty floral pattern and the design features the popular coatee effect of fashion's demands. Organdie collar, cuffs, vestee trimming and plaiting. Velvet girdle. COLORS: White with pink or white with blue. SIZES: Bust 32 to 38; skirt length 32 to 38.

PRICE, PREPAID to your home, **$3.38**

GINGHAM
8K13442
$2.98

FIGURED
VOILE
8K13441
$3.38

SHEPHERD
CHECK
8K13440
$3.38

VOILE
8K13439
$3.48
WORTH $4.00

Be sure to state SIZE and COLOR when ordering.

Dresses that Feature our Famous Values

8K13439 *A bargain without equal in this* **voile** *dress for misses, only $3.48.*

The waist portion is designed with embroidered over-blouse designed in one with sash ends. Three groups of pin tucking give charming variety to the gathered skirt. Lace edged sleeves and collar. Hemstitching. COLORS: White with blue embroidery or all white. SIZES: Bust 32 to 38; skirt length 32 to 38.

PRICE, PREPAID to your home, **$3.48**

8K13440 *For general wear the miss could not choose a more practical style than this dress.*

It is made of **woven checked material**. Soft plaits depending from a front and back yoke. Contrasting rep trimming and braid. Poplin tie. Three quarter length sleeves. A most practical and attractive dress for general wear. COLORS: Black and white with red trimming. SIZES: Bust 32 to 38. Skirt length 32 to 38.

PRICE, PREPAID to your home, **$3.38**

Most Attractive Modes of the Season!

WORTH
$10.00

SATIN
8K13451
$6.87

8K13451 *A beautiful satin dress that meets every requirement of the junior miss*

New style basque waist with sash ties. Contrasting embroidery. Dainty Georgette sleeves. COLORS: Navy blue or Copenhagen blue. SIZES: 31 to 37 bust. Skirt length 31 to 36.
PRICE, PREPAID to your home, **$6.87**

SILK POPLIN
8K13450
$4.98

8K13450 *A smart and dressy style for the junior miss in this silk poplin dress.*

Embroidery stitching adds dressiness as pictured. New style side drapery. Elbow sleeves. COLORS: Navy blue, plum or rose. SIZES: 31 to 37 bust. Skirt length 31 to 36.
PRICE, PREPAID to your home, **$4.98**

EMBR'D NET
8K13448
$7.48

ALL WOOL SERGE
8K13449
$7.48

8K13448 *Every junior girl will want this dainty and becoming dress for "best" or party wear.*

Embroidered net is used for the drop skirt and the paneled waist. The rest of the dress is made of plain net, which contrasts charmingly with the embroidery. Newest style is shown in the lace-edge pointed tunic and the over-blouse which extends below a contrasting ribbon sash. Ruffled collar and cuffs complete this girlish model. A sensational value at $7.48 COLOR: White. SIZES: 31 to 37 bust. Skirt length 31 to 36. Skirt width 64 inches.
PRICE, PREPAID to your home, **$7.48**

8K13449 *Ordinarily a dress of this style and quality could not be bought for less than $10.00.*

Only because our savings were unusually great on a large consignment of these junior misses' models are we able to sell them at $7.48. The material is an excellent quality of all wool serge, with contrasting embroidery at the neck and ¾ sleeves. The full plaited skirt is topped with a Roman striped sash, the very latest of waistline finishes. COLORS: Navy blue with Roman striped sash or wine with Roman striped sash. SIZES: 31 to 37 bust. Skirt length 31 to 36. Skirt width 70 inches.
PRICE, PREPAID to your home, **$7.48**

IMPORTANT
Be sure to state COLOR and SIZE desired when ordering.

CHICAGO, ILL.

For Index See Page 274 and Remember PHILIPSBORN'S Prepay All Transportation Charges. There Are No Express or Mailing Charges for You to Pay

35

Junior Dresses that are Charming Priced Very Low!

LINENE
8K13454
$2.88

VOILE
8K13453
$2.98

GINGHAM
8K13452
$2.88

LINENE
8K13455
$2.98

$2.98

$2.88

8K13454 *Every junior miss should have one of these practical, comfortable sailor dresses.*
This **washable linene** model is of such good quality that it would be a bargain at $4.00, but in order to give our customers the benefit of every possible saving we have marked it at $2.88. Box plaits from deep yoke. Braid trimming, as pictured. COLORS: White with Copenhagen blue or Copenhagen blue with white. SIZES: 31 to 37 bust. Skirt length 31 to 36. Skirt width 64 inches.
PRICE, PREPAID to your home, **$2.88**

8K13453 *You need not pay high prices to get the newest styles as this dress at $2.98 proves.*
It is an **embroidered voile** model, designed especially to bring out the charm of the junior miss. Elbow sleeves finished with lace-edged ruffles. Lace-trimmed collar. Contrasting ribbon sash and bow. An excellent choice for best wear. COLOR: White with blue sash. SIZES: 31 to 37 bust. Skirt length 31 to 36. Skirt width 70 inches.
PRICE, PREPAID to your home, **$2.98**

You must not! miss these Bargains

8K13452 *Among the season's newest and most practical dresses for junior misses is this model.*
Plaid gingham of very pleasing pattern is combined as illustrated with solid color linene. Patch pockets. Black tie. Button trimming. A splendid money-saving offer. COLORS: Blue and assorted plaids or pink and assorted plaids. SIZES: 31 to 37 bust. Skirt length 31 to 36. Skirt width 62 inches.
PRICE, PREPAID to your home, **$2.88**

8K13455 *A very good style for junior misses in one of the new smock dresses now so popular.*
This attractive model of good quality **linene** is made with separate skirt and smock. Hand embroidery provides a pretty trimming for the smock as pictured. Slot pockets. Opening on side. COLORS: Copenhagen blue or rose. SIZES: 31 to 37 bust. Skirt length 31 to 36. Skirt width 62 inches.
PRICE, PREPAID to your home, **$2.98**

"Queen of May"

"Prize dresses for your Daughter!"

6K11300 *A wonderfully becoming style in a girl's* **organdie** *dress.*
This pretty model is developed in an effective combination of two color organdie, and is of a quality seldom found at a reduced price. The illustration shows you the fascinating style of the surplice cross-over collar, with its wide sash terminations at the back. Contrasting organdie ruffles trim the gathered skirt, also the collar and elbow sleeves. COLORS: Light blue with white or pink with white collar, cuffs and ruffles. SIZES: 7 to 14 yrs.
PRICE, PREPAID to your home, **$3.48**

6K11301 *A favorite style in a girl's long waisted dress.*
All-over embroidered organdie fashions the semi-plaited skirt and the front of the long-waisted blouse. The back of blouse is finished with groups of cluster tucking. Dainty lace edges the revers and the short sleeves. Tucked dickey, ribbon rosettes and ribbon ends help beautify the dress. A dress that will compare favorably with models that cost from two to three dollars more elsewhere. COLOR: White only. SIZES: 7 to 14 years.
PRICE, PREPAID to your home, **$2.48**

HOW TO ORDER

If you are not sure what size to order, give age, chest measure, and length desired, and we will send you the correct size. For length, take measurement from center of neckband to edge of skirt at back.

ALL OVER
EMBR'D
ORGANDIE
6K11301
$2.48

ORGANDIE
6K11300
$3.48

6K11304 *You will be charmed with this girl's lawn dress, for which we quote a low price.* Designed in original fashion with a pointed overblouse of embroidery flouncing. Semi-plaited skirt with embroidery flouncing and cluster tucking. COLOR: White only. SIZES: 7 to 14 years. PRICE. **$1.69** PREP'D to your home,

6K11303 *Down go prices! Look at this girl's pretty dress, only $1.49 for a real $3.00 value.* Stylish becoming lawn model, made very dainty with contrasting embroidered batiste bands. Cluster tucking and hemstitching. Long waisted model. COLOR: White only. SIZES: 7 to 14 years. PRICE, PREP'D to your home, **$1.49**

LAWN
6K11304
$1.69

LAWN
6K11303
$1.49

LAWN
6K11302
98c

WORTH
$1.50

ORGANDIE
6K11305
$1.89

ORGANDIE
6K11306
$1.98

ORGANDIE
6K11307
$2.29

6K11307 *An extraordinary purchase permits the low price that we ask for this girls' organdie dress.* Note the original style of the waist, which is designed with three loose panels of embroidery with dainty lace edging. The skirt is softly plaited, and trimmed in panel effect. Cluster tucking-lace insertion and lace edging add further dressiness. Ribbon rosebuds at panels. Cluster-tucked back with invisible fastening. A dressy model at a notable saving. COLOR: White only. SIZES: 7 to 14 years. PRICE, PREPAID to your home, **$2.29**

6K11306 *Here is a surprise value from PHILIPSBORN'S —a house that ranks first in the field for values.* This charming little model is developed in beautiful quality, sheer **organdie** which contrasts effectively with the embroidery paneled waist. Further smart style is shown in the swinging patch pockets, also of embroidery trimmed with dainty lace. Satin ribbon belt and silk flower. Cluster tucking on skirt and back. A dressy model that would be a bargain at $3.00 instead of $1.98. COLOR: White only. SIZES: 7 to 14 yrs. PRICE, PREPAID to your home, **$1.98**

6K11302 *Here is a simple, girlish style in a girl's dress, and the price has been specially reduced.* The material is a good quality **lawn**, and the design is one of the long waisted models which are so generally becoming. An eyelet embroidery vestee adds dressiness, and there are clusters of pin tucks ornamenting either side of vestee. The semi-plaited skirt and girdle are tucked to correspond. Short sleeves with lace edging. Button fastening at back. A big value for the money. COLOR: White only. SIZES: 7 to 14 yrs. PRICE, PREPAID to your home, **98c**

6K11305 *Because an Eastern manufacturer sacrificed profits we can offer this dress at only $1.89.* We consider it one of our prettiest styles for girls, and we know that at this low price it is practically impossible to duplicate elsewhere. The material is an excellent grade of **organdie** combined with embroidery flouncing for the semi-plaited skirt and paneled waist. Lace-trimmed panel extends over the ribbon girdle. Ribbon rosebud trimming. Cluster-tucked back. Button fastening. Very dressy. COLORS: White only. SIZES: 7 to 14 years. PRICE, PREPAID to your home, **$1.89**

PHILIPSBORN'S

6K11311 Colored organdie *dresses are in great demand this season, and here is an especially pretty model.* Sheer, crisp organdie furnished in dainty colors is used for this exceedingly attractive dress for girls. Double picoted ruffling trim the skirt in novel pointed design and the rest of model as pictured. Deep bertha with contrasting embroidery at corners. Patch pockets. COLORS: Blue or pink. SIZES: 7 to 14 years.

PRICE, PREPAID to your home, **$3.98**

ORGANDIE
6K11311
$3.98

How to Order for Girls

If you are not sure what size to order, state age, chest measure and length desired, and we will send you the correct size. The corresponding measurements for the ages from 6 to 14 years are as follows:

6 years, 26 in. chest, length 26 in.
8 years, 28 in. chest, length 30 in.
10 years, 30 in. chest, length 34 in.
12 years, 32 in. chest, length 38 in.
14 years, 34 in. chest, length 42 in.

For length take measurement from bottom of neckband to edge of skirt at back.

IMPORTANT!
Be sure to state size and color desired

ORGANDIE
6K11310
$3.49

ORGANDIE
6K11309
$3.49

6K11310 *Look where you will, you will not find a better value for your money than this dress.*
Sheer quality **organdie** makes this model for girls. The design shows smart and up-to-date style and is very becoming. Embroidery flouncing is used for the two-tier skirt. The waist portion shows newest style in the smartly shaped front sections of embroidery which cross over as pictured. Ribbon ornament and girdle. Invisible fastening at the cluster-tucked back. COLOR: White. SIZES: 7 to 14 yrs.

PRICE, PREPAID to your home, **$3.49**

6K11309 *You could not choose a daintier style for your little daughter than this model.*
A smart and becoming feature of this **organdie** dress is the two-tier skirt formed entirely of embroidery flouncing. The embroidery paneled waist is set off with a lace-trimmed embroidered vestee. Contrasting ribbon girdle with large ribbon bows. Invisible back fastening. Cluster tucked back. COLOR: White. SIZES: 7 to 14 years.

PRICE, PREPAID to your home, **$3.49**

6K11312 Embroidered net, *a very fashionable material this season,* makes this girl's dress.
The result is as dainty and becoming a model as one could wish for, and the very moderate price which we quote puts it within the reach of every purse. Embroidery flouncing is used for the full gathered skirt, the front of waist in similar design. Lace-edged ruffle collar and cuffs. Ribbon rosebuds at collar. Ribbon ornaments on ribbon sash. COLOR: White. SIZES: 7 to 14 years.

PRICE, PREPAID to your home, **$3.88**

6K11308 *Our special price for this girls' organdie dress offers you a real cash saving.*
This very attractive model was made to sell at $4.00 but because of big discounts which we received from the manufacturers we are able to price it at only $2.48. Deep over-blouse of embroidered organdie opening over a lace-trimmed underblouse. Embroidery flouncing on skirt. COLOR: White. SIZES: 7 to 14 years.

PRICE, PREPAID to your home, **$2.48**

EMBROIDERED NET
6K11312
$3.88

ORGANDIE
6K11308 →
$2.48

Dresses that are beautiful and also Priced low!

Nifty Sailor Dresses that are always popular

6K11314 *You save fully one-third when you buy this attractive middy dress for girls at our new cut price.*
This style is very becoming to any girl. The material is a good quality **linene**. Dress is made with contrasting sailor collar, belt, cuffs, dickey and patch pocket trimming. Embroidered emblem on sleeve. Semi-plaited skirt. Contrasting braid trimming. COLORS: White and blue combination. SIZES: 7 to 14 yrs. PRICE, PREPAID to your home, **$1.98**

6K11315 *Unequaled for service and certainly a big bargain at our special price is this washable* **twill** *dress for girls.*
The model is made in regulation sailor style with large contrasting sailor collar, dickey, and cuffs. Patch pockets have button-trimmed flaps on the semi-plaited skirt. Contrasting silk braid trimming as shown. Jaunty tie. Deep, pointed yoke. COLORS: White with blue or blue with white trimming. SIZES: 7 to 14 years. PRICE, PREPAID to your home, **$2.68**

If girl is extra large for her age and you are not sure what size to order, state age, chest measure, and length desired, and we will send you the correct size.

LINENE
6K11314
$1.98

WASHABLE
TWILL
6K11315
$2.68

LINENE
6K11313

**Bargain
$1.98**
Worth
$2.50

IMPORTANT!
**Be sure to state size
and color desired**

6K11316 *Here is value for you in a girl's* **cotton serge** *dress.*
The model, which is a great favorite with young girls is made in two pieces with a separate middy blouse and a semi-plaited skirt mounted to a cambric underwaist. COLOR: Navy blue only. SIZES: 7 to 14 years. PRICE, PREPAID to your home, **$2.78**

6K11313 *Girls' smart and becoming* **linene** *sailor dress, greatly reduced in price.*
Even in pre-war days a dress of such good quality and workmanship would have been considered a find. It is made in the popular sailor style, with large attractive sailor collar and semi-plaited skirt. Contrasting braid trimming on collar and cuffs. Button-trimmed dickey. All-around buttoned belt. An ideal model for school and general wear. COLOR: Cadet Blue. SIZES: 7 to 14 yrs. PRICE, PREPAID to your home, **$1.98**

SERGE
6K11316

*Extra
Special Value*
$278

A Selection of Values and Styles that PHILIPSBORNS are proud of

6K11317 *A very dainty and becoming selection in a girl's dress of* **novelty figured voile,** *specially reduced.*
You have only to compare our prices with those charged by other mail order houses to realize that ours are the lowest, and certainly this pretty dress at our low price proves our supremacy in value-giving. The illustration shows you the unusually attractive lines,—the Tuxedo collar, vestee, and smartly shaped patch pockets. All around belt with sash in back. COLORS: Blue or pink flowered. SIZES: 7 to 14 years.
PRICE, PREPAID to your home, **$1.98**

6K11319 *You will be delighted with the attractive style of this girl's dress.*
The material is an excellent quality **gingham,** not usually found at so moderate a price. Contrasting piping. Contrasting embroidered vestee extends below the waistline. Patch pockets. A high grade dress at a worthwhile reduction. COLORS: Blue, pink and red assorted plaid. SIZES: 7 to 14 years. **$2.98**
PRICE, PREPAID to your home,

VOILE
6K11317
$1.98

GINGHAM
6K11319
$2.98

GINGHAM
6K11321
$2.98

LINENE
6K11318
$2.48

COLOR AND SIZE!
Be sure to state color and size when ordering

6K11320 *An immense bargain in a girl's dress—special at $2.98.*
Ramie linen is used for the suspender effect waist and softly gathered skirt. An under-blouse of **voile** is finished with frill collar and cuffs, prettily stitched in contrasting color. Embroidery trims waist and patch pockets. COLORS: Blue with white or pink with white voile waist. SIZES: 7 to 14 yrs.
PRICE, PREPAID to your home, **$2.98**

6K11318 *You can't imagine anything more individual in style than this stylish shirt-waist dress for girls.*
An effective combination of two-color **linene** is used for this very attractive model, which is made in two pieces as pictured. Embroidery cross stitching gives a pretty touch of color on the collar and cuffs. Silk cord tie. Cluster tucking at either side of the waist fronts. Invisible button fastening at center back. COLORS: White top with blue skirt or white top with pink skirt. SIZES: 7 to 14 yrs.
PRICE, PREPAID to your home, **$2.48**

LINENE
6K11320
$2.98

**Best Styles
Best Values
Prepaid
Besides**

6K11321 *You get 100% returns on every dollar that you spend at PHILIPSBORN'S.*
Take for example this splendid value in a girl's **checked gingham** dress. Note the clever style of the bolero waist, which is charmingly contrasted with solid color chambray for the collar, vestee, cuffs, and sash belt. Patch pockets. Rick-rack braid trimming. COLORS: Blue or lavender check. SIZES: 7 to 14 years.
PRICE, PRE'D to your home, **$2.98**

CHICAGO, ILL.

Girls' Coats Displayd on Pages 130, 131, 132, 133, 134.
† Styles and Prices Ever the Lowest

41

6K11326 *A money-saving offer in a girl's* flowered **voile** *dress at $1.88.* Even in pre-war days you would hardly expect to find a dress of this style and quality at so low a price. Contrasting linene trimming. COLORS: Blue or pink flowered. SIZES: 7 to 14 years. PRICE, PREPAID to your home, **$1.88**

6K11322 *A startling value in a girl's* **linene** *dress.* Secured at a price that has not been equaled in years. Contrasting collar and piping. Flare patch pockets. COLORS: Blue or pink. SIZES: 7 to 14 years. PRICE, PREPAID to your home, **99c**

6K11327 *One of our prettiest gingham dresses for girls.* Made of **Amoskeag plaid gingham** with solid color trimming. Embroidery at front as shown. Patch pockets. COLORS: Assorted plaid of blue, pink and tan combinations. SIZES: 7 to 14 yrs. PRICE, PREP'D to your home, **$1.98**

6K11328 *A bargain in girls' and children's bloomers.* Made of good quality **sateen** with fitted waistband and elastic at knees. Black only. SIZES: 2 to 6 years. PRICE, PREPAID to your home, **59c**

6K11329 SIZES: 8 to 14 years. PRICE, PREPAID to your home, **69c**

Be sure to state COLOR and SIZE

LINENE
6K11322
99c

VOILE
6K11326
$1.88

LINENE
6K11325
$1.98

CHAMBRAY
6K11323
$1.89

WORTH
$1.25

SATEEN
6K11328—59c
6K11329—69c

GINGHAM
6K11327
$1.98

CHAMBRAY
AND
PERCALE
COMB.
6K11324
$1.18

Nifty Models for the Growing Young Miss!

6K11323 *A most attractive style in a girl's* **chambray** *dress.* Gingham forms the rounded collar, cuffs and pocket trimming. Front of waist is daintily embroidered. Skirt designed with box plaits. Sash belt. At a saving of fully one-third. COLORS: Blue or pink. SIZES: 7 to 14 years. PRICE, PREPAID to your home, **$1.89**

6K11324 *New style shirt-waist dress for girls, only $1.18.* **Plaid percale** forms the waist and patch pockets; **plain percale** forms the softly gathered skirt. Plain percale piping as shown. Button fastening at center front. An ideal dress for school and general wear. COLORS: Blue skirt with blue plaid waist or pink skirt with pink plaid waist. SIZES: 7 to 14 years. PRICE, PREPAID to your home, **$1.18**

6K11325 *An exceedingly attractive dress for girls at a reduction.* The material—a good quality **linene** —makes the model very practical. With the addition of organdie collar, cuffs, plaiting and sash belt it is transformed into the daintiest of models. COLORS: Blue, lavender, or golden brown. SIZES: 7 to 14 yrs. PRICE, PREPAID to your home, **$1.98**

ORGANDIE
6K11331
98c

LAWN
6K11330
79c

ORGANDIE
6K11332
$1.49

6K11331 *Here's news again of important savings.*
We quote a specially reduced price on this pretty **organdie** dress for children, the equal of any $1.25 dress on the market. Embroidery flouncing forms front of waist. Cluster tucked skirt. Lace edging. Ribbon ornament. COLOR: White only. SIZES: 2 to 6 years. PRICE, PREPAID to your home, **98c**

6K11332 *A charming little dress at $1.49.*
One of our prettiest models for a child, this dress is made of **embroidered organdie flouncing** in new and attractive pattern. Cluster tucking at back. Ribbon ornament. COLOR: White only. SIZES: 2 to 6 years. PRICE, PREPAID to your home, **$1.49**

6K11333 *The most surprising of values.*
Only $1.29 for this child's dress of embroidered organdie flouncing. Made in a most attractive style with a softly plaited skirt and paneled waist. Tucked belt with ribbon ornament. COLOR: White only. SIZES: 2 to 6 yrs. PRICE, PREPAID to your home, **$1.29**

6K11337 *Another charming style offered at a price cut.*
Child's **organdie** model, made with embroidery flouncing for the two-tier skirt and paneled waist. A wonderful value. COLOR: White only. SIZES: 2 to 6 years. PRICE, PREPAID to your home, **$1.68**

A Real Bargain Dress

ORGANDIE
6K11333
$1.29

ORGANDIE
6K11337
$1.68

Dresses that Bring out the Charm of Childhood

6K11330 *Child's dress of extraordinary value.*
At our specially reduced price, this **lawn** dress for children cannot be equaled elsewhere. Long-waisted model with embroidery vestee. Cluster tucking. COLOR: White only. SIZES: 2 to 6 yrs. PRICE, PREPAID to your home, **79c**

6K11334 *This is a particularly becoming dress for children.*
Made of beautiful sheer **organdie**, with smartly shaped over-blouse. Embroidery flouncing on skirt. Ribbon girdle and ornament. COLOR: White only. SIZES: 2 to 6 years. PRICE, PREPAID to your home, **$1.49**

6K11335 *Newest style features give charm to this dress for a child.*
Embroidered organdie flouncing is used for the two-tier skirt and smartly shaped blouse. Lace and ribbon trimming. COLOR: White only. SIZES: 2 to 6 yrs. PRICE, PREPAID to your home, **$2.48**

6K11336 *An adorable style in a child's organdie dress.*
Note the charming style of the smartly shaped overblouse and softly plaited skirt. Both of embroidery flouncing. Ribbon ornament. COLOR: White only. SIZES: 2 to 6 years. PRICE, PREPAID to your home, **$1.88**

ORGANDIE
6K11334
$1.49

ORGANDIE
6K11335
$2.48

ORGANDIE
6K11336
$1.88

CHICAGO, ILL.

For Index See Page 274 and Remember PHILIPSBORN'S Prepay All Transportation Charges. There Are No Express or Mailing Charges for You to Pay

43

LINENE
6K11339
98c

GINGHAM
6K11344
$1.79

PIQUE
6K11346
$1.88

LINENE
6K11338
$1.19

FLOWERED
VOILE
6K11343
$1.49

LINENE
6K11341
$1.49

Childrens Dresses in Serviceable Styles and Materials

6K11339 *A most unusual price reduction. A real bargain.*
Child's **linene** dress with contrasting collar and cuffs. Fancy stitching on collar. Patch pockets. COLORS: Cadet blue or pink. SIZES: 2 to 6 years. PRICE, PREPAID to your home, **98c**

6K11344 *Child's very serviceable dress at a special price—$1.79.*
Combination of checked **gingham** and chambray. Novel embroidery designs. COLORS: Blue, pink, or gold. SIZES: 2 to 6 years. PRICE, PREPAID to your home, **$1.79**

6K11346 *Dainty, durable and comfortable dress for little children.*
Child's model made of **pique** with contrasting embroidery as pictured. Scalloping and embroidery. COLOR: White only. SIZES: 2 to 6 years. PRICE, PREP'D to your home, **$1.88**

6K11338 *Children's two color **linene** rompers. Wonderful comfort.*
Smocking at front. Bloomers and trimming of linene. Patch pockets. COLORS: White with tan or white with blue. SIZES: 2 to 6 years. PRICE, PREPAID to your home, **$1.19**

6K11343 *One of our daintiest and prettiest little dresses for a child.*
It is made of **flowered voile** of very artistic pattern, with embroidery as pictured. Organdie collar and cuffs lend daintiness. Patch pockets. COLORS: White with blue or pink flowers. SIZES: 2 to 6 years. PRICE, PREPAID to your home, **$1.49**

SERGE
6K11345
$1.68

CHAMBRAY
6K11340
$1.29

Bargain **$1.29**

Be sure to state COLOR and SIZE

POPLIN
6K11347
$1.98

Bargain **$1.98**

Be sure to state COLOR and SIZE

GINGHAM
6K11342—$1.49

6K11340 *Smashing price cut on a child's dress of good quality chambray.*
Embroidery designs trim either side of waist and patch pockets. **Plaid gingham** forms the novel style collar and pocket trimming. An extremely good-looking and serviceable little dress. COLORS: Cadet blue or pink. SIZES: 2 to 6 years. PRICE, PREPAID to your home, **$1.29**

6K11345 *For cool days every child should have a serge dress. Warmth and comfort.*
The model here shown is made of good quality **cotton serge**, and is made in popular sailor style. Contrasting braid trimming on collar and cuffs. Patch pockets. Cord tie. Button trimming. COLOR: Navy blue only. SIZES: 2 to 6 years. PRICE, PREPAID to your home, **$1.68**

6K11347 *One of our finest dresses for a child offered at a 25% reduction.*
Mercerized **poplin**—a material that is dressy and washes like new—is used. Underblouse of contrasting organdie. Novel silk stitched design lends charm at the front. COLORS: Light blue or pink. SIZES: 2 to 6 years. PRICE PREPAID to your home, **$1.98**

6K11342 *You save at least fifty cents in buying this dress, a worthwhile saving.*
One of our favorite styles for children, this model is fashioned of **plaid gingham** in combination with a baby waist of solid color chambray. Embroidery at front. Patch pockets. COLORS: Combinations blue or pink plaid. SIZES: 2 to 6 yrs. PRICE, PREPAID to your home, **$1.49**

6K11341 *A neat, serviceable style in a child's sailor dress at $1.49.*
This model is made of good quality **linene**, and will give you the service that you can always expect from this material. Contrasting braid trims the collar, cuffs, and patch pockets. Contrasting tie. COLOR: Cadet blue only. SIZES: 2 to 6 years. PRICE, PREPAID to your home, **$1.49**

"Goods by the Yard." A New Member of The PHILIPSBORN Family. See Pages 250 to 255

PHILIPSBORN'S

9K16266
$6.88

"The Newest Rue de la Paix" Choker Scarf!!
Fashion's Favorite

9K16269

9K16201 *Here is a style fur scarf of imitation fox specially reduced to $5.98 to introduce these new furs for spring wear.*
A good-wearing fur scarf at this low price makes this value all the more notable. The fur is dense, thick and lustrous, and will give excellent service. Made in animal style. Silk peau de cygne lining. Snap fastener in animal head and crochet ball snapper with paw. Length, 30 inches; width 7½ inches. COLORS: Black, Poiret brown or taupe grey. PRICE, PREPAID, **$5.98** to your home,

CONEY CHOKER $4.88

9K16269 *Very low priced— choker scarf of coney fur.* A fine lustrous fur which will give good service. Length 22 inches. COLORS: Black, taupe, or brown. PRICE, PREP'D to your home, **$4.88**

AMERICAN MARTEN WANTED SHADES
9K16268 **$8.98**

9K16268 *Our finest selection in a choker scarf, specially priced.* Made of the very popular American marten fur with fur on both sides. Length 22 inches. COLORS: Taupe or brown. PRICE, PREPAID to your home, **$8.98**

IMITATION FOX
9K16201
$5.98

ICELAND FOX CHOKER SCARF

9K16266 *Direct from Paris — designed by one of the foremost furriers on that famous street of shops and fashions—the Rue de la Paix.*
Here is a truly individual fur scarf made from fine selected white Iceland fox skins, with fur on both sides, giving the fashionable choker of fashion's demands. The four natural paws, the large bushy tail and animal head provide appropriate trimmings. Clamp in the mouth of the animal head. Length about 29 inches; tail 11 inches long. A wonderfully rich and dressy fur at an extremely small price. COLORS: White only. PRICE, PREPAID to your home, **$6.88**

9K16226 *Handsome fur scarf— the height of style and value.* Just the cosy warmth that one needs on chill spring days is provided in this animal scarf of good quality coney. Lined with silk peau de cygne. Clamp mouth in animal head. Length about 33 in.; width about 8 in. COLORS: Red, brown, taupe or black. PRICE, PREPAID to your home, **$6.98**

GENUINE FOX CHOKER SCARF
9K16267 **$12.98**

9K16267 *Stylish choker scarf of genuine fox fur, only $12.98.* Clamp mouth. Two natural paws. COLORS: Red, taupe, or brown. PRICE, PREPAID to your home **$12.98**

CONEY
9K16226
$6.98

FINE IMITATION FOX
9K16254
$13.98

9K16203 *Rich, luxurious fur scarf of Manchurian wolf dyed in fashionable new shades.* This scarf would be a good value even at $8.50 and it is certainly a bargain at our special reduced price. Wide animal scarf measures 35 inches in length and 8½ inches thru center. Flowered sateen lining is veiled with silk Georgette crepe in the very newest mode. COLORS: Black, brown or taupe. PRICE, PREPAID to your home, **$6.98**

IMITATION FOX
9K16228
$7.88

9K16254 *An exceedingly handsome fur scarf of fine imitation fox.* This is a long-haired, glossy fur which is very popular because of its very attractive appearance and wonderful wearing qualities. The wide ruffle edge adds dressiness. Silk peau de cygne lined. Length about 33 inches; width about 12 inches. COLORS. Brown, taupe, or black. PRICE, PREPAID to your home, **$13.98**

MANCHURIAN WOLF
9K16203
$6.98

9K16228 *Women on the lookout for bargains will admit this good-looking scarf at $7.88 to be beyond equal.* Fine selected imitation fox fur is used for the scarf, which is made in regulation animal style. It is handsomely lined with silk peau de cygne and finished with streamers to match the lining. Length about 31 inches; width about 8 inches. COLORS: Black, taupe, or brown. PRICE, PREPAID to your home, **$7.88**

CHICAGO, ILL.

PHILIPSBORN'S Simple One Price to All Policy Is Sweeping the Country. See Page 3

45

"CASTLEQUEEN" Blouses
Irene Castle's Master Waist, Design !!!

Read what she says

$3.98

"I am just over-joyed with this model - it's the prettiest I have ever created. At first it looked as though they could not produce this waist for less than $6.00 but we worked and worked on it and PHILIPSBORN'S are selling it at the wonderfully low price of

$3.98

Y-O-U must have one"!

Irene Castle

7K12300 *A fitting introduction to our waist section is this most artistic overblouse—specially low priced at $3.98. A remarkable value.* This beautiful model is developed in **silk Georgette crepe,** for which embroidery in colors contrasts charmingly. Contrasting silk braid trimming. Pointed three-quarter bell sleeves. Fastening on shoulder and either side of hip. Model extends over skirt as shown, giving a complete costume effect that is very dressy. COLORS: Navy blue with porcelain (copenhagen blue), porcelain with ecru (bisque), or zinc (French grey) with porcelain. SIZES: 34 to 44 bust.
PRICE, PREPAID to your home, **$3.98**

HOW TO ORDER
Measurement for waists should be taken loosely over dress, across center of back, under arm pits, and over largest part of bust. For extra fullness, order one size larger than actual bust measurement

For a Complete List of Irene Castle's Exclusive Designs, See the Index, Page 274

PHILIPSBORN'S

SPORT SILK
TRICOLETTE
BLOUSE
7K12302
$3.98

SILK
GEORGETTE
CREPE TIE ON
BLOUSE
7K12303
$3.98

Read what
Miss Grayson
says about
PHILIPSBORN'S
Waists and
PHILIPSBORN'S service

SILK GEORGETTE
CREPE
EATON HIP
BLOUSE
7K12301
$4.48

7K12301 *Here is the new Eton hip blouse, fashion's very latest idea in blouses.*

A decidedly superior quality of silk georgette crepe has been used in this waist, which is trimmed in Eton effect with contrasting embroidery as pictured. Hemstitched accordion plaited frills finish the neck and the three-quarter set-in sleeves. A money-saving offer in a stunning new waist. COLORS: Navy blue, white or honey dew with contrasting color embroidery. SIZES: 34 to 44 bust.
PRICE, PREPAID to your home, **$4.48**

7K12302 *New and smart is this new hip-length blouse of silk tricolette.*

It is priced at the lowest figure yet quoted on tricolette of equal quality, and when one considers that this is the season's favorite material, the offering is all the more remarkable. Blouses of this type are very much worn by fashionable women for out-door sports and general wear. The model pictured is made very rich-looking with an embroidered vestee. Fringe at sleeves and around bottom. Narrow belt. COLORS: Navy blue, rose or copenhagen blue. SIZES: 34 to 44 bust.
PRICE, PREPAID to your home, **$3.98**

7K12303 *A fascinating version of the new tie-back blouse in the forefront of fashion.*

Silk georgette crepe in lovely two-color combination makes this beautiful model. Contrasting embroidery in maple leaf design adds to its attractiveness. The model extends over the skirt as pictured and is finished with sash at the back. Full-length set-in sleeve. Collarless. COLORS: Navy blue, white or honey dew with contrasting color embroidery. SIZES: 34 to 44 bust.
PRICE, PREPAID to your home, **$3.98**

CHICAGO, ILL.

SILK
GEORGETTE CREPE
7K12305
$5.98

7K12304
$1.98

JAP SILK

7K12306 *An unusually good selection in a fine* **Jap silk** *waist which features the new frill trimming.*
At any time within a score of years the price we quote on this waist would have been considered remarkably low. Self-material fashions the finely plaited frill collar and cuffs. Collar extends down either side of waist. Three narrow box plaits at front have French knots embroidered in contrasting color. COLORS: White, navy blue or flesh. SIZES: 34 to 44 bust.
PRICE, PREPAID to your home, **$2.98**

7K12307 *An extremely dainty waist of fine* **Jap silk** *specially reduced in price.*
Wide Venise lace forms the Tuxedo collar, and trimming for the vestee, and the cuffs. Pin tucking on vestee. Small bow tie finish. Opening at side front. A wonder value, at our money-saving price. COLORS: White, flesh or navy blue. SIZES: 34 to 44 bust.
PRICE, PREPAID to your home, **$2.98**

7K12308 *A most astounding offer in one of the season's loveliest tie-back hip blouses.*
This is one of the most fashionable of models, made of **silk Georgette crepe**, and richly embroidered in colors. Sash from each side. COLORS: New shade of tomato; porcelain (Copenhagen blue) or honey dew with contrasting embroidery. SIZES: 34 to 44 bust.
PRICE, PREPAID to your home, **$2.98**

7K12309 *This blouse with kimono sleeves is again in fashion's favor.*
One of the best examples of the new modes is this **silk Georgette crepe** model, with hand embroidered front design extending around neck to back. Button fastening at back. Kimono sleeves finished with two folds. COLORS: Navy blue; brown, flesh or white. SIZES: 34 to 44 bust.
PRICE, PREPAID to your home, **$2.98**

7K12310 *Don't make the mistake of judging this new style hip blouse by the low price that we quote.*
A New York manufacturer who needed ready cash sacrificed 2,000 of these blouses to us at a price almost unbelievable. The model is made of **silk Georgette crepe**. Contrasting embroidery in pond lily design. Kimono sleeve with slashed hemstitched cuff. Slip-over style with opening at back of neck and at each side. COLORS: Navy blue with porcelain honey dew with porcelain or porcelain with bisque embroidery. SIZES: 34 to 44 bust.
PRICE, PREPAID to your home, **$2.98**

7K12311 *Here is the new Mandarin overblouse which is all the rage where fashionable women gather.*
Japanese crepe of a quality rarely seen at our low price makes the model. Hand embroidery and stitching contrasts charmingly at the square neck, the side front, on sleeves and around the bottom as pictured. Novelty slit pocket is a very new feature. Narrow sash belt. Cord and tassel finish at neck. COLORS: Rattan (gold); porcelain (Copenhagen blue); or rose, daintily hand embroidered in contrasting becoming colorings. SIZES: 34 to 44 bust.
PRICE, PREPAID to your home, **$2.98**

7K12312 *A startling blouse purchase makes possible the sensationally low price that we quote on this model.*
It is one of the new hip length slip-over blouses, fashioned of **silk tricolette** and it has the advantage of being becoming to all figure types. Chenille hand embroidery—the very latest idea in trimmings—decorate the blouse fronts and the round neck. Sash ties from each side give a charming finish. Elbow length kimono sleeve. COLORS: Neptune (nile green); brown, navy blue, rose, daintily embroidered in contrasting colors or solid black. SIZES: 34 to 44 bust.
PRICE, PREPAID to your home, **$2.98**

DON'T FORGET
In ordering be sure to state COLOR *and* SIZE *desired*

7K12304 *At a saving of exactly one-half, we offer this charming waist of* **heavy Jap silk.**

If you need a waist for general wear, we can positively say you will not have another such opportunity this season. The material is an extra heavy weight, and the style is one that any woman can wear with becomingness. Chosen in all black, this waist makes an appropriate model for mourning wear. The illustration shows you the charming style of the hemstitched Lucile collar, and the hemstitched vestee trimmed with three wide folds. Hemstitched cuffs. Button trimming as shown. Offered at a price that can't be beaten. COLORS: Flesh, white or solid black. SIZES: 34 to 44 bust.
PRICE, PREPAID to your home, **$1.98**

7K12305 *Never a question, never a doubt about our style supremacy when you see such values as this.*

Just imagine getting a waist of this wonderful new style for only $5.98. The material is **silk Georgette crepe** of excellent quality, and the style features one of the over-blouse panels which are so much in favor this year. The season's demand for embroidery is provided in the embroidery design which decorate either side of the front and the wide 3-4 length set-in sleeves have hemstitch finishing. Button trimming. Ribbon girdle. COLORS: Solid black; white with flesh embroidery; navy blue with porcelain embroidery. SIZES: 34 to 44 bust.
PRICE, PREPAID to your home, **$5.98**

48
Fashion's Latest Creations in Summer Furs Are Shown on Page 45 of This Catalog.
A Choice Assortment of Spring and Summer Dress Accessories
PHILIPSBORN'S

Your Choice $2.98 PREPAID EXTRA VALUES

7K12310

SILK GEORGETTE CREPE 7K12308

HAND EMB'D SMOCK JAPANESE CREPE 7K12311

SILK GEORGETTE CRÉPE, HAND EMB'D

FINE QUALITY JAP SILK 7K12307

7K12309

SILK GEORGETTE CRÉPE, HAND EMB'D

SILK TRICOLETTE 7K12312

FINE QUALITY JAP SILK 7K12306

For Descriptions See Page 48

CHICAGO, ILL.

IMPORTANT—Be Sure to State Color and Sizes Desired When Ordering—IMPORTANT

49

SILK
GEORGETTE
CREPE
7K12316
$3.98

SILK
GEORGETTE
CREPE
HAND
EMBR'D
7K12313
$4.98

HAND
EMBR'D

SILK
MIGNONETTE
HAND
EMBROIDERED
7K12315
$5.98

SILK GEORGETTE
CREPE, HIP BLOUSE
7K12314
$4.98

SILK
GEORGETTE
CREPE
7K12318
$3.98

SILK
GEORGETTE
CREPE
7K12319
$4.98

SILK
GEORGETTE
CREPE
7K12317
$6.88

For Descriptions See Page 51

PHILIPSBORN'S Give Away Over $500,000. See Page 3 for
This and Other Interesting Facts

3 Wonderful Styles for Misses Only

7K12322 *An effective new style in a misses' silk Georgette overblouse.* Picoted ruffles at the Kimono sleeves and tab-like hip section. Contrasting hand embroidery and pin tucking at front. COLORS: Navy blue; porcelain (Copenhagen blue); new shade tomato; new shade neptune (Nile green) daintily adorned with contrasting embroidery. SIZES: For misses' 16, 18 or 20 yrs. or sizes 34, 36, 38 bust. PRICE, PREP'D to your home, **$3.98**

7K12321 *Extremely becoming style for the miss in this new style hip line over-blouse.* Silk crepe de chine makes the model, and hand embroidery in lovely contrasting colors give a dressy effect. Jaunty tie finish at either sides. Kimono sleeve. COLORS: Flesh with porcelain; white with flesh; or navy blue with porcelain embroidery. SIZES: For misses 16, 18 or 20 yrs. or 34, 36, 38 bust. PRICE, PREPAID to your home, **$2.98**

7K12320 *A fascinating new waist designed to enhance the charm of the miss.* Made of a good quality Jap silk in the popular slip-over style with opening at back of neck. Contrasting embroidery in conventional design gives dressiness at the front. Kimono sleeve with two folds. COLORS: White with flesh embroidery or flesh with porcelain (Copenhagen blue) embroidery. SIZES: For misses 16, 18 or 20 yrs. or 34, 36, 38 bust. PRICE, PREPAID to your home, **$1.98**

Be sure to state COLOR and SIZE when ordering and thus avoid delay and disappointment.

SILK
GEORGETTE CREPE
HAND EMBR'D
7K12322
$3.98

SILK
CREPE DE CHINE
HAND EMBR'D
7K12321
$2.98

JAP SILK

7K12320
$1.98

Descriptions of Waists on Page 50

7K12313 *You can secure this handsome silk Georgette crepe overblouse for only $4.98.* Front of blouse hand embroidered in new lily design. Contrasting modified Lucile collar. COLORS: Porcelain; navy blue, zinc (French grey); or white with contrasting embroidery. SIZES: 34 to 44 bust. PRICE, PREPAID to your home, **$4.98**

7K12314 *Distinctive and exclusive describes this Mandarin overblouse of silk Georgette crepe.* Embroidery of contrasting colors decorates the front. Tucked and hemstitched hip line with plaiting at hip line. Kimono sleeves. Slip-over model with opening at neck and hips. COLORS: Tomato with navy blue; navy blue with porcelain (Copenhagen blue); bisque (ecru) with porcelain embroidery. SIZES: 34 to 44 bust. PRICE, PREPAID to your home, **$4.98**

7K12315 Mignonette, *a fibre silk material resembling tricolette fashions this overblouse.* Hand embroidery gives lovely effect as shown. Sash ties at back. Button trimming on shoulders. COLORS: Rose, Copenhagen blue; navy blue or neptune (Nile green). All with contrasting colors. SIZES: 34 to 44 bust. PRICE, PREPAID to your home, **$5.98**

7K12316 *As pretty as a picture can truly be said of this overblouse.* It is a silk Georgette model, and is decidedly underpriced for this quality. Embroidered panel. Self-material slashed "cowl collar." Sash ties at back. COLORS: Honey dew, navy blue, or porcelain with contrasting embroidery. SIZES: 34 to 44 bust. PRICE, PREPAID to your home. **$3.98**

7K12317 *Delightfully individual in style is this Cossack overblouse.* Silk Georgette crepe model with block novelty stitched in contrasting color. Latest style ostrich braid trimming finishes sailor collar and bottom of blouse. Fancy cord tie. Wide 3-4 sleeves. COLORS: Navy blue with terra cotta; flesh with porcelain (Copenhagen blue); or ecru with porcelain. SIZES: 34 to 44 bust. PRICE, PREPAID to your home, **$6.88**

7K12318 *As pretty an overblouse as you could wish, and priced low.* Fashioned of silk Georgette crepe with contrasting plaited overblouse. 3-4 sleeves have deep slashed cuffs. Hip section finished with sash tie back. COLORS: Ecru body with brown overblouse; porcelain (Copenhagen blue) with flesh; or navy blue with porcelain. SIZES: 34 to 44 bust. PRICE, PREPAID to your home, **$3.98**

7K12319 *The season's loveliest color combinations in this overblouse.* This is one of the most fashionable tie-back models, made of silk Georgette crepe, and handsomely embroidered in color. Hemstitched and button-trimmed panel. 3-4 sleeves with slashed cuffs. Sash ties across back. Wonderfully dressy. COLORS: Zinc (French grey); navy blue or flesh. SIZES: 34 to 44 bust. PRICE, PREPAID to your home, **$4.98**

CHICAGO, ILL.

For Index See Page 274 and Remember PHILIPSBORN'S Prepay All Transportation Charges. There Are No Express or Mailing Charges for You to Pay

51

7K12324 *A charming version of the slip-over blouse is offered in this* **silk Georgette** *model.*

New style is shown in the elbow length kimono sleeves finished with hemstitched slashed cuffs. Pretty embroidery design ornaments the round neck and front as shown. A dressy blouse for very little money. Easily worth $4.00. COLORS: White or flesh. SIZES: 34 to 44 bust.
PRICE, PREPAID to your home, **$2.49**

7K12325 Same style and sizes as 7K12324 but made of *silk crepe de chine.* COLORS: Navy blue, grey or white.
PRICE, PREPAID to your home, **$2.49**

7K12326 *The season's loveliest color combinations give charm to this* **silk Georgette** *blouse.*

A contrasting border with hemstitching trims the V-shaped neck. Handsome embroidery design is in contrasting color. 3-4 length set-in sleeves with hemstitched handkerchief-cuffs. Dressy slip-over model. COLORS: Flesh; porcelain (Copenhagen blue) or rattan (bisque) daintily embroidered in contrasting color. SIZES: 34 to 44 bust.
PRICE, PREPAID to your home, **$3.49**

When ordering be sure to state COLOR and SIZE desired

SILK SHANTUNG
7K12327
$2.98

SILK GEORGETTE OR SILK CREPE DE CHINE
7K12324
7K12325
$2.49

SILK GEORGETTE CREPE
7K12326
$3.49

Silk Crepe de Chine 7K12335 **$3.98**

JAP SILK
7K12323
$1.99

JAP SILK
7K12328
$1.98

Silk!
Fashion's Favorite

7K12327 *Another proof of our leadership in value-giving is this smart and stylish surplice tie-back blouse. A most splendid value.*

It is made of excellent quality **silk Shantung,** a pongee-like fabric of great beauty and durability, with full length Tuxedo collar and sash ties. COLOR: Pongee only. SIZES: 34 to 44 bust.
PRICE, PREPAID to your home, **$2.98**

7K12335 Same style and sizes but made of **silk crepe de chine.** COLORS: White, flesh or navy blue.
PRICE, PREPAID to your home, **$3.98**

7K12328 *See what you save on this pretty Jap silk blouse—a tremendous bargain.*

An embroidered front panel makes the blouse very dressy, its daintiness enhanced with hemstitched folds at either side. The self-material sailor collar terminates at either side of the front and is finished with a wide hemstitched border. Hemstitched cuffs and seams as shown. COLORS: White or flesh. SIZES: 34 to 44 bust.
PRICE, PREPAID to your home, **$1.98**

7K12323 *For the women who prefer a high-necked blouse we have designed this Jap silk model and priced it very low.*

The attractive turn-over collar is finished with a tiny bow tie as pictured. Groups of tucking trim either side of the blouse fronts. Visible button fastening. Here is a blouse that we feel sure cannot be duplicated for less than $2.50 elsewhere. Our special reduced price $1.99. COLORS: White, flesh, navy blue or black. SIZES: 34 to 44 bust.
PRICE, PREPAID to your home, **$1.99**

A New Department—"Goods by the Yard." You Cannot Equal These Values Anywhere. See Pages 250 to 255.

PHILIPSBORN'S

7K12331 *PHILIPSBORN'S special silk Georgette blouse for only $2.88.*

At our extraordinary low price of only $2.88 this pretty blouse is a bargain that no woman who is interested in saving can afford to overlook. A beautiful floral pattern embroidery trims the front panel and makes the model exceedingly dressy and becoming. Hemstitched folds define the panel as pictured. Square collar with hemstitched folds. ¾ length sleeves with hemstitched bell cuffs. COLORS: White or flesh. SIZES: 34 to 44 bust. PRICE, PREPAID to your home,

$2.88

7K12330 *The ever-popular overblouse is here shown in one of its most becoming styles.*

Heavy silk crepe de chine model compares favorably both in style and quality with blouses selling elsewhere at considerably more. Contrasting hand embroidery at the round neck and wide ¾ sleeves provides dressiness. Hip section trimmed with four hemstitched folds. Self-covered buttons at sides. Opening at sides and shoulders. COLORS: Navy blue, flesh, or white. SIZES: 34 to 44 bust. PRICE, PREPAID to your home,

$4.98

SILK
CREPE DE CHINE
7K12330
$4.98

JAP SILK
7K12329
$2.29

7K12331
$2.88

SILK
GEORGETTE

SILK
GEORGETTE
CREPE EYELET
EMBROIDERY

Silk!
Always Looks Well!

JAP SILK
7K12333
$1.98

7K12329 *Certainly for all-around wear, nothing is quite so satisfactory as Jap silk.*

The very smart and becoming blouse pictured above is made of an excellent grade of Jap silk. Rich embroidery designs adorn either side of the fronts. Smartly shaped collar has hemstitching and button trimming. Button fastening at hemstitched center plaits. COLORS: White, flesh, or honeydew (peach). SIZES: 34 to 44 bust. PRICE, PREPAID to your home,

$2.29

7K12333 *A very dressy and becoming new slip-over blouse of Jap silk at a big reduction.*

Contrasting embroidery of very rich design ornaments the model in newest fashion. Fashionable kimono sleeves finished with embroidery, hemstitching and flare cuff. A wonder of value at our low price. A real $3.50 value. COLORS: White, flesh or honeydew, with contrasting color embroidery. SIZES: 34 to 44 bust. PRICE, PREPAID to your home,

$1.98

7K12332 *Here is your chance to secure an entirely new blouse at a fraction of its real worth. Truly a remarkable value.*

This silk Georgette crepe model combines the season's favorite material, eyelet embroidery, in unusually good effect. The youthful Peter Pan collar, vestee, and turnback cuffs are of the embroidery. Small silk tie at neck. Invisible side front fastening. A big value. COLORS: White, flesh or bisque. SIZES: 34 to 44 bust. PRICE, PREPAID to your home,

$3.49

7K12332
$3.49

CHICAGO, ILL.

Waists that Have the Latest Paris touch

SILK
GEORGETTE
CREPE
CHENILLE
EMBR'Y
7K12338
$5.98

ALL
OVER
EMBR'D
SILK
GEORGETTE
CREPE
7K12337
$5.98

7K12337 All-over embroidered silk Georgette crepe makes this slip-over blouse.

A model that reflects Paris. Contrasting plaited frills give the newest of finishes as pictured. Two-tone 3-4 sleeves. Sash ties from each side. Very dressy. COLORS: Navy blue, ecru (bisque), taupe, or flesh. All with porcelain (Copenhagen blue). SIZES: 34 to 44 bust. PRICE, PREPAID to your home, **$5.98**

7K12334 Priced below actual cost to manufacture is this silk crepe de chine blouse.

The embroidered front panel makes the model very dressy and becoming. Picoted square collar. A blouse that has all the style of a high-priced model for only $2.98. COLORS: White, flesh, or honeydew (peach). SIZES: 34 to 44 bust. PRICE, PREPAID to your home, **$2.98**

Be Sure to State COLOR and SIZE.

SILK
CREPE
DE CHINE
7K12334
$2.98

SILK
GEORGETTE
CREPE
7K12339
$4.98

7K12338 This imported Parisian blouse is just another demonstration of our ability to cut prices.

The material—an excellent quality **silk Georgette crepe**—is made very effective with contrasting chenille and silk embroidery in the fashionable Greek key design. Made in slip-over style with sash ties at back. COLORS: Brown with ecru; navy blue with porcelain blue (Copenhagen blue); porcelain blue with flesh; or white with flesh. SIZES: 34 to 44 bust. PRICE, PREPAID to your home, **$5.98**

7K12339 A fascinating style in one of the new over-blouses that are all the rage with smart dressers.

Silk Georgette crepe model with contrasting embroidery at blouse front and hip sections. Cowl collar. Picoted scalloped handkerchief cuffs. Silk taffeta ribbon sash. COLORS: Zinc (French grey) with porcelain blue (Copenhagen blue); porcelain with ecru; or navy blue with porcelain. SIZES: 34 to 44 bust. PRICE, PREPAID to your home, **$4.98**

7K12336 Sacrifice prices prevail at PHILIPSBORN'S.

Here is one of the season's popular hip length over-blouses developed in **silk Georgette crepe**, and the price is only $2.39. The embroidered Peter Pan collar is an especially becoming feature. Model ties at back with sash. COLORS: Navy blue, bisque, flesh, or white, all with white collar. SIZES: 34 to 44 bust. PRICE, PREPAID to your home, **$2.39**

SILK
GEORGETTE
CREPE
7K12336
$2.39

"A Thing or Two to Remember" and Some Other Interesting Facts to Be Found on Page 5

SILK
GEORGETTE
CREPE
OVER
BLOUSE
7K12342
$5.98

SILK
MIGNONETTE
TRICOLETTE
7K12341
$5.98

SATIN
MESSALINE
OR SILK
CHIFFON
TAFFETA
7K12343
7K12344
$4.98

SILK GEORGETTE
CREPE TIE BACK
7K12340
$5.98

*"From Coast to Coast
I received letters of
approval on my last
season's waist designs
I hope you'll like these
equally as well"*

Irene Castle

7K12341 *Favored fashionable silk mignon-ette* sport blouse.
Fancy tinsel vestee of contrasting color. ¾ bell sleeves. Sash belt finished with novelty buckle. Square scalloped hip line as shown. COLORS: Navy blue, rose or porcelain blue (Copenhagen blue). SIZES: 34 to 44 bust.
PRICE, PREPAID to your home, **$5.98**

7K12342 *Fascinating over blouse of silk Georgette crepe.*
Handsomely embroidered. Straps, with ball drops drawn through picoted slots at front and back. Sash belt. COLORS: Navy blue with ecru (bisque); white with flesh; porcelain (Copenhagen blue) with navy blue or bisque with porcelain. SIZES: 34 to 44 bust.
PRICE, PREPAID
to your home, **$5.98**

7K12343 *Fashionable satin messaline tie-back blouse.*
Embroidery as pictured. COLORS: Chestnut brown, navy blue or black. SIZES: 34 to 44 bust.
PRICE, PREPAID to your home, **$4.98**

7K12344 Same style in taffeta silk. COLORS: Navy blue, black or Japan blue (Copenhagen blue). SIZES: 34 to 44 bust.
PRICE, PREPAID to your home, **$4.98**

7K12340 *Lovely two-tone overblouse of silk Georgette crepe.*
One of the new tie-back models, with embroidered over-blouse panel. V shawl collar front, square back. COLORS: Tomato with navy blue; navy blue with Neptune (Nile green) or flesh with porcelain (Copenhagen blue). SIZES: 34 to 44 bust.
PRICE, PREPAID to your home, **$5.98**

IMPORTANT!—Don't forget to state SIZE and COLOR when ordering.

SILK CREPE DE CHINE
7K12348
$3.98

7K12348 *Amazing price cut in an effective new waist for the stout woman. Wonderful value.* At only $3.98 this blouse is practically offered at the cost of the material at retail. It is fashioned of a good quality **silk crepe de chine**, richly embroidered at either side of fronts. Square collar. COLORS: Navy blue, black, white or flesh. SIZES: 46 to 54 bust. PRICE, PREPAID to your home, **$3.98**

7K12346 *Designed to give correct lines for full-formed women is this stylish, stout blouse.* Of good quality **silk crepe de chine** —seldom offered at this reduced price. Modified Lucile collar and cluster tucked vestee with pearl button finish. Dainty self-material plaiting as shown. COLORS: Black, navy blue, white or flesh. SIZES: 46 to 54 bust. PRICE, PREPAID to your home, **$3.98**

SILK CREPE DE CHINE
7K12346
$3.98

SILK GEORGETTE CREPE, HAND EMBROIDERED AND BEADS

7K12349
$5.98

7K12349 *The excellent lines of this dressy silk Georgette crepe blouse can be seen at a glance. A very desirable selection.* Specially designed for stout figures. Hand embroidered panel front. COLORS: Navy blue, black, white or flesh. SIZES: 46 to 54 bust. PRICE, PREPAID to your home, **$5.98**

SILK GEORGETTE CREPE
7K12347
$5.68

Be sure to state size and color desired

7K12345 *No smarter style for the stout woman than this semi-tailored blouse of heavy Jap silk on which we quote a cut price.* Long lines are given by the tucked front. Two rows of buttons. Square collar. Open cuffs. COLORS: Flesh, white, navy blue or black. SIZES: 46 to 54 bust. PRICE, PREPAID to your home, **$2.88**

7K12347 *Dressy style with slenderizing lines distinguish this handsome silk Georgette crepe waist for stout women. A very becoming model.* Contrasting and self-tone embroidery. Elbow sleeves with handkerchief points and picot edge. COLORS: Navy blue, black, flesh, or white. SIZES: 46 to 54 bust. PRICE, PREPAID to your home, **$5.68**

JAP SILK
7K12345
$2.88

Save Real Money!

Buy any or all of these three
Great Specials!! Our Mr.
H. Philipsborn telegraphed—

WESTERN UNION
TELEGRAM

RECEIVED AT

COLLECT

25 NEW YORK NY 535P JAN 7 1921

PHILIPSBORN'S

CHICAGO ILLINOIS

I AM SENDING THE THREE GREATEST WASH WAIST STYLE AND VALUES FOR PAGE
FIFTY SEVEN I EVER LAID MY EYES ON. DESTROY OLD PAGE AND USE THESE
INSTEAD

H. PHILIPSBORN

We had this page all ready to put
in our catalog, when this message
came!!!

HERE THEY ARE!

The 3 Greatest Values Ever!
Order at our risk · We know
you'll agree!!

**VOILE
HAND
EMBROIDERED
7K12356
$1.88**

**VOILE
7K12358
$1.88**

**VOILE
7K12357
$1.88**

7K12357 *Entirely new and extremely becoming is this tie-back voile blouse, special at $1.88*

Newest style is displayed in the all-over embroidered front, with box plaits at either side. New coat collar with hemstitching finish and string tie. Small opening at front as pictured. The mode ties at the side with a self-material sash. An extraordinary value. COLORS: White, flesh or bisque. SIZES: 34 to 44.

PRICE, PREPAID to your home, **$1.88**

7K12356 *Where could you find a blouse of equal beauty for only $1.88? A real $3.00 value.*

This charming **voile** model is designed in the new tie-back style with sash ties from each side. Hand embroidered scroll design at front and around neck. Small pockets as pictured. Kimono sleeves with embroidery stitching and scalloping. COLORS: Orchid, honey dew (peach shade); Copenhagen blue, white or rose. SIZES: 34 to 44.

PRICE, PREPAID to your home, **$1.88**

7K12358 *The picture can only suggest the daintiness of this blouse—a voile model of exquisite beauty.*

It is one of the newest versions of the popular tie-back blouses, and is a real find at our bargain price. Dainty lace is inset at the top of the vestee and at the bottom of the over-blouse section, also at the ¾ length sleeves. Tucked and lace-trimmed bands extend down either side of fronts, collar to correspond. Sash ties at back. COLORS: White or flesh. SIZES: 34 to 44.

PRICE, PREPAID to your home, **$1.88**

VOILE
7K12362
$2.98

Special!
$2.98

VOILE
7K12360
$2.98

"Hand Made Collars & Cuffs"

7K12359
$1.98

The Latest Styles !!! Priced Low!

VOILE
7K12361
$2.49

FLOWERED VOILE
7K12363
$1.98

VERY IMPORTANT
Don't forget to state SIZE and COLOR desired when ordering.

7K12361 *Extremely effective style in a tie-back blouse.*

The material is of good quality **voile** with lace-edged folds composing the front of waist as pictured. Wide hip section with sash ties. Lace-trimmed collar and cuffs. COLORS: Bisque with white, flesh with white, or all white. SIZES: 34 to 44 bust.
PRICE, PREPAID to your home, **$2.49**

7K12359 *Exquisite in its daintiness is this batiste blouse.*

The season's demand for hand-work finds charming accord in the hand-drawn work which ornaments the Lucile collar and cuffs. Box plait effect front. Novelty buttons. Priced very low for such daintiness. COLORS: Flesh with white, or all white. SIZES: 34 to 44 bust.
PRICE, PREPAID to your home, **$1.98**

7K12360 *A charming version of the new hip line blouse.*

For only $2.98 you can secure this very dainty blouse of **all-over embroidered voile**. Wide Venise lace hip section with ribbon belt tying on side. Venise lace-trimmed collar. Turn-back cuffs. COLORS: White or flesh. SIZES: 34 to 44 bust.
PRICE, PREPAID to your home, **$2.98**

7K12363 *An especially good bargain in a pretty tie-back blouse.*

Novelty figured voile in attractive colors is used for this model. Self-material Tuxedo collar. 3-4 length sleeves. Tucked vestee. Hip section with sash ties. Lace trimming as shown. COLORS: Navy blue with gold or rose or copenhagen blue with white. SIZES: 34 to 44 bust.
PRICE, PREPAID to your home, **$1.98**

58

All Merchandise in This Catalogue is Covered by Our Broad Guarantee. See Page 3

PHILIPSBORN'S

7K12368 *Where could you duplicate this stylish voile blouse at our money-saving price?*
Newest style is shown in the embroidered front, which is designed with a wedge-shaped button-trimmed vestee in fashionable Eton effect. Youthful Peter Pan collar with two rows of Val. lace. Lace-trimmed vestee and ¾ sleeves. COLOR: All white. SIZES: 34 to 44 bust. PRICE, PREPAID to your home, **$1.19**

All! Hand Made

Filipino Open Work

VOILE
7K12368
$1.19

FIGURED VOILE
7K12367
$1.79

7K12364
$2.93

VOILE HIP BLOUSE
VENISE TRIMMED
7K12365
$2.79

VOILE
7K12366
$1.88

Sheer Waists of Novel Designs

7K12364 *Hand made blouses are all the rage and here is a wonderful value in a dainty batiste blouse.*
We imported this pretty model from the Philippine Islands. It features the Filipino hand-drawn work for which these people are famous and is hand made throughout. Fronts and collar are decorated as pictured. Tucking. Hemstitching. The smartest in blouse styles. COLOR: White only. SIZES: 34 to 44. PRICE, PREPAID to your home, **$2.93**

7K12365 *Was there ever a blouse fashion more charming and becoming than the hip-line blouse?*
Here is the very latest version of this popular style, developed in good quality voile. All-over lace forms the collar, vestee front and hip section. Lace-edged ¾ sleeves. Ribbon lacing at waistline. COLORS: White or flesh. SIZES: 34 to 44 bust. PRICE, PREPAID to your home, **$2.79**

7K12366 *The high-necked blouse never fails to please, because it is always trim and tailored.*
Here is a money-saving offer in a dainty voile blouse which rivals in charm the hand-made models now so popular. The hemstitched bosom front, turn-over collar and turnback cuffs are most effective. Tucking. Button fastening. COLORS: White or flesh. SIZES: 34 to 44. PRICE, PREPAID to your home, **$1.88**

7K12367 *Fashion turns to frill effects in blouses.*
The charming model here shown in dainty floral design voile, which is furnished in the new spring shades. Flat plaited frill collar and cuffs, both finished with silk ties. A most becoming blouse at a big saving. COLORS: Light pink or light blue. SIZES: 34 to 44. PRICE, PREPAID to your home, **$1.79**

DON'T FORGET
In ordering be sure to state
SIZE and COLOR desired

Misses
Voile
and
Organdie

7K12373

Choice $1.39 Worth $2.00

VOILE
7K12374

VOILE
7K12370

7K12373 *A charmingly youthful blouse, specially designed for misses and small women—special at $1.39.*

For this model of good quality **voile**, contrasting color organdie provides a delightful touch of color in the "Peter Pan" collar and turnover cuffs. Note the effective style of the new style "bosom" front which is made of pin-tucked voile in criss-cross design. Black bow tie. Button fastening at center front. COLORS: White with orchid; white with rose or white with Copenhagen blue organdie. SIZES: 32 to 40 bust. **PRICE, PREPAID to your home,** **$1.39**

7K12374 *Here is the latest tie-back blouse in voile. A most attractive garment.*

All-over embroidery fashions the plastron front and turnback cuffs on the ¾ sleeves. Smart, collarless neck with black silk tie. Slip-over model. Sash ties from either side across back. COLORS: White or flesh. SIZES: 34 to 44 bust. **PRICE, PREPAID to your home,** **$1.39**

7K12370 *Remarkable bargain in a new voile blouse Stunningly effective.*

This pretty model features the new jabo effect which is achieved with wide lace edging, forming collar. Lace-trimmed turnback cuff. Black silk tie. Hemstitching. COLOR: White only. SIZES: 34 to 44 bust. **PRICE, PREPAID to your home,** **$1.39**

Be sure and state SIZE and COLOR desired

VOILE
7K12372

VOILE
7K12371

VOILE
7K12369

7K12369 *A splendid offer in a new style voile blouse, reduced to a very low price.*

Large square collar with embroidery, lace medallion and lace edging. Lace-trimmed and tucked vestee. Lace-edged turnover cuffs. COLOR: All white. SIZES: 34 to 44 bust. PRICE, PREPAID to home, **$1.39**

7K12371 *An exquisite style is shown in this pretty new voile blouse, yet the price is very low.*

Embroidered organdie trims either side of front. Pin-tucked vestee with black ribbon tie slipped through slots. Round collar. COLOR: All white. SIZES: 34 to 44 bust. PRICE, PREPAID to your home, **$1.39**

7K12372 *Extremely dressy and becoming is this voile blouse with its smart style collar.*

Embroidery and Venise lace trims both collar and blouse fronts. Embroidery sprays at either side. Black silk tie. COLORS: White or flesh. SIZES: 34 to 44 bust. PRICE, PREPAID to your home, **$1.39**

ALL OVER
EMBR'D VOILE
7K12378

VOILE
7K12376

**Choice
98¢
Worth
$1 50**

VOILE
AND
ORGANDIE
7K12379

7K12378 *An unlooked-for saving in a
stylish blouse. A real bargain.*

All-over embroidery voile of unusually attractive
pattern fashions this model. Square collar of
organdie with contrasting embroidered edge. Button fastening. COLORS: White with rose or
white with blue. SIZES: 34 to 44 bust.
PRICE, PREPAID
to your home,   **98c**

7K12376 *An extraordinary bargain in a
voile blouse. Extraordinary value.*

One of the prettiest of the new spring models: this
blouse features a round hemstitched yoke below
which becoming fulness is laid. Turnback cuffs.
Slip-over model. COLORS: All black or all
white. SIZES: 34 to 44 bust.
PRICE, PREPAID
to your home,   **98c**

IMPORTANT
*Be sure to state COLOR
and SIZE desired*

7K12379 *We bought several thousand of
these blouses at a big sacrifice—therefore the
low price. Don't miss this opportunity to
save.*

This pretty model combines two very dainty
materials, **voile** and **embroidered organdie.**
Square collar and neckline edged with dainty lace.
Side front fastening. Very dressy. COLOR: All
white. SIZES: 34 to 44 bust.
PRICE, PREPAID
to your home,   **98c**

7K12380
*Misses
Voile*

VOILE
7K12377

VOILE AND
ORGANDIE
7K12375

7K12380 *Smart and becoming
voile blouse, specially designed for
misses and small, youthful women.*

**All-over embroidered "Peter
Pan" collar** and turnback cuffs,
lace edging and black bow tie as
pictured. Button fastening. COLORS: White or flesh. SIZES: 32
to 40 bust. PRICE, PREPAID to your home,   **98c**

7K12377 *A smart kimona sleeve
blouse of good quality voile at less
than today's wholesale prices.*

Contrasting embroidery as pictured. Tuxedo collar. Tucked
vestee. ¾ sleeves. Very dressy
and becoming. COLORS: White
with rose; white with blue. SIZES:
34 to 44 bust. PRICE,
PREPAID to your home,   **98c**

7K12375 *Savings that put money
into your pocket—this dainty voile
blouse at a low price.*

Contrasting organdie plaited frills
add a charming color touch as
pictured. COLORS: White with
blue; white with rose plaiting.
SIZES: 34 to 44 bust.
PRICE, PREPAID
to your home,   **98c**

CHICAGO, ILL.

*PHILIPSBORN'S Bargain Prices Include Delivery to Your Door.
No Extra Charges for Express or Mailing*

61

7K12386
$1.00

VOILE
7K12385
$1.39

7K12384
99c

TAILORED LINON

SUSETTE, FAST BLACK

7K12386 *Here is a tailored blouse which is unusually smart and it is priced at the remarkably low price of only $1.00.*
A decidedly superior quality of **linon** is used in this model. Designed with convertible collar which may be buttoned high as in the illustration or left open as in miniature. Patch pocket. Button fastening at center front. COLOR: All white. SIZES: 34 to 44 bust.
PRICE, PREPAID to your home. **$1.00**

7K12384 *For the woman who likes a blouse with a convertible collar we offer this new model. Very up-to-date style.*
The material is **susette**, a cotton fabric finished to look like silk and guaranteed absolutely fast color. Collar buttons high, as miniature, if desired. Two patch pockets trimmed with box plaits. Button fastening at center front. COLOR: Black. SIZES: 34 to 44 bust.
PRICE, PREPAID to your home, **99c**

7K12385 *You will be delighted if you select this blouse. It has all the style features of the higher-priced model.*
In good quality **voile**. Floral embroidery in handsome eyelet pattern adorns either side of the blouse fronts. Smartly shaped collar and pointed handkerchief cuffs with dainty lace edging. Button fastening. COLOR: All white. SIZES: 34 to 44 bust.
PRICE, PREPAID to your home, **$1.39**

PETER PAN VOILE AND ORGANDIE
7K12382
98c

Misses Specials

VOILE
7K12383
98c

LINON
7K12381
79c

7K12382 *Misses' stylish voile blouse priced at a very low figure for this style and quality. A wonderful value.*
Contrasting plaited organdie frills trim the Peter Pan collar, turnback cuffs and center plait. Button fastening. COLORS: White with blue or white with rose. SIZES: 32 to 40 bust. PRICE, PREPAID to your home, **98c**

7K12381 *Here is an exceptional value in a misses' middy blouse of good quality linon. Splendid value.*
Made in regulation middy style with patch pocket and black tie. Short sleeves. COLORS: All white, all rose or all Copenhagen blue. SIZES: 32 to 40. PRICE, PREPAID to your home, **79c**

7K12383 *Here is the latest collarless blouse of good quality voile at less than the cost of making.*
Embroidered front panel is trimmed with lace, hemstitched, button trimmed and fastened as pictured. Very dainty and becoming—big value. COLOR: All white. SIZES: 34 to 44 bust. PRICE, PREPAID to your home **98c**

Always be sure to state size and color desired.

7K12395
$1.98

*Two-Tone
Hand
Emb.*

A word to the Wise!!
Buy these Bargains!

7K12395 *As attractive a smock as you will find this season, and certainly remarkably low priced.*
Good quality **ramie linen** makes the model. Two-tone hand-embroidery decorates the front as pictured. Contrasting trimming and embroidery stitching. Round collar, Patch pockets. Sash belt. ¾ length sleeves. COLORS: Copenhagen blue with gold, rose with gold or gold with Copenhagen blue. SIZES: 34 to 44 bust.
PRICE, PREPAID to your home, **$1.98**

7K12397 *The smartest idea in middy blouses is this stylish pure silk model.*
It is made of an excellent quality **washable silk** in regulation unbelted style. Sailor collar finished with mercerized sailor tie. Patch pocket. Elbow sleeves. An unequaled bargain at this low price.
COLOR: White. SIZES: 34 to 44 bust.
PRICE, PREPAID to your home, **$2.28**

7K12396 *Smart style in a regulation unbelted middy with deep yoke.*
Made of good quality **jean** with contrasting emblem on sleeve. Mercerized tie. Sailor collar. Slip-over model. A wonderful value. COLOR: White. SIZES: 34 to 44 bust.
PRICE, PREP'D to your home, **$1.69**

*All
Silk
Middy*

7K12397
$2.28

*Regulation
Middy Jean*
7K12396
$1.69

7K12392
98c
Jean

7K12394 *Here is the best smock the season offers, both as regards style and value. Tremendous Value.*
It is fashioned of a good quality **French linon** and at our low price it is a competition-defying bargain without equal. Note the very dainty effect of the contrasting hand embroidery which ornaments the square neck, the ¾ length sleeves and the patch pockets. Sash belt. Model slips over head. Button fastening at shoulders. COLORS: Rose, Copenhagen blue, green or white. SIZES: 34 to 44 bust.
PRICE, PREPAID to your home, **$1.88**

7K12392 *Here's news again of how to reduce costs in this splendid middy offer. A big price-saving value.*
You can see for yourself that a middy of good quality **jean** is a wonderful bargain at only 98c. Slip-over model made in regulation unbelted style with lacings at the front. Contrasting trimming on the sailor collar, cuffs and single patch pocket. Plain dickey. A money-saving value without equal. COLORS: White with navy blue trimming or white with Copenhagen blue. SIZES: 34 to 44 bust.
PRICE, PREPAID to your home, **98c**

7K12393 *You could not begin to duplicate this smart smock elsewhere at our price. This is a splendid value.*
For the material we have selected a good quality **linon**, a close-woven fabric which resembles linen but is not nearly so expensive. The smock is made in very latest style with three eyelet lacings at the square neck. Embroidery in "V" effect at the front of smock. Embroidered ¾ sleeves and patch pockets. Sash belt. COLORS: Copenhagen blue, rose or white, all with contrasting embroidery. SIZES: 34 to 44 bust.
PRICE, PREPAID to your home, **$1.39**

7K12393
$1.39
*Linon
Hand
Emb.*

7K12394
*French Linon
Hand Emb.*
$1.88

***Be sure to state SIZE and
COLOR desired***

Real Hand Embroidered Models

Hand Wool Emb
7K12400
$2.38

7K12400 *Hand embroidery adds to the effect of this new style* **linene** *smock.* Contrasting wool embroidery. French knots on the new style slashed collar and cuffs. Conventional lily design and stitching at lower part of model. Sash belt. Slip-over model. COLORS: Copenhagen blue, rose, green or gold. SIZES: 34 to 44 bust. PRICE, PREPAID to your home, **$2.38**

7K12402 *No wonder smocks are so very popular when they are as attractive as this.* It is made of **Trouville cloth.** New style is shown in the bosom effect yoke with embroidery stitching. Contrasting trimming. Embroidery sprays. Sash belt. Slot pockets. COLORS: Copenhagen blue with gold, rose with gold or white with Copenhagen blue. SIZES: 34 to 44 bust. PRICE, PREPAID to your home, **$2.28**

7K12402
$2.28
Two-Tone Hand wool Emb.

7K12399 *Regulation* **jean** *middy with detachable wool flannel collar.* Collar has contrasting braid and button trimming. Mercerized sailor tie. Plain dickey. Pointed yoke with slit pocket. Embroidered emblem on sleeve. Open buttoned cuffs. Slip-over style. COLORS: White with navy blue or white with red. SIZES: 34 to 44 bust. PRICE, PREPAID to your home **$1.69**

Wool-Flannel Detachable Collar **2 in One**

All Silk or Middy Jean

7K12399
$1.69

7K12403
$2.98
7K12404
$1.47

7K12403 *All silk middy blouses are all the rage—this model very low priced.* Made of **washable Jap silk** in regulation unbelted style with lacings at front. Single patch pocket. Open buttoned cuffs. A wonderful value. COLOR: White. SIZES: 34 to 44 bust. PRICE, PREPAID to your home, **$2.98** **7K12404** Same style as 7K12403 but made of good quality jean. COLOR: White. PRICE, PREPAID to your home, **$1.47**

7K12401 *An unusually pretty style in a two-color* **ramie linen** *smock at a saving.* Contrasting linon is used for the square yoke, the cuffs and wide border around bottom. Embroidery sprays add dressiness on the yoke and border. ¾ length sleeves. Sash belt through loops. Dressy and very becoming. COLORS: Copenhagen blue, rose, gold or white. SIZES: 34 to 44 bust. PRICE, PREPAID to your home, **$2.49**

7K12398 *A wonderfully effective style is presented in this* **French linon** *smock.* The very low price, too, is an added attraction, only $1.98 for a model which would sell for considerably more in the shops. Elaborate floral embroidery decorates the front and scalloped sleeves. Sash belt. Opening at shoulders. COLORS: Copenhagen blue, rose, gold or white. SIZES: 34 to 44 bust. PRICE, PREPAID to your home, **$1.98**

7K12401
$2.49

Two Tone Hand Emb.

Always be sure to state COLOR *and* SIZE *desired*

French Linon Hand Emb. 7K12398 $1.98

A New Department—"Goods by the Yard." You Cannot Equal These Values Any Where. See Pages 250 to 255

PHILIPSBORN'S

VOILE
7K12389
$1.69

VOILE
7K12388
$1.98

7K12387 *The slenderizing lines of this style blouse makes it possible for the stout women to follow the mode in the most becoming fashions.*
This is one of the popular collarless models, made of a good quality **voile** and designed with an embroidered panel front. Venise lace trims the round yoke and ¾ pointed sleeves. Hemstitched seams as shown add daintiness. Priced at a very low figure. COLOR: All white. SIZES: 46 to 54 bust. PRICE, PREPAID to your home, **$2.49**

VOILE
7K12387
$2.49

VOILE
7K12390
$2.48

7K12389 *Still lower prices on stout women's blouses — this* **voile** *model at $1.69.* Daintily combined with trimmed organdie collar. Very effective and a most practical style. Button fastening at center front. Clusters of tucking trim either side of fronts. COLOR: All white. SIZES: 46 to 54 bust. PRICE, PREPAID to your home, **$1.69**

VOILE
7K12391
$2.78

7K12388 *A further example of the excellent values we offer in blouses for stout women.*
This very dainty model is made of **voile** combined with organdie vestee and collar, and at the low price that we quote can scarcely be duplicated. Embroidered panels at either side of the front add dressiness. Venise lace trims the collar and turnback cuffs. Hemstitching as shown. Button fastening. COLOR: All white. SIZES: 46 to 54 bust. PRICE, PREP'D to your home, **$1.98**

7K12390 *An unusually dressy style in a blouse for stout women, quoted at the reduced price of $2.48.*
This model developed in a good quality **voile** and combined with organdie and embroidery band insertion on Lucile collar and vestee front. Val lace adds a further dainty touch. Long sleeves have lace-trimmed turnback cuffs. Invisible side front fastening. A big value. COLOR: All white. SIZES: 46 to 54 bust. PRICE, PREPAID to your home, **$2.48**

7K12391 *We bought these waists at pre-war prices, and are sharing our saving with our customers.*
The stout woman will be delighted with the exclusive and becoming style of this **voile** blouse, and the very moderate price will be an added attraction. Designed with ¾ length sleeves with slashed cuff. Embroidery sprays and filet pattern lace insertion. Lace-trimmed square collar and lace-trimmed cuffs. COLOR: All white. SIZES: 46 to 54 bust. PRICE, PREPAID to your home, **$2.78**

CHICAGO, ILL.

PHILIPSBORN'S Is Beyond Question the Lowest Priced Mail Order House in America. See Page 3

65

"Be a Leader Set the Pace! Wear Castle-Styles This new Model is one of my favorites!" *Irene Castle*

Descriptions for Page 67

7K12350 *A most attractive and dressy new blouse for a small sum of money. It is fashioned of* **silk Georgette** *with a wide panel in over-blouse effect.*

Handsomely embroidered and trimmed with contrasting folds of self-material. ¾ sleeves. Sash ties at back. COLORS: Navy blue with porcelain (Copenhagen blue) trimming and embroidery; white with flesh; or all black. SIZES: 34 to 44 bust.
PRICE, PREPAID to your home, **$4.98**

7K12354 *The season's most fashionable material—* **silk tricolette** *— makes this beautiful new blouse, designed in popular overblouse style.*

Embroidered net fashions the hip section and the trimming band on the flare cuffs. Round neck with contrasting piping. Button trimming at front. Opening at sides. COLORS: Copenhagen blue, navy blue with contrasting embroidery or rose with contrasting embroidery. SIZES: 34 to 44 bust.
PRICE, PREPAID to your home, **$2.98**

7K12355 *Unusually rich and dressy is this* **two-tone silk Georgette** *overblouse with upper part of model in contrasting color with lower part.*

Kimono sleeves with slashed cuffs. Silk and bead embroidery. Sash ties. COLORS: Ecru and navy blue with honey dew (peach color) embroidery; navy blue and porcelain (Copenhagen blue) with navy blue and porcelain; or white and flesh with flesh and porcelain. SIZES: 34 to 44 bust.
PRICE, PREPAID to your home, **$4.98**

8K13465 *Here is a dressy* **taffeta silk** *skirt at a very moderate price. Worn with different blouses, one can have frequent changes for a very small outlay of money.*

The model is especially charming when worn with our blouse model 7K12350. Pointed tunic with silk twist stitching and button groups. Self-material belt. COLORS: Navy blue or black. SIZES: Waistband 24 to 30. Front length 34 to 42 inches.
PRICE, PREPAID to your home, **$5.98**

8K13466 *There is nothing more satisfactory for general wear than a good plaid skirt. This model is made of* **all wool plaid** *in artistic patterns.*

It is made in a very attractive style with full knife plaiting, and a box plait at one side. Large novelty buttons. Self-material belt. COLORS: Tan and blue or blue and tan plaid. SIZES: Waistband 24 to 30. Front length 34 to 42 inches.
PRICE, PREPAID to your home, **$5.98**

8K13467 *Latest style for spring and summer is shown in this* **all wool serge** *skirt, one of the season's best values at our money-saving price.*

Full knife-plaited model, three-tone stitching and silk braid trimming in circular design all around the lower part. Wide belt. COLORS: Navy blue or black. SIZES: Waistband 24 to 30. Front lengths 34 to 42 inches   PRICE, PREPAID to your home, **$4.88**

ALL WOOL
SERGE
AND SILK
SATIN
8K13461
$7.75

8K13461 *Irene Castle, PHILIPSBORN'S famous designer and style expert, is responsible for this smart skirt.*

All wool serge, in a stylish combination with satin messaline is used for the model. Eight braid-bound panels with new style eyelet trimming open over a full drop skirt of the messaline. All-around self-material belt. Exceedingly attractive and becoming. A wonder of value at our low price. COLOR: Navy blue and black. SIZES: Waistband 24 to 30. Front length of skirt 34 to 42.
PRICE, PREPAID to your home, **$7.75**

HOW TO ORDER

In ordering skirts, give waist and hip measures; front length and color desired. To obtain front length, measure from natural waistline in front down to desired length.

For a Complete List of Irene Castle's Exclusive Designs, See the Index, Page 274

PHILIPSBORN'S

You'll be the best dressed woman for miles around in one of these New French Skirt Styles!

SILK GEORGETTE CREPE, HAND EMBROIDERY AND BEADED
7K12355
$4.98

SILK TRICOLETTE
7K12354
$2.98

SILK GEORGETTE CREPE—HAND EMBR'D
7K12350
$4.98

ALL WOOL SERGE SKIRT
8K13467
$4.88

ALL WOOL PLAID SKIRT
8K13466
$5.98

TAFFETA SILK SKIRT
8K13465
$5.98

For Descriptions See Page 66

SILK
GEORGETTE
CREPE
7K12353
$3.49

SILK
GEORGETTE
CREPE
HAND EMB'D
7K12352
$5.98

SILK
GEORGETTE
CREPE
7K12351
$3.98

SILK POPLIN
SKIRT
8K13462
$3.48

TAFFETA SILK
SKIRT
8K13463
$5.98

ALL WOOL SERGE
SKIRT
8K13464
$5.88

For Descriptions See Page 69

For a Complete List of Irene Castle's Exclusive Designs,
See the Index, Page 274

7K12351 *There is no more popular style this season than the overblouse, of which this model is a good example and a wonderful value.*

It is developed in good quality **silk Georgette**, with heavy contrasting embroidery in scalloped design. Square collarless neck finished with contrasting piping. Wide three-quarter sleeves. Finished with two trimming folds. Sash ties at back. A wonderfully dressy and becoming model at a decidedly low price. COLORS: Navy blue with ecru; white with flesh; or flesh with porcelain blue (Copenhagen blue). SIZES: 34 to 44 bust.
PRICE, PREPAID to your home, **$3.98**

7K12352 *A most becoming version of the fashionable overblouse is shown in this silk Georgette model.*

It is designed in jumper effect with contrasting underblouse. Contrasting silk floss embroidery adorns the overblouse. Shirred vestee with bow tie. Novel sleeve with pointed overcuff. Sash ties at back. COLORS: Neptune (Nile green) and navy blue with Neptune and ecru embroidery; ecru and brown with ecru and brown embroidery; or zinc (French grey) and porcelain (Copenhagen blue). SIZES: 34 to 44 bust.
PRICE, PREPAID to your home. **$5.98**

7K12353 *An unparalleled offer in a silk Georgette overblouse made in the newest style and reduced to $3.49.*

This is another of the tie-back models which fashionable women are wearing this season. Contrasting embroidery in conventional scroll design decorates the blouse fronts and hip section as pictured. No woman who needs a dressy blouse should overlook this splendid offer. COLORS: Burgundy with ecru and tomato-colored embroidery; navy blue with porcelain (Copenhagen blue) and navy blue; or all black. SIZES: 34 to 44 bust.
PRICE, PREPAID to your home, **$3.49**

8K13462 *Here is a dressy silk poplin skirt, and the price is unusually low for a model of this sort.*

Soft gathers laid below a deep yoke give becoming fulness, and three wide tucks laid all around the bottom provide dressy trimming. Two wide straps at either side are laid in soft folds and are caught under at the first row of tucks as shown. Very dressy when worn with any of the blouses shown on this page. COLORS: Burgundy, navy blue or black. SIZES: Waistband 24 to 30. Front length 34 to 42 inches.
PRICE, PREPAID to your home, **$3.48**

8K13463 *Plaid, taffeta silk of very rich and beautiful patterns and colorings makes this dressy new skirt.*

We bought these models when the cost of silks dropped and consequently paid much less than the usual market prices. Knife plaits are laid at the front and back of model, the sides trimmed with pointed patch pockets with tassel finish. A style and value that cannot be duplicated elsewhere at our money-saving price. COLORS: Navy blue and green plaid. SIZES: Waistband 24 to 30 inches. Front length 34 to 42 inches.
PRICE, PREPAID to your home, **$5.98**

8K13464 *Seldom does a cloth skirt feature such dressy lines as this new PHILIPSBORN'S model of all wool serge. Splendid wearing qualities.*

The season's vogue for tucked effects is provided in the cluster tucking which encircles the lower part of skirt. Contrasting embroidery adds a charming color touch on the patch pocket flap and the braid-bound sash belt. Extremely new and smart. COLORS: Navy blue with bisque and Copenhagen blue embroidery; brown with bisque and red embroidery. SIZES: 24 to 30 waist. Skirt length 34 to 42.
PRICE, PREPAID to your home, **$5.88**

Be sure to state COLOR and SIZE desired when ordering.

8K13468 Silk tricolette—*which is considered by fashion experts to be the material of the day*—is used for this stylish new skirt.

The material is furnished in dark as well as delicate light shades which make it particularly appropriate for summer wear with light blouses. It does not wrinkle readily, and its rich lustre gives it a very dressy appearance. Smartly shaped flaps with button trimming mark the pockets. All-around belt. The beauty of this model cannot be over-emphasized, and at our special price every woman can have one of these models. COLORS: White, rose, navy blue, or French blue. SIZES: Waistband 24 to 30. Front length 34 to 42 inches.
PRICE, PREPAID to your home, **$6.98**

8K13469 *Fashion's preference for silk braid trimming is charmingly expressed in this smart and distinctive skirt of all wool serge.*

Cluster plaits centered with box plaits are laid all around, and are easily re-pressed at home. Silk braid is applied in diagonal fashion, entirely encircling the skirt both front and back as pictured. Self-material belt is finished with tasseled sash. If you have shopped around, you know what an unusual value an all wool serge at our low price is, and that it is practically impossible to duplicate this value elsewhere for anywhere near this figure. COLORS: Navy blue or black. SIZES: Waistband 24 to 30. Front length 34 to 42 inches.
PRICE, PREPAID to your home, **$5.98**

SILK TRICOLETTE
8K13468
$6.98

ALL WOOL SERGE
8K13469
$5.98

WORTH
$7.50

8K13470 *Why wait until the end of the season for clearance sales to buy your new skirt? Buy now at these amazingly low prices when you can get a whole season of wear.*

When you come to examine the quality of this **all-wool serge**, you will be agreeably surprised, as we were when we first saw these models. We bought them from a manufacturer who needed ready cash and who accepted our spot cash offer of 25 per cent below regular market prices. This sensational offer is the result. The illustration shows you the smart and becoming lines, the cluster side plaits which are laid both front and back. Silk braid in novel design trims the sides, button groups as pictured. An all-around self-material belt with button finish completes the model. If you wish a skirt that will wear well and always keep its trim, tailored appearance send for this model. It is just the right weight for spring and summer, and is so generally serviceable that you will make no mistake in selecting the model. COLORS: Navy blue or black. SIZES: Waistband 24 to 30. Front length 34 to 42 inches.
PRICE, PREPAID to your home, **$5.98**

8K13471 *Because of the great volume of business that we do each season, we are able to obtain big discounts for cash, which are not possible for smaller houses.*

Here is a splendid offering in a stylish, up-to-date and becoming new skirt of **all-wool poplin**. Usually a skirt of this style and quality would cost you considerably more but owing to the fact that a big manufacturer sacrificed these models to us at a very small margin of profit, we are able to name this remarkably low price and pass on the saving to you. This price is all the more remarkable when you consider that it includes all transportation charges. Note the smart style features which this skirt shows—the twelve rows of tucking all-around the lower part, and the novel trimming straps which form pockets at the top. The straps fold under in newest fashion at the bottom row of tucks and are finished at the top with smartly shaped flaps with button and buttonhole. Wide self-material belt with button finish. COLORS: Navy blue or black. SIZES: Waistband 24 to 30. Front length 34 to 42 inches.
PRICE, PREPAID to your home, **$5.98**

HOW TO ORDER

In ordering women's skirts, give waist and hip measures; front length and color desired. To obtain front length, measure from natural waistline down to length desired. If a larger size than 30 waistband is required, order from our stout sizes.

IMPORTANT!
Be Sure to state SIZE and COLOR desired.

PHILIPSBORN'S

SKIRTS OF THIS CHARACTER A YEAR AGO WOULD HAVE SOLD FOR
$8.50

ALL WOOL POPLIN
8K13471
$5.98

ALL WOOL SERGE
8K13470
$5.98

31 years of faithful service PHILIPSBORN'S Proud Record!

8K13472 *Important savings for you in one of the season's newest and most desirable skirts; but this saving is not at the expense of quality nor at the sacrifice of style.*

The material is an excellent quality **all-wool plaid** of attractive color combination and pattern. The tailoring and workmanship leave nothing to be desired, and if you will compare this skirt with those selling at retail for $8.00 and more you will appreciate the wonderful bargain that *PHILIPSBORN'S* offers you in this smart model. The model is laid in side plaits centered with narrow box plaits, the back a duplicate of the front. The sides are plain and finished with smartly shaped pocket flaps with button trimming. All-around self-material belt with button finish. If you would be in style this season, you must have one of these plaid skirts. Women of fashion are choosing them to wear with dark-colored odd jackets, giving an effect that is very new and smart. Equally appropriate worn with a sweater or top coat. COLORS: Blue and tan plaid. SIZES: Waistband 24 to 30. Front length 34 to 42 inches.

PRICE, PREPAID to your home, **$6.48**

8K13473 *Thirty-one years ago PHILIPSBORN'S put out their first catalog, and every year since we have learned something of how to gather styles and to decrease costs.*

Take for example this very smart and becoming **all-wool serge** skirt which offers you the very latest style at a special reduction of 25 per cent. In fact such good workmanship and such splendid materials are rarely found in garments at double the price. Like many of the season's favored models, this skirt is laid in knife plaits with a wide box plait at the front and wide side plaits at the sides. Diagonal rows of silk braid cross in the front of skirt as pictured and make a novel trimming. The model is completed with a wide self-material belt which extends all-around and is finished with braid and button trimming. The material is of proper weight for spring and summer, and will give wonderful service and entire satisfaction. If you want one of the best skirts ever sold at this money-saving price, then send for this model. COLOR: Navy blue. SIZES: Waistband 24 to 30. Front length 34 to 42 inches.

PRICE, PREPAID to your home, **$5.98**

IMPORTANT!

Do not delay your order by failing to give SIZE and COLOR desired.

Full instructions for taking measurements are given in the order blank at the back of this book, also on opposite page.

CHICAGO, ILL.

ALL WOOL SERGE
8K13473
$5.98

WORTH
$7.00

WORTH
$8.00

ALL WOOL PLAID
8K13472
$6.48

See Page 274 for Index and Don't Forget When Ordering to State the Color and Size Desired

Descriptions for Page 73

8K13475 *It would be hard to imagine a more stylish and distinctive skirt than this new accordion-plaited model. The very low price makes it one of the season's best offerings.*

The material is **wool mixed plaid** in smart new shades and pattern. The material is cut on the bias, giving an effect that is altogether new and attractive. The wide self-material belt is finished with button trimming. If you want one of the newest and most fashionable of the season's skirts, send for this model. We have reduced the price so as to place it within the reach of every woman's pocketbook. COLOR: Assorted blue, tan, brown plaids. SIZES: Waistband 24 to 30. Front length 34 to 42 inches. PRICE, PREPAID to your home, **$5.98**

8K13476 *This skirt bargain proves beyond the shadow of doubt that PHILIPSBORN'S have smashed prices to the limit. The model has all the smart style of skirts costing $8.00 to $15.00 elsewhere.*

The material is an excellent quality **all-wool serge**, which we are furnishing in light and dark shades. Many women are choosing all white serge skirts to accompany their light blouses, giving a finished costume that is very pleasing and appropriate for summer. For such purposes this model makes a most desirable selection. The illustration shows you the smart, plaited style with cluster plaits laid all-around and a wide box plait at the center. All-around self-material belt with button finish. For general spring and summer wear you will find no more satisfactory style than this model. COLORS: Navy blue or white. SIZES: Waistband 24 to 30. Front length 34 to 42 inches. PRICE, PREPAID to your home, **$5.88**

8K13477 *Manufacturers' misfortunes are your good fortune. Many of them have been forced to dispose of heavy reserve stocks at less than cost. This lot of skirts secured at a sensational price cut.*

It has been many months since you have seen such values as this **all-wool serge skirt** for only **$4.75**. If you have shopped for skirts recently we don't need to tell you that similar models are selling in the shops at $4.00 to $5.60 more than we ask. Individuality of style is displayed in the three groups of tucks which decorate the lower part of model, a wide lapped fold with button trimming finishing the left side. Patch pockets feature braid-trimmed straps and button groups. One of the best skirts you could buy for general service, offering you style and quality at far less than prevailing retail prices. COLORS: Navy blue or black. SIZES: Waistband 24 to 30. Front length 34 to 42 inches. PRICE, PREPAID to your home, **$4.75**

HOW TO ORDER

In ordering women's skirts, give waist and hip measure; front length and color desired. To obtain front length, measure from natural waistline down to length desired. If a larger size than 30 waistband is required, make your selection from our stout sizes.

ALL WOOL SERGE
8K13474
$4.98

Here's the Best Bargain in a Plaited All-Wool Serge Skirt.
Price a year ago would have been $7.98

8K13474 *Before buying your spring clothes, shop around and satisfy yourself of the goods that others have to offer. Then compare our styles and prices, and we feel sure that you will send your order to us.*

You really could not find a greater combination of style and value anywhere than we offer in this **all-wool serge** skirt. It is made in the new plaited style with clusters of side plaits alternating with wide box plaits. A very dressy touch is afforded in the sash belt which is weighted with silk tassels. When you see this stylish skirt and examine the material you will agree with us that it is a wonderful bargain at our special cut price. COLORS: Navy blue, gray, or brown. SIZES: Waistband 24 to 30. Front length 34 to 42 inches. PRICE, PREPAID to your home, **$4.98**

ALL WOOL SERGE
8K13477
$4.75

Stylish Shirts at Popular Prices

WOOL MIXED
PLAID
8K13475
$5.98

ALL
WOOL
SERGE
8K13476
$5.88

For Descriptions See Page 72

CHICAGO, ILL.

The Newest Conceits in Neckwear Are Here at PHILIPSBORN'S.
See Pages 103 and 104 of This Catalog

Here's the Skirt You've Been Waiting For

8K13479 *A swagger style in an all-wool plaid skirt at considerably less than prevailing retail prices.*
An odd skirt of this sort is so very practical that no woman should be without one, especially when the price is only $4.88. Novel trimming straps which conceal convenient pockets also form loops for the all-around belt. COLORS: Blue and tan assorted plaids. SIZES: 24 to 30 waistband. Front length 34 to 42.
PRICE, PREPAID to your home, **$4.88**

8K13478 *Here is a money-saving chance—a real bona fide bargain offer by an all-wool serge skirt at $4.48.*
One of the best examples of the popular plaited skirts, this model is designed with six box plaits across the front and back and side plaits at the sides. Wide all-around belt with button trimming. Very smart and serviceable COLORS: Navy blue or black. SIZES: 24 to 30 waistband. Front length 34 to 42.
PRICE, PREPAID to your home, **$4.48**

8K13480 *An up-to-the-minute version of the popular plaited skirt is presented in this smart all-wool serge model.*
Clusters of side plaits alternate with wider side plaits to make this skirt extremely effective. Silk braid trims the lower part of skirt and finishes the button groups as pictured. A tailored model of much distinction. COLORS: Navy blue or black. SIZES: 24 to 30 waistband. Front length 34 to 42.
PRICE, PREPAID to your home, **$4.88**

Be sure to state SIZE and COLOR when ordering

ALL WOOL SERGE
8K13478—$4.48

ALL WOOL SERGE
8K13480—$4.88

ALL WOOL PLAID
8K13479
$4.88
WORTH
$6.50

All Wool Double Warp Serge **Challenge Price!** **$2.88**

WORTH
$4.00

ALL WOOL SERGE
8K13481
$2.88

8K13481 *Here is a skirt value that will cause a sensation among thrifty shoppers everywhere.*
An all-wool serge skirt at only $2.88 is indeed a find, and this model is particularly smart and stylish. Novelty braid trims the tailored flaps which conceal pockets. All-around belt. COLORS: Navy blue or black. SIZES: 24 to 30 waistband. Skirt length 34 to 42.
PRICE, PREPAID to your home, **$2.88**

Bargains in Practical Skirts—Latest Styles

8K13482 *No woman anxious to get the most for her clothes money can afford to overlook this extraordinary opportunity.*

Think of getting a skirt of this wonderful style for only $2.88. The material is a serviceable **fancy plaid** containing about one-half wool and cotton, and the design is the favorite full knife-plaited style so much worn this season. All-around belt. COLORS: Black and white assorted plaid or blue and white assorted plaid. SIZES: 24 to 30 waistband. Front length 34 to 42.
PRICE, PREPAID to your home, **$2.88**

8K13484 *Wise women shoppers will recognize how unusual this serviceable* **mohair** *skirt is at our special reduced price.*

If you can duplicate goods of the same quality at a lower price elsewhere, we want to know it, and we will gladly refund your money. The model shows smart design in the novel pocket flaps with braid and button trimming. All-around belt. COLORS: Black or navy blue. SIZES: 24 to 30 waistband. Front length 34 to 42.
PRICE, PREPAID to your home, **$3.68**

8K13485 *Our foresighted policy in buying is responsible for this remarkable offer in a dressy* **silk poplin** *skirt at $2.48.*

We laid in a plentiful supply of these models when the market reached its lowest point, and now we are giving you the benefit of our wise purchase. The picture shows you the dressy style of the model, with three trimming folds below the deep yoke. COLORS: Black, navy blue or plum. SIZES: 24 to 30 waistband. Front length 34 to 42.
PRICE, PREPAID to your home, **$2.48**

8K13483 *Positively the greatest skirt value in years—snap it up while you have the chance—only $2.97 for a real $4.00 value.*

Surf satin—a material which has every appearance of satin, only it is cotton-backed and infinitely more serviceable—is used for this dressy skirt. Fancy patch pockets have trimming straps, cording and button groups. Shirrings at the waistline give becoming fullness under the all around self-material belt. Very stylish and dressy. COLOR: Black. SIZES: 24 to 3 waistband. Skirt length 34 to 42. PRICE, PREPAID to your home, **$2.97**

MOHAIR
8K13484
$3.68

FANCY PLAID
8K13482
$2.88

8K13485
All Silk Poplin
Challenge Price!
$2.48

WORTH
$3.75

SURF SATIN
8K13483
$2.97

No Talk!
Just Values
We bought this
silk at the Market's
Lowest Point !!
Here's the
Result!

SILK
TAFFETA
8K13487
$5.78

SILK
TAFFETA
8K13488
$6.88

SILK
TAFFETA
8K13486
$3.98

For Descriptions See Page 77

"Goods by the Yard." A New Member of The PHILIPSBORN Family.
See Pages 250 to 255   PHILIPSBORN'S

Descriptions for Page 76

8K13486 *Unusually dressy style in this* **taffeta silk** *skirt, a wonderful value.* Shirred sections at the sides form patch pockets with button trimmed straps above as shown. Wide belt. COLOR: Black. SIZES: Waistband 24 to 30. Front length 34 to 42 inches. PRICE, PREPAID to your home, **$3.98**

8K13487 *The new wrapped effect tunic gives newest style to this* **taffeta silk** *skirt.* Wide folds in tunic effect are trimmed with silk twist stitching. Fancy patch pocket. Fringed sash at side. COLOR: Black. SIZES: Waistband 24 to 30. Front length 34 to 42 inches. PRICE, PREPAID to your home, **$5.78**

8K13488 *A favorite skirt style this season is this tunic model of rich* **taffeta silk.** Irregular line tunic laid in narrow box plaits. Contrasting silk stitching. Braid binding on edge. COLOR: Black. SIZES: Waistband 24 to 30. Front length 34 to 42 inches. PRICE, PREPAID to your home, **$6.88**

8K13489 *Dressy* **taffeta silk** *skirt for stout women.* Accordion plaited sections at either side of panel front and back. Trimming straps and buttons across front. COLOR: Black. SIZES: Waistband 32 to 40. Front length 36 to 44 inches. PRICE, PREP'D to your home, **$6.98**

8K13490
Adjustable Skirt!
All Wool Serge!
Perfect Fit Guaranteed!
$6.68

8K13490 *The new adjustable skirt for stout women and maternity purposes* Made of a splendid quality **all wool serge.** The feature of this model is the adjustable back, which forms an overlapping panel with snappers at the waistline, which can be let out as desired. Pockets with tailored flaps and buttons. COLORS: Navy blue or black. SIZES: Waist band 32 to 40. Front length 36 to 44 inches. PRICE, PREP'D to your home, **$6.68**

8K13491 *Wonderfully good lines for the stout women feature this skirt. Worth $6.00.* The material is **all wool panama,** a fabric that does not require frequent pressing. The model is plaited in newest fashion with knife plaits forming a wide panel at front and back, and box plaits on the sides. Soutache braid and button trimming. COLORS: Navy blue or black. SIZES: Waistband 32 to 40. Front length 36 to 44 inches. PRICE, PREP'D to your home, **$4.98**

ALL WOOL PANAMA
8K13491
$4.98

TAFFETA SILK
8K13489
$6.98

The World's Greatest Power—"Public Opinion."
See Page 3

PHILIPSBORN'S

Misses Skirts at Big Feature Values!

FANCY PLAID
8K13500

$2.46

MOHAIR
8K13501
$3.98
WORTH
$5.00

SILK PLAID
8K13504
$4.98

ALL SILK POPLIN
8K13502
$3.48

8K13503

$4.48

ALL WOOL SERGE

8K13500 *See what you save on this attractive skirt for misses, and an unusually smart style.*

Made of good quality **fancy plaid skirting** in very pretty color combinations and patterns. Becoming fulness is laid at the waistline under the all-around self-material belt, and there are patch pockets with novel overlapping sections. Button trimming and soutache braid buttonholes trim the model as shown. COLOR: Assorted plaids. SIZES: Waistband 22 to 28. Front length 32 to 38 inches.
PRICE, PREPAID to your home, **$2.46**

8K13501 *Fashion's latest word in skirt styles for the miss is this new accordion-plaited model.*

It is made of good quality **mohair**, a material that retains plaiting for a long time. Contrasting silk twist stitching forms a pretty trimming all-around the lower part of model as pictured. Self-material sash belt has stitching to correspond and tassel finish. This dressy and becoming skirt proves our ability to save you money. COLORS: Navy blue or black. SIZES: Waistband 22 to 28. Front length 32 to 38.
PRICE, PREPAID to your home, **$3.98**

Important! Be sure to state SIZE and COLOR desired.

8K13503 *A neat and practical selection in a misses all wool serge skirt at only $4.48.*

Narrow box plaits laid all-around give the season's correct style in plaited effects. All-around self-material belt with button finish. COLORS: Navy blue or black. SIZES: Waistband 22 to 28. Full length 32 to 38 inches.
PRICE, PREPAID to your home, **$4.48**

8K13502 *Never was there a time when embroidery was so much used, and this skirt for misses is charming.*

The material is **all silk poplin**, its beauty enhanced with harmonizing silk embroidery all around the lower part. Designed with deep yoke with tasseled sash ends at the front. Very low priced for this style and quality. COLOR: Navy blue, plum or Copenhagen blue. SIZES: Waistband 22 to 28. Front length 32 to 38 inches.
PRICE, PREPAID to your home, **$3.48**

8K13504 *The miss who likes to dress in the very latest style will appreciate this very attractive satin plaid skirt.*

The material comes in very pretty pattern and color combinations, and is a remarkable value at our money-saving price. Model is laid in box plaits all-around. Self-material belt with button trimming. COLOR: Assorted blue, green, red—plaids. SIZES: Waistband 22 to 28. Front length 32 to 38 inches. PRICE, PREPAID to your home, **$4.98**

Wash Shirts! You need them for "All Sport" Wear!

8K13505 *Surf satin stencilled in color is used for this skirt.*

Box-plaited model with wide border stencilled in contrasting color and artistic design. All-around belt with button finish. A style that is destined for great favor this season, and a notable value at our low price. COLOR: White with black stencil. SIZES: Waistband 24 to 30. Front length 34 to 42 inches.

PRICE, PREPAID to your home, **$2.98**

8K13506 *A smashing bargain at our money-saving price.*

This stylish and becoming gabardine skirt features flat-stitched folds at either side of the front in panel effect, button groups as pictured. Four rows of tucking extend all around lower part. Belt through self loops. COLOR: White. SIZES: Waistband 24 to 30. Front length 34 to 42 inches.

PRICE, PREPAID to your home, **$1.98**

8K13507 *One of the season's smartest novelties is this gabardine skirt.*

Tucking in black design ornaments the entire model and there is a smartly shaped front panel with pockets set in underneath. Button trimming. All-around belt. An extra special bargain. COLOR: White. SIZES: Waistband 24 to 30. Front length 34 to 42 inches.

PRICE, PREPAID to your home, **$2.48**

COLOR and SIZE
Be sure to state COLOR and SIZE when ordering

SURF SATIN
8K13505
$2.98

GABARDINE
8K13507
$2.48

GABARDINE
8K13508
$2.48

GABARDINE
8K13506
$1.98

8K13508 *When you see this pretty embroidered gabardine skirt you will marvel at its low price.*

It is one of the season's newest and most favored styles, and except for a special purchase on which we received a big discount we would have to charge considerably more. Elaborate embroidery in self-tone adorns the lower part of skirt. Pockets with crossed straps and buttons. COLOR: White. SIZES: Waistband 24 to 30. Front length 34 to 42 inches.

PRICE, PREPAID to your home, **$2.48**

In Ordering, Be Sure to Give Size and Color Desired. Without This Information We Cannot Fill Your Order Promptly

8K13511 *Every woman needs plenty of wash skirts for summer.*

This smart and becoming **gabardine** skirt offers you a substantial saving. Two groups of tucks give distinctive style to the lower part of skirt. Pockets marked with smartly-shaped and button-trimmed flaps. COLOR: White. SIZES: Waistband 24 to 30. Front length 34 to 42 inches.
PRICE, PREPAID to your home, **$1.88**

8K13509 *Dressy material and smart style combine in this skirt.*

The model is fashioned of **surf satin**, one of the dressiest and most satisfactory of wash fabrics. Made with a deep semi-attached yoke. Smartly shaped tailored flaps with button trimming mark the pockets. COLOR: White. SIZES: Waistband 24 to 30. Front length 34 to 42 inches.
PRICE, PREPAID to your home, **$2.50**

8K13512 *You will like this skirt for its smart and unusual style.*

Fashioned of **gabardine**, we consider it one of our greatest bargains both in style and quality. A wide lapped fold with button trimming and three smaller folds trim the left side of model. Single patch pocket forms loop for the all-around belt. COLOR: White. SIZES: Waistband 24 to 30. Front length 34 to 42 inches.
PRICE, PREPAID, to your home, **$1.69**

GABARDINE
8K13511
$1.88

GABARDINE
8K13510
$1.96

SURF
SATIN
8K13509
$2.50

GABARDINE
8K13512
$1.69

Priced Low! so you should buy more than one !!

8K13510 *You will congratulate yourself every time you wear this dressy embroidered skirt.*

At the low price that we quote it is practically impossible to duplicate, either in style or material at other mail order houses. The material is an excellent quality of washable **gabardine** embroidered in self-tone all-around bottom. Patch pockets in plait effect with buttons. COLOR: White. SIZES: Waistband 24 to 30. Front length 34 to 42 inches.
PRICE, PREPAID to your home, **$1.96**

CHICAGO, ILL. *A New Department—"Goods by the Yard." You Cannot Equal These Values Any Where. See Pages 250 to 255* 81

5 Bargain Values!

SHEPHERD CHECK
8K13516
$1.47

GABARDINE
8K13513
$1.69

SERGE
8K13515
$1.48

GABARDINE
8K13514
$1.48

8K13517
$1 19

RAMIE LINENE

8K13513 *We bought several thousand of these skirts at a big sacrifice—therefore the low price.*

The material is **gabardine**—one of the most satisfactory of wash skirtings. Newest style is displayed in the patch pockets, for which tucking and button-trimmed straps provide a novel trimming. Wide all-around self-material belt is finished with button and button-hole. A value that proves our ability to underbuy and to undersell all competitors. A good model for general wear. COLOR: White. SIZES: Waistband 24 to 30. Front length 34 to 42 inches.
PRICE, PREPAID
to your home, **$1.69**

8K13516 *For real, practical service a checked skirt of this type has no equal.*
This very attractive model is fashioned of a durable woven check and made with smartly shaped pocket flaps. Button trimming. All-around belt.
COLOR: Black and white check.
SIZES: Waistband 24 to 30. Front length 34 to 42 inches.
PRICE, PREPAID
to your home, **$1.47**

8K13517 *Cotton ramie linen, a very popular wash skirting, makes this new model.*
At only $1.19 it offers convincing proof of the astonishing values possible at Philipsborn's. Patch pockets have button-trimmed straps and tucking. All-around belt. COLOR: White. SIZES: Waistband 24 to 30. Front length 34 to 42 inches.
PRICE, PREPAID
to your home **$1.19**

8K13515 *A big bargain in a cotton serge skirt of smart and distinctive design.*
Made with a deep, fitted yoke. Patch pockets with button trimming. A serviceable model that cannot be duplicated elsewhere at our low price.
COLORS: Black or navy blue. SIZES: Waistband 24 to 30. Front length 34 to 42 inches.
FRICE, PREPAID
to your home, **$1.48**

8K13514 *Have you ever seen a prettier skirt or a better value at this money-saving price?*
This is a very becoming style, made in serviceable **gabardine**. Patch pockets designed with cording in criss-cross effect and button trimming. Panel front. COLOR: White. SIZES: Waistband 24 to 30. Front length 34 to 42 inches.
PRICE, PREPAID
to your home, **$1.48**

PHILIPSBORN'S Simple One Price to All Policy Is Sweeping the Country. See Page 3

PHILIPSBORN'S

All the Rage!
These three new Sweater Styles
All Wool

ALL
WORSTED
LINKS & LINKS
9K18300
$2.98

ALL WOOL
AND ANGORA
HAND WOOL
EMBROIDERED
9K18301
$6.49

ALL WOOL
9K18302
$4.48

IMPORTANT
*Be sure to state COLOR and
SIZE desired when ordering*

9K18301 *Smartly dressed women and misses make these sweaters their choice.*

Here is one of our smartest Tuxedo sweater coats knit from fine selected **all wool yarns, every thread 100% wool.** If you have shopped for sweaters recently we need not tell you what an unusual offering this model is at the special reduced price that we name. The style features all that is charming and becoming. The Angora wool collar and cuffs afford a striking note of contrast, which is further emphasized on the collar with the contrasting wool yarn, hand embroidery design in color to harmonize with the sweater. The Tuxedo reveres turn back and extend to the edge of sweater, while a sash belt with tassels holds the model to trim lines. Two patch pockets add a smart touch. Quoted at a price that you will agree is very moderate when you see the quality of this sweater. A usual $10.00 value. COLORS: Black with white; brown with white; purple with white; light blue with white, or tan with white. SIZES: 32 to 44 bust.

PRICE, PREPAID to your home, **$6.49**

9K18300 *Fashion's latest fancy in sweater styles is this new tie-on sweater blouse.*

This is a **guaranteed 100% all wool worsted** sweater, knit in the popular link-and-link stitch. All that is newest and prettiest is embodied in this model. The style, as you can see, is most becoming with its full length surplice collar extending to the waistline. Contrasting crochet stitching gives a pretty finish on the edge of both collar and cuffs. The sleeves are 3-4 length and the cuffs turn back as pictured. The sweater extends well over the skirt, and is finished with a sash belt with tassels. The model is furnished in practical colors, and is one of the most serviceable and satisfactory sweaters that you could possibly buy. May be worn with or without a blouse underneath. We are quoting a special reduced price on this model to introduce this style, which usually retails for not less than $5.00. COLORS: Black with white edging; navy blue with red edging; or buff with brown edging. SIZES: 32 to 44 bust.

PRICE, PREPAID to your home, **$2.98**

9K18302 *Smart and becoming new slip-on sweater quoted at an unequaled low price.*

Think of getting an **all wool worsted** sweater for only $4.48 and **guaranteed to be 100% all wool** at that. We bought a big supply of these sweaters at sacrifice prices, hence the low price that we are able to name. The value is so unusual that we cannot hope to duplicate this offer for many months to come, so early selection is advisable while our stocks are complete. The picture shows you the wonderfully becoming lines. It is knit in fancy stitch and trimmed with crochet shell stitch at the neck. Fancy double frill cuffs give newest style to the elbow sleeves. Patch pockets are trimmed in corresponding style, both cuffs and pockets finished with button-trimmed straps. A braided cord girdle provides the very latest of waistline finishes. Model slips over head. An exceptionally fine value, at a moderate cost.

COLORS: Navy blue, peacock blue, buff, or purple. SIZES: 32 to 44 bust.

PRICE, PREPAID to your home, **$4.48**

New Tie-on Novelty

9K18305 *Here is the new tie-on sweater blouse at an unexpected saving in price.*

This is an **all-wool** model knit in a stylish new weave. The wide sash belt crosses over at the front and terminates in long tasseled ends at the back. A very stylish model for very little money. COLORS: Peacock blue, rose, emerald green, navy blue or black. SIZES: 34 to 44. PRICE, PREPAID to your home, **$2.88**

WOOL SCARF

9K18303 **$1.69**

TUXEDO

ALL WOOL
9K18305
$2.88

Sweaters for every occasion at Bargain Prices

9K18306 *Here is a big bargain in a stunning new Tuxedo sweater coat.* Knit from **wool mixed yarns.** Very durable. Contrasting stripes trim the Tuxedo collar as shown in the picture. Patch pockets. COLORS: Peacock blue, American beauty or taupe. SIZES: 34 to 44 bust. PRICE, PREPAID to your home, **$2.88**

9K18303 *Smart and stylish stole scarf of* **brushed wool yarn.** Contrasting border. Self fringe. A rare bargain at our low price. COLORS: Purple and grey; brown and buff; rose and Copenhagen blue or Copenhagen blue and rose. PRICE, PREPAID to your home, **$1.69**

9K18307 *Smart and serviceable sweater coat of all* **wool yarn.** Made with sailor collar, patch pockets and all-around belt. Contrasting trimming. COLORS: American beauty and buff, peacock blue and buff or navy blue and buff. SIZES: 34 to 44 bust. PRICE, PREPAID to your home, **$3.98**

9K18308 *New style tie-on sweater blouse with "ostrich" trimming.* Knit from **all wool** yarns with fancy contrasting "ostrich" stitch edge. Sash ties. COLORS: Black and white; navy blue and white; buff and brown or peacock blue and buff. SIZES: 34 to 44 bust. PRICE, PREPAID to your home, **$3.69**

9K18304 *Tie-on sweater blouses are all the rage and this one is a bargain.* It is made from good quality **cotton** in an attractive new weave, and it is just as smart and effective as sweaters which are selling elsewhere for considerably more. The model is made with a surplice collar and sash belt which crosses over at the front and ties at the back. An exceedingly popular style at a very low price. COLORS: Black, navy blue, gendarme blue or American beauty. SIZES: 36 to 44 bust. PRICE, PREPAID to your home, **$1.89**

IMPORTANT
Be sure to state SIZE and COLOR desired when ordering

9K18306
$2.88

LINKS AND LINKS
ALL WOOL
OSTRICH EDGE

9K18308
$3.69

ALL WOOL
9K18307
$3.98

TIE ON
BLOUSE
9K18304
$1.89

Remember, There Are No Extra Charges for Express and Mailing When You Shop Here. We Prepay All Transportation Charges

PHILIPSBORN'S

Silk Bargain!

9K18314 *Imagine getting a pure silk sweater coat for only $6.98.*

This handsome sweater is knit in fancy block design with full length Tuxedo revers, and tasseled sash belt. Furnished in the season's newest shades. COLORS: Navy blue, seal brown, kelly green, rose, peacock blue, turquoise blue, orchid, or purple. SIZES: 32 to 44 bust.

PRICE, PREPAID to your home, **$6.98**

PURE SILK

9K18314
$6.98

9K18312
$4.98

LINKS
AND LINKS
OSTRICH
EDGES

WOOL
9K18309
$2.99

Sweater Novelties at attractive Prices!

9K18311 *An exceedingly smart sweater coat of all wool worsted yarns in link-and-link stitch.*

The Tuxedo revers are knit in two-tone basket-weave stitch. Cuffs to correspond. Border in similar pattern. COLORS: Brown and buff; navy blue and buff; black and white; or buff and brown. SIZES: 32 to 44 bust.

PRICE, PREPAID to your home, **$4.88**

9K18312 *The new "Ostrich" trimming gives newest effect to this all wool worsted sweater coat.*

Contrasting ostrich stitch used at the edge of the Tuxedo collar and cuffs. Cord girdle. COLORS: Black and white; buff and brown; navy blue and buff; or peacock blue and buff. SIZES: 32 to 44 bust.

PRICE, PREPAID to your home, **$4.98**

9K18309 *Stylish new coatee scarf of fine wool yarn with brushed Angora-like finish.*

All-around belt with buckle. Two patch pockets. Fringe trimming. COLORS: Brown and buff; purple and steel grey; emerald green and white; white and black; rose and Copenhagen blue; or Copenhagen blue and rose.

PRICE, PREPAID to your home, **$2.99**

9K18313 *One of the season's smartest Tuxedo sweater coats at a special reduced price.*

Knit from all wool worsted yarn, 100% wool and set off with Angora wool Tuxedo revers and cuffs. COLORS: Black and white; purple and white; navy blue and white; or brown and buff. SIZES: 32 to 44 bust.

PRICE, PREPAID to your home, **$4.88**

TUXEDO
ALL
WORSTED

ALL WORSTED
AND
ANGORA FINISH

9K18310 *The very newest version of the fashionable tie-back sweater blouse is here shown.*

This is a 100% all wool garment, knit in regulation sweater stitch, and made very attractive and becoming with a Tuxedo collar and cuffs of contrasting Angora wool. The wide girdle crosses over at the front and terminates in sash ends at the side. An unbeatable value. COLORS: Black and white; American beauty and white; peacock blue and white; or brown and buff. SIZES: 32 to 44 bust.

PRICE, PREPAID to your home, **$3.49**

VERY IMPORTANT
Be always sure to state
COLOR and SIZE
desired

9K18311
$4.88
WORTH
$6.00

WORSTED AND
ANGORA
TIE BACK
9K18310
$3.49

9K18313
$4.88
WORTH
$6.00

CHICAGO, ILL.

Order at Our Risk. You Are the Judge—Your Money Back If You Are Not Satisfied

85

9K18316 Novelty wool *sweater coat with scarf.* Angora finish, Belted and pocketed. COLORS: Dark brown, dark blue, buff or Copenhagen blue, all with fancy plaid. SIZES: 34 to 44. PRICE, PREPAID to your home, **$5.88**

Womens' Knitted Sweater Novelties

9K18317 *New style knitted jersey cape with checked Angora trimming.* Stunningly attractive, Patch pockets. Belt. COLORS: Navy blue with navy blue and buff, dark brown with brown and buff or black with black and white. SIZES: Small, medium and large. PRICE, PREPAID to your home, **$7.98**

9K18315 All wool *coatee scarf with fringed contrasting collar as shown.* Angora. Narrow patent leather belt. Patch pockets. COLORS: Brown and buff, purple and grey, peacock blue and buff or rose and Copenhagen blue. PRICE, PREPAID to your home, **$3.98**

WOOL CAPE SCARF 9K18315 **$3.98**

KNITTED COAT AND SCARF 9K18316 **$5.88**

KNITTED JERSEY ANGORA CAPE 9K18317 **$7.98**

Misses and Childrens Sweater Bargains

ALL WOOL 9K18321 **$3.88**

9K18322 **$1.69**

9K18320 **$2.98**

SLIP OVER TIE BACK 9K18318 **$2.39**

9K18323—**$1.98**

9K18322 *Child's Merino yarn sweater coat at a real worth-while saving.* 20% wool, 80% cotton. COLORS: White, rose or Copenhagen blue. SIZES: 2 to 6 years. PRICE, PREPAID to your home, **$1.69**

9K18321 *Misses' all wool Tuxedo sweater coat.* COLORS: Peacock blue with navy blue stripes, rose with Copenhagen blue, buff with brown or navy blue with Copenhagen blue. SIZES: 6 to 14 years. PRICE, PREPAID to your home, **$3.88**

9K18320 *Misses' all wool sweater with new ripple effect.* Very attractive. COLORS: Peacock blue and buff, buff and peacock blue or rose and Copenhagen blue. SIZES: 6 to 14 years. PRICE, PREPAID to your home, **$2.98**

9K18323 *Child's worsted slip-over sweater.* Fine links and links. COLORS: Peacock blue and white, rose and white or all white. SIZES: 2 to 6 years. PRICE, PREPAID to your home, **$1.98**

9K18318 *Girls' slip-over tie-back wool-mixed sweater.* Very new and smart. Contrasting trimming. Sash. COLORS: Copenhagen blue with buff, buff with brown or rose with Copenhagen blue. SIZES: 6 to 12 years. PRICE, PREPAID to your home, **$2.39**

9K18319 *Misses' All-wool sweater coat with sailor collar.* Big value. COLORS: American beauty, Kelly green, peacock blue or white. SIZES: 6 to 14 years. PRICE PREPAID **$2.98**

Be sure to state SIZE and COLOR desired.

9K18319—**$2.98**

PHILIPSBORN'S

This Stunning Castle Creation Leads the Grand March of suit styles for 1921

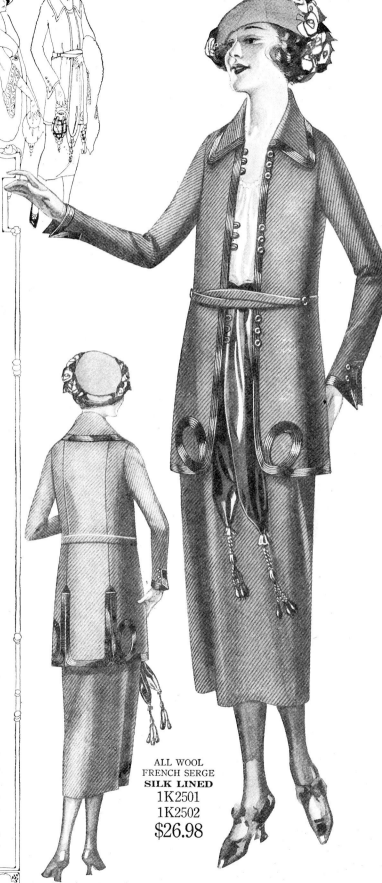

1K2501 *Irene Castle's cleverness and skill as a designer are revealed in every line of this, her own creation. the smartest suit of the season of 1921. In any fashion revue this model will easily take first place.*

Fashion's tendency to box coat effects—than which there is no style more youthful and smart—is charmingly interpreted in this **all wool French Serge** suit. Silk braid contributes a dressy and effective trimming, forming large circular designs at both front and back of the 30-inch coat. Panel back with deep slashings at either side. New style square coat collar. Open flare sleeves. Narrow cross-over shoestring belt. Small loops and buttons fasten the coat to the neckline. The tailored skirt is finished in newest fashion with a silk satin sash with ornamental pendants. Tailored pockets. The coat is lined with fancy silk. Only to Philipsborn's customers comes the opportunity to possess this stunning Castle creation. Why not you? COLORS: Navy blue or tan. SIZES: 32 to 44 bust. Skirt length 36 to 42.

PRICE, PREPAID to your home, **$26.98**

1K2502 For misses and small women. SIZES: 32 to 38 bust. Skirt length 32 to 38.

PRICE, PREPAID to your home, **$26.98**

HOW TO ORDER

In ordering women's and small women's suits, be sure to give bust measure, size of waistband, and front length of skirt. Full instructions for taking these measurements are given in the order blank at the back of this catalog.

IT IS IMPORTANT TO GIVE ALL THREE MEASUREMENTS, as without this information we cannot fill your order promptly.

Do not order a larger size than is cataloged. For these, refer to our stout sizes. Also state color of suit desired.

ALL WOOL
FRENCH SERGE
SILK LINED
1K2501
1K2502
$26.98

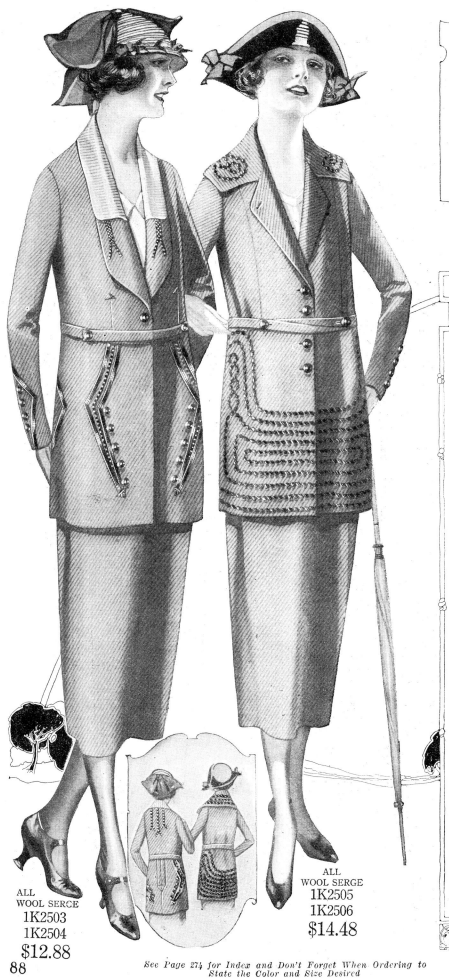

Down! Go! Prices!

"Two Great Values - Very Last Minute Bargain Prices" Save $5 cash and delivery charges!!

1K2503 *The way in which Philipsborn's have forced prices back to normal is convincingly shown in this* **all wool serge suit** *at $12.88.*

A clear saving of $5.00 plus free transportation to your door makes this the biggest suit value of the year. Silk braid and silk twist stitching give charming style to the new 28-inch length coat. Self-material shawl collar with poplin over-collar. Flowered sateen lining. Tailored skirt with belted and gathered back. Smart and dressy. COLORS: Navy blue or tan. SIZES: 32 to 44 bust. Skirt length 36 to 42.
PRICE, PREPAID to your home, **$12.88**

1K2504 Same style for misses and small women. SIZES: 32 to 38 bust. Skirt length 32 to 38.
PRICE, PREPAID
to your home **$12.88**

1K2505 *Not in many seasons have you seen an* **all wool serge** *suit of such superior style and excellent workmanship quoted at so low a price, $14.48.*

Only our foresighted buying when the cost of materials dropped makes such a splendid saving possible at this time. The stylish 28-inch coat shows newest style tendencies in the semi-box effect and the elaborate use of silk braid trimming, as in the large illustration and in miniature. Large becoming cape collar. Narrow cross-over belt. Flowered sateen lining. Tailored skirt with belted and gathered back. Unusually dressy and becoming. COLORS: Navy blue or tan. SIZES: 32 to 44 bust. Skirt length 36 to 42.
PRICE, PREPAID to your home, **$14.98**

1K2506 Same style for misses and small women. SIZES: 32 to 38 bust. Skirt length 32 to 38.
PRICE, PREPAID
to your home, **$14.48**

IMPORTANT
Be sure to state COLOR and SIZE desired when ordering

ALL WOOL SERGE
1K2503
1K2504
$12.88

ALL WOOL SERGE
1K2505
1K2506
$14.48

Best Value ↑ Latest Style

Everything Prepaid and Money Back Guarantee!

3 Reasons why everything points to "PHILIPSBORN'S"

1K2507 *A glance is enough to show you the attractive style of this suit, tailored in one of the season's favorite designs and quoted at a cash saving.*

Our usual three-fold guarantee of best value, latest style and prepaid transportation charges goes with the suit. The material is **all wool serge**. The coat cut in fashionable new spring length (28 inches) has accordion-pleated sides and center back. Silk braid and button trimming add dressiness. Self-material Tuxedo collar with poplin over-collar. Fancy tussah silk lining. Skirt has all-around belt. A rare value. COLOR: Navy blue. SIZES: 32 to 44 bust. Skirt length 36 to 42.
PRICE, PREPAID to your home, **$15.98**

1K2508 Same style for misses and small women. SIZES: 32 to 38 bust. Skirt length 32 to 38.
PRICE, PREPAID to your home, **$15.98**

1K2509 *If you are in doubt about the sort of suit to select for spring, why not choose this model of* **all wool serge.**

The price that we quote is unusually moderate for this quality and the style is sure to please you. Harmonizing silk stitching massed in panel effect gives just the right touch of trimming to the very distinctive 29-inch coat. The miniature shows you the smart style of the back. Tuxedo collar of self-material contrasts pleasingly with the pongee over-collar. New style slashed sleeves. All-around self-material shoe string belt. Flowered tussah silk lining. Skirt has tailored pockets and all-around belt. COLORS: Navy blue. SIZES: 32 to 44 bust. Skirt length 36 to 42.
PRICE, PREPAID to your home, **$21.98**

1K2510 Same style for misses and small women. SIZES: 32 to 38 bust. Skirt length 32 to 38.
PRICE, PREPAID to your home, **$21.98**

IMPORTANT
Do not delay your order by failing to state SIZES and COLOR desired.

ALL WOOL SERGE
1K2509
1K2510
$21.98

ALL WOOL SERGE
1K2507
1K2508
$15.98

CHICAGO, ILL.

The Best-Dressed Women Everywhere Wear PHILIPSBORN'S Clothes. Prices Always the Lowest, Quality Always the Highest

89

A Suit we are really proud of because of its Style & Value

1K2511 *Never in our thirty-one years' experience in making stylish suits have we offered a model to surpass this in style and value.*

All wool men's wear serge of splendid quality makes the suit, and silk embroidery with bright touches of color adds to its attraction. The coat is cut in stylish 26-inch length with set-in sections at the front and sides in a slightly rippled effect that is very new and becoming. Panel effect pockets at the sides. Shawl collar. Flare cuffs. Cording and button trimming. Flowered tussah silk lining. Skirt has tailored pockets and all-around belt. COLORS: Navy blue or tan. SIZES: 32 to 44 bust. Skirt length 36 to 42.
PRICE, PREPAID to your home, **$24.98**

1K2512 Same style for misses and small women. SIZES: 32 to 38 bust. Skirt length 34 to 38.
PRICE, PREPAID to your home, **$24.98**

ALL WOOL MEN'S WEAR SERGE
1K2511
1K2512
$24.98

Descriptions for Page 91

1K2513 *No detail has been overlooked, no pains have been spared that would make this suit one of the finest ever offered at our low price.*

It is an original Irene Castle design, for which we have chosen a very durable **all wool men's wear serge.** Newest style is shown in the smartly shaped loose coat back which is cut in one with the collar, its style heightened with hand embroidery at the top and bottom. Two rows of cording at the waistline give the newest of finishes and terminate in cord ornaments at the side fronts. Embroidered sleeve with new style kimono cuff. **Flowered silk lining.** Coat 30 inches long. Tailored skirt with slot pockets and all-around belt. Extremely dressy. COLOR Navy blue. SIZES: 32 to 44 bust. Skirt length 36 to 42.
PRICE, PREPAID to your home, **$34.98**

1K2514 Same style for misses and small women. SIZES: 32 to 38 bust. Skirt length 34 to 38.
PRICE, PREPAID to your home, **$34.98**

1K2515 *Many a woman believes that she is lacking in style simply because she has never found a style that suited her particular type.*

In this smart new suit of **all wool poplin,** PHILIPSBORN'S style expert and designer, Irene Castle, has created a wonderful new model for the woman who ordinarily is hard to fit. Note the effective lines of the 27-inch unbelted box coat which is made very dressy and becoming with harmonizing stitching and silk arrowhead trimming. Inverted plaits at the sides and back. Tailored button-trimmed cuffs. Deep shawl collar. Flowered tussah silk lining. Tailored skirt with eight rows of silk twist stitching to correspond with coat. It has slot pockets and all-around belt. A youthful model of great charm. COLOR: Navy blue, or tan. SIZES: 32 to 44 bust. Skirt length 36 to 42.
PRICE, PREPAID to your home, **$27.50**

1K2516 Same style for misses and small women. SIZES: 32 to 38 bust. Skirt length 34 to 38.
PRICE, PREPAID to your home, **$27.50**

1K2517 *Still another charming suit style from the hands of Irene Castle, is this* **all wool tricotine** *model for which we quote an amazingly low price.*

The stylish 28-inch box coat has trimming effectively distributed in the fancy silk and gold braided vestee and the silk braid binding. The Tuxedo collar extending to the bottom of coat gives very becoming lines, which are further accented with the novel treatment of the sides. Six rows of tucking with three tabs in pocket effect contribute a very new trimming touch. All-around self-material shoestring belt. **Flowered silk lining.** Skirt has slot pockets and all-around belt. Here is your chance to secure one of the season's finest suits at a big saving. COLORS: Navy blue or black. SIZES: 32 to 44 bust. Skirt length 36 to 42.
PRICE, PREPAID to your home, **$29.98**

1K2518 Same style for misses and small women. SIZES: 32 to 38 bust. Skirt length 34 to 38.
PRICE, PREPAID to your home, **$29.98**

IMPORTANT!
Be sure to state SIZE and COLOR desired when ordering— DON'T FORGET!

I only intended one Suit for this Page-But these three Models are so pretty I could not choose

Irene Castle

SILK LINED
ALL WOOL MEN'S
WEAR SERGE
1K2513
1K2514
$34.98

ALL WOOL
POPLIN
1K2515
1K2516
$27.50

SILK
LINED
ALL WOOL
TRICOTINE
1K2517
1K2518
$29.98

For Descriptions See Page 90

1K2521 *Without exaggeration here is one of the most remarkable offerings to be found this season in an all wool French serge suit.*

At our special low price we defy competition to match this value. There is charm in every line of the model, from the smart Tuxedo collar with its becoming touch of white in the silk over-collar to the silk twist stitching which ornaments both front and back. (See miniature.) The coat is cut in fashionable new spring length (28 inches) and is fastened with two buttons and loops as pictured. Narrow tie belt held with fancy loop. Tussah silk lining. Skirt with slot pockets and all-around belt. COLORS: Navy blue or tan. SIZES: 32 to 44 bust. Skirt length 36 to 42.
PRICE, PREPAID to your home, **$21.98**

1K2522 Same style for misses and small women. SIZES: 32 to 38 bust. Skirt length 34 to 38.
PRICE, PREPAID to your home, **$21.98**

1K2523 *A charming example of the new box coats is shown in this all wool serge suit—an exclusive Philipsborn's model at a reduced price.*

A very aristocratic air is contributed by the elaborate silk braid embroidery which adorns the stylish 28-inch box coat as pictured. See miniature for embroidered panel back with button trimming. Contrasting French knot embroidery gives a charming touch of color as shown. Further smart style is displayed in the bell sleeves and slot pocket. Shawl collar. Flowered tussah silk lining. All-around belted skirt with tailored slot pockets. Unequaled for youthful charm and style. COLORS: Navy blue or tan. SIZES: 32 to 44 bust. Skirt length 36 to 42.
PRICE, PREPAID to your home, **$19.98**

1K2524 Same style for misses and small women. SIZES: 32 to 38 bust. Skirt length 34 to 38.
PRICE, PREPAID to your home, **$19.98**

1K2525 *If you are looking for style, fine tailoring, and excellent materials you'll find them in this suit at a very low price.*

One of the advance spring models for 1921, it is fashioned of all wool serge. The smartly tailored 28-inch coat is designed in newest pointed effect at the sides where pockets are provided. Splendid trimming is given in the silk twist stitching and silk braid with button groups as pictured. Smartly shaped. Long roll collar. All-around self-material shoestring belt crossed over at front. Flowered tussah silk lining. Skirt has slot pockets and belted back. COLOR: Navy blue. SIZES: 32 to 44 bust. Skirt length 36 to 42.
PRICE, PREPAID to your home, **$16.98**

1K2526 Same style for misses and small women. SIZES: 32 to 38 bust. Skirt length 34 to 38.
PRICE, PREPAID to your home, **$16.98**

How to Order Women's Suits

State bust measure, size of waistband, and front length of skirt. IT IS IMPORTANT TO GIVE ALL THREE MEASUREMENTS. Also, do not order a larger size than is catalogued. For these, refer to our stout sizes.

Be sure to state SIZE and COLOR desired

ALL WOOL
POPLIN
SILK LINED
1K2519
1K2520

SPECIAL
$24.88
PREPAID

Wonder of Wonders - is this Suit - a Real Big!! Value!

1K2519 *Don't wait until the end of the season sales to buy your new suit, for you will never find a better value than this.*

We bought this suit of **all wool poplin** when the cost of materials dropped, and consequently paid less than the usual market price. You get the benefit in these reduced prices. 27-inch semi-box coat with new style slashed sides and back. Braid and button trimming. Flowered taffeta lining. Belted and pocketed skirt. COLORS: Navy blue or tan. SIZES: 32 to 44 bust. Skirt length 36 to 42.
PRICE, PREPAID to your home, **$24.88**

1K2520 Same style for misses and small women. SIZES: 32 to 38 bust. Skirt length 34 to 38.
PRICE, PREPAID to your home, **$24.88**

America's
3 Best
Suit Styles
Order At Our Risk

ALL WOOL SERGE
1K2525
1K2526
$16.98

ALL WOOL
SERGE
1K2523
1K2524
$19.98

ALL WOOL WORSTED SERGE
1K2521
1K2522
$21.98

For Descriptions
See Page 92

ALL WOOL
MANNISH SERGE
1K2531
1K2532 } $29.75

ALL WOOL
POPLIN
1K2527
1K2528
$24.98

ALL WOOL
SERGE
1K2533
$19.98

ALL WOOL
SERGE
1K2529
1K2530
$14.88

For Descriptions See Page 95

PHILIPSBORN'S

Descriptions for Page 94

1K2527 *Trim, tailored lines make this suit of* **all wool poplin** *unusually distinctive and becoming.*

Smart 28-inch coat has three rows of cording through the center back, with narrow box plait from waistline to bottom. Silk braid and silk stitching in triangle effect. Smartly shaped overlapping sections with set-in pockets. Shoestring belt. Flowered tussah lining. Tuxedo collar. Belted and pocketed skirt. COLORS: Navy blue or tan. SIZES: 32 to 44 bust. Skirt length 36 to 42. PRICE, PREPAID to your home, **$24.98**

1K2528 For misses and small women. SIZES: 32 to 38 bust. Skirt length 34 to 38. PRICE, PREPAID to your home, **$24.98**

1K2529 *One of the greatest reductions ever offered in an* **all wool serge** *suit of this quality.*

Note the smart style of the irregular line 28-inch coat with its silk braid trimming and button groups. The back is just as smart and distinctive as the front with plait and button trimming through the center. Tuxedo collar with striped silk over-collar. Flowered sateen lining. Belted and pocketed skirt. COLOR: Navy blue. SIZES: 32 to 44 bust. Skirt length 36 to 42. PRICE, PREPAID to your home, **$14.88**

1K2530 For misses and small women. SIZES 32 to 38 bust. Skirt length 34 to 38. **$14.88** PRICE, PREPAID to your home,

1K2531 *Refined and artistic taste were never better displayed than in this handsome suit.*

It features the box coat effect now so much in vogue, and is made of splendid quality **men's wear all wool serge.** An elaborate embroidery design combines with silk braid to make the most effective of trimmings. Smart details are the new style square collar with long sash ties with ornamental pendants, the breast pockets, and slashed flare sleeves. Tussah silk lining. Skirt with slot pockets and all-around belt. COLORS: Navy blue or tan. SIZES: 32 to 44 bust. Skirt length 36 to 42. PRICE, PREPAID to your home, **$29.75**

1K2532 For misses and small women. SIZES: 32 to 38 bust. Skirt length 34 to 38. PRICE, PREPAID to your home, **$29.75**

1K2533 *Specially designed to bring out the charms of the miss is this stunning new suit.*

The material is **all wool serge**, and the design is the favored box coat effect. Gold tinsel embroidery lends a very dressy trimming all-around the bottom, through the center back and front of the 26-inch coat as pictured. Button trimming at either side. Corded square collar. Wide full length flare sleeves. Tussah silk lining. Skirt has slot pockets and all-around belt. COLORS: Navy blue. SIZES: 32 to 38 bust. Skirt length 34 to 38. PRICE, PREPAID to your home, **$19.98**

IMPORTANT!
Do not delay your order by failing to state SIZE *and* COLOR *desired. Important!*

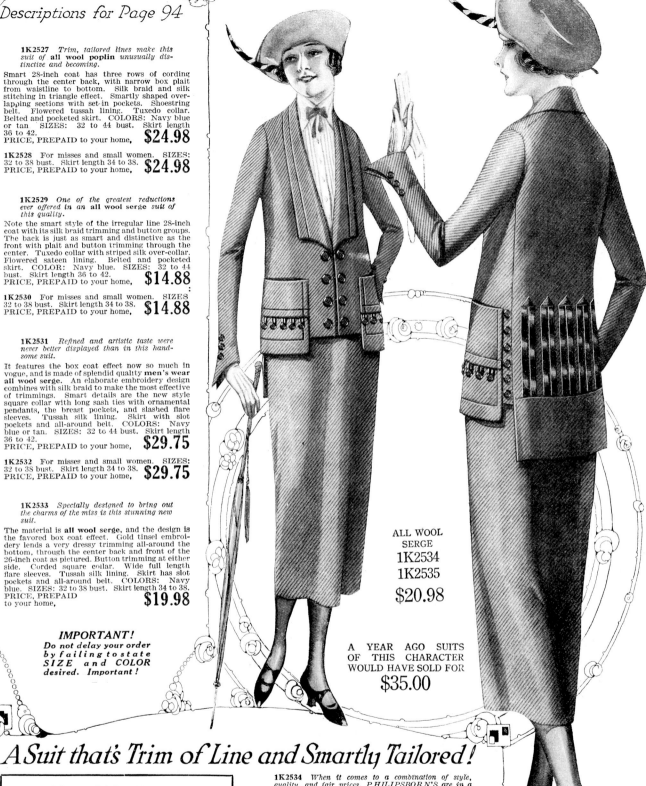

ALL WOOL
SERGE
1K2534
1K2535

$20.98

A YEAR AGO SUITS OF THIS CHARACTER WOULD HAVE SOLD FOR
$35.00

A Suit that's Trim of Line and Smartly Tailored!

HOW TO ORDER

In ordering women's suits, be sure to state bust measure, size of waistband, and front length of skirt.

IT IS IMPORTANT TO GIVE ALL THREE MEASUREMENTS.

Full instructions for taking measurements will be found in the order blank at the back of this catalog.

Do not order a larger size than is cataloged, but for these, refer to our stout sizes.

Also, state color of suit desired.

1K2534 *When it comes to a combination of style, quality, and fair prices,* P H I L I P S B O R N'S *are in a class by themselves.*

A comparison of our prices with those charged by other mail order houses will convince you that you will save money by shopping here. Take, for example, this **all wool serge** suit— the season's latest version of the box coat effect. Silk braid and button trimmed back. Novel patch pockets with loops and button trimming as in the front illustration. Tuxedo collar. Flowered tussah silk lined. Tailored skirt with slot pockets and all-around belt. A bargain offering. COLORS: Navy blue or black. SIZES: 32 to 44 bust. Skirt length 36 to 42. PRICE, PREPAID to your home, **$20.98**

1K2535 For misses and small women. SIZES: 32 to 38 bust. Skirt length 34 to 38. PRICE, PREPAID to your home, **$20.98**

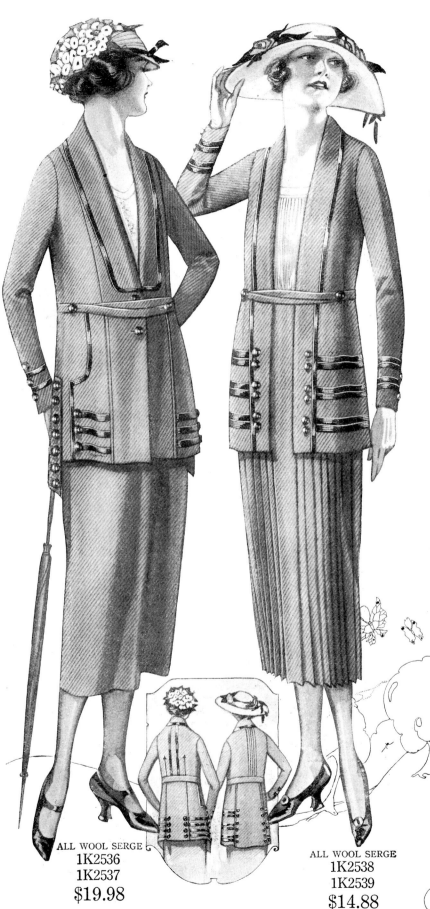

31 Years!
of suit knowledge back of every PHILIPSBORN suit! Read what others say · · ·

1K2536 *During our many years of making suits, we have learned to create beauty and becomingness.*

You will be delighted with the dressy appearance of this **all wool serge** suit with its fashionable silk braid trimming decorating the 29-inch coat. All-around self-material shoestring belt. Tuxedo collar. Button trimming. Flowered tussah silk lining. Felted and pocketed skirt. One of the season's best suit offerings at an amazingly low price. COLOR: Navy blue. SIZES: 32 to 44 bust. Skirt length 36 to 42.
PRICE, PREPAID to your home, **$19.98**

1K2537 For misses and small women. SIZES: 32 to 38 bust. Skirt length 34 to 38.
PRICE, PREPAID to your home, **$19.98**

1K2538 *A stylish and becoming suit which pays tribute to our thirty-one years' tailoring knowledge.*

All wool serge makes the model, a striking feature of which is the side and box-plaited skirt, a style that is destined for great favor this season. 28-inch coat smartly trimmed with silk braid as shown in the illustrations. Full length Tuxedo collar. Shoestring belt. Flowered tussah silk lining. Skirt has all-around belt. COLORS: Navy blue or black. SIZES: 32 to 44 bust. Skirt length 36 to 42.
PRICE, PREPAID to your home, **$14.88**

1K2539 For misses' and small women. SIZES: 32 to 38 bust. Skirt length 34 to 38.
PRICE, PREPAID to your home, **$14.88**

Be sure to state SIZE and COLOR desired when ordering.

ALL WOOL SERGE
1K2536
1K2537
$19.98

ALL WOOL SERGE
1K2538
1K2539
$14.88

Two wonderful Values for Stout figures . . . .

Worth $~~22.00~~

Our Special Price

$18.88

1K2540 *To the woman who knows, the style of this suit will carry instant conviction of the striking values that we offer.*

This good-looking suit of **all wool serge** has the height-giving lines and splendid wearing qualities which the stout woman wants in a suit for all around service. A very becoming line is effected by the front and back panel, with silk braid trimming terminating at the sides. Tailored notch collar with a silk poplin over-collar. Tailored slot pockets. Button trimming and fastening. Serviceably lined with twill. The skirt has becoming fulness gathered under the half belt at the back. Style and serviceability at a very small outlay of money. COLORS: Navy blue or black. SIZES: 37 to 53 bust. Skirt length 36 to 42.
PRICE, PREPAID
to your home,   **$18.88**

1K2541 *When you get this suit home and learn what others are paying for similar styles, you will see that it is a big bargain.*

It is an **all wool serge** model, especially designed for the stout woman. Note the clever style of the fashionable 31-inch coat, which is made very dressy with silk twist stitching. The back is designed with a wide panel with soft plaits below the waistline, button groups at either side as pictured. Convenient pockets formed at the sides have silk twist stitching and button trimming as in miniature. Shawl collar. Shoe string belt. Flowered tussah silk lining. Skirt has tailored pockets, belted and gathered back. An unmatchable value at our low price. COLORS: Navy blue or black. SIZES: 37 to 53 bust. Skirt length 36 to 42.
PRICE, PREPAID
to your home,   **$18.88**

DON'T FORGET
When ordering be sure to state SIZE and COLOR desired

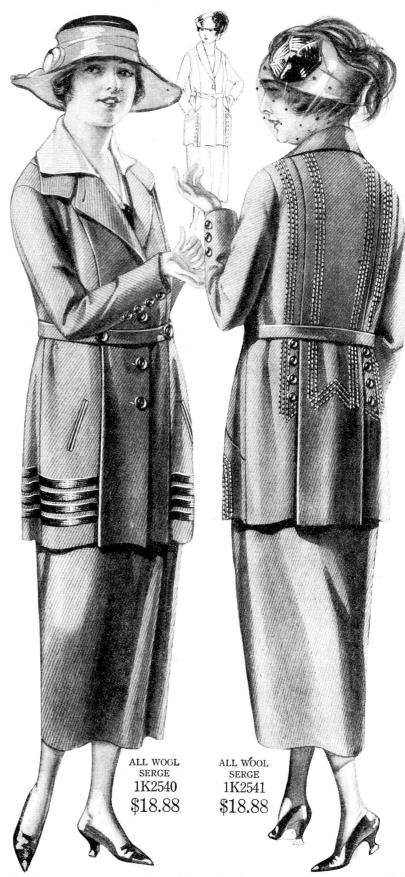

ALL WOOL
SERGE
1K2540
$18.88

ALL WOOL
SERGE
1K2541
$18.88

CHICAGO, ILL.

Furs of Distinction for Spring and Summer Wear Are Shown on Page 45 of This Catalog. Prices Extremely Low

97

ALL
WOOL SERGE
1K2542
$16.68

ALL
WOOL
SERGE
1K2544
$22.98

ALL
WOOL MEN'S
WEAR SERGE
1K2543
$24.98

*Three Stouts
Suits - All!
Extra Value!*

1K2542 *A splendid style for the stout woman in a moderately priced suit.*
The material is **all wool serge** of great durability. Silk braid in fancy design trims the 30-inch coat as pictured. Slot pockets. Narrow cross-over belt. Long shawl collar. Flowered tussah silk lining. Skirt has gathered back and all-around belt. Very smart and becoming. COLORS: Navy blue or black. SIZES: 37 to 53 bust. Skirt length 36 to 42.
PRICE, PREPAID
to your home, **$16.68**

1K2544 *Dressy style for the stout woman features this all wool serge suit.*
Stylish 30-inch coat with soutache braid embroidered pockets. Notch collar with silk arrow head trimming, and long revers. Fashionably narrow cross-over belt. Set-in pockets. Braid trimmed sleeves. Flowered tussah silk lining. Tailored skirt with pockets and all-around belt. COLORS: Navy blue or black. SIZES: 37 to 53 bust. Skirt length 36 to 42.
PRICE, PREPAID
to your home, **$22.98**

1K2543 *The lines sought by fashionable women are cleverly adapted for the stout woman here.*
All wool men's wear serge of wonderful serviceability makes the model. Silk braid at the coat sides and sleeves makes an effective trimming. Tailored notch collar with revers. Narrow cross-over belt. Panel front. Inverted plait through center back. Flowered tussah silk lining. Skirt with slot pockets and all-around belt. COLORS: Navy blue or black. SIZES: 37 to 53 bust. Skirt length 36 to 42.
PRICE, PREPAID
to your home, **$24.98**

IMPORTANT!—Be sure to state SIZE and COLOR desired.

My present to you—the loveliest misses suit I have ever designed! I want Y-O-U to have one!!

Irene Castle

1K2550 *No designer knows so well the art of dressing the American miss as Irene Castle. Her skill was never better displayed than in the charming suit here pictured.*

A model of last minute style ideas, it is developed in men's wear **all-wool serge**, a material which we selected specially because of its great durability and splendid appearance. The trim, smart lines of the box coat are irresistibly youthful and becoming. They are accented with twin box plaits through the back, centered with contrasting piping. Box plaits to correspond finish either side of the fronts, a vestee of contrasting material providing a new style effect at the center front. The novel style roll collar is set off with self-material tie and finished with self-ornaments—the very newest idea in neckline finishes. Six rows of silk braid with contrasting piping trim the coat at the sides. Braid and piping on collar to correspond. Handsome novelty buttons trim the coat as pictured. It is cut in a new short length, about 24 inches and is lined with flowered taffeta silk. The skirt is designed on trim, tailored lines, and is finished with slot pockets and an all-around belt. A wonderful style and value. COLORS: Navy blue with tan vestee and piping or tan with Copenhagen blue trimming. SIZES: 32 to 38 bust. Skirt length 32 to 38.
PRICE, PREPAID to your home, **$24.98**

HOW TO ORDER

In ordering misses' suits, be sure to state bust measure, front length of skirt, and size of waistband. DO NOT ORDER BY AGE, as it is impossible for us to determine correct sizes without exact measurements.
If a larger size than 38 bust is desired, refer to our women's suits.
Complete directions for taking measurements will be found in the order blank at the back of this catalog, and to avoid delay and disappointment be sure to always state COLOR and SIZE desired.

ALL WOOL
MEN'S WEAR
SERGE
1K2550
$24.98
SILK LINED

ALL WOOL
SERGE

1K2552
$16.98

WORTH
$20.00

ALL WOOL
SERGE
1K2551
$14.88
WORTH
$17.00

SERGE
1K2553
$10.88
WORTH
$14.00

Smart Suits for Petite Figures

1K2551 *One of the best suit styles that the miss or small youthful woman can select,*

This **all** wool serge model features a smart 28-inch coat with novel trimming panels at the sides. Silk braid and contrasting stitching ornament panels. Contrasting stitching on the Tuxedo collar. Braid-trimmed back. Flowered tussah silk lining. Skirt is gathered and belted across back. COLOR: Navy blue. SIZES: 32 to 38 bust. Skirt length 32 to 38.

PRICE, PREPAID
to your home, **$14.88**

1K2552 *A new and becoming suit for the miss at a price that makes it a real economy.*

All wool serge of excellent quality makes the model. Note the clever style of the exceedingly fashionable 28-inch box coat. Inch-wide box plaits extend all around the bottom, silk braid trimming as pictured. Long shawl collar with fancy silk overcollar. Flowered tussah silk lining. Belted skirt. COLOR: Navy blue. SIZES: 32 to 38 bust. Skirt length 32 to 38 inches.

PRICE, PREPAID
to your home, **$16.98**

1K2553 *The miss will find this suit of wool mixed serge a dressy and becoming style.*

The back of the 28-inch coat is made very distinctive with a graduated panel in wedge shape. Silk braid and button-trimmed sections at the side fronts further emphasize the smart style. Tailored notch collar with revers. Shoestring belt. Flowered sateen lining. Skirt has gathered and belted back. A remarkable value. COLOR: Navy blue. SIZES: 32 to 38 bust. Skirt length 32 to 38 inches.

PRICE, PREPAID
to your home, **$10.88**

ALL WOOL
MEN'S WEAR
SERGE
1K2556
$24.98
WORTH
$30.00

ALL WOOL
SERGE
1K2555
$19.98
WORTH
$25.00

ALL
WOOL
SERGE

1K2554
$17.50
WORTH
$20.00

Styles that Paris Raves about

1K2556 *A charming style for misses is this suit of* **men's wear all wool serge.**
The style is new and out of the ordinary. The smart lines of the 26-inch coat accented with silk twist stitching in two-tone triangle effect. See miniature for back view. Stylish Tuxedo collar. Flare sleeves. Flowered tussah silk lining. Full side plaited skirt with tasseled sash belt. A style of much distinction.
COLOR: Navy blue. SIZES: 32 to 38 bust. Skirt length 34 to 38 inches.
PRICE, PREPAID to your home, **$24.98**

1K2555 *A Parisian inspiration,* **all wool serge** *suit for misses—an advance 1921 model.*
The very youthful 24-inch box coat shows newest style in the semi-attached self-material straps at the back. Sides are smartly slashed, silk braid trimming all around the bottom as shown. Button groups. Braid-bound Tuxedo collar. Flared cuff sleeves. Tussah silk lining. Belted and pocketed skirt.
COLOR: Navy blue. SIZES: 32 to 38 bust. Skirt length 34 to 38 inches.
PRICE, PREPAID to your home, **$19.98**

1K2554 *One of the most desirable suits ever shown for misses at our low price.*
This **all-wool serge** model creates instant attention by the unusual design of the 27-inch coat. Silk twist stitching at front and back, with novel scalloped edge and plaits. Tuxedo collar with white poplin over-collar. Shoestring belt. Flowered tussah silk lining. Belted and pocketed skirt. COLOR: Navy blue. SIZES: 32 to 38 bust. Skirt length 34 to 38 inches.
PRICE, PREPAID to your home **$17.50**

Values that speak Volumes!

1K2558 *Charmingly youthful is this* **all wool serge** *suit for misses and small women.*

The style trend of the season is seen in the 26-inch box coat. Gold and tinsel trimmed vestee with button trimming. Silk embroidery all around bottom. New style coat collar. Tussah silk lining. Belted and pocketed skirt. COLOR: Navy blue. SIZES: 32 to 38 bust. Skirt length 34 to 38 inches.
PRICE, PREPAID to your home, **$18.98**

1K2557 *Very new style details give charming variety to this* **all wool serge** *suit for misses.*

Plaited panels trimmed with contrasting silk twist stitching add dressiness to the 27-inch coat. Silk satin sash with silk fringe. Panel effect back. Shawl collar. Tussah silk lined. Skirt with slot pockets and all-around belt. A big value at our low price. COLOR: Navy blue. SIZES: 32 to 38 bust. Skirt length 34 to 38 inches.
PRICE, PREPAID to your home, **$19.98**

SERGE
1K2559
$11.98
WORTH
$14.00

ALL WOOL SERGE
1K2560
$16.98

ALL WOOL SERGE
1K2558
$18.98

ALL WOOL SERGE
1K2557
$19.98

Two Junior Styles that are Right

1K2559 *The junior miss will be delighted with the smart and becoming style of this* **PHILIPSBORN'S** *suit.*

Good quality **wool** mixed serge makes the model, and the style leaves nothing to be desired, newest features being shown throughout. The nobby 26-inch coat is distinctively designed with graduated sides, smartly trimmed with silk braid and button groups. The smartly shaped shawl collar is made very becoming with a white poplin over-collar and button trimming. Braid and button trimmed sleeves. Flowered sateen lining. The tailored skirt has slot pockets and gathered and belted back. COLOR: Navy blue. SIZES: 31 to 37 bust. Skirt length 32 to 37 inches.
PRICE, PREPAID to your home, **$11.98**

1K2560 *Made right and priced right is this fashionable suit for junior misses. A bargain at our price.*

The model is made of **all wool serge**, with coat in the popular box effect so much favored this season. It is cut in jaunty 24-inch length, and is smartly slashed at the side seams. Silk twist and gold tinsel trimming form modish panels at the front and back, braid-bound slot pockets placed below the trimming at the front. The soft rolling shawl collar has braid binding. Flare sleeves with button trimming. Coat fastening with loops and buttons. Tussah silk lining. Belted and pocketed skirt. COLOR: Navy blue. SIZES: 31 to 37 bust. Skirt length 32 to 37 inches.
PRICE, PREPAID to your home, **$16.98**

9K17300 *Net guimpe and vestee with attached collar.* Picoted ruffles. COLORS: Cream or white. PRICE, PREPAID to your home, **$1.98**

9K17310 *Organdie vestee and collar with novelty tucking.* COLOR: White. PRICE, PREPAID to your home, **89c**

9K17301 *Fashionable net and Val. lace vestee with collar.* Tucking as shown. COLORS: Cream or white. PRICE, PREPAID to your home, **79c**

9K17302 *Extremely pretty net and Val. lace vestee.* Roll collar. COLOR: White. PRICE, PREPAID to your home, **59c**

9K17325 *Fichu collar of net with plaited frill edging and Val. lace.* COLOR: White. PRICE, PREPAID to your home, **49c**

9K17305 *New style guimpe and vestee of net and Val. lace.* COLOR. Light ecru. PRICE, PREPAID to your home, **98c**

9K17309 *Tucked and lace-trimmed organdie vestee.* COLOR: White. PRICE, PREPAID to your home, **75c**

9K17329 *A bargain value in a stylish new collar.* Made entirely of Venise lace. Greatly underpriced. COLOR: Cream. PRICE, PREPAID to your home, **39c**

9K17330 *Attractive collar, greatly reduced.* Made of filet pattern lace in points as pictured. COLOR: Light ecru. PRICE, PREPAID to your home, **39c**

Your Choice *in this Group!* 39c

9K17306 *White pique vestee Buster Brown collar.* PRICE, PREPAID to your home, **49c**

9K17328 *Novelty tucked organdie roll collar and cuffs.* COLOR: White. PRICE, PREPAID to your home, **39c**

9K17313 *Stylish roll collar of heavy Venise lace.* COLOR: Cream. PRICE, PREPAID to your home, **39c**

9K17334 *Embroidered organdie collar.* COLOR: White. PRICE, PREPAID to your home, **39c**

9K17314 *White lace collar and cuffs.* PRICE, PREPAID to your home, **69c**

9K17333 *Organdie collar, cuffs.* COLOR: White with ecru. PRICE, PREPAID to your home, **39c**

9K17336 *Venise roll collar.* COLOR: White or cream. PRICE, PREPAID to your home, **88c**

9K17332 *Net and filet lace collar.* COLOR: Natural. PRICE, PREPAID to your home, **39c**

9K17337 *Collar and cuffs of embroidered batiste with Venise lace.* COLOR: Cream. PRICE, PREPAID to your home, **69c**

9K17331 *Smart pique collar and cuff set.* COLOR: White. PRICE, PREPAID to your home, **39c**

9K17324 *Point collar of Venise lace.* COLOR: Light ecru. PRICE, PREPAID to your home, **39c**

9K17307 *Tricolene vestee.* COLORS: Rose, Copenhagen, bisque, taupe, navy, brown. PRICE, PREPAID to your home, **98c**

9K17303 *Val. lace vestee and collar.* COLOR: Light ecru. PRICE, PREPAID to your home, **79c**

9K17323 *Square collar of embroidered net and Val. lace.* COLOR: Cream. PRICE, PREP'D to your home, **69c**

9K17311 *Eyelet embroidery vestee and collar.* COLOR: Cream. PRICE, PREPAID to your home, **69c**

Net-Voile or Organdie

Ruffled Flouncing by the yard

9K17317 *Organdie,* width 39 in. COLORS: Pink, white, Copenhagen blue, lavender, or maize.

9K17319 *Voile,* width, colors, as above.

9K17318 *Net.* Width, 39 in. COLORS: White or Cream. PRICE, PREPAID to your home, **$1.39**

9K17315 *Shadow lace point collar.* Gives the newest of neckline finish for a dress or blouse. COLORS: Cream or white. PRICE, PREPAID to your home, **35c**

9K17308 *Eyelet embroidered batiste vestee and collar.* COLOR: Ecru. PRICE, PREPAID to your home, **59c**

9K17326 *Organdie roll collar and cuffs with tucking and Val. lace.* COLOR: white. PRICE, PREPAID to your home, **49c**

9K17312 *New style two-tier collar of Venise lace over net and Val. lace.* COLOR: Ecru. PRICE, PREPAID to your home, **49c**

9K17316 *Popular middy tie of pure silk—special at 69c.* COLORS: Scarlet, cardinal, navy blue, black, Kelly green, white or gold. PRICE, PREPAID to your home, **69c**

9K17320 *Children's voile skirting.* 26-27 inches wide. Tucking and three rows of ruffling. COLORS: Pink, light blue or white. PRICE, PREPAID to your home, **$1.19**

9K17321 *26-27 inch Children's net skirting,* with ruffling as above. COLORS: White or cream. PRICE, PREP'D. **$1.19**

9K17322 *26-27 inch Children's organdie skirting.* COLORS: Pink, light blue, or white. PRICE, PREPAID to your home, **$1.19**

9K17327 *Silk messaline Windsor tie.* COLORS: Scarlet, navy blue, cardinal, black, Kelly green, brown, royal blue, white, Copenhagen blue, Scotch plaid, or shepherd checks. PRICE, PREPAID to your home, **23c**

Marabou and Curled Ostrich
9K16395
$7.39

Stylish Smart Marabou
Ostrich Fur Effects!
First Quality!
The Lasting Kind!!
All Silk Lined

All Marabou
9K16396
$7.98

9K16398
$11.98

Marabou and Curled Ostrich
9K16392
$4.98

9K16396 *Stunning new marabou cape, moderately priced.* 28 marabou tails. Silk taffeta streamers with marabou pompons. Silk peau de cygne lining. COLORS: Black, brown or taupe. PRICE, PREPAID to your home, **$7.98**

9K16395 *Effective new cape of marabou and ostrich.* It has 18 marabou tails and a wide ostrich border. Silk cord ties with marabou pompons. Silk peau de cygne lining. COLORS: Black, brown or taupe. PRICE, PREPAID to your home, **$7.39**

9K16398 *Here is a distinctive new full length marabou stole.* Ostrich bands extend down either side as pictured. Eight marabou tails and two ostrich tails. Taffeta ribbon streamers. Silk peau de cygne lined. COLORS: Black, brown or taupe. PRICE, PREP'D, **$11.98**

All Marabou
9K16393
$2.98

9K16397
$9.69

9K16393 *Marabou choker scarf at a specially reduced price.* Made with marabou on both sides, and finished with two large silk corded tassels. Very smart with a suit or dress. COLORS: Black, brown or taupe. PRICE, PREPAID, **$2.98** Value, $3.75.

9K16399
$6.88
Marabou and Curled Ostrich

Marabou and Curled Ostrich

9K16394
$4.68

Very Special Value!

All Marabou

9K16392 *Smart and stylish new marabou cape at a noteworthy price reduction.* Wide border of ostrich as shown. Silk streamers with ostrich pompons. Silk peau de cygne lining. COLORS: Black, brown or taupe. PRICE, PREPAID, **$4.98**

9K16399 *New style marabou cape trimmed with three bands of ostrich at back.* Trimmed with eight marabou tails and three ostrich tails. Silk cord ties. Silk peau de cygne lined. COLORS: Black, brown or taupe. PRICE, PREPAID to your home, **$6.88**

9K16397 *A handsome marabou cape at a small expense—real $12.00 value, $9.69. A splendid bargain.* Trimmed with wide ostrich band which encircles neck and forms stole effect at front as in miniature. Silk taffeta streamers with ostrich pompons. Silk peau de cygne lined. COLORS: Black, brown or taupe. PRICE, PREP'D to your home, **$9.69**

9K16394 *Here is one of our less expensive marabou capes, one of the season's best bargains.* Made entirely of good grade marabou and lined with silk peau de cygne. Silk taffeta streamers finished with marabou pompons. Very stunning and effective. COLORS: Black, brown or taupe. PRICE, PREP'D to your home, **$4.68**

You Take No Risk When You Shop Here—Your Money Back If You Are Not Satisfied

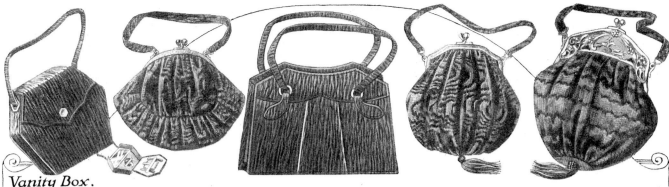

Vanity Box.
9K17366 *"Vanity box" mirror, powder box, coin purse, file, large mirror.* **Black crepe grained leather,** 6½x6¾. PRICE, PREPAID to your home, **$2.98**

9K17362 Moire silk bag *in fashionable shades.* Fancy seco silk lining. COLORS: Black, taupe, navy blue or brown. PRICE, PREPAID to your home, **$1.39**

9K17367 *New swagger bag of* crepe **grained leather.** Brocaded silk lining. Two inside compartments. COLORS: Black or tan. PRICE, PREPAID to your home. **$3.89**

9K17356 *Dressy bag at a real cash saving.* Made of **moire poplin.** Engraved metal frame. COLORS: Black or navy blue. PRICE, PREPAID to your home, **98c**

9K17361 *Handsome* **moire silk** bag—*very special.* Fancy metal frame. COLORS: Black, navy blue, taupe grey, or brown. PRICE, PREPAID to your home, **$1.49**

Hand Beaded

9K17371 *Novelty* **leather** belt—*white front with black ¾ way round.* Two buckles. SIZES: 28 to 40. PRICE, PREP'D to your home, **45c**

9K17372 *Open work belt of black* **patent leather**—*very new and smart.* A big value. SIZES: 28 to 40. PRICE, PREP'D to your home, **39c**

9K17377 *New style belt of* **black patent leather**—*nickel rings.* Specially reduced. SIZES: 28 to 38. PRICE, PREPAID to your home, **35c**

9K17370 *Novelty cut-out design belt of good quality* **leather.** White, brown or black. Very dressy. SIZES: 28 to 40. PRICE, PREPAID to your home, **45c**

9K17375 *New* **patent leather** belt *in your choice of black or red.* A special bargain. SIZES: 28 to 40. PRICE, PREPAID to your home, **23c**

9K17374 *Narrow belt in your choice of black or red* **patent leather.** Reduced price. SIZES: 28 to 40. PRICE, PREP'D to your home, **23c**

9K17376 *Eyelet open work belt of* **black** or tan **leather.** A big value. SIZES: 28 to 40. PRICE, PREP'D to your home. **39c**

9K17373 *An inexpensive belt of good quality* black or tan **leather.** Reduced price. SIZES: 28 to 40. PRICE, PREPAID. **19c**

9K17365 *New style dress bag oval frame.* Good quality **poplin.** Mirror inside oval frame. Attached coin purse. Seco silk lining. Black, navy blue, taupe or brown. **$2.98**

Hand Beaded

All Silk

9K17360 Hand-beaded poplin bag *at a saving of exactly one-third.* Metal frame. Seco silk lining. COLORS: Black, navy blue, taupe grey or brown. PRICE, PREPAID to your home, **$1.88**

Hand Beaded

9K17363 Moire silk bag *with hand beaded frame.* COLORS: Black, navy blue, taupe grey or brown. PRICE, PREPAID to your home, **$2.98**

9K17369 *Handsome hand-tooled fine* **leather bag.** Metal frame. Three inside compartments. COLORS: Black or tan PRICE, PREPAID to your home, **$2.25**

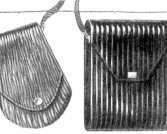

9K17350 *Kodak bag of* **crepe grain leather** *in brown, blue, grey or black.* Silk lined. PRICE, PREP'D, **$1.39**

9K17355 *Kodak bag of* **black imitation patent leather.** Brocaded lining. SIZE: 5½x7. PRICE, PREPAID to your home, **98c**

9K17359 *A bargain in a black* **pin seal leather** bag — *Kodak style.* Metal frame. PRICE, PREP'D to your home, **$1.45**

9K17368 *Kodak bag of hand-tooled* **sheep skin**—*very new and dressy, black or tan.* Moire lined. PRICE, PREP'D to your home, **$1.89**

9K17354 *Hand-tooled bag of* **black pin grained skiver leather,** *only 89c.* Kodak open top style. Well lined. Three compartments. A rare value. PRICE, PREP'D to your home, **89c**

9K17357 *Kodak bag of* **pin seal grain leather.** A big value. COLORS: Black or tan. PRICE, PREPAID, **$1.29**

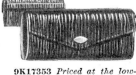

9K17351 *Envelope purse of good quality* **black leather.** Three inside compartments. Silk-mixed lining. Back strap handle as illustrated. PRICE, PREP'D to your home, **49c**

9K17358 *Black* **sheepskin shopping bag,** 6½ x8 inches. Engraved metal frame. Safety lock. Usual fittings. A good bag at a small price. PRICE, PREPAID to your home, **$1.39**

9K17352 *Envelope purse of black* **karatol leatherette,** *59c.* Back strap handle and strap with snap for fastening. Silk mixed lining. 3 compartments. PRICE, PREP'D to your home, **59c**

9K17364 Moire poplin bag, *attractive new shirred oval top.* Engraved oval frame has mirror inside. Seco silk lining. COLORS: Navy blue, black, brown or taupe. PRICE, PREPAID to your home, **$2.39**

9K17353 *Priced at the lowest figure yet quoted on purses of equal quality.* Envelope purse of black imitation **patent leather.** Three inside compartments. Metal frame. Back strap handle. Silk-mixed lining. PRICE, PREPAID to your home, **49c**

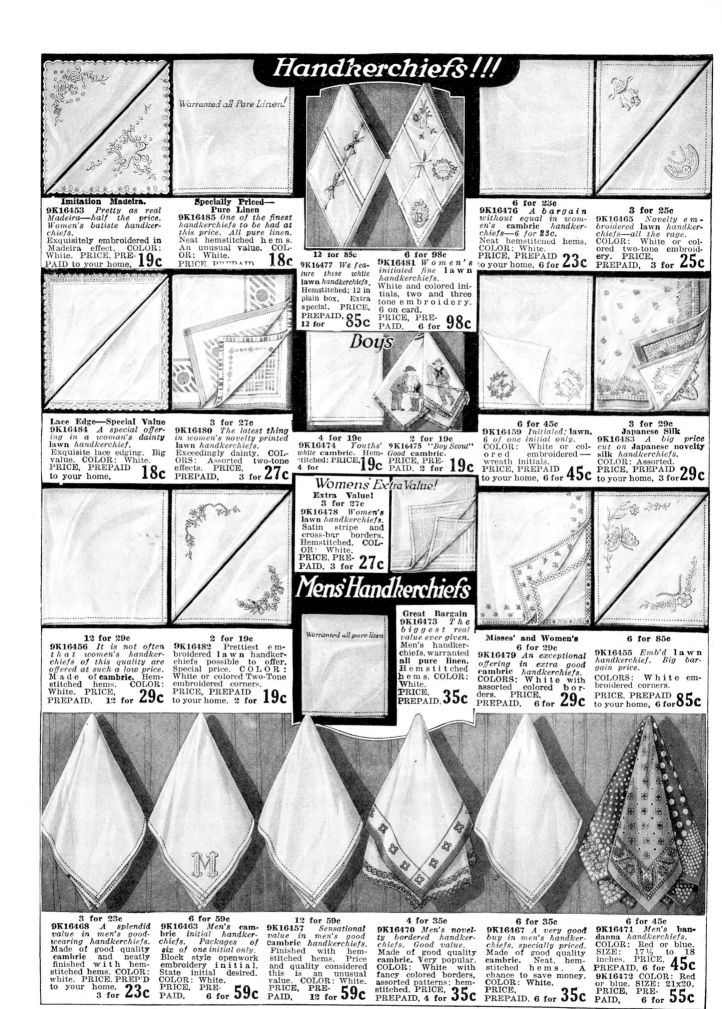

Handkerchiefs!!!

Warranted all Pure Linen!

Imitation Madeira.
9K16453 *Pretty as real Madeira—half the price.* Women's batiste handkerchiefs. Exquisitely embroidered in Madeira effect. COLOR: White. PRICE, PRE-PAID to your home, **19c**

Specially Priced—Pure Linen
9K16485 *One of the finest handkerchiefs to be had at this price.* All pure linen. Neat hemstitched hems. An unusual value. COLOR: White. PRICE, PREPAID **18c**

12 for 85c
9K16477 *We feature these white lawn handkerchiefs.* Hemstitched; 12 in plain box. Extra special. PRICE, PREPAID, 12 for **85c**

6 for 98c
9K16481 *Women's initialed fine lawn handkerchiefs.* White and colored initials, two and three tone embroidery. 6 on card. PRICE, PRE-PAID. 6 for **98c**

6 for 23c
9K16476 *A bargain without equal in women's cambric handkerchiefs—6 for 23c.* Neat hemstitched hems. COLOR: White. PRICE, PREPAID to your home, 6 for **23c**

3 for 25c
9K16465 *Novelty embroidered lawn handkerchiefs—all the rage.* COLOR: White or colored two-tone embroidery. PRICE, PREPAID, 3 for **25c**

Lace Edge—Special Value
9K16184 *A special offering in a woman's dainty lawn handkerchief.* Exquisite lace edging. Big value. COLOR: White. PRICE, PREPAID to your home, **18c**

3 for 27c
9K16480 *The latest thing in women's novelty printed lawn handkerchiefs.* Exceedingly dainty. COLORS: Assorted two-tone effects. PRICE, PREPAID, 3 for **27c**

Boys

4 for 19c
9K16474 *Youths' white cambric.* Hemstitched: PRICE, 4 for **19c**

2 for 19c
9K16475 *"Boy Scout"* Good cambric. PRICE, PREPAID, 2 for **19c**

6 for 45c
9K16159 *Initialed; lawn. 6 of one initial only.* COLOR: White or colored embroidered—wreath initials. PRICE, PREPAID to your home, 6 for **45c**

3 for 29c
Japanese Silk
9K16483 *A big price cut on Japanese novelty silk handkerchiefs.* COLOR: Assorted. PRICE, PREPAID to your home, 3 for **29c**

Womens' Extra Value!
Extra Value!
3 for 27c
9K16478 *Women's lawn handkerchiefs.* Satin stripe and cross-bar borders. Hemstitched. COLOR: White. PRICE, PRE-PAID, 3 for **27c**

Mens' Handkerchiefs

Warranted all pure linen

Great Bargain
9K16473 *The biggest real value ever given.* Men's handkerchiefs, warranted all pure linen. Hemstitched hems. COLOR: White. PRICE, PREPAID, **35c**

12 for 29c
9K16456 *It is not often that women's handkerchiefs of this quality are offered at such a low price.* Made of cambric. Hemstitched hems. COLOR: White. PRICE, PREPAID, 12 for **29c**

2 for 19c
9K16482 *Prettiest embroidered lawn handkerchiefs possible to offer.* Special price. COLOR: White or colored Two-Tone embroidered corners. PRICE, PREPAID to your home, 2 for **19c**

Misses' and Women's
6 for 29c
9K16479 *An exceptional offering in extra good cambric handkerchiefs.* COLORS: White with assorted colored borders. PRICE, PREPAID, 6 for **29c**

6 for 85c
9K16455 *Emb'd lawn handkerchief. Big bargain price.* COLORS: White embroidered corners. PRICE, PREPAID to your home, 6 for **85c**

3 for 23c
9K16468 *A splendid value in men's good-wearing handkerchiefs.* Made of good quality cambric and neatly finished with hemstitched hems. COLOR: white. PRICE, PREP'D to your home, 3 for **23c**

6 for 59c
9K16463 *Men's cambric initial handkerchiefs. Packages of six of one initial only.* Block style openwork embroidery initial. State initial desired. COLOR: White. PRICE, PREPAID, 6 for **59c**

12 for 59c
9K16457 *Sensational value in men's good cambric handkerchiefs.* Finished with hemstitched hems. Price and quality considered this is an unusual value. COLOR: White. PRICE, PREPAID, 12 for **59c**

4 for 35c
9K16470 *Men's novelty bordered handkerchiefs. Good value.* Made of good quality cambric. Very popular. COLOR: White with fancy colored borders, assorted patterns; hemstitched. PRICE, PREPAID, 4 for **35c**

6 for 35c
9K16467 *A very good buy in men's handkerchiefs, specially priced.* Made of good quality cambric. Neat, hemstitched hems. A chance to save money. COLOR: White. PRICE, PREPAID, 6 for **35c**

6 for 45c
9K16471 *Men's bandanna handkerchiefs.* COLOR: Red or blue. SIZE: 17½ to 18 inches. PRICE, PREPAID, 6 for **45c**
9K16472 COLOR: Red or blue. SIZE: 21x20. PRICE, PREPAID, 6 for **55c**

Be Stylish! Save Money!

"Wear this Coat Style!" says Irene Castle

$17.88

"*I tore up at least 20 designs before I hit upon this, I tested it with a dozen different materials and trimmings before I selected this combination. If you want style and real saving here it is.*"

Irene Castle

1K2572 The creative genius of Irene Castle is responsible for this handsome new spring "wrap" coat of all wool velour.

We put the price at a very low figure and placed the model on the first page of our coat section, because it so perfectly shows the latest style trend to "wrappy" coat effects. Fancy silk twist stitching adorns the flare back as in miniature. Scalloped cape collar (17 inches deep). Silk twist stitching as pictured. Sash belt extends underneath back. Button trim at sides. Flowered silk poplin lining throughout. Exceedingly dressy and becoming. COLORS: Havana brown, Pekin blue, or tan. SIZES: 32 to 44 bust. Length 46 inches.
PRICE, PREPAID to your home, **$17.88**
1K2573 For misses and small women. SIZES: 32 to 38 bust. Length 46 inches.
PRICE, PREPAID to your home, **$17.88**

HOW TO ORDER

In ordering women's and misses' coats, state bust measure a size larger than for a dress

ALL WOOL
VELOUR
1K2572
1K2573
$17.88

CHICAGO, ILL.

For a Complete List of Irene Castle's Exclusive Designs, See the Index, Page 274

$11.98 PREPAID

Worth $15.00

Down go Prices!! Up goes your bank account! Values like these do the Work!!

ALL WOOL VELOUR
1K2574
1K2575
$11.98

1K2574 *Several million good shrewd shoppers add to their bank account by buying from PHILIPSBORN'S—why not you?*

Here is a good example of the remarkable values that PHILIPSBORN'S have to offer you in this all wool velour sport coat for women and misses. You would consider it a snap at a much higher price, but our special reduced price is only $11.98. Contrasting stitching in ornamental designs provides the very newest of trimmings exactly as pictured. Panel back with two lapped seams. Button trimming. Cape collar. Narrow cross-over belt. Patch pockets. No lining. Very dressy and becoming. COLORS: Havana brown or tan. SIZES: 32 to 44 bust. Length 39 inches.
PRICE, PREPAID to your home, **$11.98**

1K2575 Same style and colors for misses and small women. SIZES: 32 to 38 bust. Length 39 inches.
PRICE, PREPAID to your home, **$11.98**

IRENE CASTLE, the World's Foremost Style Authority, Now Designs for PHILIPSBORN'S. For a Complete List of Her Designs, See the Index, Page 274. **PHILIPSBORN'S**

Every way you look at this coat its a Beauty!
Low priced too!

1K2576 *Anyway, every way you look at this stunning coat of **all-wool heather velour** you will marvel at the becoming style. The low price is in its favor too.*

It has all the style that you could possibly expect, as the five different illustrations show. Harmonizing silk twist stitching. Novel set-in pockets. Box plait at back. Large cape collar. Unlined. COLORS: Havana brown, Peking blue **or** tan. SIZES: 32 to 44 bust. Length 48 inches.
PRICE, PREPAID
to your home, **$16.68**
1K2577 For misses and small women. SIZES: 32 to 38 bust. Length 48 inches.
PRICE, PREPAID to your home, **$16.68**

$16.68

ALL WOOL
HEATHER VELOUR
1K2576
1K2577
$16.68

1K2588 *Considering that these wrap capes with fashionable women are the very latest style, our price of $12.98 is very low.*

Silk braid and silk floss embroidery lends a delightful contrast for the deep shirred cape collar of this **all wool velour** model. A sleeveless wrap made on a yoke foundation with armhole openings. Yoke silk lined. A wonderful economy in one of the season's most fashionable wraps. COLORS: Reindeer, Pekin blue, or Havana brown; all with embroidery to harmonize. SIZES: 32 to 44 bust. Length 47 inches.

PRICE, PREPAID to your home, **$12.98**

1K2589 For misses and small women. SIZES: 32 to 38 bust. Length 47 inches.

PRICE, PREPAID to your home, **$12.98**

1K2590 *All wool velour furnished in the season's most popular colors, is used for this new sport coat.*

One of the dressiest of the short coats, this model is made very attractive with a large cape collar and deep cuffs of contrasting wool velour. Further smart style is added in the contrasting silk twist stitching which adorns the model as pictured. Patch pockets. Button-trimmed panel back. Novel buckle on the narrow self-material belt. Unlined. An unusual value at our special reduced price. COLORS: Tan and Pekin blue or Pekin blue and tan. SIZES: 32 to 44 bust. Length 38 inches.

PRICE, PREPAID to your home, **$13.98**

1K2591 For misses and small women. SIZES: 32 to 38 bust. Length 38 inches.

PRICE, PREPAID to your home, **$13.98**

1K2592 *Here is another illustration of the wonderful coat values which PHILIPSBORN'S have to offer you this season.*

We consider this coat of **all wool polo velour** one of our most distinctive models, which we offer at the sensationally low price of $14.98. Note the smart style of the loose, ripple back and the ornamental silk stitching, in self color. Wide pocket flaps. Deep cape collar. Belted front. Unlined. COLORS: Tan, Pekin blue, or reindeer. SIZES: 32 to 44 bust. Length 46 inches.

PRICE, PREPAID to your home, **$14.98**

1K2593 For misses and small women. SIZES: 32 to 38 bust. Length 46 inches.

PRICE, PREPAID to your home, **$14.98**

HOW TO ORDER

Always state bust measure in ordering coats. Take measurements loosely over a dress, and order a size larger than you would take in a dress. For example if you take 38-inch bust in dress, order your coat in size 40 bust.

Be sure to state SIZE and COLOR desired when ordering

1K2580
1K2581
$13.98
WORTH
$16.00

ALL WOOL VELOUR

ALL WOOL VELOUR
1K2578
1K2579
$9.88

Sport Wear Coats at Special Values

1K2580 *One of the most attractive of the new sport coats is this model of all wool velour for women and misses. The very low price of $13.98 makes the coat doubly attractive to shrewd shoppers. It's worth every cent of $16.00.*

Note the unusually smart style of the self-cording which trims the back of model, continuing to the front as shown in miniature. The raglan sleeves and inverted plait at the center back further emphasize the smart style. Deep cape collar and cuffs with cording. Fashionably narrow self-material belt crossed over at front. The coat is trimmed with large self-material buttons and fastened with novelty buttons. Unlined. Unequaled for style and value. COLORS: Tan, Pekin blue, or Havana brown. SIZES: 32 to 44 bust. Length 37 inches.

PRICE, PREPAID to your home, **$13.98**

1K2581 Same style for misses and small women. SIZES: 32 to 38 bust. Length 37 inches.

PRICE, PREPAID to your home, **$13.98**

1K2578 *Sport coats are always so youthful and becoming that they never seem to lose their appeal or to go out of style. Here is a particularly smart model developed in all wool velour.*

Grace of line and becomingness are achieved in the deep shawl collar of self-material which forms a cape effect at the back. The panel style patch pockets are a very new feature and are set off with large self-covered buttons. The sash belt of self-material is button trimmed through the back and finished with ornamental ball pendants. The coat is of a weight that makes a lining unnecessary. A model that offers you the best possible value at a very low price. COLORS: Pekin blue, Havana brown, or tan. SIZES: 32 to 44 bust. Length 36 inches.

PRICE, PREPAID to your home, **$9.88**

1K2579 Same style for misses and small women. SIZES: 32 to 38 bust. Length 36 inches. Average sweep 62 inches.

PRICE, PREPAID to your home, **$9.88**

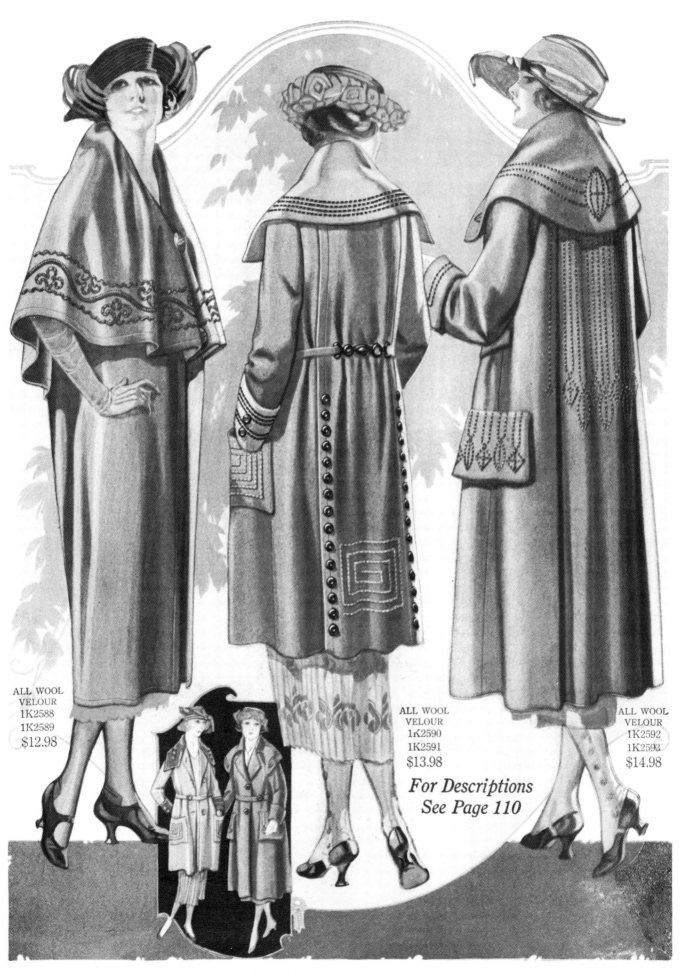

ALL WOOL
VELOUR
1K2588
1K2589
$12.98

ALL WOOL
VELOUR
1K2590
1K2591
$13.98

*For Descriptions
See Page 110*

ALL WOOL
VELOUR
1K2592
1K2593
$14.98

For Descriptions See Page 113

Descriptions for Page 112

1K2582 *The woman or miss who wishes the very latest will choose this* **all wool velour** *sport model.*

Particularly new style is shown in the plaid material which fashions the stylish Tuxedo collar, the cuffs, and flaps for the patch pockets. All-around self-material belt. Handsome novelty buttons trim the coat. Unlined. Here is a spring and summer coat which is equally appropriate for sports or for general wear. Full set in sleeves. COLORS: Pekin blue and tan trimming; or brown and tan trimming. SIZES: 32 to 44 bust. Length 36 inches.
PRICE, PREPAID to your home, **$9.98**
1K2583 For misses and small women. SIZES: 32 to 38 bust. Length 36 inches.
PRICE, PREPAID to your home, **$9.98**

1K2584 *Fashion's favorite coat style for 1921 is this very becoming wrap cape for women and misses.*

All wool velour, a handsome and popular coating, makes the model. The deep cape collar of self-material extending well below the waistline (26 inches deep through center back) is trimmed with self cording and harmonizing silk twist stitching. Sleeveless. Unlined. COLORS: Brown, Pekin blue, or taupe. SIZES: 32 to 44 bust. Length 48 inches.
PRICE, PREPAID to your home, **$10.88**
1K2585 For misses and small women. SIZES: 32 to 38 bust. Length 48 inches. **$10.88**
PRICE, PREPAID to your home,

1K2586 *An all wool serge coat of this style makes a very practical selection for general wear.*

Contrasting serge is used for the large cape collar, cuffs, and pocket flaps, which are made very dressy with the addition of silk floss embroidery of unusually effective design. The back of model is designed in loose, rippled effect, the front smartly belted. Unlined. COLORS: Navy blue with tan; or tan with Copenhagen blue trimming. SIZES: 32 to 44 bust. Length 48 inches.
PRICE, PREPAID to your home, **$13.98**
1K2587 For misses and small women. SIZES: 32 to 38 bust. Length 48 inches. **$13.98**
PRICE, PREPAID to your home,

HOW TO ORDER

In ordering women's coats, give bust measure. Take measurement loosely over a dress, as directed in the order blank at the back of this catalog. Order a size larger than you would take in a dress, that is, if you take a 38-inch bust in a dress, order your coat in size 40 bust.

2
Special Coat Bargains

ALL WOOL POPLIN

1K2596
1K2597 } $18.98

1K2594
1K2595
$12.98

ALL WOOL VELOUR

1K2596 *When you see this coat you will marvel that merchandise of such excellent quality and superior workmanship may be had at such a modest outlay of money.*
But for the fact that manufacturers reduced prices to us we would not be able to sell this **all wool poplin** coat for $18.98. Contrasting trimming bands add a delightfully new finish on the deep cape collar, cuffs, and large overflaps on the patch pockets. Loose, ripple back. Belted front. Unlined. COLORS: Navy blue with Havana brown trimming; or tan with Copenhagen blue trimming. SIZES: 32 to 44 bust. Length 48 inches. Average sweep 80 inches.
PRICE, PREPAID to your home, **$18.98**
1K2597 Same style for misses and small women. SIZES: 32 to 38 bust. Length 48 inches. Average sweep 80 inches.
PRICE, PREPAID to your home, **$18.98**

1K2594 *Here is the new wrap cape which has taken the world of fashion by storm—one of the most graceful and becoming wraps ever designed for women and misses.*
All wool velour makes the model. Contrasting silk stitching in novel design adds dressiness at the deep shirred cape collar and bottom of model. Slot pockets. Made sleeveless with fitted yoke and armholes underneath. Unlined. Depth of collar 26 inches. Button trimming as pictured. A wonderful value at our low price. COLORS: Havana brown, Pekin blue, or reindeer. SIZES: 32 to 44 bust. Length 48 inches. Average sweep 54 inches.
PRICE, PREPAID to your home, **$12.98**
1K2595 Same style for misses and small women. SIZES: 32 to 38 bust. Length 48 inches. Average sweep 54 inches.
PRICE, PREPAID to your home, **$12.98**

Fashionable New Styles!

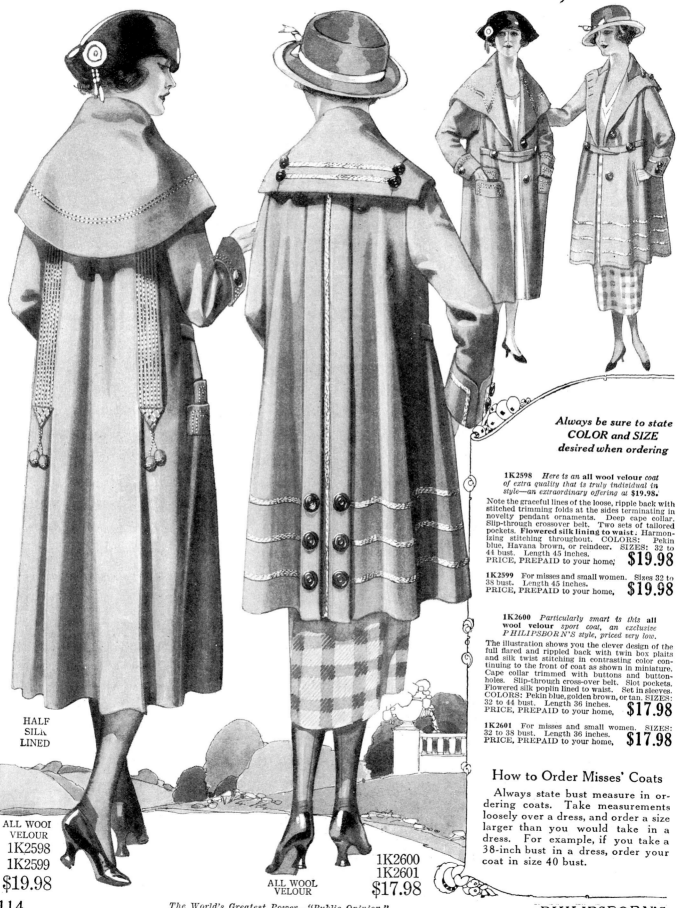

Always be sure to state
COLOR and SIZE
desired when ordering

1K2598 *Here is an all wool velour coat of extra quality that is truly individual in style—an extraordinary offering at $19.98.*
Note the graceful lines of the loose, ripple back with stitched trimming folds at the sides terminating in novelty pendant ornaments. Deep cape collar. Slip-through crossover belt. Two sets of tailored pockets. Flowered silk lining to waist. Harmonizing stitching throughout. COLORS: Pekin blue, Havana brown, or reindeer. SIZES: 32 to 44 bust. Length 45 inches.
PRICE, PREPAID to your home, **$19.98**

1K2599 For misses and small women. Sizes 32 to 38 bust. Length 45 inches.
PRICE, PREPAID to your home, **$19.98**

1K2600 *Particularly smart is this all wool velour sport coat, an exclusive PHILIPSBORN'S style, priced very low.*
The illustration shows you the clever design of the full flared and rippled back with twin box plaits and silk twist stitching in contrasting color continuing to the front of coat as shown in miniature. Cape collar trimmed with buttons and button-holes. Slip-through cross-over belt. Slot pockets. Flowered silk poplin lined to waist. Set in sleeves. COLORS: Pekin blue, golden brown, or tan. SIZES: 32 to 44 bust. Length 36 inches.
PRICE, PREPAID to your home, **$17.98**

1K2601 For misses and small women. SIZES: 32 to 38 bust. Length 36 inches.
PRICE, PREPAID to your home, **$17.98**

How to Order Misses' Coats

Always state bust measure in ordering coats. Take measurements loosely over a dress, and order a size larger than you would take in a dress. For example, if you take a 38-inch bust in a dress, order your coat in size 40 bust.

HALF
SILK
LINED

ALL WOOL
VELOUR
1K2598
1K2599
$19.98

1K2600
1K2601
$17.98

ALL WOOL
VELOUR

The World's Greatest Power—"Public Opinion."
See Page 3

PHILIPSBORN'S

at Lowest! Prices !!!

IMPORTANT
Be sure to always state
COLOR and SIZE
when ordering

1K2602 *If you did not know the price on this handsome new coat, you would take it to be a very high-priced model.*

The distinctive design and the rich quality of the material—an **all wool velour**—give it every appearance of a model costing considerably more. It is fashioned on new and becoming lines, with modified wrap effect sleeves. Self-tone silk twist stitching and large novelty buttons through the center back lend a dressy touch that is altogether new and charming. Deep cape collar with shawl effect at front trimmed with silk stitching; deep cuffs to correspond. Slip-through sash belt holds coat to figure, as it extends all around. Flowered poplin lining to waist. A wonderful coat at a worthwhile reduction. COLORS: Golden brown, tan, or Pekin blue. SIZES: 32 to 44 bust. Length 48 inches.
PRICE, PREPAID to your home, **$19.98**

1K2603 For misses and small women. SIZES: 32 to 38 bust. Length 48 inches.
PRICE, PREPAID to your home, **$19.98**

1K2604 *This extraordinarily low price is made possible only because of a jobber's heavy sacrifice.*

Here is a coat of an excellent quality **all wool serge** which was made to sell at considerably more money, but because of the reduced price at which we secured this consignment we are able to quote the model at only $14.98. The season's demand for embroidery is interpreted in lavish terms in this model, with silk braid in novel design adorning the deep cape collar and bell-shaped cuffs. All-around self-material belt. Slot pockets. Tussah silk lining to waist, full set in sleeves. COLORS: Navy blue. SIZES: 32 to 44 bust. Length 48 inches.
PRICE, PREPAID to your home, **$14.98**

1K2605 For misses and small women. SIZES: 32 to 38 bust. Length 48 inches.
PRICE, PREPAID to your home, **$14.98**

ALL WOOL
VELOUR

1K2602
1K2603
$19.98

ALL WOOL SERGE

1K2604
1K2605
$14.98

Correct Styles!

ALL WOOL
POLO
VELOUR
1K2606
1K2607
$9.48

WORTH
$12.00

TAFFETA
SILK
1K2608
1K2609
$13.88

ALL WOOL
VELOUR
1K2610
1K2611
$14.98

1K2606 *Here's the sort of bargain in a coat that interests every woman who wants to economize and still wants to be well dressed.*

One of the smartest versions of the new short coats, this sport model of **all wool polo cloth** compares favorably with models sold elsewhere at high prices. Contrasting silk twist stitching is one of its many attractive features. An inverted plait at the center back, the deep cape collar, smart cross-over belt, and patch pockets make the model very attractive and becoming. Unlined. A splendid model for general wear. COLORS: Tan, Havana brown, or Pekin blue; all with contrasting stitching. SIZES: 32 to 44 bust. Length 35 inches.
PRICE, PREPAID to your home, **$9.48**

1K2607 Same style for misses and small women. SIZES: 32 to 38 bust. Length 35 inches.
PRICE, PREPAID to your home, **$9.48**

Be Sure to State COLOR and SIZE When Ordering

1K2608 *One of the most attractive silk coats that we have ever offered is this* **taffeta silk model.** *Special at $13.88.*

For dressy wear a model of this sort is really indispensable, while for a spring and summer motor coat it is unsurpassed because it is light weight and does not hold the dust. The material is a **soft finished taffeta silk** of rich lustrous appearance, and is admirably suited to the graceful design. Deep cape collar finished with an accordion-pleated edge. Full gathered back. All-around self-material belt. Patch Pockets. Self button trimming and fastening. Unlined. COLOR: All black. SIZES: 32 to 44 bust. Length 46 inches.
PRICE, PREPAID to your home, **$13.88**

1K2609 Same style for misses and small women. SIZES: 32 to 38 bust. Length 46 inches.
PRICE, PREPAID to your home, **$13.88**

1K2610 *This coat offers you last-minute style at a price that you would usually pay for ordinary styles.*

The large illustration and the one in miniature give you an idea of the clever lines, but you will have to get this coat home and try it on to appreciate its real beauty and becomingness. The material is an excellent quality **all wool velour.** The smart design features the new "wrap" effect so much desired, with loose, rippled back and modified raglan sleeves. Roomy and very comfortable. Self-tone silk twist stitching in fancy design. Deep cape collar. Button trimming and fastening. Unlined. COLORS: Golden brown, Pekin blue, or reindeer. SIZES: 32 to 44 bust. Length 47 inches.
PRICE, PREPAID to your home, **$14.98**

1K2611 For misses and small women. SIZES: 32 to 38 bust. Length 47 inches.
PRICE, PREPAID to your home, **$14.98**

ALL WOOL VELOUR
1K2616
1K2617
$16.98

ALL WOOL
SERGE
1K2612
1K2613
$9.98

WORTH
$12.00

1K2614
1K2615
$8.88

ALL WOOL
POLO

Big Bargain!

1K2616 *Recent large purchases from over-stocked manufacturers resulted in wonderful savings for us and for you.*

We are giving our customers the benefit of every cent saved when we quote this handsome coat of **all wool velour** at our present low price. Distinctive new style is shown in the back, which may be worn in loose-rippled style or belted all around. Back designed in panel effect with folds, plaits, and cording. Large becoming square cape collar. Panel effect pockets. Slip-through self-material belt. Harmonizing stitching and button trimming as pictured. Unlined. Full drop sleeves. COLORS: Golden brown or taupe. SIZES: 32 to 44 bust. Length 46 inches.

PRICE, PREPAID to your home, **$16.98**

1K2617 For misses and small women. SIZES: 32 to 38 bust. Length 46 inches.

PRICE, PREPAID to your home, **$16.98**

1K2612 *Here is a remarkable coat which no one would expect to buy even in pre-war days at such an unheard of price of only $9.98.*

All wool serge makes the model, and the design is especially smart and becoming. Harmonizing silk †twist stitching forms an attractive design at the center back. The deep cape collar is trimmed with stitching to correspond. New style patch pockets of odd design have stitching and button trimming. Deep cuffs with stitching and button trimming. All-around self-material belt. Two-tone novelty button trimming and fastening. Unlined. Stylish and serviceable. COLORS: Navy blue or black. SIZES: 32 to 44 bust. Length 46 ins.

PRICE, PREPAID to your home, **$9.98**

1K2613 For misses and small women. SIZES: 32 to 38 bust. Length 46 inches.

PRICE, PREPAID to your home, **$9.98**

1K2614 *A smart and dressy version of the popular sport coat is here presented in this* **all wool polo cloth** *coat—a big bargain at our low price.*

A coat of this type makes an ideal purchase because it is suitable not only for sports but for general all around wear. Smart style is shown in the box-pleated back with cording at either side. Finished with silk arrow heads. Harmonizing silk twist stitching—a trimming that is used on the season's most expensive coats, makes the model very dressy. Fancy patch pockets. Cape collar. Unlined. Set in sleeves. COLORS: Tan or Pekin blue. SIZES: 32 to 44 bust. Length 34 inches.

PRICE, PREPAID to your home, **$8.88**

1K2615 For misses and small women. SIZES: 32 to 38 bust. Length 34 inches.

PRICE, PREPAID to your home, **$8.88**

Be sure to state SIZE and COLOR desired when ordering

CHICAGO, ILL.

Smashing! Values in

1K2618 *Rarely does one find a coat of such excellent style and material for so little money* as this new *PHILIPSBORN'S* model of **all wool serge.**

A strikingly handsome effect is produced with contrasting wool embroidery which adorns the deep cape collar and hip line. Model is designed on the new "wrap" lines and is lined to the waist with flowered sateen. Unbelted. COLORS: Navy blue or tan with Copenhagen blue trimming. SIZES: 32 to 44 bust. Length 46 inches, full drop sleeves.
PRICE, PREPAID to your home, **$12.88**

1K2619 Same style for misses and small women. SIZES: 32 to 38 bust. Length 46 inches.
PRICE, PREPAID to your home, **$12.88**

When ordering be sure to state **COLOR** *and* **SIZE** *desired.*

ALL WOOL HEATHER VELOUR
1K2620
1K2621
$6.98

ALL WOOL SERGE
1K2622
1K2623
$12.88

ALL WOOL SERGE, WOOL EMBROIDERY
1K2618
1K2619
$12.88

1K2620 *Here is an unequaled opportunity to secure a serviceable new coat at less than pre-war prices.*

If you are ready for your spring coat, we can positively assure you the greatest bargain of the season in this **all wool heather velour** tailored sport coat. It is one of the best examples of the popular short length coats and is designed on newest lines with raglan sleeves, slot pockets, full flared back, belted front and cape collar. Silk stitching and button trimming. Unlined. COLORS: Tan or golden brown. SIZES: 32 to 44 bust. Length 35 inches.
PRICE, PREPAID to your home, **$6.98**

1K2621 For misses and small women. SIZES: 32 to 38 bust. Length 35 inches.
PRICE, PREPAID to your home, **$6.98**

1K2622 *Shop where you will you will not find a coat of such good style and quality at our money-saving price.*

An immense purchase of this material from a manufacturer who needed ready cash accounts for the amazing price cut. The material is a good quality **all wool serge** and the design features the new "wrap" effect. Deep shirred cape collar has four rows of silk braid. Pockets set in at hip line. Modified dolman sleeves, roomy and comfortable. Unlined. Very stylish and becoming. COLORS: Navy blue or black SIZES: 32 to 44 bust. Length 48 inches.
PRICE, PREPAID to your home, **$12.88**

1K2623 For misses and small women. SIZES: 32 to 38 bust. Length 48 inches.
PRICE, PREPAID to your home, **$12.88**

PHILIPSBORN'S Simple One Price to All Policy Is Sweeping the Country. See Page 3

PHILIPSBORN'S

Coats of the Hour!

1K2628 *Here is your chance to secure one of the new wrap capes at an extraordinary reduction—an exclusive* **all wool serge** *model.*

Graduated cape collar measuring 21 inches through center and 34 inches at sides. Contrasting silk twist stitching all around cape and at bottom of garment. Patch pockets. Sleeveless. Unlined. COLORS: Navy blue with Copenhagen blue or tan with Copenhagen blue stitching. SIZES: 32 to 44 bust. Length 48 inches.
PRICE, PREPAID to your home, **$7.88**
1K2629 For misses and small women. SIZES: 32 to 38 bust. Length 48 inches.
PRICE, PREPAID to your home, **$7.88**

Be sure to state SIZES and COLOR when ordering

VELOUR PLAID
1K2624
1K2625
$4.98
WORTH
$6.00

ALL WOOL SERGE
1K2626
1K2627
$7.97

ALL WOOL SERGE
1K2628
1K2629
$7.88

1K2624 *Another proof of the unexampled bargain values which PHILIPSBORN'S can give you in wearing apparel.*

A Sport coat of **checked flannel velour**, specially reduced. An inverted plait at the center back, the large patch pockets, the contrasting broadcloth inlay on the deep cape collar are features that give style and distinction to the model. All around self-material belt with button trimming at front and back. Unlined. COLORS: Blue and white check. SIZES: 32 to 44 bust. Length 34 inches.
PRICE, PREPAID to your home, **$4.98**
1K2625 For misses and small women. SIZES: 32 to 38 bust. Length 34 inches.
PRICE, PREPAID to your home, **$4.98**

1K2626 *You are always assured of correct style and 100% value for your money when you shop at PHILIPSBORN'S.*

In taking advantage of this offer you secure an **all wool serge** coat of newest style at a remarkable saving. A very becoming effect is afforded in the deep cape collar of self-material with an over-collar of contrasting silk poplin. Pockets are marked with smartly shaped overflaps. All-around belt. No lining. COLORS: Navy blue with Pekin blue overcollar, or black with gold overcollar. SIZES: 32 to 44 bust. Length 47 inches.
PRICE, PREPAID to your home, **$7.97**
1K2627 For misses and small women. SIZES: 32 to 38 bust. Length 47 inches.
PRICE, PREPAID to your home, **$7.97**

1K2634 *Again, Irene Castle designs a stunning new coat for PHILIPSBORN'S customers, and as ever, the price is astonishingly low.*

In this **all wool velour** model, the unbelted, flare back is interpreted in terms of great becomingness, and the smart new length adds dashing lines. Contrasting silk twist stitching contributes a pleasing touch of color, appearing in fancy design all around bottom of back, on the smartly shaped cape collar, cuffs, and pocket flaps. Panel effect pockets. Button trimming as pictured. No lining. Full set-in sleeves. COLORS: Tan and Pekin blue or Pekin blue and henna trimming. SIZES: 32 to 44 bust. Length 38 inches.
PRICE, PREPAID to your home, **$15.98**

1K2635 For misses and small women. SIZES: 32 to 38 bust. Length 38 inches.
PRICE, PREPAID to your home, **$15.98**

1K2636 *Another very handsome coat designed by Irene Castle is this* **all wool poplin** *model in smart belted style, and the low price speaks for itself.*

Contrasting material is used for the large becoming cape collar, giving a color note that is very pleasing and effective. Silk twist stitching to match the collar trims the back in novel design. Stitching on collar, cuffs, and patch pockets to correspond. Fashionably narrow self-material belt has novelty composition buckle at back; crossed over at front. The model is suitable weight for spring and is unlined. A big bargain. COLORS: Navy blue with tan trimming; or tan with Pekin blue trimming. SIZES: 32 to 44 bust. Length 45 inches.
PRICE, PREPAID to your home, **$18.98**

1K2637 For misses and small women. SIZES: 32 to 38 bust. Length 45 inches.
PRICE, PREPAID to your home, **$18.98**

1K2638 *Irene Castle presents a charming version of the fashionable "wrap" coat, which is destined to be so very popular this season.*

This clever model derives its name from the way in which it wraps the figure in its graceful folds, tapering at the bottom to a new stylish width. The material—an excellent quality **all wool velour**—is well suited to the design. The model is styled with modified kimono sleeves, deep cape collar, and fancy patch pockets. Harmonizing silk twist stitching, cording, and arrow heads as pictured, add a very dressy trimming. Unbelted model lined to hips with fancy tussah silk. COLORS: Pekin blue, reindeer or Havana brown. SIZES: 32 to 44 bust. Length 46 inches.
PRICE, PREPAID to your home, **$18.88**

1K2639 For misses and small women. SIZES: 32 to 38 bust. Length 46 inches.
PRICE, PREPAID to your home, **$18.88**

How to Order Women's Coats

Always state bust measure required. Take bust measure loosely over dress, and order a size larger than you would take in a dress; that is, if you take a 38-inch bust in a dress, order your coat in size 40 bust.

Also always be sure to state COLOR and SIZE desired

ALL WOOL
VELOUR
1K2630
1K2631
$14.98

ALL SILK
TAFFETA
1K2632
1K2633
$16.98

1K2630 *A glance is enough to assure you of the smart and becoming lines that are featured in this new* **all wool velour** *coat.*

Loose, flared back, with folds and cord trimming. Front as in miniature. Slot pockets. Deep cape collar. Cording and button trimming. All-around slip-through belt. Set-in sleeves. Unlined. COLORS: Golden brown, tan, or Pekin blue. SIZES: 32 to 44 bust. Length 46 inches.
PRICE, PREPAID to your home, **$14.98**

1K2631 For misses and small women. SIZES: 32 to 38 bust. Length 46 inches.
PRICE, PREPAID to your home, **$14.98**

1K2632 *There is an elegance to silk which is scarcely equaled by any fabric, and it certainly makes an ideal summer wrap.*

This beautiful coat is developed in a rich, lustrous quality of **all silk taffeta.** Extra deep cape collar with self-covered button trimming at either side of fronts. Sash belt. Patch pockets. Set-in sleeves. Unlined. A marvelous offering in a high grade coat. COLOR: Black. SIZES: 32 to 44 bust. Length 48 inches.
PRICE, PREPAID to your home, **$16.98**

1K2633 For misses and small women. SIZES: 32 to 38 bust. Length 48 inches.
PRICE, PREPAID to your home, **$16.98**

ALL WOOL
DUVETYN
VELOUR
1K2634
1K2635
$15.98

ALL
WOOL
VELOUR
1K2638
1K2639
$18.88

3

Wonderfully
Tailored Coats
Castle
Designed!
Wonderfully
Low Priced!

For Descriptions
See Page 120

CHICAGO, ILL.

ALL
WOOL POPLIN
1K2636
1K2637 $18.98

For a Complete List of Irene Castle's Exclusive Designs,
See the Index, Page 274

1K2644
1K2645
$9.88

ALL WOOL
HEATHER
VELOUR

ALL WOOL
WORSTED
SERGE
1K2642
1K2643
$14.98

ALL WOOL VELOUR
1K2640
1K2641
$12.98

*For Descriptions
See Page 123*

*PHILIPSBORN'S Give Away Over $500,000. See Page 3 for
This and Other Interesting Facts*

PHILIPSBORN'S

1K2640 *Here is a very swagger new sport coat developed in all wool heather velour—a style that is preferred by smart women this season.*

Soft plaits with contrasting silk twist stitching, and button trimming give charming variety to the loose, unbelted back. Stitching on collar and cuffs to correspond. Right side of coat has two pockets; left side made with one pocket. All-around slip-through belt. No lining. Extremely smart and becoming. COLORS: Havana brown, Pekin blue or tan. SIZES: 32 to 44 bust. Length 36 inches. PRICE, PREPAID to your home, **$12.98**

1K2641 Same style for misses and small women. SIZES: 32 to 38 bust. Length 36 inches. PRICE, PREPAID to your home, **$12.98**

1K2642 *A big cash purchase on which we received a very liberal discount allows us to name an especially moderate price on this new all wool serge coat.*

Self-tone silk stitching is distributed effectively on the smartly flared unbelted back as shown in the illustration. The large cape collar is made very becoming with a border of contrasting broadcloth and silk twist stitching. Tailored pockets with stitching. Slip-through belt. Unlined. Drop sleeves. Greatly underpriced. COLORS: Navy blue with Copenhagen blue or tan with Copenhagen blue trimming. SIZES: 32 to 44 bust. Length 48 inches. PRICE, PREPAID to your home, **$14.98**

1K2643 Same style for misses and small women. SIZES: 32 to 38 bust. Length 48 inches. PRICE, PREPAID to your home, **$14.98**

1K2644 *The woman who is particular about the little things in dress will appreciate the careful attention which PHILIPSBORN S give to details.*

Take for example this stunning new sport coat of all wool heather velour, effectively combined with contrasting velour for the collar, cuffs, and pocket trimming. Back has inverted plait finished with silk arrowhead. Silk twist stitching in contrasting color trims both front and back. Flowered twill lining to waistline. COLORS: Heather taupe with Pekin blue trimming or heather brown with Pekin blue. SIZES: 32 to 44 bust. Length 38 inches. PRICE, PREPAID to your home, **$9.88**

1K2645 Same style for misses and small women. SIZES: 32 to 38 bust. Length 38 inches. PRICE, PREPAID to your home, **$9.88**

How to Order Women's Coats

Always state bust measure required. Take bust measure loosely over dress, and order a size larger than you would take in a dress; for example, if you take a 38-inch bust in a dress, order your coat in size 40 bust.

Also always be sure to state COLOR and SIZE desired

ALL SILK LINED

Real Paris Swagger Models

ALL WOOL TRICOTINE	ALL WOOL VELOUR
1K2648	1K2646
1K2649	1K2647
$32.98	$16.98

1K2648 *Our handsomest coat style is this new "wrap" model of silk lined all wool tricotine.*

Contrasting collar and cuffs with handsome embroidery to match. Full length Tuxedo style collar. Novel panel back as in miniature. Slip-through belt. Full silk lining. Very dressy and very latest in style. COLORS: Dark tan with navy blue trimming; or navy blue with tan. Embroidery to match. SIZES: 32 to 44 bust. Length 45 inches. PRICE, PREPAID to your home, **$32.98**

1K2649 For misses and small women. SIZES: 32 to 38 bust. Length 45 inches. PRICE, PREPAID to your home, **$32.98**

1K2646 *Paris sponsors this smart coat of all wool velour in the new sport length.*

Full flared and plaited back with cording, button trimming, and silk arrowheads. Stitched cape collar and patch pockets. Flowered tussah silk lining to waistline. Full drop sleeves. A big value and a very handsome coat. COLORS: Golden brown, Pekin blue, or tan. SIZES: 32 to 44 bust. Length 37 inches. PRICE, PREPAID to your home, **$16.98**

1K2647 For misses and small women. SIZES: 32 to 38 bust. Length 37 inches. PRICE, PREPAID to your home, **$16.98**

ALL
SILK
TAFFETA
1K2651
$16.98

ALL
WOOL
SERGE
1K2650
$12.98

ALL WOOL
WORSTED
SERGE
1K2652
$16.98

WORTH $15.00

1K2651 *The stout woman cannot fail to be delighted with the smart and dressy style of this all silk taffeta coat.*

A beautiful lustrous quality of taffeta not usually found at this very moderate price makes the model. The miniature shows you the distinctive style of the back, which is trimmed with eight narrow plaits stitched to the hip-line. Very becoming style is displayed in the new style upstanding collar of self-material, a charming version of the Quaker collar now so fashionable. The collar is shirred and laid in soft plaits and trimmed at the revers with self-covered buttons. Cuffs of novel design are trimmed with self-covered buttons. Fancy patch pockets with button trimming. Fashionably narrow self-material belt extends all around and crosses over at the front. Unlined. Here is one of the dressiest coats one could select for spring and summer, and at our special cut price it represents an unusual value. COLORS: Navy blue or black. SIZES: 37 to 53 bust. Length 48 inches.
PRICE, PREPAID
to your home, **$16.98**

1K2650 *It is seldom that one finds so good-looking a coat for the stout woman as this all wool serge model at so moderate a price.*

Height-giving lines are introduced at the back of model with a wide panel which is laid in soft plaits below the waistline, and trimmed with self-tone silk twist stitching. An especially becoming feature is seen in the large cape collar of silk poplin (measuring 11 inches at the center back.) The front of coat is finished with two large patch pockets as shown in miniature. Smartly shaped cuffs, both pockets and cuffs set off with silk twist stitching and buttons. All-around self-material belt. Serviceably lined to the waistline with sateen. The stout woman can add immeasurably to her appearance with the right sort of coat. We especially recommend this model to the woman who is looking for good, conservative style at a decidedly low price. A money-saving value that is hard to equal. COLORS: Navy blue or black. SIZES: 37 to 53 bust. Length 48 inches.
PRICE, PREPAID to your home, **$12.98**

1K2652 *All wool worsted serge is used for this very attractive new spring coat, designed for the stout woman.*

For general service, a model of this description makes one of the most practical coats a woman can buy. Just the right touch of dressiness is given by harmonizing silk twist stitching which adorns the large cape collar, slot pockets, cuffs, and back of model. The back of coat is designed in panel effect with soft plaits at either side from the waistline down, and silk stitching to correspond with rest of model. Narrow self-material belt extends all around. Collar is shirred at back and designed in shawl effect at front. Lined with flowered tussah silk to waist line. COLORS: Navy blue or black. SIZES: 37 to 53 bust. Length 48 inches.
PRICE, PREPAID
to your home, **$16.98**

ALL WOOL
MEN'S WEAR
SERGE
1K2655
$22.98

SILK
POPLIN
1K2653
$13.98

ALL WOOL
SERGE
1K2654
$14.98

WORTH $17.00

1K2655 *This good-looking coat has the height-giving lines and splendid wearing qualities for the stout woman.*

It is developed in **all wool men's wear serge,** a material of proven durability, which retains its appearance through many months of wear. Excellent style is given by the cording and plaiting at the panel effect back, button groups as pictured. The large cape collar has shawl effect at front, trimming of silk twist stitching interspersed with tinsel stitching. Side fronts of coat are laid in plaits and finished with set-in pockets with cord trimming. Sash belt with self pendants. Flowered tussah silk lining to hips. Full set in sleeves. COLORS: Navy blue or black. SIZES: 37 to 53 bust. Length 48 inches.

PRICE, PREPAID to your home, **$22.98**

1K2653 *The stout woman who is in doubt about the proper kind of coat to select will find her problem successfully solved in this model.*

The material of itself is very dressy—a splendid weight **silk poplin**—and the design is not too elaborate for general wear. And when you consider that the price is only $13.98 you can see for yourself what a wonderful value it is. Soft gathers laid at the waistline under the all-around self-material belt give becoming figure lines. A novel trimming treatment is accorded the large cape collar of self-material. Stitched down plaits in fold effect and button groups contribute a new and smart finish, as pictured. Shirred patch pockets. Unlined. Full set in sleeves. The stout woman who has but a limited amount of money to spend will find this coat one of the best investments she can make. It offers her dressy style and general serviceability for a very small outlay of money. COLOR: Black. SIZES: 37 to 53 bust. Length 45 inches.

PRICE, PREPAID to your home, **$13.98**

1K2654 *It seems too good to be true that one can secure such a stunning coat as this* **all wool worsted serge** *model for so little money.*

It is a stout woman's model, skillfully designed on the slenderizing lines that are so becoming to full figures. Self-tone stitching, a trimming that is used on the season's newest and smartest coats, is effectively distributed. The back is stitched through the center and designed in panel effect with deep plaits at either side from the waistline down, while the front is set off with large overflaps on the patch pockets, stitching and button trimming as pictured. The large attractive cape collar has stitching to correspond with rest of coat. Deep cuffs with stitching and button trimming. All-around self-material belt. The stout woman who wants to get her money's worth in style and satisfactory service will make no mistake in ordering this clever model. It positively cannot be duplicated elsewhere at our low price. COLORS: Navy blue or black. SIZES: 37 to 53 bust. Length 48 inches.

PRICE, PREPAID to your home, **$14.98**

Important! Be sure to state SIZE and COLOR desired

CHICAGO, ILL.

See Page 274 for Index and Don't Forget When Ordering to State the Color and Size Desired

1K2660
69c

1K2658 *Stylish and becoming raincoat of rubberized waterproof poplin at a very moderate cost.*
Model has patch pockets with overflaps and all-around self-material buckled belt. Cape collar. Can be worn as a regular street coat. COLORS: Navy blue or tan. SIZES: 32 to 44 bust. Length 52 inches.
PRICE, PREPAID to your home, **$6.98**
1K2660 Tam o'Shanter rain hat to match above coat. PRICE, PREPAID to your home, **69c**

1K2661
79c

RUBBERIZED
BOMBAZINE
1K2656
$4.50

Style and Wearing Quality Combined in our Raincoats!!

1K2656 *One of the best selections you could make in a moderately priced raincoat.*

It is made of **rubberized waterproof bombazine cloth** and is roomy enough to slip over a suit with comfort. Deep, diagonal pockets. Strap cuffs. All-around belt. A money-saving value which only a house with our tremendous purchasing power can offer. COLOR: Tan only. SIZES: 32 to 44 bust. Length 52 inches.
PRICE, PREPAID to your home, **$4.50**

RUBBERIZED
TWEED MIXTURE
1K2659—$8.98

RUBBERIZED
POPLIN
1K2658—$6.98

1K2657 *Smart raincoat of rubberized waterproof covert cloth.*
This shower-proof material resembles a regular coating. The model is smartly styled with large flap patch pockets, fancy coat collar and all-around belt. COLOR: Olive-tan. SIZES: 32 to 44 bust. Length 52 inches. PRICE, PREPAID to your home, **$5.98**

1K2659 *Our finest raincoat of rubberized waterproof tweed mixture.*
Fancy cape collar, strap cuff and slot pockets. Full belted. A stylish and serviceable coat. COLORS: Pepper and salt mixture or brown mixture. SIZES: 32 to 44 bust. Length 52 inches. PRICE, PREPAID to your home, **$8.98**
1K2661 Tam o'Shanter rain hat to match. PRICE, PREPAID to your home, **79c**

RUBBERIZED
COVERT CLOTH
1K2657—$5.98

Good!
Better!!
BEST!!

Irene Castle was not satisfied with her first Misses coat design which we said was GOOD! nor even with the next which we said was better! She did not rest until she had turned Good into Better!! and Better into BEST and here it is !!!

The One Best! Misses Coat Design Ever Offered!!

1K2670 *Irene Castle's superb genius as a designer was never more convincingly shown than in this new wrap cape for misses.*

For the development of this model we have chosen an excellent grade of **all wool velour**, one of the most popular of the season's coatings. The charm and grace of the lines can scarcely be over emphasized, the two illustrations giving an idea of their cleverness. A very unusual effect is introduced in the extra cape section which depends from the deep yoke. Contrasting silk twist stitching contributes the right touch of trimming on the cape section and the deep shirred cape collar. Button groups as pictured. Tailored arm openings, no sleeves. Unlined. To introduce this style to our customers we have named a very low price. We predict that it will be the model of the season. COLORS: Tan or Pekin blue. SIZES: 32 to 38 bust. Length 42 inches.

PRICE, PREPAID to your home, **$13.88**

Be sure to state COLOR and SIZE desired

HOW TO ORDER

In ordering misses' coats, give bust measure. DO NOT ORDER BY AGE as it is impossible for us to determine correct size without actual bust measure. Allow size larger than for a dress.

ALL WOOL VELOUR
1K2670
$13.88

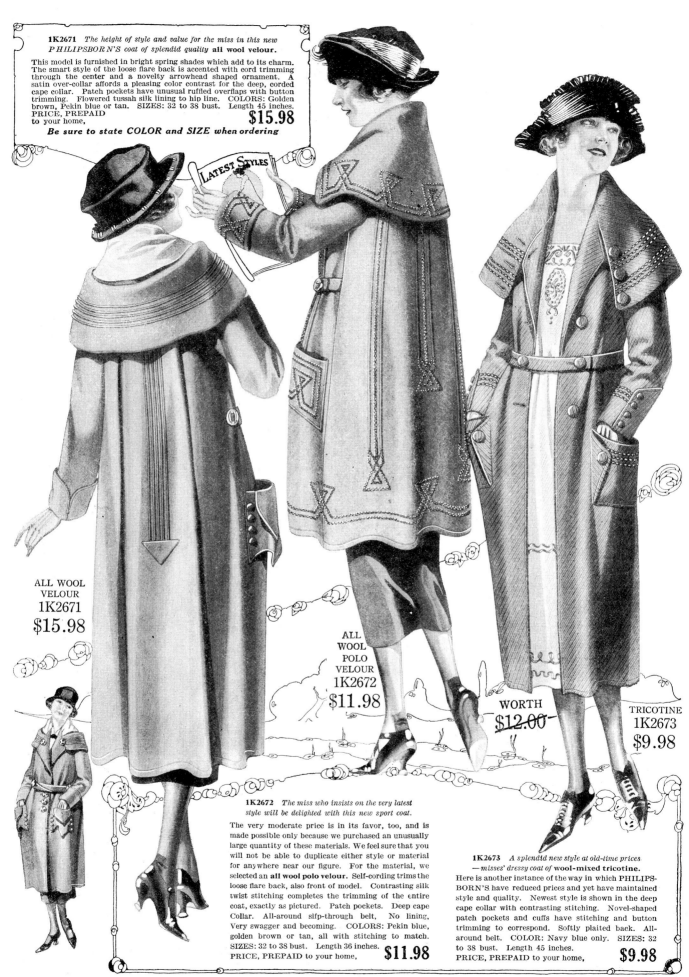

1K2671 *The height of style and value for the miss in this new PHILIPSBORN'S coat of splendid quality* **all wool velour.**

This model is furnished in bright spring shades which add to its charm. The smart style of the loose flare back is accented with cord trimming through the center and a novelty arrowhead shaped ornament. A satin over-collar affords a pleasing color contrast for the deep, corded cape collar. Patch pockets have unusual ruffled overflaps with button trimming. Flowered tussah silk lining to hip line. COLORS: Golden brown, Pekin blue or tan. SIZES: 32 to 38 bust. Length 45 inches.
PRICE, PREPAID
to your home, **$15.98**

Be sure to state COLOR and SIZE when ordering

LATEST STYLES

ALL WOOL
VELOUR
1K2671
$15.98

ALL
WOOL
POLO
VELOUR
1K2672
$11.98

WORTH
$12.00

TRICOTINE
1K2673
$9.98

1K2672 *The miss who insists on the very latest style will be delighted with this new sport coat.*

The very moderate price is in its favor, too, and is made possible only because we purchased an unusually large quantity of these materials. We feel sure that you will not be able to duplicate either style or material for anywhere near our figure. For the material, we selected an **all wool polo velour.** Self-cording trims the loose flare back, also front of model. Contrasting silk twist stitching completes the trimming of the entire coat, exactly as pictured. Patch pockets. Deep cape Collar. All-around slip-through belt, No lining, Very swagger and becoming. COLORS: Pekin blue, golden brown or tan, all with stitching to match. SIZES: 32 to 38 bust. Length 36 inches.
PRICE, PREPAID to your home, **$11.98**

1K2673 *A splendid new style at old-time prices — misses' dressy coat of* **wool-mixed tricotine.**
Here is another instance of the way in which PHILIPSBORN'S have reduced prices and yet have maintained style and quality. Newest style is shown in the deep cape collar with contrasting stitching. Novel-shaped patch pockets and cuffs have stitching and button trimming to correspond. Softly plaited back. All-around belt. COLOR: Navy blue only. SIZES: 32 to 38 bust. Length 45 inches.
PRICE, PREPAID to your home, **$9.98**

1K2674 *Rarely have we offered a coat style for the miss which surpassed this model in design.*

All wool heather mixture, a soft-napped wool fabric which comes in bright new shades, is used for the model. Loose flare back with graduating trimming strap, finished with very large buttons. Deep cape collar with contrasting cloth over-collar. Patch pockets have overflaps to match over-collar. Slip-through belt. Unlined. COLORS: Tan (heather) with Copenhagen blue trimming, or Pekin blue (heather) with tan trimming. SIZES: 32 to 38 bust. Length 45 inches.
PRICE, PREPAID to your home, **$10.98**

VELOUR
PLAID

3
Coats for the Miss that will Please and Charm the Wearer

1K2675
$5.88

ALL WOOL
HEATHER
VELOUR
1K2676
$7.98
WORTH
$10.00

Also always be sure to state COLOR and SIZE desired

ALL
WOOL
HEATHER
MIXTURE

1K2676 *Every miss likes to be dressed in the height of fashion, and yet not have to pay exorbitant prices.*

Here is one of the new wrap capes which answers every demand of fashion for the unusual, and the low price offers you an un-hoped-for saving. Developed in **all wool heather velour.** Contrasting stitching adorns the lower part of wrap and a single row appears on the cape collar (22 inches deep). Made sleeveless without lining. Furnished in smart spring shades. A wrap that cannot be duplicated elsewhere at our low price. COLORS: Golden brown, tan or Pekin blue. SIZES: 32 to 38 bust. Length 45 inches.
PRICE, PREPAID to your home **$7.98**

1K2675 *It is just like finding money to secure a coat of this style and material at our sensationally low price.*

The jaunty style will be particularly becoming to misses and small women. The material is **flannel velour,** in attractive plaid design. The model is cut in the new sport length, which gives it a dashing air which every miss likes. Smart style is shown in the large cape collar, designed in shawl effect at the front and inlaid with contrasting velour. Novel shaped patch pockets. Unlined. All-around belt. COLORS: Blue and white plaid. SIZES: 32 to 38 bust. Length 34 inches.
PRICE, PREPAID to your home, **$5.88**

1K2674— $10.98

1K2679 *If you are looking for a bargain in a misses' coat, here it is.*

We name a special reduced price on this model, which is made possible only by the fact that we received tremendous discounts from the manufacturer. The material is a very durable **all wool serge**, which will give good hard wear and always look well. Self-tone silk braid embroidery in Greek key design trims the lower part of model, all-around cape collar and deep cuffs. Novel patch pockets. All-around slip-through belt. Unlined. Raglan sleeves. COLORS: Navy blue or Copenhagen blue. SIZES: 32 to 38 bust. Length 36 inches.
PRICE, PREPAID to your home, **$11.88**

1K2680 *The miss will be glad to find the new wrap coat included in our styles for her.*

What could be more charming than this **all wool velour** model, on which we quote a special reduced price. It is designed in the new "wrapped" effect seen on the season's best models, the lines tapering slightly to the bottom. Silk twist stitching in distinctive design trims the lower part of model and deep cape collar. Silk stitching in over-collar effect. Raglan sleeves. Stitched and button-trimmed cuffs. Slot pockets. Made without a lining. COLORS: Pekin blue, tan or Havana brown. SIZES: 32 to 38 bust. Length 44 inches.
PRICE, PREPAID to your home, **$11.88**

1K2681 *A delightful version of the wrap cape is here presented in a misses' model.*

It is developed in **all wool serge** and is a wonderful value at our low price, considering that this is one of the season's most wanted styles. Silk braid in an unusual arrangement ornaments the deep cape collar which extends well below the waistline. A clever style touch is provided in the fancy shirred patch pockets with buttons and buttonholes. Sleeveless model. Unlined. All the style of a high-priced model at a very low price. COLOR: Navy blue. SIZES: 32 to 38 bust. Length 44 inches.
PRICE, PREPAID to your home, **$11.88**

HOW TO ORDER

In ordering misses' coats, give bust measure. **DO NOT ORDER BY AGE**, as it is impossible for us to determine correct sizes without actual bust measure. Allow a size larger than for a dress.

IMPORTANT!
Be sure to state SIZE and COLOR desired when ordering

ALL
WOOL
HEATHER
POLO
1K2677
$8.75

ALL WOOL
SERGE
1K2678
$8.75

Our Junior Specials

A year ago coats of this character would have sold for $15.00

1K2678 *Great serviceability and smart style combine in this coat for junior misses.*

It is developed in **all wool serge** and is distinguished with newest style features. Note the attractive lines of the large cape collar with contrasting silk poplin over-collar. Patch pockets with silk poplin trimming to match over-collar. All-around self-material belt. Unlined. Greatly underpriced at this low figure.
COLORS: Navy blue with Pekin blue trimming. SIZES: 31 to 37 bust. Length 43 inches.
PRICE, PREPAID to your home, **$8.75**

1K2677 *An unprecedented offer in a junior misses' smart new coat at a cut price.*

All wool heather polo cloth makes the model. Designed in jaunty sport length, a style that is particularly becoming to small figures. Cording and buttons provide an effective trimming. Loose flare back. Panel effect pockets. Stitched cape collar. Unlined. COLORS: Tan, brown or Pekin blue. SIZES: 31 to 37 bust. Length 32 inches.
PRICE, PREPAID
to your home, **$8.75**

ALL WOOL
SERGE
1K2681
$11.88

ALL WOOL VELOUR
1K2680
$11.88

ALL WOOL SERGF
1K2679
$11.88

**For Descriptions
See Page 130**

Your Choice $11.88

*Our Famous "EVERDAINTY" Underwear Chosen by Millions of Women as the Best
in Quality, Style, and Service. See Index, Page 274*

1K2684 *At only $11.98 this handsome all wool velour coat for misses clearly demonstrates our ability to reduce prices.*
The model is designed with the new unbelted ripple back, trimmed thru the center with large buttons. Double throw collar with tassel. Contrasting fancy stitching, self-material belt across front. COLORS: Tan or Pekin blue. SIZES: 32 to 38. Length, 32 inches.
PRICE, PREPAID to your home. **$11.98**

1K2685 **Scotch heather velour** *fashions this stunning coat for misses—one of the season's smartest models.*
Contrasting rosettes with silk twist stitching and buttons trim the 16-inch cape collar and novel patch pockets. Narrow sash belt. Unlined. COLORS: Tan with porcelain blue (copenhagen blue); or Pekin blue with tan trimming. SIZES: 32 to 38. Length 45 inches.
PRICE, PREPAID to your home. **$11.98**

ALL
WOOL
SERGE

1K2682
$8.98

HEATHER
VELOUR
1K2683
$8.98

ALL
WOOL
VELOUR
1K2684
$11.98

SCOTCH
HEATHER
VELOUR
1K2685—$11.98

1K2682 *The very newest idea in coats is this new "wrappy" model for junior misses offered at a saving of fully one-third.*
And when you consider that the material is a fine quality **all wool serge**, the very low price of $6.98 which we ask is all the more remarkable. The model envelops the figure in the most approved fashion, its attractiveness enhanced with an extra deep cape collar which measures 24 inches in depth and extends well below the waistline. Contrasting silk twist stitching ornaments the cape section and the bottom of wrap exactly as pictured. This garment is without sleeves. COLORS: Navy blue. SIZES: 31 to 37 bust. Length 45 inches. PRICE, PREPAID to your home, **$8.98**

1K2683 *An astonishing coat offer made possible because of a special purchase from a manufacturer at a new low price.*
This exceptionally attractive sport coat for misses and junior misses is fashioned of **heather velour**, a wool-mixed material that is new and is destined for widespread popularity this season. Trimming sections with contrasting piping give style to the smartly shaped collar, cuffs, and patch pockets. Button trimming and fastening. Narrow self-material belt. Cording in panel effect at back. Unlined. COLORS: Rose with Pekin blue trimming or Pekin blue with tan trimming. SIZES: 31 to 37. Length 35 inches.
PRICE, PREPAID to your home. **$8.98**

COLOR AND SIZE—Don't Forget to Give This Information When Ordering. COLOR AND SIZE.

Coats at Prices that say Buy!

1K2686 *Big returns in style and satisfaction.* This coat of **all wool serge.** Contrasting silk poplin collar and trimming as pictured. Smartly shaped patch pockets. All around belt.
COLOR: Navy blue with Pekin blue trimming. SIZES: 8 years, length 32 inches; 10 years, length 34 inches; 12 years, length 36 inches; 14 years, length 38 inches.
PRICE, PREPAID to your home, **$6.98**

1K2689 *No girl should be without a raincoat when one can be bought for only $3.98.* Good quality **rubberized cloth.** Convertible collar. Large patch pockets with smartly shaped overflaps. All-around belt. COLORS: Dark grey or tan. SIZES: 8 to 14 years.
PRICE, PREPAID to your home **$3.98**
1K2689X Girl's Tam O' Shanter rain hat to match.
PRICE, PREPAID to your home, **59c**

HAT
1K2689X
59c

RUBBERIZED
1K2689
$3.98

ALL
WOOL
SERGE
1K2686
$6.98

The Style that's the talk of the Town

ALL WOOL
SERGE
1K2688
$6.98

Very Special! **$6.48**

ALL WOOL
VELOUR
1K2690
$8.98

1K2690 *One of our finest coats for girls in this* **all wool velour model.** Smartest style is seen in the deep cape collar. Silk twist stitching. Patch pockets with smartly shaped overflaps. Unlined. COLORS: Golden brown or Pekin blue. SIZES: 8 years, length 32 inches; 10 years, length 34 inches; 12 years, length 36 inches; 14 years, length 38 inches.
PRICE, PREPAID to your home, **$8.98**

1K2688 *A splendid money-saving offer in a girls'* **all wool serge** coat. Contrasting silk twist stitching extends around back, terminating at front pocket sections. Deep cape collar. Contrasting silk poplin overcollar. COLORS: Navy blue with tan trimming, or tan with Copenhagen blue trimming. SIZES: 8 to 14 yrs.; lengths as quoted under 1K2690.
PRICE, PREPAID to your home, **$6.98**

1K2687 *The very newest in girls' wraps is this smart cape.* It is one of the accordion plaited models so much in demand, and is made of **wool-and-cotton-mixed tricotine.** Large gathered collar of fancy brocaded silk finished with cord ties. Unlined. Extremely dressy. COLOR: Navy blue. SIZES: 8 to 14 years.
PRICE, PREPAID to your home, **$6.48**

TRICOTINE
1K2687
$6.48

1K2694 *Child's* **all wool serge** *coat,* *special at $4.68*
Cape collar with embroidered organdie overcollar. Pockets with button-trimmed pointed flaps. Sateen lining. COLOR: Navy blue with white overcollar. SIZES: 2 to 6 years.
PRICE, PREPAID to your home, **$4.68**

1K2691 *Girls' raincape with attached hood at a price that means real economy.*
Made of **rubberized covert cloth.** Attached hood is fitted with elastic, and lined with fancy satin. Tailored flaps at arm openings. A big value. COLORS: Olive tan. SIZES: 8 to 14 years. PRICE, PREPAID to your home, **$2.98**

Special **$4.98**

Can't be Beat!! is Mother's Verdict

1K2695 *Because we bought a manufacturer's surplus lot we are able to offer this dressy coat at only $4.98.*
Mercerized silk poplin model, contrasting moire silk forms the large cape collar, belt and sash ends. Shirred patch pockets. Sateen lining. Button trimming. COLORS: Navy blue with copenhagen blue trimming or tan with copenhagen blue. SIZES: 2 to 6 years.
PRICE, PREPAID to your home, **$4.98**

1K2693 *Here is a very dressy new coat for girls at one of the most remarkable price concessions of the year.*
The material is good quality **all wool heather velour** and the smart design features a full, flared back and belted front. Silk twist stitching provides a dressy trimming as pictured. Pockets with double button-trimmed flaps. Sateen lining to waist. COLORS: Pekin blue or tan. SIZES: 8 to 14 yrs. Lengths: 8 yrs., 32 inches; 10 yrs., 34 inches; 12 yrs., 36 inches; 14 yrs., 38 inches.
PRICE, PREPAID to your home, **$7.98**

ALL WOOL SERGE
1K2694
$4.68

RUBBERIZED
1K2691
$2.98

MERCERIZED POPLIN
1K2695
$4.98

1K2692 *Intermediate girls' coat of good quality* **all wool serge.**
Silk poplin trimming. Large sailor collar. Contrasting silk poplin pockets. Sateen lining throughout. All-around belt. COLOR: Navy blue with Pekin blue trimming. SIZES: 7 yrs., length 31 inches; 8 yrs., length 32 inches; 9 yrs., length 33 inches.
PRICE, PREPAID to your home, **$6.48**

1K2696 *Child's dressy Empire style coat of good quality* **all wool serge.**
Made with box-plaited skirt portion with narrow self-material belt joining the high waist. Shawl collar of self-material with large overcollar of embroidered organdie. Button trimming. Sateen lining. COLORS: Navy blue or copenhagen blue. SIZES: 2 to 6 years.
PRICE, PREPAID to your home, **$5.98**

ALL WOOL SERGE
1K2696
$5.98

ALL WOOL SERGE
1K2692
$6.48

ALL WOOL HEATHER VELOUR
1K2693—$7.98

PHILIPSBORN'S

Glove Bargains!! and Glove Hints! from PHILIPSBORN'S

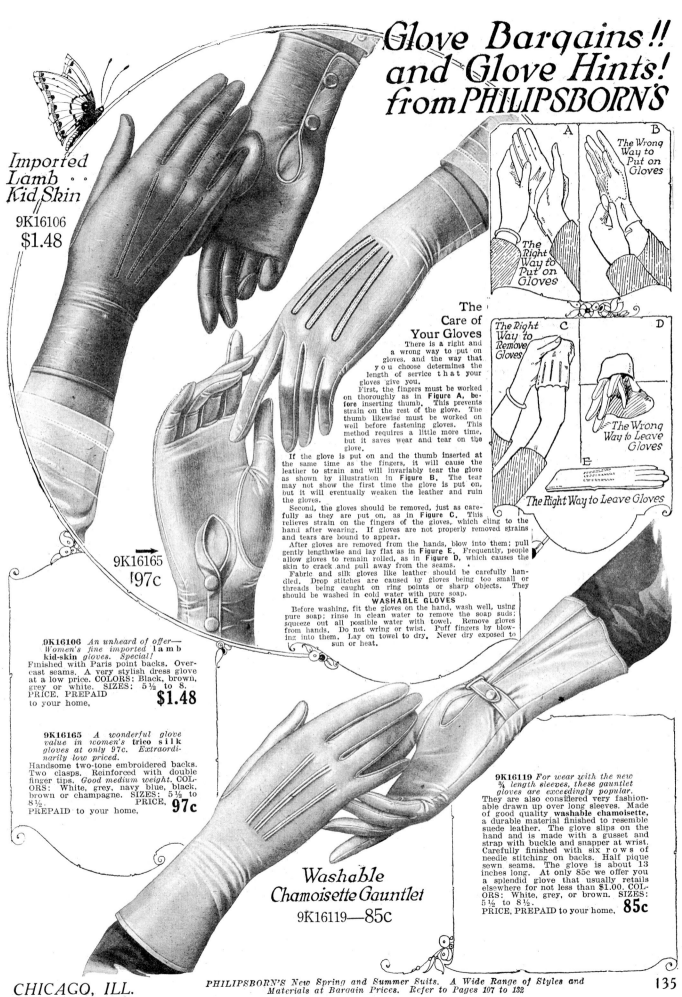

Imported Lamb Kid Skin
9K16106
$1.48

9K16165
97c

A
B — The Wrong Way to Put on Gloves
The Right Way to Put on Gloves

C — The Right Way to Remove Gloves
D — The Wrong Way to Leave Gloves
E — The Right Way to Leave Gloves

The Care of Your Gloves

There is a right and a wrong way to put on gloves, and the way that you choose determines the length of service that your gloves give you.

First, the fingers must be worked on thoroughly as in **Figure A**, before inserting thumb. This prevents strain on the rest of the glove. The thumb likewise must be worked on well before fastening gloves. This method requires a little more time, but it saves wear and tear on the glove.

If the glove is put on and the thumb inserted at the same time as the fingers, it will cause the leather to strain and will invariably tear the glove as shown by illustration in **Figure B**. The tear may not show the first time the glove is put on, but it will eventually weaken the leather and ruin the gloves.

Second, the gloves should be removed, just as carefully as they are put on, as in **Figure C**. This relieves strain on the fingers of the gloves, which cling to the hand after wearing. If gloves are not properly removed strains and tears are bound to appear.

After gloves are removed from the hands, blow into them; pull gently lengthwise and lay flat as in **Figure E**. Frequently, people allow gloves to remain rolled, as in **Figure D**, which causes the skin to crack and pull away from the seams.

Fabric and silk gloves like leather should be carefully handled. Drop stitches are caused by gloves being too small or threads being caught on ring points or sharp objects. They should be washed in cold water with pure soap.

WASHABLE GLOVES

Before washing, fit the gloves on the hand, wash well, using pure soap; rinse in clean water to remove the soap suds; squeeze out all possible water with towel. Remove gloves from hands. Do not wring or twist. Puff fingers by blowing into them. Lay on towel to dry. Never dry exposed to sun or heat.

9K16106 *An unheard of offer— Women's fine imported **lamb kid-skin** gloves. Special!* Finished with Paris point backs. Overcast seams. A very stylish dress glove at a low price. COLORS: Black, brown, grey or white. SIZES: 5½ to 8. PRICE, PREPAID to your home, **$1.48**

9K16165 *A wonderful glove value in women's **trico silk** gloves at only 97c. Extraordinarily low priced.* Handsome two-tone embroidered backs. Two clasps. Reinforced with double finger tips. *Good medium weight.* COLORS: White, grey, navy blue, black, brown or champagne. SIZES: 5½ to 8½. PRICE, PREPAID to your home, **97c**

Washable Chamoisette Gauntlet
9K16119—85c

9K16119 *For wear with the new ¾ length sleeves, these gauntlet gloves are exceedingly popular.* They are also considered very fashionable drawn up over long sleeves. Made of good quality **washable chamoisette**, a durable material finished to resemble suede leather. The glove slips on the hand and is made with a gusset and strap with buckle and snapper at wrist. Carefully finished with six rows of needle stitching on backs. Half pique sewn seams. The glove is about 13 inches long. At only 85c we offer you a splendid glove that usually retails elsewhere for not less than $1.00. COLORS: White, grey, or brown. SIZES: 5½ to 8½. PRICE, PREPAID to your home, **85c**

CHICAGO, ILL.

PHILIPSBORN'S New Spring and Summer Suits. A Wide Range of Styles and Materials at Bargain Prices. Refer to Pages 107 to 132

135

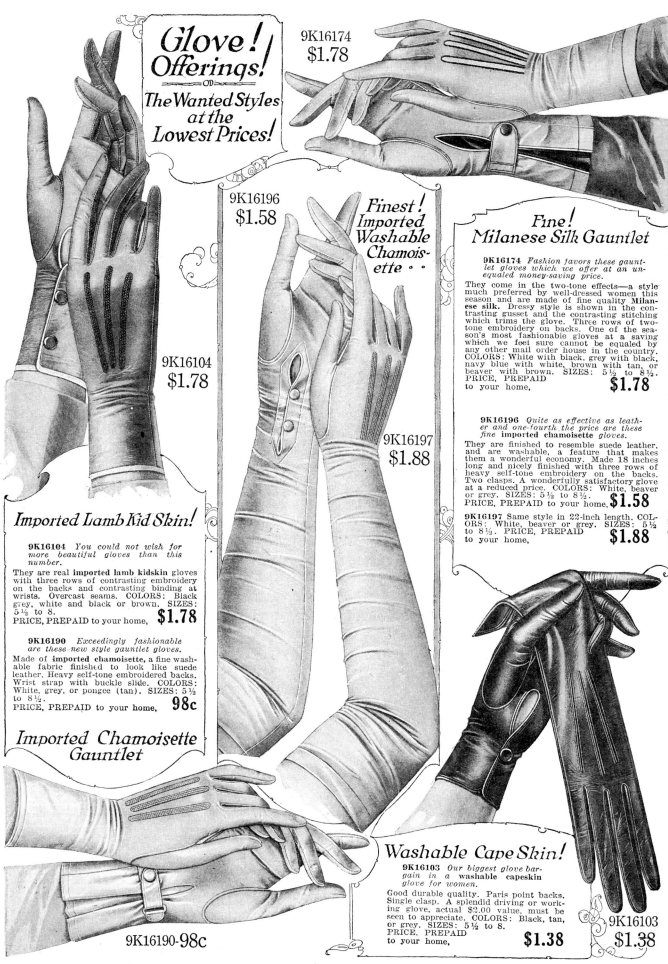

Glove! Offerings!

The Wanted Styles at the Lowest Prices!

9K16174 $1.78

9K16196 $1.58

9K16104 $1.78

9K16197 $1.88

Finest! Imported Washable Chamoisette

Fine! Milanese Silk Gauntlet

9K16174 *Fashion favors these gauntlet gloves which we offer at an unequaled money-saving price.*

They come in the two-tone effects—a style much preferred by well-dressed women this season and are made of fine quality Milanese silk. Dressy style is shown in the contrasting gusset and the contrasting stitching which trims the glove. Three rows of two-tone embroidery on backs. One of the season's most fashionable gloves at a saving which we feel sure cannot be equaled by any other mail order house in the country. COLORS: White with black, grey with black, navy blue with white, brown with tan, or beaver with brown. SIZES: 5½ to 8½. PRICE, PREPAID to your home, **$1.78**

9K16196 *Quite as effective as leather and one-fourth the price are these fine imported chamoisette gloves.*

They are finished to resemble suede leather, and are washable, a feature that makes them a wonderful economy. Made 18 inches long and nicely finished with three rows of heavy self-tone embroidery on the backs. Two clasps. A wonderfully satisfactory glove at a reduced price. COLORS: White, beaver or grey. SIZES: 5½ to 8½. PRICE, PREPAID to your home, **$1.58**

9K16197 Same style in 22-inch length. COLORS: White, beaver or grey. SIZES: 5½ to 8½. PRICE, PREPAID to your home, **$1.88**

Imported Lamb Kid Skin!

9K16104 *You could not wish for more beautiful gloves than this number.*

They are real **imported lamb kidskin** gloves with three rows of contrasting embroidery on the backs and contrasting binding at wrists. Overcast seams. COLORS: Black grey, white and black or brown. SIZES: 5½ to 8. PRICE, PREPAID to your home, **$1.78**

9K16190 *Exceedingly fashionable are these new style gauntlet gloves.*

Made of **imported chamoisette**, a fine washable fabric finished to look like suede leather. Heavy self-tone embroidered backs. Wrist strap with buckle slide. COLORS: White, grey, or pongee (tan). SIZES: 5½ to 8½. PRICE, PREPAID to your home, **98c**

Imported Chamoisette Gauntlet

9K16190-98c

Washable Cape Skin!

9K16103 *Our biggest glove bargain in a washable capeskin glove for women.*

Good durable quality. Paris point backs. Single clasp. A splendid driving or working glove, actual $2.00 value, must be seen to appreciate. COLORS: Black, tan, or grey. SIZES: 5½ to 8. PRICE, PREPAID to your home, **$1.38**

9K16103 $1.38

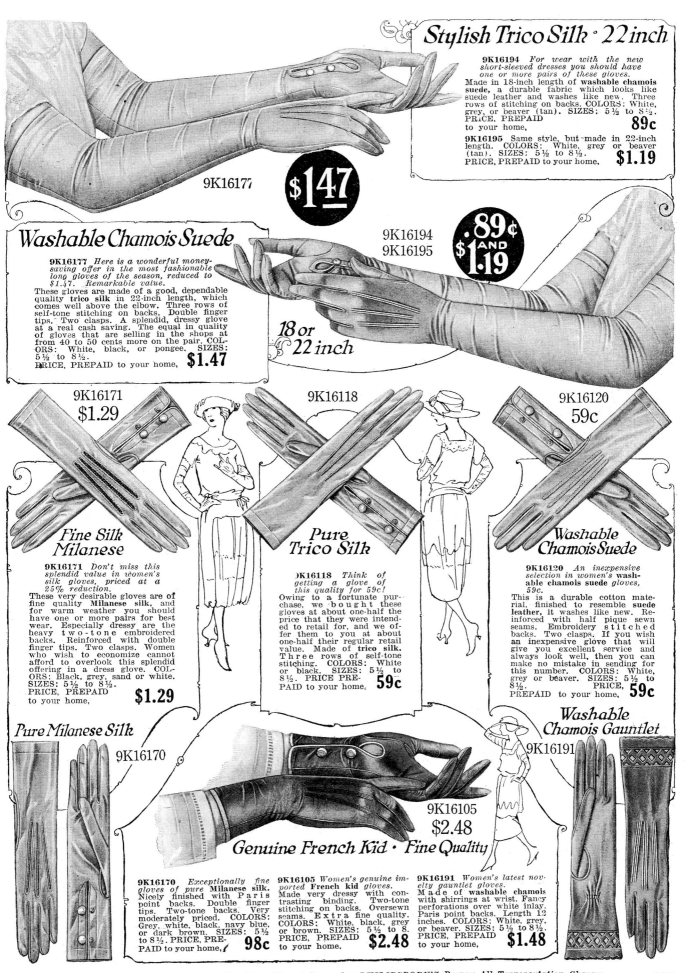

Stylish Trico Silk · 22 inch

9K16194 *For wear with the new short-sleeved dresses you should have one or more pairs of these gloves.* Made in 18-inch length of **washable chamois suede**, a durable fabric which looks like suede leather and washes like new. Three rows of stitching on backs. COLORS: White, grey, or beaver (tan). SIZES: 5½ to 8½. PRICE, PREPAID to your home **89c**

9K16195 Same style, but made in 22-inch length. COLORS: White, grey or beaver (tan). SIZES: 5½ to 8½. PRICE, PREPAID to your home, **$1.19**

9K16177

$1.47

9K16194
9K16195

.89¢ AND $1.19

18 or 22 inch

Washable Chamois Suede

9K16177 *Here is a wonderful money-saving offer in the most fashionable long gloves of the season, reduced to $1.47. Remarkable value.* These gloves are made of a good, dependable quality **trico silk** in 22-inch length, which comes well above the elbow. Three rows of self-tone stitching on backs. Double finger tips. Two clasps. A splendid, dressy glove at a real cash saving. The equal in quality of gloves that are selling in the shops at from 40 to 50 cents more on the pair. COLORS: White, black, or pongee. SIZES: 5½ to 8½. PRICE, PREPAID to your home, **$1.47**

9K16171 $1.29

9K16118

9K16120 59c

Fine Silk Milanese

9K16171 *Don't miss this splendid value in women's silk gloves, priced at a 25% reduction.* These very desirable gloves are of fine quality **Milanese silk**, and for warm weather you should have one or more pairs for best wear. Especially dressy are the heavy **two-tone** embroidered backs. Reinforced with double finger tips. Two clasps. Women who wish to economize cannot afford to overlook this splendid offering in a dress glove. COLORS: Black, grey, sand or white. SIZES: 5½ to 8½. PRICE, PREPAID to your home, **$1.29**

Pure Trico Silk

9K16118 *Think of getting a glove of this quality for 59c!* Owing to a fortunate purchase, we bought these gloves at about one-half the price that they were intended to retail for, and we offer them to you at about one-half their regular retail value. Made of **trico silk**. Three rows of self-tone stitching. COLORS: White or black. SIZES: 5½ to 8½. PRICE PREPAID to your home, **59c**

Washable Chamois Suede

9K16120 *An inexpensive selection in women's washable chamois suede gloves, 59c.* This is a durable cotton material, finished to resemble **suede leather**, it washes like new. Reinforced with half pique sewn seams. Embroidery stitched backs. Two clasps. If you wish an inexpensive glove that will give you excellent service and always look well, then you can make no mistake in sending for this number. COLORS: White, grey or beaver. SIZES: 5½ to 8½. PRICE, PREPAID to your home, **59c**

Pure Milanese Silk

9K16170

Washable Chamois Gauntlet

9K16191

9K16105 $2.48

Genuine French Kid · Fine Quality

9K16170 *Exceptionally fine gloves of pure* **Milanese** *silk.* Nicely finished with Paris point backs. Double finger tips. Two-tone backs. Very moderately priced. COLORS: Grey, white, black, navy blue, or dark brown. SIZES: 5½ to 8½. PRICE, PREPAID to your home, **98c**

9K16105 *Women's genuine imported* **French kid** *gloves.* Made very dressy with contrasting binding. Two-tone stitching on backs. Oversewn seams. Extra fine quality. COLORS: White, black, grey or brown. SIZES: 5½ to 8. PRICE, PREPAID to your home, **$2.48**

9K16191 *Women's latest novelty gauntlet gloves.* Made of **washable chamois** with shirrings at wrist. Fancy perforations over white inlay. Paris point backs. Length 12 inches. COLORS: White, grey, or beaver. SIZES: 5½ to 8½. PRICE, PREPAID to your home, **$1.48**

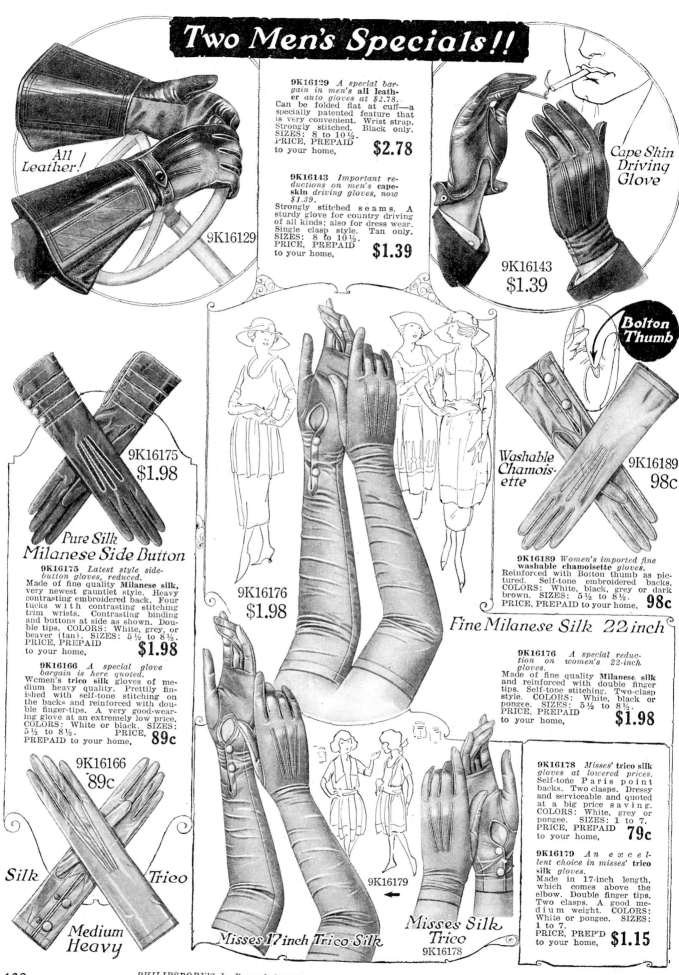

Two Men's Specials!!

9K16129 *A special bargain in men's* **all leather** *auto gloves at $2.78.* Can be folded flat at cuff—a specially patented feature that is very convenient. Wrist strap. Strongly stitched. Black only. SIZES: 8 to 10½. PRICE, PREPAID to your home, **$2.78**

9K16143 *Important reductions on men's* **capeskin** *driving gloves, now $1.39.* Strongly stitched seams. A sturdy glove for country driving of all kinds; also for dress wear. Single clasp style. Tan only. SIZES: 8 to 10½. PRICE, PREPAID to your home, **$1.39**

All Leather!

9K16129

Cape Skin Driving Glove

9K16143 $1.39

Bolton Thumb

Pure Silk Milanese Side Button

9K16175 $1.98

9K16175 *Latest style side-button gloves, reduced.* Made of fine quality **Milanese silk,** very newest gauntlet style. Heavy contrasting embroidered back. Four tucks with contrasting stitching trim wrists. Contrasting binding and buttons at side as shown. Double tips. COLORS: White, grey, or beaver (tan). SIZES: 5½ to 8½. PRICE, PREPAID to your home, **$1.98**

9K16166 *A special glove bargain is here quoted.* Women's **trico silk** gloves of medium heavy quality. Prettily finished with self-tone stitching on the backs and reinforced with double finger-tips. A very good-wearing glove at an extremely low price. COLORS: White or black. SIZES: 5½ to 8½. PRICE, PREPAID to your home, **89c**

9K16166 89c

Silk

Trico

Medium Heavy

9K16176 $1.98

Washable Chamoisette

9K16189 98c

9K16189 *Women's imported fine* **washable chamoisette** *gloves.* Reinforced with Bolton thumb as pictured. Self-tone embroidered backs. COLORS: White, black, grey or dark brown. SIZES: 5½ to 8½. PRICE, PREPAID to your home, **98c**

Fine Milanese Silk 22 inch

9K16176 *A special reduction on* **women's 22-inch** *gloves.* Made of fine quality **Milanese** silk and reinforced with double finger tips. Self-tone stitching. Two-clasp style. COLORS: White, black or pongee. SIZES: 5½ to 8½. PRICE, PREPAID to your home, **$1.98**

9K16178 *Misses' trico silk gloves at lowered prices.* Self-tone Paris point backs. Two clasps. Dressy and serviceable and quoted at a big price saving. COLORS: White, grey or pongee. SIZES: 1 to 7. PRICE, PREPAID to your home, **79c**

9K16179 *An excellent choice in misses'* **trico** *silk gloves.* Made in 17-inch length, which comes above the elbow. Double finger tips. Two clasps. A good medium weight. COLORS: White or pongee. SIZES: 1 to 7. PRICE, PREP'D to your home, **$1.15**

9K16179

Misses 17 inch Trico Silk

Misses Silk Trico
9K16178

138   *PHILIPSBORN'S Is Beyond Question the Lowest Priced Mail Order House in America. See Page 3*

PHILIPSBORN'S

PHILIPSBORN'S
Spring Millinery Display is in Full Bloom!
The Choicest Styles!
Direct from the Boulevards of Paris

3K5203
$4.95

3K5204
$3.98

3K5205
$5.98

3K5203 *Your spring hat will surely come from the PHILIPSBORN'S assortment if you wish style and to save money.*

Here is just one of the countless bargains that we have to offer you this season—a smart and becoming off-the-face hat, developed in the **new luster braid and hemp Batavia cloth.** These are the season's most popular millinery fabrics, and as the picture shows you the effect is unusually rich and dressy. **Imitation aigrette in Paradise effect** gives dash and distinction to the model. COLORS: Black, peacock blue, pheasant, or navy blue.
PRICE, PREPAID
to your home. **$4.95**

3K5205 *Without doubt one of the prettiest hats in our entire display is this large transparent dress model.*

The brim is made of two thicknesses of **silk maline;** the crown and flange of **maline hair braid.** Satin morning glories and daisies placed inside the crown give newest trimming effect. Wide silk messaline ribbon completes this beautiful model. COLORS: Black with black ribbon, natural purple morning glories; black with Copenhagen blue ribbon, rose color flowers; or black with cream yellow ribbon and yellow flowers.
PRICE, PREPAID
to your home. **$5.98**

3K5204 *A great favorite among younger women and misses is this charming hat which features a curtain veil.*

It is a roll-brim model, made of **Hemp Batavia cloth,** one of the season's most fashionable millinery materials. The silk embroidery facing gives a lovely color note, and there is a deep **curtain edge of silk Chantilly lace** extending over the brim exactly as pictured. The lace forms a large soft bow at the back. Silk grosgrain ribbon around crown. The season's newest hat at a bargain price. COLORS: Black, brown, pheasant, peacock blue; all with black lace.
PRICE, PREPAID
to your home, **$3.98**

3K5209
$4.98

3K5213
$4.98

3K5213 *Stunning and distinctive turban of the* **new luster braid.**
All silk messaline crown. Novelty trimming in paradise aigrette effect. COLORS: Black, navy blue, cherry red, dark brown or pheasant.
PRICE, PREPAID to your home, **$4.98**

3K5208 *Entirely new off-the-face hat of* **silk taffeta.**
Grosgrain ribbon around crown. The facing is of **genuine haircloth** with fringed ends. Novelty trimming pin. A most effective style.
COLORS: Navy blue with pheasant (light reddish brown) facing; black with peacock blue, brown with sand, or all black.
PRICE, PREPAID to your home. **$5.98**

3K5209 *All* **feather** *hats are the rage, and this fashionable off-the-face style is very low priced.*
Trimmed with contrasting ostrich in pompon effect. COLORS: Black; navy blue; peacock blue with navy blue ostrich; brown with peacock blue ostrich. **$4.98**
PRICE, PREPAID to your home.

Style!!
in every
Line!

3K5210 *Beautiful over-drape with curtain edge of silk chantilly lace.*
Hat is of smooth **silk braid.** Novelty flower cluster of silk and velvet blossoms. COLORS: Black, white, peacock blue or navy blue.
PRICE, PREPAID to your home, **$5.98**

3K5208
$5.98

3K5210
$5.98

3K5212
$4.98

3K5212 *Transparent hat.* **Silk Georgette crepe** *brim with eight fine ostrich tips.*
The crown is of **lustrous straw braid** with a band of silk grosgrain ribbon. COLORS: Black, navy blue, white or Copenhagen blue.
PRICE, PREPAID to your home, **$4.98**

3K5206 *Dressy all* **silk Georgette crepe** *hat.*
Latest curtain edge of same material. Silk and velvet flowers appliqued with silk floss stitching. Silk grosgrain ribbon band. COLORS: Navy blue with white facing; black with Copenhagen blue; all white; all pink; or all Copenhagen blue.
PRICE, PREPAID to your home, **$4.98**

IMPORTANT!
Don't forget to state
COLOR desired when
ordering.

3K5214 *Transparent hat developed in* **fancy maline hair braid.**
Trimmed with twisted ribbon band and bow of silk grosgrain ribbon. Novelty wreath of violets and fruit. Frameless transparent crown. COLORS: Black with natural purple violets or black with yellow violets.
PRICE, PREPAID to your home, **$3.98**

3K5214
$3.98

3K5206 $4.98

3K5211 *A very* **chic** *dress hat for the matron is here shown.*
A good quality **lustrous straw** braid, it features a cornet trimming of glycerined ostrich which adds height-giving lines. Crown is encircled with a crushed silk messaline band. COLORS: Black, brown or navy blue.
PRICE, PREPAID to your home, **$4.98**

3K5207 *Taffeta silk hats are very popular this season, and here is a particularly charming model.*
A decidedly superior grade of **taffeta silk** is used for this hat, which is made with the short front and back now so fashionable. Two accordion-plaited ruffles trim the upper brim. Draped taffeta band. Wide bow at back. A wonderful value at our price. COLORS: Navy blue, black, white, pink or dark brown. **$3.97**
PRICE, PREPAID to your home,

3K5207
$3.97

3K5211
$4.98

PHILIPSBORN'S

3K5222 *The woman who wants the very latest in millinery will make no mistake in choosing this transparent hat.*

The fascinating and becoming style of this hat cannot be shown in a picture. You will have to get this model home to appreciate its real loveliness. It is one of the fashionable transparent brim models, made with a draped **crown of taffeta silk and a brim of Chantilly lace.** Large fancy bow of taffeta silk. COLORS: Black or white.

PRICE, PREPAID to your home, **$3.98**

3K5217
$3.98

3K5222
$3.98

Style! Style! Style! That's what this Hat Spells!

3K5218
$4.98

3K5217 *No matter where you look you will find no smarter hat than this new style turban.*

The price, too, is exceedingly moderate for this style and quality. **The crown sides are of feathers, the top of fancy luster braid.** A double wing ornament across the back adds dash and smartness of line. A wonderfully becoming style. COLORS: Copenhagen blue feathers with black braid; Nile green with navy blue; all navy blue; burnt orange with black, or all black.

PRICE, PREPAID to your home, **$3.98**

3K5218 *The new "Sipper" straw combines with taffeta silk to make this off-the-face hat.* Novelty quill trimming. A smart hat at a big price reduction. COLOR: Black.
PRICE, PREPAID **$4.98**

3K5223
$4.98

3K5215
$3.98

3K5215 *A style that is certain to be admired and a big value at our price.*

This **Milan hemp** hat is made very attractive with Cuban lace braid which is inserted around the upturned brim as pictured. A wreath of satin buttercups with silk buds and foliage encircles the crown. Ribbon ends. COLORS: Black with rose color flowers; navy blue with Copenhagen blue; Copenhagen blue with rose; white with cream yellow; all ribbons to match hats.

PRICE, PREPAID to your home, **$3.98**

3K5219 *A stunning new style in a straight brim* **Milan hemp** *sailor.*

A very new trimming feature is seen in the soft ribbon flange which encircles the brim edge. Half wreath composed of silk velvet daisy, grapes and taffeta silk leaves. COLORS: Black with Copenhagen blue daisy; black with yellow daisy; navy blue with white daisy; brown with yellow daisy; or white with yellow daisy.

PRICE, PREPAID to your home, **$4.48**

3K5219
$4.48

3K5223 *Simply unapproachable at our low price is this mushroom brim dress hat.*

Made of good quality **chip**. Entire top of upper brim is covered with layer of single ply contrasting ostrich. Single ply ostrich tip at side. One of the dressiest hats ever offered at our money-saving price. It compares favorably with hats selling elsewhere at $7.50. COLORS: Black with Copenhagen blue trimming; all black, navy blue with sand; or white with Copenhagen blue.

PRICE, PREPAID to your home, **$4.98**

3K5221
$4.38

3K5221 *Distinctive off-the-face hat with popular glycerined ostrich aigrettes.*
Crown of lustrous **all-over braid.** COLORS: All black.
PRICE, PREPAID to your home, **$4.38**

3K5216
$3.98

3K5216 *A sensational value in a beautiful transparent off-the-face hat.*
Made of fancy **Maline hair braid.** Applique trimming of fine quality satin and velvet morning glories set off with silk floss embroidery stitching. Ribbon trimming. COLORS: Black with rose color flowers; black with natural purple flowers; or black with Copenhagen blue flowers.
PRICE, PREPAID to your home, **$3.98**

3K5220 *"Cellophane."* The very latest millinery in splendid style for the matron.
One of our most stylish turbans, it is made with full coronet of **new lustrous cellophane with satin brim and crown top.** Trimmed around crown with good quality glycerined ostrich and satin rose with foliage. COLORS: Black only with rose color flower.
PRICE, PREPAID to your home, **$4.68**

3K5220
$4.68

3K5226
$3.48

3K5228
$3.88

Feather Trimming the last word of Fashion!

3K5224
$4.48

3K5227
$3.75

3K5227 *Plumed hats rank first in fashion's favor this season.*
Certainly, you could not wish for a more charming or dressier hat than the beautiful model here pictured and the price is unbelievably low. The model is made of **chip braid** and is specially designed for matrons. Large ostrich plume gracefully arranged at side. Silk grosgrain ribbon bow. COLORS: Black with white plume; navy blue with peacock blue plume; or all black.
PRICE, PREPAID to your home, **$3.75**

3K5226 *Here is an advance spring hat that is winsome to the last degree.*
This is a **polished chip straw** model with brim binding of fancy barnyard braid. Band and bow of silk grosgrain ribbon. Tightly crushed roses on the attractively flared and scalloped brim. An unusual value at our low price. COLORS: Black with rose color roses; black with American beauty red roses; navy blue with Copenhagen blue roses; brown with rose color roses; white with Copenhagen blue roses.
PRICE, PREPAID to your home, **$3.48**

3K5225
$4.95

3K5224 *Here is a new off-the-face hat that will be admired for its chic.*
It is a Milan hemp model with facing of genuine haircloth. Trimmed with three rows of beads. COLORS: White with navy blue facing; black with peacock blue; sand with brown; pheasant with peacock blue; all black, or all navy blue.
PRICE, PREPAID to your home, **$4.48**

3K5228 *Straight-brim sailor. Of fine* **chip braid fancy woven edge of** patent Milan.
Velvet poppies appliqued on crown. Silk grosgrain ribbon. COLORS: Black with poppy red flowers; brown with peacock blue; navy blue with pheasant; white with peacock blue flowers and peacock blue edge.
PRICE, PREPAID to your home, **$3.88**

VEIL
3K5309
98c

3K5309 *Large silk veil with chenille dots.* Full drape size. COLORS: Black, brown, navy blue, taupe, black with Copenhagen blue dots; or navy blue with henna. PRICE, PREPAID to your home, **98c**

3K5229 *Roll brim sailor of Milan hemp.*
Two silk velvet and satin daisies. Ribbon lacing. COLORS: Sand with Copenhagen blue trimming; black with Copenhagen blue; navy blue with sand color ribbon and white daisies; white with rose color ribbon and Copenhagen blue daisies
PRICE, PREPAID to your home, **$3.49**

3K5229
$3.49

3K5231
$3.88

3K5225 *A very dressy hat trimmed with tightly curled ostrich feathers.*
Chip crown with silk Georgette brim. Silk grosgrain ribbon. COLORS: Black crown with peacock blue brim and trimming; brown with sand; navy blue with henna; navy blue with white; or all black.
PRICE, PREPAID to your home, **$4.95**

3K5232
$3.88

3K5231 *A particularly dressy hat made of good quality* **silk messaline.**
It features a short-back mushroom brim. Base of crown and edge of brim finished with row of fancy barnyard braid. Half wreath of mixed fruit in natural colorings. COLORS: Black, navy blue, sand or white.
PRICE, PREPAID to your home, **$3.88**

3K5230 *Semi-transparent brim style. Shortback mushroom hat.*
Brim is of net and is trimmed on top with glycerined ostrich. Contrasting silk warp ribbon binding and trimming. COLORS: Black with Copenhagen blue trimming; black with sand trimming; or all black.
PRICE, PREPAID to your home, **$3.49**

3K5232 *Milan hemp off-the-face hat with flange of fancy hair braid.*
Three clusters of grapes with foliage across the front. Faille ribbon trimming. COLORS: Black, navy blue, taupe, brown or sand; all with natural color grapes.
PRICE, PREPAID to your home, **$3.88**

3K5230
$3.49

The Rage on Champs Elysees Paris!

3K5234
$3.48

3K5235
$3.75

3K5240
$2.98

3K5238
$3.69

3K5237
$3.48

3K5234 *Here is a splendid chance for the matron to secure a stylish hat at a saving.*
Medium-sized turban of **polished chip** with brim facing of silk mixed crepe. Trimming of glycerined ostrich-aigrette. COLORS: Black with copenhagen blue facing and trimming, navy blue with sand color, all navy blue, or all brown.
PRICE, PREPAID to your home, **$3.48**

3K5240 *The last word in chic style this tam-o-shanter turban, a direct importation from Paris.*
The top is composed entirely of **feather**, the sides are of a new lustrous **artificial silk braid** that is very rich and dressy. A novelty pin gives just the right touch of trimming at the side front. A bargain offering at our low price. COLORS: Black, copenhagen blue, cherry red, pheasant, or navy blue.
PRICE, PREPAID to your home, **$2.98**

3K5235 *A picturesque style is offered in this* **Milan hemp** *hat with its flower trimming.*
A spray consisting of a large French rose with a half blown bud and foliage is placed at one side as pictured. Bands and long ends of silk warp ribbon. COLORS: Sand with copenhagen blue ribbon and rose color flower; black with copenhagen blue ribbon and rose color flower; peacock blue with navy blue ribbon and American beauty red flower, or white with white ribbon and rose color flower.
PRICE, PREPAID to your home, **$3.75**

3K5237 *The straight-brim sailor returns again to favor—no doubt because it is so generally becoming to so many types.*
Here is a particularly smart and dressy model of **Milan hemp**. Trimming consists of silk warp ribbon band and half wreath of novelty mixed dahlias, fruits and buds. You have only to make comparisons with the prices that others are charging to see what you save when you buy this hat. COLORS: Black, white, sand, copenhagen blue, navy blue, or pheasant
PRICE, PREPAID to your home, **$3.48**

3K5238 *A dress hat that charms with its beauty and grace.*
Transparent brim model with brim of **silk Chantilly lace** silk and **crown of taffeta**. Half wreath of satin and muslin flowers and foliage. COLORS: Black with copenhagen blue flowers, or white with copenhagen blue flowers.
PRICE, PREPAID to your home, **$3.69**

3K5241
$2.98

3K5233
$3.98

3K5233 *A small hat of undisputed charm designed for misses.*
It is made with a four-piece **silk taffeta** crown and off-the-face brim of combination color artificial silk braid. Two large ribbons. Appliqued on brim. COLORS: Navy blue crown with navy blue and red brim, brown with sand and brown, black with black and red, sand with sand and brown; all ribbon trimmings to match crown.
PRICE, PREPAID to your home, **$3.98**

3K5241 *Ostrich-trimmed hats are destined for great popularity this season.*
This chin-chin model is of **polished chip** with crown trimming of two single layer ostrich feathers and two tiny satin covered buds. A splendid value. COLORS: Black with peacock-blue feathers, all black, all navy blue, or all brown.
PRICE, PREPAID to your home, **$2.98**

3K5239 *A favorite style with youthful women is this chin-chin hat with plaited silk taffeta brim.*
The bell-shaped crown is of **Milan hemp**. Band and bow of silk grosgrain ribbon. A rich looking hat which is universally becoming. COLORS: All navy blue; peacock blue crown with pheasant brim; black with cherry red; sand with brown; or all black.
PRICE, PREPAID to your home, **$2.98**

3K5239
$2.98

3K5236 *Very new is this off-the-face hat of Milan hemp.*
It features a new style corrugated brim, trimmed with silk grosgrain ribbon. COLORS: All black, all pheasant color, black with peacock blue ribbon, navy blue with henna, or brown with sand ribbon.
PRICE, PREPAID to your home, **$3.47**

3K5236
$3.47

3K5244
$2.98

3K5247
$3.69

3K5245
$3.98

3K5243
$2.79

3K5244 *Attractive Chin Chin hat of* **Milan hemp** *and* **chip** *sewed row on row in pretty color combinations.*

Trimmed with five double satin daisies on facing. COLORS: Black hat; peacock blue and navy blue; sand and copenhagen blue; or brown and sand all with daisies in harmonizing two-tone colorings.
PRICE, PREPAID to your home, **$2.98**

3K5248 *New style* **chip** *hat with short-back poke brim.*

Wide **messaline ribbon**, prettily draped. Two clusters of berries. COLORS: Black with copenhagen blue ribbon; navy blue with emerald green; white with copenhagen blue; sand with navy blue; all black or all brown.
PRICE, PREPAID to your home, **$3.39**

DON'T FORGET
In ordering to state
COLOR desired

3K5243 *It is not often that you find a hat of this smart style at the money-saving price that we quote.*

This is a matrons' model made of **chip straw** with a fashionable, medium high crown and a small brim flared at a becoming angle. Trimming consists of a wreath of natural colored berries with foliage branched on twisted rubber stems. Silk grosgrain ribbon band completes this attractive hat. COLORS: Black, brown, or navy blue; all fruit of natural mixed colors.
PRICE, PREPAID to your home, **$2.79**

3K5247 *You are always sure of getting the very latest styles at PHILIPSBORN'S, yet our prices are never high as this offer proves.*

This is a very smart and very popular Chin Chin hat of **transparent braid** at a real saving. It features the "corrugated" brim so very fashionable this season. Large, effective bow and band of silk velvet. COLORS: Black with French blue; black with American beauty; black with burnt orange; or all black.
PRICE, PREPAID to your home, **$3.69**

3K5245 *This pretty sailor makes two claims to popularity—its very fashionable material—***silk Georgette crepe**—*and its stylish veil.*

Metallic braid around the crown and brim gives a bright touch of color. The silk veil is of attractive open mesh and is finished with a wide ribbon edge. COLORS: Sand with navy blue veil; black with black veil; navy blue with navy blue veil; dark brown with brown veil; or all henna with navy blue veil.
PRICE, PREPAID to your home, **$3.98**

3K5242 *Here is an appealingly youthful sailor that is up to the minute in style.*

The model is made with a double brim of contrasting **lustrous straw braid** of extra fine quality. **Picot-edged messaline ribbon** drapes the crown, and is drawn through the side of hat in newest fashion, forming sash ends as shown. COLORS: Brown with sand facing; navy blue with pheasant; black with peacock blue; or sand with peacock blue.
PRICE, PREPAID to your home, **$3.78**

New Chic French Effect

3K5242
$3.78

3K5248
$3.39

3K5246
$3.98

3K5246 *A chic off-the-face hat.*
Facing and side crown of **diamond porcupine braid** in combination with **taffeta silk**. Fancy bow COLORS: Black, navy blue, pheasant, sand, or dark brown.
PRICE, PREPAID to your home, **$3.98**

3K5250 *Here is a conservative style turban for the older woman, special at $2.48.*
Lustrous Jap straw model with an effective trimming of grosgrain ribbon. The large, attractive bow is placed at one side in splendid height-giving lines. A wonderful value. COLORS: Black, brown or navy blue.
PRICE, PREPAID to your home, **$2.48**

3K5249 *An unusually attractive and becoming* **chip** *hat with* **metallic tricotine** *facing.*
Three satin daisies inlaid in brim. Two daisies at front of crown with silk floss embroidery. COLORS: Black with copenhagen blue daisies; black with yellow; navy blue with white; brown with yellow.
PRICE, PREPAID to your home, **$2.89**

3K5250
$2.48

3K5249
$2.89

3K5254
$3.98

3K5255
$3.48

3K5256
$2.98

3K5254 *Sailors are always in favor—particularly when they are as original in design as this model.*

Barnyard braid, one of the season's newest millinery fancies, is used for the crown. Extra quality **chip brim** with wide flange on upper brim. Messaline trimming with two straw cabachons. COLORS: Black, brown, navy blue or pheasant

PRICE, PREPAID
to your home.   **$3.98**

3K5255 *An entirely new design in a close-fitting turban for misses and very moderately priced.*

A striking feature is the two-tone cushion brim of **Milan hemp** in stripe effect. Six-piece crown of new lustrous artificial silk braid. Silk cord and tassel. COLORS: Red crown with red and navy blue brim; brown with brown and sand; navy blue with henna and navy blue; peacock blue with peacock blue and taupe; or black with black and red.

PRICE, PREPAID
to your home,   **$3.48**

3K5253 *You will be delighted with the smart and original style of this off-the-face hat of good quality* **chip.**

It is a model that will be found most becoming to misses and youthful women. Half wreath of silk-covered fruit and tinted leaves with velveteen ribbon provide a rich trimming. COLORS: White, black, navy blue, or brown; all with wreath of dainty mixed shades.

PRICE, PREPAID
to your home,   **$2.98**

3K5259 *The last word in millinery styles for misses and youthful women.*

Off-the-face hat with tam effect crown, of new lustrous artificial silk braid with ribbon top. Silk embroidery stitching. Silk grosgrain ribbon bow COLORS: Black braid with Copenhagen blue ribbon; black with cherry red; brown with sand; henna with navy blue; or all navy blue.

PRICE, PREPAID
to your home,   **$3.98**

3K5259
$3.98

3K5253
$2.98

Very Newest Style!

3K5251
$3.48

3K5256 *Dressy and distinctive mushroom brim hat of* **polished chip.**

Trimmed with two satin daisies branched with grass aigrettes and natural wheat on chenille stems. COLORS: Black with yellow daisies; black with Copenhagen blue; navy blue with white; brown with yellow or white with yellow.

PRICE, PREPAID
to your home,   **$2.98**

3K5251 *One of the best examples of the popular transparent hats.*

This is a straight-brim sailor made of **imitation hair braid,** sewed row on row with patent Milan. Patent Milan flange on brim. Two clusters of cherries. Velveteen ribbon trimming. COLORS: Black with cherry red ribbon or all black.

PRICE, PREPAID
to your home,   **$3.48**

3K5258
$1.88

3K5258 *Floppy brim hat of* **chip** *with contrasting silk warp ribbon.*

COLORS: White with Copenhagen blue ribbon; white with navy blue; sand with brown; Copenhagen blue with navy blue; or all black.

PRICE, PREPAID
to your home,   **$1.88**

3K5252
$2.98

3K5252 *Soft, double brim turban with two tone brim.*

Made of **Milan hemp.** Crown band and side bow trimming of silk grosgrain ribbon. COLORS: Navy blue with pheasant facing; black with peacock blue; brown with sand; emerald green with white; or all black; all ribbons to match top of hat.

PRICE, PREPAID
to your home,   **$2.98**

3K5257 *New style poke hat turned up at back as shown.*

This model of **polished chip** will charm you with its becoming lines. Contrasting facing and crown band of silk warp crepe Half wreath of satin roses, buds, and foliage. COLORS: Black with peacock blue facing.

PRICE, PREPAID
to your home,   **$2.48**

3K5257
$2.48

3K5261 *The very latest corrugated chin chin sailor. Remarkably attractive and good value.*
Polished chip with embroidered crepe crown. Grosgrain ribbon trimming. COLORS: Black brim with peacock blue crown; navy blue with pheasant; all brown; or white with peacock blue.
PRICE, PREPAID
to your home, **$3.49**

3K5269 *Soft finished close fitting turban with full drape of good quality faille silk. Very becoming.*
Stylish silk tassel trimming. COLORS: White with burnt orange trimming; white with navy blue; all black; black with peacock blue; sand with brown or all navy blue.
PRICE, PREPAID
to your home, **$2.48**

3K5261
$3.49

3K5269
$2.48

3K5262
$2.49

3K5260
$2.48

IMPORTANT!

Be Sure To State COLOR Desired.

3K5260 *Here is a small sized dress hat at a special reduction.*

It is one of the popular **polished chip** models, with an alluring tilt to the brim. Contrasting silk warp crepe is used to face the underbrim. A double satin wild rose with small buds and leaves provide dressy trimming. Faille ribbon. COLORS: Black with peacock blue facing; black with sand; brown with peacock blue; navy blue with sand; all roses in color to harmonize.
PRICE, PREPAID
to your home, **$2.48**

3K5265 *A youthful style in a fine hand-woven braided straw hat reduced to $1.98.*
Wreath of twelve cherries with foliage encircles hat. Two-tone grosgrain ribbon band and streamers. A model that compares favorably with high-priced hats elsewhere. COLORS: White, black, peacock blue, gold or sand; all with harmonizing ribbon and natural color cherries.
PRICE, PREPAID
to your home, **$1.98**

A Straw Tam of unusual charm

3K5266 *An exclusive design in a fine Milan hemp Tam o'Shanter.* Contrasting silk fringe furnishes the very latest in trimmings, while silk soutache braid around the sides completes the smart effect. COLORS: Black, navy blue, henna, sand or red.
PRICE, PREPAID
to your home, **$2.88**

BATAVIA CLOTH—a new millinery fabric destined for widespread popularity this season,— is found in a variety of charming styles in Philipsborn's hats for the spring and summer of 1921.

This fabric is made of hemp in an open mesh weave, which lends itself admirably to embroidery. It is also effective plain without embroidery.

Particularly good examples of this new fabric are shown on pages 139, 146, 149, 150, and 156 of this catalog. Pheasant, a reddish brown, and henna are the season's best new shades.

Important! Do not delay your order by forgetting to give color of hat desired.

3K5262 *Smart roll brim hat of peanit straw with Batavia facing. Special bargain. Unusually becoming.*
Batavia fold and two rosettes around crown. All in two-tone combinations. COLORS: Black with pheasant facing; navy blue with peacock blue; brown with sand; or white with gold.
PRICE, PREPAID
to your home, **$2.49**

3K5266
$2.88

3K5264
$1.69

3K5263
$1.19

3K5268
$3.38

3K5267
$3.48

3K5263 *Here is an especially stylish selection in an automobile cap—Special.*
The mode is made of good grade **poplin** and is one of the biggest bargains ever offered at this low price. Corded Tam o'Shanter crown. Veil loops. Elastic head band. Vizor brim. COLORS: Navy blue, sand, brown or Copenhagen blue.
PRICE, PREPAID to your home, **$1.19**

3K5268 *Patent Milan hats never lose their popularity—special at $3.38.*
Attractive medium-sized roll-brim model with silk warp crepe trimming folded and draped about crown. Large attractive bow held with novelty ornament. COLORS: Black with pheasant color trimming; navy blue with pearl gray trim; brown with sand trim; all white; sand color with peacock blue.
PRICE, PREPAID to your home, **$3.38**

3K5264 *Another of our wonderful values—this* **two-tone braided straw sailor.**
Ribbon band and bow. Very artistic color combinations. COLORS: Navy blue with white combination; navy blue with henna; brown with sand; black with white; peacock blue with brown; all ribbons to match dark color in hats.
PRICE, PREPAID to your home, **$1.69**

3K5267 *No need to pay high prices when you can get a hat of this style for $3.48.*
This very smart turban shows an effective combination of **rough straw braid and taffeta.** Large wing effect bows of taffeta embroidered with silk floss. COLORS: Brown taffeta with peacock blue braid; all black; navy blue with henna; all cherry red; all embroidery to match braid.
PRICE, PREPAID to your home, **$3.48**

3K5265
$1.98

3K5275
$1.98

3K5274
$1.29

Fine Panama Hats! Woven by Hand!

3K5275 *An extraordinary offer in a hand-woven Panama hat.*

This is a medium-size model. Trimmed with a cluster of six cherries with foliage and a velveteen ribbon band and ends. One of the most satisfactory hats you could buy at this price. COLORS: White with black ribbon and red cherries; or white with red ribbon and red cherries.
PRICE, PREPAID to your home, **$1.98**

3K5278
$1.95

3K5278 *A new style in a soft finish Panama crusher.*

Contrasting hand embroidery as pictured. COLORS: White with mixed color embroidery.
PRICE, PREPAID to your home, **$1.95**

3K5274 *Here is a striking value in an untrimmed Panama hat.*

Mushroom model with pencil curl on edge of brim. For trimming suggestions, see page 153 of this catalog. The equal of any $2.00 hat on the market. COLORS: Cream white.
PRICE, PREPAID to your home, **$1.29**

3K5270
$1.68

3K5272
$3.48

3K5270 *Untrimmed hat with soft floppy brim.*

Very effective **trimmed with flowers and ribbon streamers.** A wonderful bargain. COLORS: Cream white.
PRICE, PREPAID to your home, **$1.68**

3K5273 $2.96

3K5271 *Untrimmed straight brim sailor.*

The hats shown on this page are the biggest bargains ever put out in Panama hats. COLORS: Cream white.
PRICE, PREPAID to your home, **$1.79**

3K5276 *One of the prettiest hats in our entire showing, is this hand-woven Panama.*

Large flop-brim model. Contrasting faille ribbon and a full aster wreath. COLORS: White with copenhagen blue ribbon and mixed wreath; white with gold ribbon and mixed wreath; or white with navy blue and mixed wreath.
PRICE PREPAID to your home, **$2.79**

3K5273 *Grace itself is reflected in this large floppy brim hat.*

Half wreath with crushed roses; satin buttercups and fruit. Satin-backed velvet ribbon streamers. Easily worth $4.98. COLORS: White with black ribbon; wreath in mixed harmonizing colors.
PRICE, PREPAID to your home, **$2.96**

3K5272 *Dressy and becoming flop-brim Panama hat.*

Trimming consists of full wreath of field flowers and satin-backed velvet ribbon with streamers as shown. Extremely low priced. COLORS: White with black ribbon and natural red and corn flower, blue mixed flowers.
PRICE, PREPAID to your home, **$3.48**

3K5277 *A big bargain in a Panama sailor at only $1.79.*

Styled with pencil curl on edge of brim and trimmed with silk grosgrain ribbon band and bow. Correct, tailored style at a bargain price. COLORS: White with white band; white with peacock blue; or white with navy blue.
PRICE, PREPAID to your home, **$1.79**

3K5271
$1.79

3K5276
$2.79

3K5277
$1.79

3K5280 *Smart and becoming style in this hat for the Miss.*
This attractive model is made of **patent Milan** in the new mushroom brim poke effect. Silk messaline ribbon draped about the crown and two large satin daisies trim the hat. For misses 14 to 18 years. COLORS: All black; peacock blue; navy blue; or sand with brown ribbon, or black with Copenhagen blue ribbon. PRICE, PREPAID to your home, **$3.48**

3K5280
$3.48

3K5281
$2.98

←A Big Value!
Last Minute Style

3K5281 *This season's favorite hat model for the Miss.*
Off-the-face style of fine quality **Patent Milan** trimmed with band and double bow of fine grosgrain ribbon. Suitable for misses 15 to 18 years. COLORS: Black, or navy blue. PRICE, PREPAID to your home, **$2.98**

3K5285
$2.48

3K5287 **Patent Milan** *hat with contrasting faille ribbon lacing in brim.*
Half wreath of twelve cherries. Girls 12 to 15 years. COLORS: Black with Copenhagen blue ribbon; navy blue with red; brown with sand or Copenhagen blue with navy blue. PRICE, PREPAID to your home, **$2.98**

When we quote hats for girls 12 to 14 years it means that the hat will fit a large 12 year old girl, a small 14 year old or an average girl of 13 years.

3K5282
$2.59

3K5288
$2.79

3K5285 *Misses' floppy brim hat of* **patent Milan** *and Milan hemp sewed row on row.*
Silk warp grosgrain ribbon streamers. COLORS: Sand and Copenhagen blue; navy blue and white; brown and Copenhagen blue; black and red; all ribbons to match lighter color in hat. PRICE, PREPAID to your home, **$2.48**

3K5287
$2.98

3K5288 *A youthful and becoming style for misses.*
Poke hat of very fine quality **fancy Milan**, featuring a chin strap and streamers of silk warp ribbon. Half wreath of satin dahlias, asters, and small buds. Misses 14 to 18 years. COLORS: Black; navy blue; peacock blue; sand or henna. PRICE, PREP'D to your home, **$2.79**

3K5283
$1.75

3K5282 *Distinctive and stylish rolling brim sailor of* **fancy Milan**—*for Misses.*
Good grosgrain ribbon streamers. COLORS: Navy blue with Copenhagen blue flange; black with gold; white with brown or Copenhagen blue with rose. PRICE, PREPAID to your home, **$2.59**

3K5283 *Misses' hat of hand woven straw in two-tone combination. Convertible brim.*
Silk warp ribbon band and streamers. COLORS: Sand and Copenhagen blue; navy blue and red; sand and brown; black and red; all ribbons to match dark color in hat. PRICE, PREPAID to your home, **$1.75**

3K5308
$1.38

3K5286 *Remarkably low priced hat of hand woven* **chip straw.**
Grosgrain ribbon band finished at back with a flat tailored bow and streamers. Five daisies appliqued on crown. For misses 14 to 16 years. COLORS: Navy blue, brown, black or peacock blue. PRICE, PREPAID to your home, **$1.98**

3K5284
$2.19

3K5286
$1.98

3K5289 *Misses' off-the-face hat of* **polished chip.**
Four rows of contrasting insertion in brim. Silk moire ribbon drape and short streamers, with bead pendants. COLORS: Peacock blue with navy blue insertion; sand with brown; black with Copenhagen blue; or navy blue with peacock blue. PRICE, PREPAID to your home, **$2.48**

3K5289
$2.48

3K5308 *Fine quality* **patent Milan straw** *hat for girls 12 to 15 years.*
We offer you this hat either untrimmed as in the large picture or trimmed with good grosgrain ribbon band and streamers. COLORS: Copenhagen blue with sand insertion; black with Copenhagen blue; navy blue with sand or brown with coral.
3K5308 Untrimmed. PRICE, PREPAID to your home, **$1.38**
3K5284 Trimmed. PRICE, PREPAID to your home, **$2.19**

PHILIPSBORN'S

3K5294
$2.68

3K5293
$4.88

3K5293 *One of the most attractive small hats in our entire collection.*
All Batavia braid, entire top embroidered with silk floss and metallic thread. Trimmed with long silk fringe. A very becoming and rich-looking hat at a notably low price. COLORS: Copenhagen blue, jade green, navy blue, dark brown, or black. All hats with colored embroidery.
PRICE, PREPAID to your home, **$4.88**

3K5298 *A very new model in one of the popular "off-the-face" hats.*
Shiny straw crown with brim of silk embroidered Batavia. Novelty trimming pin at front gives a chic finish. COLORS: Black crown with pheasant color brim as illustrated; navy blue with peacock blue brim; sand with brown brim; black with jade green brim.
PRICE, PREPAID to your home, **$4.98**

3K5297 *Smart, tailored lines give style to this hat.*
Lustrous straw model with smartly upturned brim faced with embroidered Batavia cloth. Novelty fruit and ribbon trimming, at side front. A very becoming model that will be suitable for either misses or older women. COLORS: Navy blue, dark brown, or black; all with harmonizing embroidery.
PRICE, PREPAID to your home, **$3.48**

3K5296 *Stunning model with entire facing of feathers.*
Pictured at the right hand corner of this page is a particularly desirable and unusually low priced hat. It is made with a chip straw crown, and satin upper brim. COLORS: Black with burnt orange facing; navy blue with peacock blue facing; brown with sand facing; black with peacock blue facing; or all black.
PRICE, PREPAID to your home, **$4.68**

3K5290
$3.48

3K5294 *Soft finish ribbon hat. Can be worn in any desired shape.*
Sewed row on row with milan hemp braid. Trimmed with five straw rosettes and silk floss. COLORS: Jade green, burnt-orange, peacock blue, gold or navy blue. PRICE, PREPAID to your home, **$2.68**

3K5290 *Charming, youthful style in this hat.*
Made of novelty chain straw. Trimmed with a wreath of field flowers and bow of silk ribbon. COLORS: White, peacock blue, wistaria or gold; all with mixed flowers as illustrated.
PRICE, PREPAID to your home, **$3.48**

3K5291 *An unusually becoming style in a small roll brim.*
This model attractively combines an all-over straw brim with a feather crown and long ostrich fibre trimming. Extremely dressy. COLORS: Red, peacock blue, navy blue, or black. PRICE, PREPAID to your home, **$3.97**

3K5292 *Fashion's popular whim is this large transparent hair braid hat.*
Five large daisies inserted in brim. Narrow silk ribbon trimming. COLORS: Black with yellow daisies; black with copenhagen blue, or black with white daisies. PRICE, PREPAID to your home, **$4.98**

3K5295 *A moderately priced hat of youthful charm.*
Milan hemp model with wide, floppy brim. Trimmed with fruit "trailer" and grosgrain ribbon. COLORS: Sand with Copenhagen blue flange; black with peacock blue flange; white with gold flange; or brown with burnt orange flange. PRICE, PREPAID to your home, **$4.48**

Be Sure to Always State COLOR Desired When Ordering, Thus Avoiding Delay and Disappointment.

3K5291
$3.97

3K5292
$4.98

3K5295
$4.48

3K5298
$4.98

3K5297
$3.48

3K5296
$4.68

3K5299 *An exquisite dress hat made entirely of* **silk Georgette crepe.** Plaited brim. Wool yarn hand embroidered around front and sides of crown. Ends of Georgette folded across back of brim. COLORS: Pink with combination burnt orange; copenhagen blue and pink embroidery; white, cream yellow or navy blue; all with beautiful mixed embroidery trimming. **$5.98** PRICE, PREPAID to your home,

3K5300 *Stunning hat made with* **lustrous** straw *crown and soft taffeta silk brim with all over wool embroidery.* Silk cord trimming pin. COLORS: Cherry red; navy blue with copenhagen blue; brown with sand; black with burnt orange; or black with peacock blue embroidery. PRICE, PREPAID to your home, **$3.98**

3K5302 **Taffeta silk** *Tam O'Shanter trimmed with good quality grosgrain ribbon. Elastic band to fit all heads.* COLORS: Peacock blue with navy blue ribbon; sand with brown ribbon; all red; all black; or burnt orange with white ribbon. PRICE, PREPAID to your home, **$2.29**

3K5303 *Only $1.69 for this smart sailor of* **glossy straw** *with contrasting facing.* Wide ribbon band and bow. COLORS: Navy blue with peacock blue facing; black with peacock blue facing; brown with sand facing; or red with navy blue facing. PRICE, PREPAID to your home, **$1.69**

3K5301 *Attractive small-sized hat with* **hemp crown.** Upper brim covered with silk-mixed crepe. Faille ribbon. Wreath of satin roses. COLORS: Black with gold crepe; black with peacock blue crepe; sand with peacock blue crepe; navy blue with sand crepe; or all gold. PRICE, PREPAID to your home, **$2.48**

3K5306 *Charming style in this* **chip** *hat with facing of rich looking* **silk embroidered Batavia.** *Silk tassel.* COLORS: Black with burnt orange facing; navy blue with peacock blue facing; sand with peacock blue facing; all black; white with navy blue facing. All with harmonizing embroidery and all tassels to match hat. PRICE, PREPAID to your home, **$2.98**

3K5307 *One of our dressiest Tam hats, made of rich looking* **embroidered Batavia** *with silk tassel.* COLORS: Pheasant with copenhagen blue embroidery as illustrated; peacock blue with rose; navy blue with jade green; brown with sand; cherry red with navy blue. PRICE, PREPAID to your home, **$3.48**

3K5305 *An off-the-face hat of much charm is this* **Milan hemp** *model trimmed with ten crush roses.* Silk warp ribbon trimming. COLORS: Brown with cream yellow roses; navy blue with pink roses; black with pink roses; white with pink roses; sand with copenhagen blue roses. PRICE, PREPAID to your home, **$3.75**

3K5304 *Here is a hat that will charm you with its dressy lines.* Medium-sized **chip** model with contrasting crepe facing. Wreath of twelve cherries with foliage. Ribbon band and streamers. A special price reduction. COLORS: Black with rose facing; black with peacock blue facing; navy blue with sand facing; white with jade green facing. PRICE, PREPAID to your home, **$3.75**

3K5300 $3.98

3K5304 $3.75

3K5299 $5.98

3K5302 $2.29

3K5303 $1.69

3K5301 $2.48

3K5307 $3.48

3K5306 $2.98

3K5305 $3.75

3K5314 *New style off-the-face hat for a child.* **Imitation Panama** with fancy all-over cloth facing. For children 4 to 6 years. COLORS: Rose, copenhagen blue, white, or navy blue. PRICE, PREPAID to your home, **98c**

3K5311 *Child's silk embroidered toque. Children 3 or 4 years.* Narrow ribbed **poplin Silk messaline** ribbon bow. COLORS: White with pink or white with light blue. PRICE, PREPAID to your home, **98c**

3K5319 *Girls' two-tone Patent Milan straw hat.* For girls 9 to 12 years old. Convertible brim. Extra long ribbon streamer. COLORS: Brown with white brim; navy blue with white; black with white; or all black PRICE, PREPAID to your home, **$1.98**

3K5314 **98c**

3K5311 **98c**

3K5315 **59c**

3K5312 **98c**

3K5319 **$1.98**

3K5315 *Child's soft washable pique hat.* For children 3 or 4 years old. Prettily shirred crown. Silk cord trimming. COLORS: White with pink cord or white with light blue cord. PRICE, PREPAID to your home. **59c**

3K5312 *Child's soft organdie hat.* For children 3 to 4 years. Organdie band and bow. COLORS: White, pink, or light blue. PRICE, PREPAID **98c**

3K5320 *Two-tone mushroom brim.* For girls 5 to 7 years. Made of **fancy Milan.** Silk floss cabachon and ribbon streamers. COLORS: Copenhagen blue crown with sand; navy blue with white; black with red; or all black. PRICE, PREPAID to your home, **$2.45**

3K5320 **$2.45**

Extra Special

3K5316 *Two-tone Milan hat. Convertible brim.* Girls 12 to 14 years old. COLORS: Black with white; sand with copenhagen blue; white with navy blue; or navy blue with green insertion. PRICE, PREPAID to your home, **$2.29**

3K5321 *Fine quality* **Patent Milan** *hat.* Silk grosgrain ribbon band and streamer. Girls 13 to 15 years. COLORS: Black, navy blue, or sand. PRICE PREPAID, to your home, **$2.88**

3K5313 *Attractive* **Milan** *hemp Tam.* Trimmed with quill and straw cabachon. Elastic band. Children from 3 to 5 years. COLORS: Black, navy blue, or copenhagen blue. PRICE, PREPAID to your home, **$1.98**

3K5316 **$2.29**

3K5322 *Convertible brim hat of* **Patent Milan** *for girls 4 to 6.* Silk warp ribbon trimming. COLORS: Black, navy blue or sand. PRICE, PREPAID to your home, **$1.69**

3K5318 *Convertible brim hat of* peanit straw. Silk warp ribbon binding and trimming. Children 11 to 14 years. COLORS: Black, navy blue, brown or cardinal. PRICE, PREPAID to your home, **$1.79**

3K5317 **Hand-woven** straw hat. Convertible brim. Silk grosgrain ribbon band and streamers. Children 4 to 6 years. COLORS: Sand and copenhagen blue; white and brown; black and red; navy blue and copenhagen blue combination, or all black. PRICE, PREPAID to your home, **$1.49**

When we quote hats for girls 4 to 6 years it means that the hat will fit a large 4 year old girl, a small 6 year old, or an average girl of 5 years.

3K5322 **$1.69**

3K5321 **$2.88**

3K5313 **$1.98**

3K5317 **$1.49**

3K5318 **$1.79**

3K5332 $2.88

3K5332 Milan hemp *short-back poke hat. For girls 9 to 12 years.* Flower cluster and messaline ribbon streamers. COLORS: Black with Copenhagen blue ribbon; white with Copenhagen blue; all navy blue; or sand with brown ribbon. PRICE, PREPAID to your home, **$2.88**

3K5328 *An extraordinary bargain in a girl's hat. For girls 10 to 12 years.* Mushroom brim model of **shiny straw braid with silk warp ribbon trimming.** COLORS: Copenhagen blue crown with sand brim; red with navy blue; all navy blue; or all black. PRICE, PREPAID to your home, **$1.19**

3K5328 $1.19

3K5327 $1.98

3K5326 *An extremely becoming hat for girls 6 to 8 years.* Rolling brim sailor of **fancy Milan braid with silk messaline ribbon trimming** as shown. Satin daisy at front and back. Very dressy. COLORS: Black with Copenhagen blue trim; black with gold; navy blue with Copenhagen blue; sand with brown; or Copenhagen blue with rose. PRICE, PREPAID to your home, **$2.78**

3K5337 $2.48

3K5327 *Dressy style in a girls' peanit straw hat.* Half wreath of four asters. Bow and streamers of silk warp ribbon. Ribbon binding on edge. Suitable for girls 10 to 13 years. COLORS: Black, navy blue, red, or brown. PRICE, PREPAID to your home, **$1.98**

3K5326 $2.78

3K5337 *Child's two-tone* **patent Milan hat.** Daisy trimming on rolling brim. Ribbon streamers. For children 6 to 8 years. COLORS: White crown with navy blue brim; white with black; sand with navy blue; all black; all navy blue. Daisies to harmonize. PRICE, PREPAID to your home, **$2.48**

3K5329 $1.98

3K5336 $2.49

3K5330 $2.89

3K5331 $1.59

3K5329 **Child's** *short-back poke hat of* **patent Milan.** Silk grosgrain ribbon streamers, and three lawn roses. For children 4 to 6 years. COLORS: Navy blue, black, brown; white with navy blue ribbon; all flowers to harmonize. PRICE, PREPAID to your home, **$1.98**

Be sure to state COLOR desired.

3K5330 *Child's rolling brim sailor of* **chip straw.** Mixed flower wreath and ribbon streamers. For children 6 to 9 years. COLORS: Sand with Copenhagen blue; black with rose; navy blue with Copenhagen blue; or white with rose. PRICE, PREPAID to your home, **$2.89**

Genuine Panama Hat

3K5336 Fine Toyo Panama hat. Silk grosgrain ribbon streamers. For girls 10 to 12 yrs. COLORS: White with black or white with navy blue. PRICE, PREPAID to your home, **$2.49**

3K5331 *An unusual value at our reduced price.* Girls' mushroom brim hat of **patent Milan.** Half wreath of daisies, silk warp ribbon band and streamers. For girls 10 to 13 years. COLORS: White with navy blue ribbon; sand with Copenhagen blue; black with Copenhagen blue, or navy blue with Copenhagen blue. PRICE, PREPAID to your home, **$1.59**

3K5333 $1.59

3K5335 $2.69

Genuine Panama Hat

When we describe a hat for girls from 10 to 12 years, we mean that it will fit a large 10 year old, a small 12 year old, or an average size 11 year old girl.

3K5334 $1.98

Novelty Bargain A Big Special!

3K5335 Genuine Panama hat. *For girls 9 to 12 years.* Lustrous silk ribbon band and streamers. Mixed novelty half wreath. COLORS: White with navy blue ribbon; white with brown; or white with black. PRICE, PREPAID to your home, **$2.69**

3K5333 *Girl's woven hat of* **Milan braid.** Trimmed with cherry wreath, silk grosgrain ribbon bows and streamers. For girls 9 to 12 years. COLORS: Red and navy blue combination; sand and Copenhagen blue; black and red; or sand and brown. PRICE, PREPAID to your home, **$1.59**

3K5334 *Charming style for a child.* Mushroom brim hat of **patent Milan with chin strap.** Silk messaline ribbon trimming. Clusters of cherries. For children 3 to 5 years. COLORS: Red, black, navy blue, or white with navy blue ribbon. PRICE, PREPAID to your home, **$1.98**

Order at Our Risk. You Are the Judge—Your Money Back if You Are Not Satisfied.

PHILIPSBORN'S

3K5358 *Cherry wreath—an always popular and effective trimming. 24 cherries with foliage.*
COLORS: Natural cherry red.
PRICE, PREPAID to your home, **58c**

3K5359 *Novelty ring wreath of two satin daisies, wheat and grass aigrette on stems.*
COLORS: White, yellow, Copenhagen blue, or rose, all with grass in harmonizing combinations. PRICE, PREPAID to your home, **63c**

3K5345 *New style satin rose ring with four satin leaves and small buds.*
COLORS: Rose, maize, Copenhagen blue or jacque.
PRICE, PREPAID to your home, **98c**

Bargains in Millinery Trimmings—The Rage

3K5353 *Very dainty forget-me-not wreath.*
Made of 54 velvet flowers.
COLORS: Pink, light blue, or pink and light blue mixed.
PRICE, PREPAID to your home, **23c**

3K5351 *Eight double satin daisies in wreath.*
COLORS: White, maize, Copenhagen blue, Copenhagen blue and rose mixed, or white, yellow and black mixed.
PRICE, PREPAID to your home, **44c**

3K5344 *Big value in a half wreath of six satin pansies.* Made with shaded leaves and silk buds. COLORS: Natural purple, natural yellow, or purple and yellow mixed. PRICE, PREPAID **63c**

3K5349 *Imitation wheat wreath—very new and stunningly effective.*
COLORS: Pheasant, black, white, peacock blue, cherry red, or sand.
PRICE, PREPAID to your home, **75c**

← 3K5354 *Very fashionable flower wreath.* June roses and six velvet asters. COLORS: Rose or Copenhagen blue, all with asters in harmonizing combination. PRICE, PREP'D to your home, **58c**

3K5352 *Fashionable mixed flower wreath at a money-saving price.*
Three muslin asters branched with satin buttercups and fruit; satin and muslin foliage. COLORS: Lavender, Copenhagen blue, dark red, and mixed natural shades.
PRICE, PREPAID to your home, **$1.25**

3K5341 *The season's newest idea in novelty flower wreath of finest quality.*
Satin velvet and taffeta daisy, buttercups and buds. Very rich and dressy. Unequaled for value at our price. Natural mixed colors.
PRICE, PREPAID to your home, **$1.75**

3K5350 *Here is the very latest idea in hat trimming, specially reduced.*
Flower wreath made of cellaphane. A new high luster material of very rich appearance. COLORS: Henna, rose, Copenhagen blue, navy blue, cherry red or brown.
PRICE, PREPAID to your home, **$1.19**

Feather **3K5343** *Handsome ostrich wreath in the season's favored colors.* *Novelty*
Fine quality, tightly curled. COLORS: Black, white, Copenhagen blue, pheasant, navy blue, brown or cherry red.
PRICE, PREPAID to your home, **$1.75**

3K5361 *At a special price—cluster of eight cherries with foliage.*
COLOR: Natural cherry red.
PRICE, PREP'D to your home, **21c**

3K5348 *Effecting cluster of five large pansies and three buds, on long stems.*
COLORS: Natural purple or yellow.
PRICE, PREPAID to your home, **29c**

3K5346 *Three muslin half blown roses with muslin and satin leaves.*
COLORS: Rose, maize, Copenhagen blue, or jacque.
PRICE, PREP'D to your home, **49c**

3K5360 *Flat rose of satin and velvet with taffeta leaves.*
COLORS: Rose, maize, Copenhagen blue or American beauty.
PRICE, PREP'D to your home, **39c**

3K5357 *Novelty silk tassel, with silk cord pendant.*
COLORS: Black, white, peacock blue, cherry red, navy blue, brown or pheasant.
PRICE, PREP'D to your home, **49c**

3K5363 *Latest straw ornament.*
COLORS: Rose and Copenhagen blue; henna and navy blue; black and peacock blue; or royal blue and red.
PRICE, PREPAID to your home, **69c**

3K5355 *Satin poppy with wheat.*
COLORS: Poppy red, Copenhagen blue, rose, or gold.
PRICE, PREP'D to your home **44c**

3K5362 *Straw head pin—the very latest in trimming.*
COLORS: Peacock blue, henna, navy blue, brown, cherry red or burnt orange. PRICE,
PREPAID to your home, **39c**

3K5347 *Cluster of twelve silk-covered grapes with foliage, at a low price.*
COLORS: Purple, rose, Copenhagen blue or nile green.
PRICE, PREPAID to your home, **33c**

3K5342 *Rose with two cherries and five leaves. Tremendous value.*
Makes a very rich trimming. COLORS: Rose, Copenhagen blue, maize or jacque.
PRICE, PREPAID to your home, **25c**

3K5356 *Bead head trimming pin—very fashionable and extremely low priced.*
Can be used alone without other trimming. COLOR: Black only.
PRICE, PREPAID to your home, **45c**

For Index See Page 274 and Remember PHILIPSBORN'S Prepay All Transportation Charges. There Are No Express or Mailing Charges for You to Pay

CHICAGO, ILL. 153

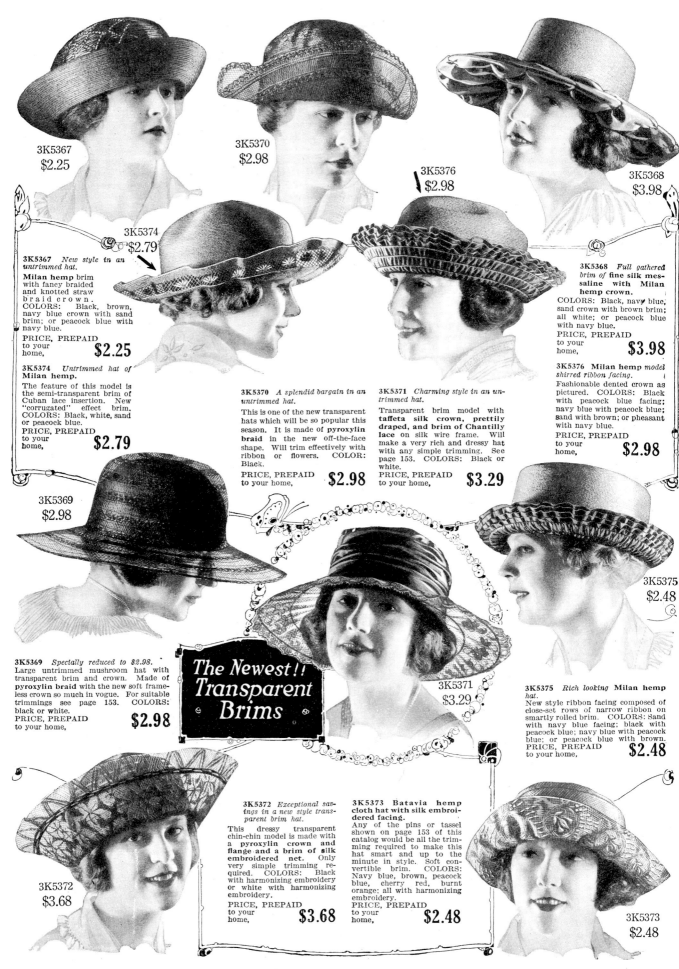

3K5367
$2.25

3K5370
$2.98

3K5376
$2.98

3K5368
$3.98

3K5374
$2.79

3K5367 *New style in an untrimmed hat.*
Milan hemp brim with fancy braided and knotted straw braid crown.
COLORS: Black, brown, navy blue crown with sand brim; or peacock blue with navy blue.
PRICE, PREPAID to your home, **$2.25**

3K5374 *Untrimmed hat of* **Milan** hemp.
The feature of this model is the semi-transparent brim of Cuban lace insertion. New "corrugated" effect brim. COLORS: Black, white, sand or peacock blue.
PRICE, PREPAID to your home, **$2.79**

3K5370 *A splendid bargain in an untrimmed hat.*
This is one of the new transparent hats which will be so popular this season. It is made of **pyroxylin braid** in the new off-the-face shape. Will trim effectively with ribbon or flowers. COLOR: Black.
PRICE, PREPAID to your home, **$2.98**

3K5371 *Charming style in an untrimmed hat.*
Transparent brim model with **taffeta silk crown, prettily draped, and brim of Chantilly lace** on silk wire frame. Will make a very rich and dressy hat with any simple trimming. See page 153. COLORS: Black or white.
PRICE, PREPAID to your home, **$3.29**

3K5368 *Full gathered brim of* **fine silk messaline with Milan hemp crown.**
COLORS: Black, navy blue, sand crown with brown brim; all white; or peacock blue with navy blue.
PRICE, PREPAID to your home, **$3.98**

3K5376 **Milan hemp** *model shirred ribbon facing.*
Fashionable dented crown as pictured. COLORS: Black with peacock blue facing; navy blue with peacock blue; sand with brown; or pheasant with navy blue.
PRICE, PREPAID to your home, **$2.98**

3K5369
$2.98

3K5375
$2.48

3K5369 *Specially reduced to $2.98.*
Large untrimmed mushroom hat with transparent brim and crown. Made of **pyroxylin braid** with the new soft frameless crown so much in vogue. For suitable trimmings see page 153. COLORS: black or white.
PRICE, PREPAID to your home, **$2.98**

The Newest!! Transparent Brims

3K5371
$3.29

3K5375 *Rich looking* **Milan hemp** *hat.*
New style ribbon facing composed of close-set rows of narrow ribbon on smartly rolled brim. COLORS: Sand with navy blue facing; black with peacock blue; navy blue with peacock blue; or peacock blue with brown.
PRICE, PREPAID to your home, **$2.48**

3K5372
$3.68

3K5372 *Exceptional savings in a new style transparent brim hat.*
This dressy transparent chin-chin model is made with a pyroxylin crown and flange and a brim of silk embroidered net. Only very simple trimming required. COLORS: Black with harmonizing embroidery or white with harmonizing embroidery.
PRICE, PREPAID to your home, **$3.68**

3K5373 **Batavia hemp** cloth hat with silk embroidered facing.
Any of the pins or tassel shown on page 153 of this catalog would be all the trimming required to make this hat smart and up to the minute in style. Soft convertible brim. COLORS: Navy blue, brown, peacock blue, cherry red, burnt orange; all with harmonizing embroidery.
PRICE, PREPAID to your home, **$2.48**

3K5373
$2.48

3K5399 *Unusual smartness of line distinguishes this untrimmed* **Milan hemp** *hat.*

It is a turban model which features a new style corrugated side, and can be worn by either young or mature women. Stylish edging of diamond porcupine braid. An entirely new model. COLORS: Black, brown or navy blue.
PRICE, PREPAID to your home, **$3.29**

3K5399
$3.29

3K5403
$1.98

3K5403 *A splendid model for general wear at a money-saving price.*

This untrimmed close-fitting poke model is made entirely of **Milan hemp.** Pencil curl on edge of brim. Designed particularly for misses and young women. COLORS: Black, white, navy blue, or cherry red.
PRICE, PREPAID to your home, **$1.98**

3K5402
$2.48

3K5402 *New and smart style features this rolling brim untrimmed hat.*

It is made of **Milan hemp** with pencil curl on edge of brim and fashionable bell crown. A ribbon band and ornament will make a stylish trimming. COLORS: Black, navy blue, sand, peacock blue, or white. PRICE, PREPAID to your home, **$2.48**

3K5404 *Very latest of* **Milan hemp.**

It is equally becoming turned up in the back as shown in the illustration or as an off-the-face style. COLORS: Black, white, henna, cherry red or sand.
PRICE, PREPAID to your home, **$2.29**

3K5404
$2.29

3K5398
$1.85

3K5397
$3.49

The Newest Shape from Paris!!

3K5395
$1.98

3K5398 **Milan** hemp *chin-chin with new corrugated brim.*

You will find appropriate trimming on page 153 of this catalog. A special bargain at our money-saving price. Worth $2.50. COLORS: Black, white, sand, peacock blue, or cherry red.
PRICE, PREPAID to your home, **$1.85**

3K5400 *A good selection for style and value in this untrimmed hat.*

It is one of the popular off-the-face models made entirely of **Milan hemp.** Use any simple trimming of flowers or fancies as shown on page 153 of this catalog. COLORS: Black, brown, navy blue, henna or sand.
PRICE, PREPAID to your home, **$2.48**

3K5401
$1.98

3K5406
$3.39

3K5395 *Large size untrimmed hat at a special reduction.*

Made entirely of **Milan hemp** with attractive side rolling brim. Will trim effectively with any of the flowers or fancies shown on page 153 of this catalog. COLORS: Black, white, sand, or navy blue.
PRICE, PREPAID to your home, **$1.98**

3K5405 *A smart and becoming style designed for matrons.*

Close fitting untrimmed hat of **Milan hemp.** The medium high crown and slightly rolled brim give particularly smart lines to the model. It is an exceptionally good value at our low price. COLORS: Black, brown or navy blue.
PRICE, PREPAID to your home, **$1.49**

3K5396
$2.48

3K5397 *Entirely new untrimmed off-the-face hat of* **Milan hemp.** *Wide corrugated flare.*
COLORS: Black, navy blue, pheasant (new light brown) peacock blue or white. PRICE, PREPAID to your home, **$3.49**

3K5401 *Large-sized straight brim* **Milan hemp** *sailor.*
An extraordinary value. COLORS: Black, white, sand, navy blue, or peacock blue.
PRICE, PREPAID to your home, **$1.98**

3K5406 **Milan hemp** *off-the-face hat—new braid edge.*
COLORS: Black, brown, navy blue, henna, with navy blue edge; or sand with peacock blue.
PRICE, PREPAID to your home, **$3.39**

3K5396 *New style untrimmed* **Milan hemp** *mushroom hat.*
Wide flare sides. COLORS: Black, white, navy blue or Copenhagen blue.
PRICE, PREPAID to your home, **$2.48**

3K5400
$2.48

3K5405
$1.49

CHICAGO, ILL.

Our "EVERDAINTY" Underwear Is the Best for Style, Service, and Quality. Refer to Pages 216 to 24!

155

3K5387 *Untrimmed Chin-chin sailor at a noteworthy price cut.*

Of **lustrous Jap straw** with embroidered Batavia facing. Only simplest trimming required. COLORS: Black with pheasant facing; white with peacock blue; peacock blue with navy blue; all navy blue or all black.
PRICE, PREPAID to your home, **$2.78**

3K5410 For those desiring a less expensive hat, we offer the same style made of chip braid. Colors same as 3K5387.
PRICE, PREPAID to your home, **$2.15**

3K5382
$2.88

3K5387
$2.78

Novelty Style

3K5391
98c

3K5386 *Lustrous Jap straw hat with silk embroidered Batavia facing.*

COLORS: Black with Copenhagen blue facing; black with henna; sand with navy blue; white with burnt orange.
PRICE, PREPAID to your home, **$2.78**

3K5409 For those desiring a less expensive hat, we offer the same style made of chip braid. Colors same as 3K5386.
PRICE, PREPAID to your home, **$1.98**

3K5386
$2.78

3K5382 *Lustrous Jap straw untrimmed hat — embroidered Batavia facing.*

COLORS: Black with Copenhagen blue facing; sand with brown; navy blue with Copenhagen blue; brown with sand; or white with rose.
PRICE, PREPAID to your home, **$2.88**
3K5407 Same style colors as above. Made of chip.
PRICE, PREPAID **$2.19**

3K5391 *An excellent style—untrimmed turban for matrons.*

This smart hat of **polished chip** combines a medium high crown with smartly flared brim as shown. Very effective with any simple ornament. See page 153. COLORS: Black, brown, or navy blue.
PRICE, PREPAID to your home, **98c**

3K5390
$1.38

3K5389
$1.29

3K5384
$2.58

3K5380
$1.38

3K5390 *Chin-chin sailors are always exceedingly becoming.*

This **polished chip** model is especially smart and good-looking. Suitable trimmings shown on page 153 of this catalog. COLORS: Black, white, navy blue, or peacock blue.
PRICE, PREPAID to your home, **$1.38**

3K5381 *Distinctive untrimmed polished chip hat for matrons.*

The smart, upturned brim has contrasting crepe facing. Easy to trim. COLORS: Black with Copenhagen blue facing; black with sand; brown with Copenhagen blue, or navy blue with sand.
PRICE, PREPAID to your home, **$1.69**

3K5383
$2.98

3K5384 *A very new and attractive style in an untrimmed hat.*

Made of **shiny Jap straw** with insertion of Cuban lace braid. Will make a dressy and becoming hat with flower or ribbon trimming. Greatly under priced. COLORS: Black, white, Copenhagen blue, sand, or brown.
PRICE, PREPAID to your home, **$2.58**

3K5383 *Untrimmed roll brim lustrous Jap straw sailor.*

Embroidered Batavia facing. COLORS: Black with pheasant facing; white with Copenhagen blue; navy blue with sand, or all black.
PRICE, PREPAID to your home, **$2.98**
3K5408 For those desiring a less expensive hat, we offer the same style made of chip braid. COLORS: Same as 3K5383.
PRICE, PREPAID to your home, **$2.29**

3K5385 **$1.79**

3K5381
$1.69

3K5389 *Large untrimmed mushroom brim hat, only $1.29.*

Made of **polished chip.** One of our most becoming styles, greatly reduced. COLORS: Black, white, Copenhagen blue, pheasant, navy blue.
PRICE, PREPAID to your home, **$1.29**

3K5380 *Very fashionable this season.*

This medium-sized untrimmed sailor is made of a good quality **polished chip.** Trim with flowers or fancies. COLORS: Black, white, navy blue, or peacock blue.
PRICE, PREPAID to your home, **$1.38**

3K5388 *A splendid style for the matron in this untrimmed hat.*

Polished chip model. Contrasting crepe facing. COLORS: Black with Copenhagen blue facing; black with sand; navy blue with Copenhagen blue; or brown with sand.
PRICE, PREPAID to your home, **$1.79**

3K5385 *Flop brim hat of novelty chain weave straw.* Unequaled for style and value at our low price. For suitable trimming see page 153. COLORS: Black, white, brown, peacock blue, navy blue or gold.
PRICE, PREPAID to your home, **$1.79**

3K5388
$1.79

EASY MEASURE CHART

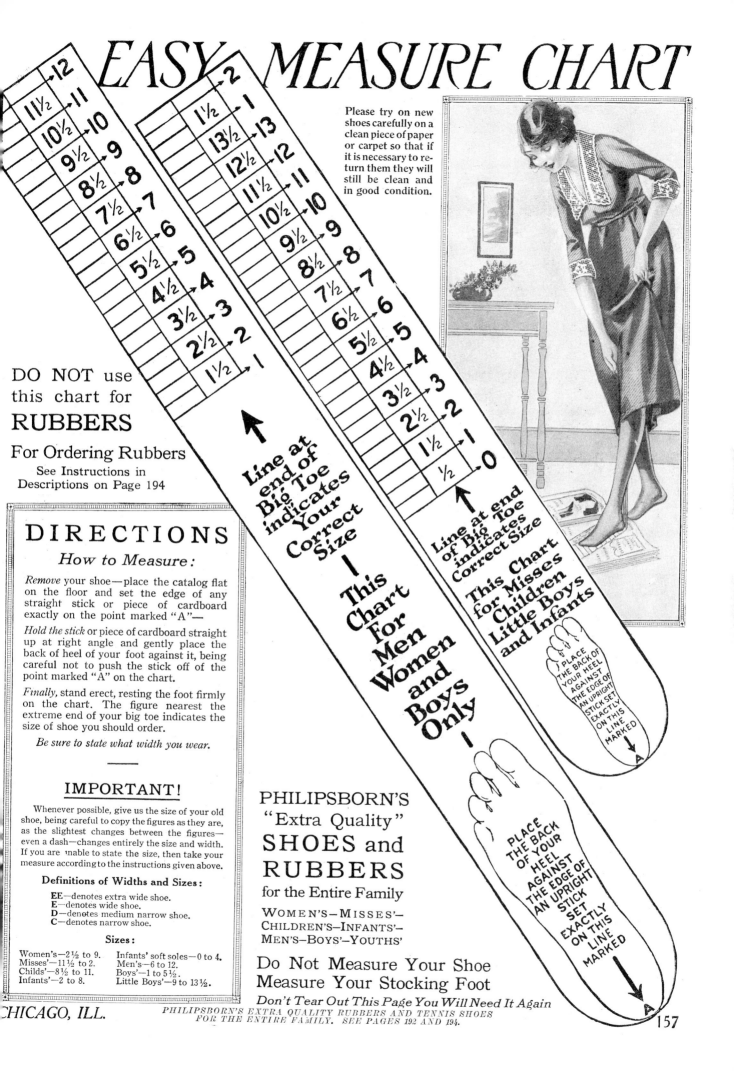

Please try on new shoes carefully on a clean piece of paper or carpet so that if it is necessary to return them they will still be clean and in good condition.

DO NOT use this chart for RUBBERS

For Ordering Rubbers
See Instructions in Descriptions on Page 194

Line at end of Big Toe indicates Your Correct Size
This Chart For Men Women and Boys Only

Line at end of Big Toe indicates Correct Size
This Chart for Misses Children Little Boys and Infants

PLACE THE BACK OF YOUR HEEL AGAINST THE EDGE OF AN UPRIGHT STICK SET EXACTLY ON THIS LINE MARKED →A

PLACE THE BACK OF YOUR HEEL AGAINST THE EDGE OF AN UPRIGHT STICK SET EXACTLY ON THIS LINE MARKED →A

DIRECTIONS

How to Measure:

Remove your shoe—place the catalog flat on the floor and set the edge of any straight stick or piece of cardboard exactly on the point marked "A"—

Hold the stick or piece of cardboard straight up at right angle and gently place the back of heel of your foot against it, being careful not to push the stick off of the point marked "A" on the chart.

Finally, stand erect, resting the foot firmly on the chart. The figure nearest the extreme end of your big toe indicates the size of shoe you should order.

Be sure to state what width you wear.

IMPORTANT!

Whenever possible, give us the size of your old shoe, being careful to copy the figures as they are, as the slightest changes between the figures—even a dash—changes entirely the size and width. If you are unable to state the size, then take your measure according to the instructions given above.

Definitions of Widths and Sizes:

EE—denotes extra wide shoe.
E—denotes wide shoe.
D—denotes medium narrow shoe.
C—denotes narrow shoe.

Sizes:

Women's—2½ to 9.	Infants' soft soles—0 to 4.
Misses'—11½ to 2.	Men's—6 to 12.
Childs'—8½ to 11.	Boys'—1 to 5½.
Infants'—2 to 8.	Little Boys'—9 to 13½.

PHILIPSBORN'S "Extra Quality" SHOES and RUBBERS
for the Entire Family

WOMEN'S—MISSES'—CHILDREN'S—INFANTS'—MEN'S—BOYS'—YOUTHS'

Do Not Measure Your Shoe Measure Your Stocking Foot

Don't Tear Out This Page You Will Need It Again

LATEST AND SMARTEST STYLES
Extra Quality

These Shoes Designed by IRENE CASTLE. STAMPED BY PHILIPSBORN'S

5K7384 *In the very fore front of fashion is this woman's pump, the newest idea in strap models.*
Attractive strap pump made of fine genuine black kid leather with fashionable cut-outs on strap. Beautiful butterfly ornament. Louis heel with vanity plate. SIZES: 2½ to 8. WIDTHS: EE, E, D and C.
PRICE, PREPAID to your home, **$3.68**

5K7383 *The fashionable Egyptian anklet tie pump is here charmingly designed for you by Irene Castle, herself.*
This handsome genuine black kid leather pump is made very effective with new style cut-outs on the strap and sides. Mercerized silk ribbon ties. Louis heel with vanity heel plate. SIZES: 2½ to 8. WIDTHS: EE, E, D and C. PRICE, PREPAID to your home, **$3.78**

5K7385 *Your money's worth and more in this latest, stylish and most daintily designed pump for women.*
One of the newest of the novelty one-strap pumps so fashionable this season, this model is made of genuine **black kid leather**. It is made over a slim toe last, and has fashionable cut-outs on the sides. Novelty bead ornaments trim both vamp and strap. New style Parisian Cuban heel. A smart and dressy pump offered at a special reduction in price. SIZES: 2½ to 8. WIDTHS: EE, E, D and C. PRICE, PREPAID to your home, **$3.68**

5K7386 *The latest in women's novelty footwear—unusually low priced at $3.98.*
Here is the new Princess instep strap pump. It is made of genuine **black kid leather**, with new style perforations over a white inlay as pictured. Parisian Cuban heel with vanity heel plate. It would be hard to find a more effective and graceful style than this pump, and the price is extremely moderate for the style and quality. Ideal for dress wear. SIZES: 2½ to 8. WIDTHS: EE, E, D and C. PRICE, PREPAID to your home, **$3.98**

PHILIPSBORN'S Give Away Over $500,000. See Page 3 for This and Other Interesting Facts

PHILIPSBORN'S

WOMEN'S NOVELTY SHOES
Lowest Prices

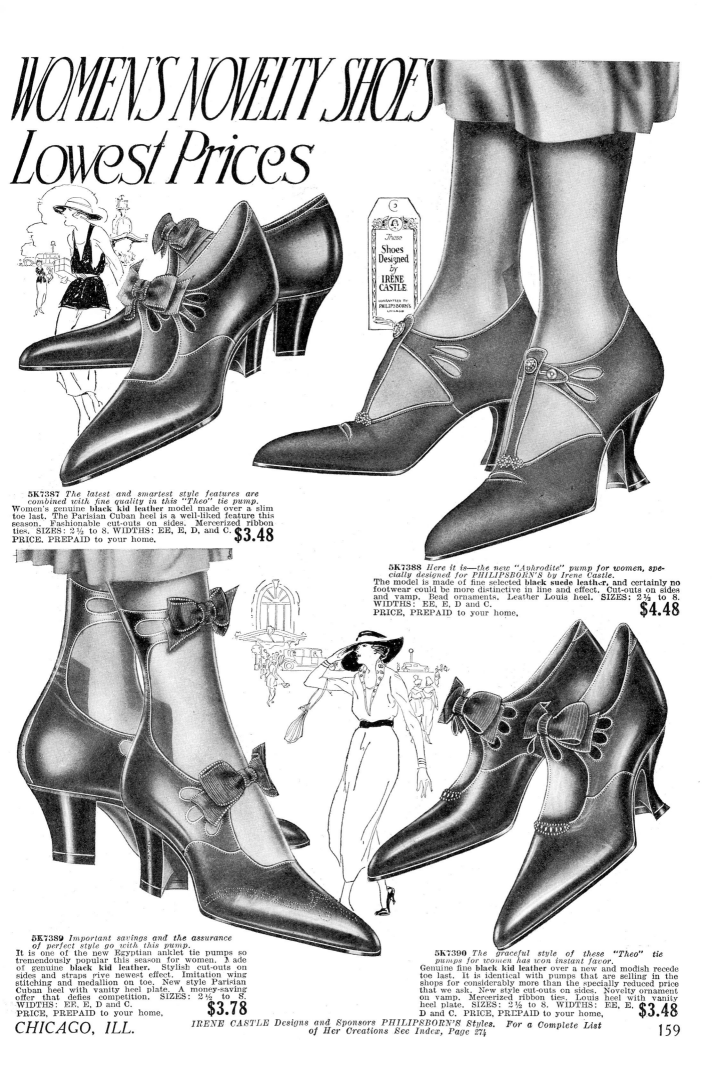

5K7387 *The latest and smartest style features are combined with fine quality in this "Theo" tie pump.* Women's genuine **black kid leather** model made over a slim toe last. The Parisian Cuban heel is a well-liked feature this season. Fashionable cut-outs on sides. Mercerized ribbon ties. SIZES: 2½ to 8. WIDTHS: EE, E, D, and C. PRICE, PREPAID to your home, **$3.48**

These Shoes Designed by IRENE CASTLE GUARANTEED BY PHILIPSBORN'S CHICAGO

5K7388 *Here it is—the new "Aphrodite" pump for women, specially designed for PHILIPSBORN'S by Irene Castle.* The model is made of fine selected **black suede leather**, and certainly no footwear could be more distinctive in line and effect. Cut-outs on sides and vamp. Bead ornaments. Leather Louis heel. SIZES: 2½ to 8. WIDTHS: EE, E, D and C. PRICE, PREPAID to your home, **$4.48**

5K7389 *Important savings and the assurance of perfect style go with this pump.* It is one of the new Egyptian anklet tie pumps so tremendously popular this season for women. Made of genuine **black kid leather**. Stylish cut-outs on sides and straps give newest effect. Imitation wing stitching and medallion on toe. New style Parisian Cuban heel with vanity heel plate. A money-saving offer that defies competition. SIZES: 2½ to 8. WIDTHS: EE, E, D and C. PRICE, PREPAID to your home, **$3.78**

5K7390 *The graceful style of these "Theo" tie pumps for women has won instant favor.* Genuine fine **black kid leather** over a new and modish recede toe last. It is identical with pumps that are selling in the shops for considerably more than the specially reduced price that we ask. New style cut-outs on sides. Novelty ornament on vamp. Mercerized ribbon ties. Louis heel with vanity heel plate. SIZES: 2½ to 8. WIDTHS: EE, E, D and C. PRICE, PREPAID to your home, **$3.48**

CHICAGO, ILL.

IRENE CASTLE Designs and Sponsors PHILIPSBORN'S Styles. For a Complete List of Her Creations See Index, Page 274

WOMEN'S LATEST STYLE
Lowest Prices Pre-

5K7391 *Women's new "THEO" tie pump* of **black chrome patent leather,** *greatly underpriced.* New style cut-outs. Louis heel. A splendid value. SIZES: 2½ to 8. WIDTHS: EE, E, D and C. PRICE, PREPAID to your home, **$3.68**

5K7364 *Women's fashionable "THEO" tie pump developed in* fine **black kid-finished leather.** Perforations. Smartest walking heel. SIZES: 2½ to 8. WIDTHS: EE, E, D, and C. PRICE, PREPAID to your home, **$2.78**

5K7376 *The season's popular "THEO" tie pump, and a splendid bargain, too, at this low price.* Women's handsome **black suede leather** model has fashionable cut-outs on sides. Ribbon ties. Louis heel. SIZES: 2½ to 8. WIDTHS: EE, E, D, and C. PRICE, PREPAID to your home, **$3.98**

5K7363 *Big values instead of big profits has always been the PHILIPSBORN'S policy.* Women's handsome two-eyelet pump of **black chrome patent leather.** Another example of savings we give you. Louis heel. SIZES: 2½ to 8. WIDTHS: EE, E, D, and C. PRICE, PREPAID to your home, **$2.78**

5K7392 *The latest creation in Women's footwear—one-strap pump.* Made of fine **black chrome patent leather.** Novelty cut-outs on sides. Parisian walking heel. SIZES: 2½ to 8. WIDTHS: EE, E, D, and C. PRICE, PREPAID to your home, **$3.78**

5K7309 *A favorite style in a Women's Colonial pump.* Made of fine soft genuine **black kid leather.** Handsome cut steel buckle. Louis heel. A rare value. SIZES: 2½ to 8. WIDTHS: EE, E, D, and C. PRICE, PREPAID to your home, **$3.48**

5K7394 *To be in perfect style this season, every woman should have a pair of these handsome "THEO" tie pumps at this greatly reduced price.* **Black chrome patent leather** model with stylish cut-outs. Medium walking heel. SIZES: 2½ to 8. WIDTHS: EE, E, D, and C. PRICE, PREPAID to your home, **$3.68**

NOVELTY SHOE CREATIONS
-Paid To Your Home

5K7359 *Women's two eyelet tie pump* of **fine black kid-finished leather.** *Less than cost.* Pointed tongue. Ribbon ties. Louis heel. SIZES: 2½ to 8. WIDTHS: EE, E, D. and C. PRICE, PREPAID to your home, **$2.78**

5K7393 *The very newest is this woman's crossed-strap pump of* **black chrome patent leather.** Cut-outs on sides. Louis heel. Smart and dressy. SIZES: 2½ to 8. WIDTHS: EE, E, D, and C. PRICE, PREPAID to your home, **$3.78**

5K7381 *Fashion's latest creation in women's foot-wear — the Egyptian anklet tie pump.* This very distinctive model is made of **fine quality black suede leather.** Cut-outs on strap and sides. Parisian Cuban heel. SIZES: 2½ to 8. WIDTHS: EE, E, D, and C. PRICE, PREPAID to your home, **$4.48**

5K7312 *The splendid saving in this woman's pump is another proof of our wonderful values.* Made of **black kid-finished leather** with a smart walking heel, this pump gives a wonderfully trim appearance to the foot. SIZES: 2½ to 8. WIDTHS: EE, E, D, and C. PRICE, PREPAID to your home, **$2.98**

5K7380 *Decidedly smart and up-to-date is this woman's cut-out crossed-strap pump of genuine fine* **black kid leather.** *Very fashionable and dressy.* This model features the new Parisian walking heel with vanity heel plate, the very latest in modern shoe making. SIZES: 2½ to 8. WIDTHS: EE, E, D, and C. PRICE, PREPAID to your home, **$3.68**

5K7304 *Here is a money-saving shoe value that is second to none.* Woman's stylish Oxfords made of fine **black chrome patent leather** over a dressy last. Louis heel. SIZES: 2½ to 8. WIDTHS: EE, E, D, and C. PRICE, PREPAID to your home, **$2.78**

5K7368 *For dress wear you choose this woman's Colonial pump.* Made of **black chrome patent leather.** Handsome novelty buckle. Cuban walking heel. A big value. SIZES: 2½ to 8. WIDTHS: EE, E, D, and C. PRICE, PREPAID to your home, **$3.68**

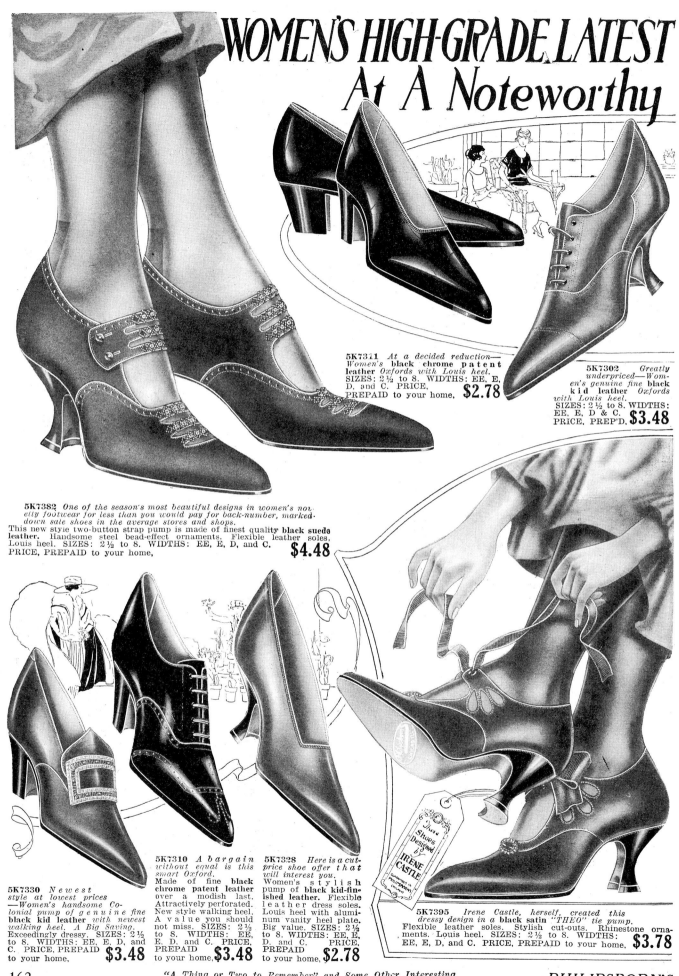

WOMEN'S HIGH-GRADE LATEST
At A Noteworthy

5K7311 *At a decided reduction*— Women's **black chrome patent leather** *Oxfords with Louis heel.* SIZES: 2½ to 8. WIDTHS: EE, E, D, and C. PRICE, PREPAID to your home, **$2.78**

5K7302 *Greatly underpriced*—Women's genuine fine **black kid leather** *Oxfords with Louis heel.* SIZES: 2½ to 8. WIDTHS: EE, E, D & C. PRICE, PREP'D. **$3.48**

5K7382 *One of the season's most beautiful designs in women's novelty footwear for less than you would pay for back-number, marked-down sale shoes in the average stores and shops.* This new style two-button strap pump is made of finest quality **black suede leather.** Handsome steel bead-effect ornaments. Flexible leather soles, Louis heel. SIZES: 2½ to 8. WIDTHS: EE, E, D, and C. PRICE, PREPAID to your home, **$4.48**

5K7330 *Newest style at lowest prices* —Women's handsome Colonial pump of *genuine fine* **black kid leather** *with newest walking heel.* A Big Saving. Exceedingly dressy. SIZES: 2½ to 8. WIDTHS: EE, E, D, and C. PRICE, PREPAID to your home, **$3.48**

5K7310 *A bargain without equal is this smart Oxford.* Made of fine **black chrome patent leather.** Attractively perforated. New style walking heel. A value you should not miss. SIZES: 2½ to 8. WIDTHS: EE, E, D, and C. PRICE, PREPAID to your home, **$3.48**

5K7328 *Here is a cut-price shoe offer that will interest you.* Women's stylish pump of **black kid-finished leather.** Flexible leather dress soles. Louis heel with aluminum vanity heel plate. Big value. SIZES: 2½ to 8. WIDTHS: EE, E, D, and C. PRICE, PREPAID to your home, **$2.78**

5K7395 *Irene Castle, herself, created this dressy design in a black satin "THEO" tie pump.* Flexible leather soles. Stylish cut-outs. Rhinestone ornaments. Louis heel. SIZES: 2½ to 8. WIDTHS: EE, E, D, and C. PRICE, PREPAID to your home, **$3.78**

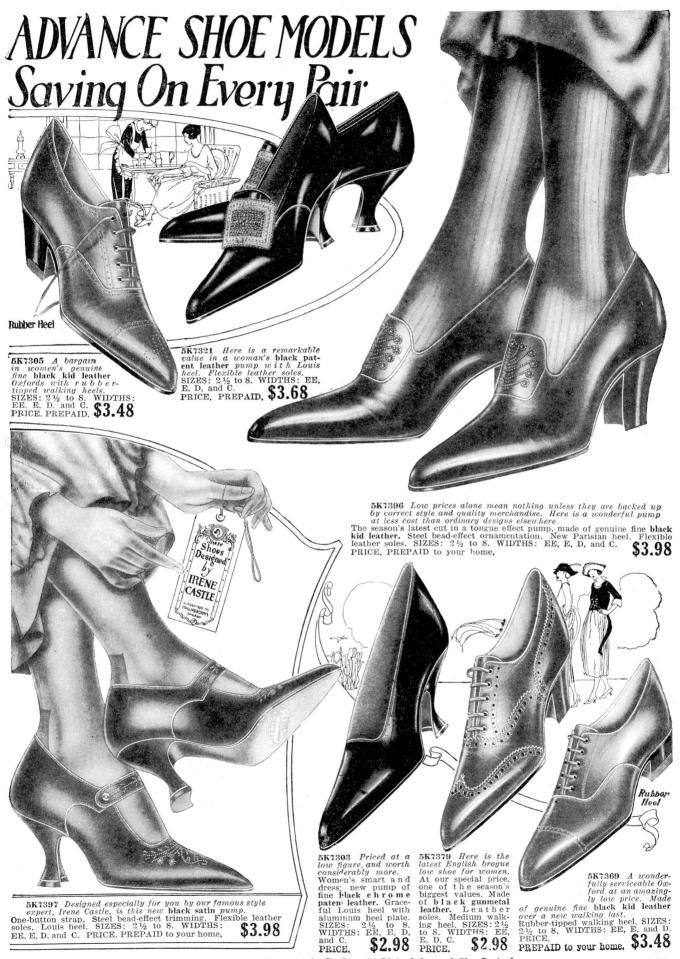

ADVANCE SHOE MODELS
Saving On Every Pair

Rubber Heel

5K7305 *A bargain in women's genuine fine black kid leather Oxfords with rubber-tipped walking heels.* SIZES: 2½ to 8. WIDTHS: EE, E, D, and C. PRICE, PREPAID. **$3.48**

5K7321 *Here is a remarkable value in a woman's* **black patent leather** *pump with Louis heel. Flexible leather soles.* SIZES: 2½ to 8. WIDTHS: EE, E, D, and C. PRICE, PREPAID, **$3.68**

5K7396 *Low prices alone mean nothing unless they are backed up by correct style and quality merchandise. Here is a wonderful pump at less cost than ordinary designs elsewhere.* The season's latest cut in a tongue effect pump, made of genuine fine **black kid leather.** Steel bead-effect ornamentation. New Parisian heel. Flexible leather soles. SIZES: 2½ to 8. WIDTHS: EE, E, D, and C. PRICE, PREPAID to your home, **$3.98**

These Shoes Designed by IRENE CASTLE

5K7397 *Designed especially for you by our famous style expert, Irene Castle, is this new* **black satin** *pump.* One-button strap. Steel bead-effect trimming. Flexible leather soles. Louis heel. SIZES: 2½ to 8. WIDTHS: EE, E, D, and C. PRICE, PREPAID to your home, **$3.98**

5K7303 *Priced at a low figure, and worth considerably more.* Women's smart and dress new pump of fine **black chrome** **paten** leather. Graceful Louis heel with aluminum heel plate. SIZES: 2½ to 8. WIDTHS: EE, E, D, and C. PRICE. **$2.98**

5K7379 *Here is the latest English brogue low shoe for women.* At our special price, one of the season's biggest values. Made of **black gunmetal** leather. Leather soles. Medium walking heel. SIZES: 2½ to 8. WIDTHS: EE, E, D, C. PRICE. **$2.98**

Rubber Heel

5K7369 *A wonderfully serviceable Oxford at an amazingly low price.* Made of genuine fine **black kid** leather over a new walking last. Rubber-tipped walking heel. SIZES: 2½ to 8. WIDTHS: EE, E, and D. PRICE. PREPAID to your home. **$3.48**

MOST POPULAR SPRING and SUMMER
Great Price Reductions!

Flexible Leather Soles and Rubber Heels

Rubber Heel

5K7308 Women's one-strap slippers of black glazed kid-finished leather, *house or street wear.* Made with flexible leather soles and rubber-tipped heels. A wonderfully comfortable slipper at a big saving. SIZES: 3 to 8. Wide width. PRICE, PREPAID to your home, **$1.88**

5K7702 *The reductions that you have been waiting for are offered you in these wonderful shoe values.* Here are women's fine **Russia leather** sandals at only $1.98. They have two adjustable straps and are made by the famous Goodyear stitch-down welt process. Strong leather soles. Rubber heels. SIZES: 2½ to 8. WIDTHS: EE, E, and D. PRICE, PREPAID to your home. **$1.98**

5K7335 PHILIPSBORN'S *popular baby-doll last pump in the very latest crossed-strap design.* Made of fine **black chrome patent leather** and is one of the biggest values ever offered at this low price. Straps are smartly cut out, novelty ornament on the vamp. SIZES: 2½ to 8. WIDTHS: EE, E, and D. PRICE, PREP'D to your home. **$2.98**

5K7372

5K7401

5K7339

5K7372 *Here are prices that are a direct challenge to profiteers.* Imagine getting one of the season's most stylish Oxfords at the price we ask. Made of fine **black kid-finished leather** over a new last. Graceful Louis heel with Vanity plate. An immense value. SIZES: 2½ to 8. WIDTHS: EE, E, and D. PRICE, PREPAID, **$2.48**

5K7339 *When you see this slipper you will marvel that such fine leather and such superior workmanship may be had for so little money. You get all the savings.* It is just another of the wonderful values offered by PHILIPSBORN'S, the lowest priced mail order house in the U. S. A. The slipper is in one-strap style and is made of fine glazed **black kid**-finished leather. SIZES: 2½ to 8. WIDTHS: EE, E, and D. PRICE, PREPAID, **$1.88**

5K7401 *Worn with any of the new hosiery shown on pages 209 to 215 of this catalog, this new two-eyelet pump will be very dressy and up to date.* Fine **black kid**-finished leather, and is a marvelous value, which you will find impossible to duplicate elsewhere at our cut price. It is nattily finished with ribbon bows. Cuban heel. Economical, and extremely stylish. SIZES: 2½ to 8. WIDTHS: EE, E, and D. PRICE, PREPAID, **$1.98**

$1.98 PREPAID

5K7336 *Another very popular style in a baby-doll pump for women.* This pump is an extraordinary value. It is made of fine **black patent leather** over a baby-doll last. Low heel. SIZES: 2½ to 8. WIDTHS: EE, E, and D. PRICE, PREPAID to your home, **$1.98**

STYLES in WOMEN'S LOW-CUT SHOES
Satisfaction Guaranteed

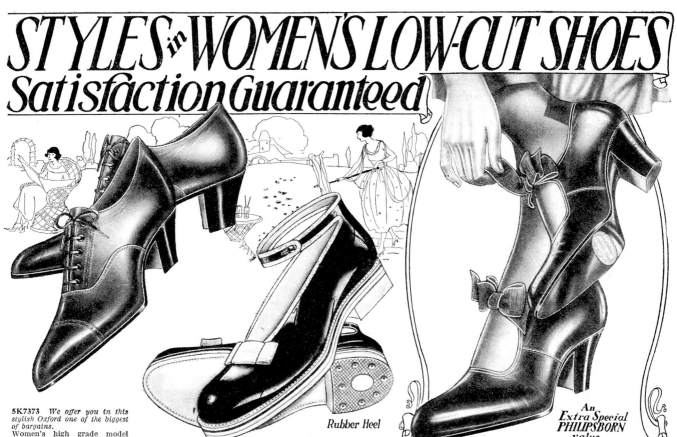

5K7373 We offer you in this stylish Oxford one of the biggest of bargains.
Women's high grade model made of **black kid-finished leather.** Medium recede toe finished with perforated tip. Leather soles. Cuban heel. SIZES: 2½ to 8. WIDTHS: EE, E and D.
PRICE, PREP'D to your home, **$2.48**

Rubber Heel

5K7713 Our tremendous cash purchases have made it possible to offer this truly wonderful value in women's popular pump of fine **black chrome patent leather.**
White binding and white tailored bow. Made by the famous stitch-down welt process. White ivory leather soles and low rubber heels. SIZES: 2½ to 8. WIDTHS: EE, E, and D. PRICE, PREPAID to your home, **$2.48**

An Extra Special PHILIPSBORN value

5K7400 An outright substantial saving on every pair of these stylish extra quality "THEO" tie pumps.
Made of fine **black kid-finished leather** over a modish new last. Ribbon ties. Flexible leather soles. Cuban walking heel. SIZES: 2½ to 8. WIDTHS: EE, E and D PRICE, PREPAID to your home, **$1.98**

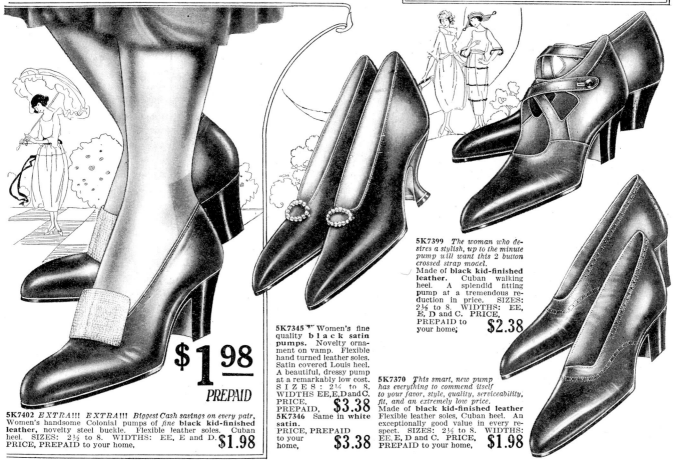

$1.98 PREPAID

5K7402 *EXTRA!!! EXTRA!!!* Biggest Cash savings on every pair, Women's handsome Colonial pumps of fine **black kid-finished leather,** novelty steel buckle. Flexible leather soles. Cuban heel. SIZES: 2½ to 8. WIDTHS: EE, E and D. PRICE, PREPAID to your home, **$1.98**

5K7345 Women's fine quality **black satin pumps.** Novelty ornament on vamp. Flexible hand turned leather soles. Satin covered Louis heel. A beautiful, dressy pump at a remarkably low cost. SIZES: 2½ to 8. WIDTHS EE, E, D and C. PRICE, PREPAID, **$3.38**
5K7346 Same in white satin. PRICE, PREPAID to your home, **$3.38**

5K7399 The woman who desires a stylish, up to the minute pump will want this 2 button crossed strap model.
Made of **black kid-finished leather.** Cuban walking heel. A splendid fitting pump at a tremendous reduction in price. SIZES: 2½ to 8. WIDTHS: EE, E, D and C. PRICE, PREPAID to your home, **$2.38**

5K7370 This smart, new pump has everything to commend itself to your favor, style, quality, serviceability, fit, and an extremely low price.
Made of **black kid-finished leather** Flexible leather soles. Cuban heel. An exceptionally good value in every respect. SIZES: 2½ to 8. WIDTHS: EE, E, D and C. PRICE, PREPAID to your home, **$1.98**

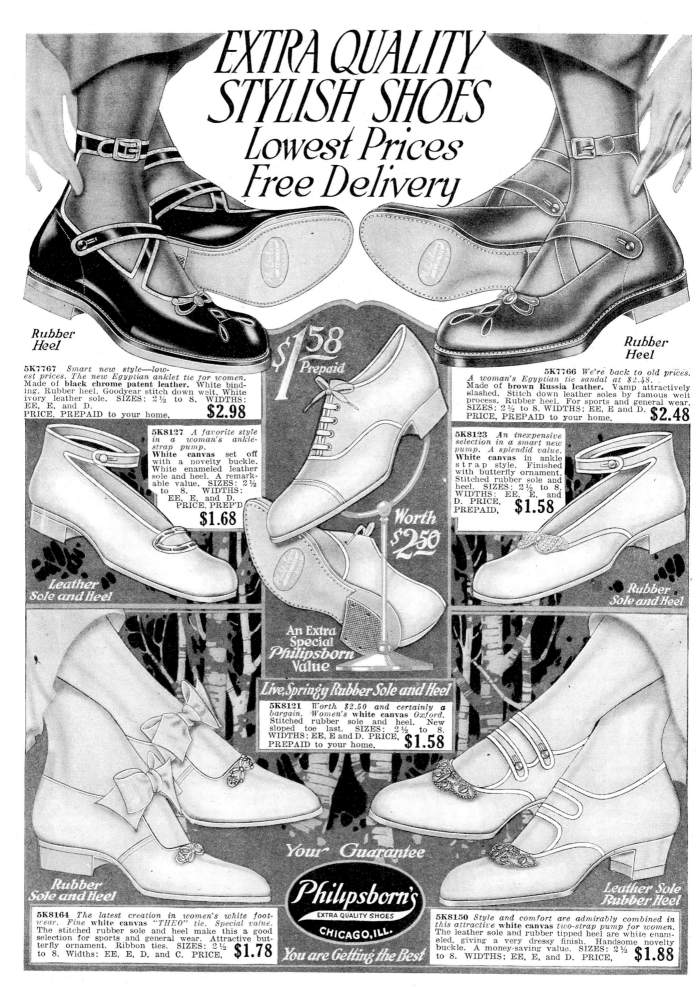

EXTRA QUALITY STYLISH SHOES
Lowest Prices
Free Delivery

Rubber Heel

5K7767 *Smart new style—lowest prices. The new Egyptian anklet tie for women.* Made of **black chrome patent leather.** White binding. Rubber heel. Goodyear stitch down welt. White ivory leather sole. SIZES: 2½ to 8. WIDTHS: EE, E, and D. PRICE, PREPAID to your home, **$2.98**

5K8127 *A favorite style in a woman's ankle-strap pump.* **White canvas** set off with a novelty buckle. White enameled leather sole and heel. A remarkable value. SIZES: 2½ to 8. WIDTHS: EE, E, and D. PRICE, PREP'D **$1.68**

Leather Sole and Heel

$1⁵⁸ Prepaid

Worth $2⁵⁰

An Extra Special Philipsborn Value

Live, Springy Rubber Sole and Heel

5K8121 *Worth $2.50 and certainly a bargain.* Women's **white canvas** *Oxford.* Stitched rubber sole and heel. New sloped toe last. SIZES: 2½ to 8. WIDTHS: EE, E and D. PRICE, PREPAID to your home, **$1.58**

Rubber Heel

5K7766 *We're back to old prices. A woman's Egyptian tie sandal at $2.48.* Made of **brown Russia leather.** Vamp attractively slashed. Stitch down leather soles by famous welt process. Rubber heel. For sports and general wear. SIZES: 2½ to 8. WIDTHS: EE, E and D. PRICE, PREPAID to your home, **$2.48**

5K8123 *An inexpensive selection in a smart new pump. A splendid value.* **White canvas** in ankle strap style. Finished with butterfly ornament. Stitched rubber sole and heel. SIZES: 2½ to 8. WIDTHS: EE, E, and D. PRICE, PREPAID, **$1.58**

Rubber Sole and Heel

Rubber Sole and Heel

5K8164 *The latest creation in women's white footwear. Fine* **white canvas** *"THEO" tie. Special value.* The stitched rubber sole and heel make this a good selection for sports and general wear. Attractive butterfly ornament. Ribbon ties. SIZES: 2½ to 8. Widths: EE, E, D, and C. PRICE, **$1.78**

Your Guarantee

Philipsborn's
EXTRA QUALITY SHOES
CHICAGO, ILL.
You are Getting the Best

Leather Sole Rubber Heel

5K8150 *Style and comfort are admirably combined in this attractive* **white canvas** *two-strap pump for women.* The leather sole and rubber tipped heel are white enameled, giving a very dressy finish. Handsome novelty buckle. A money-saving value. SIZES: 2½ to 8. WIDTHS: EE, E, and D. PRICE, **$1.88**

PHILIPSBORN'S INDIVIDUAL CREATIONS for Every OCCASION

5K7765 *The season's newest shoe style in an Havana brown genuine kid leather* Egyptian anklet pump. Fashionable cut-outs. Louis heel. SIZES: 2½ to 8. WIDTHS: EE, E, D and C. PRICE, PREPAID to your home, **$3.98**

5K7773 *Latest novelty strap pump in the new* "Morning Mist" *grey colored kid-finished leather.* Parisian-Cuban heel. SIZES: 2½ to 8. WIDTHS: EE, E, D and C. PRICE, PREPAID to your home, **$3.98**

5K7586 *Here is the new* "tongueless" *boot of* Midnight Blue kid-finished leather. *Height 10 inches.* Louis heel with vanity heel plate. SIZES: 2½ to 8. WIDTHS: EE, E, D and C. PRICE, PREPAID to your home, **$5.98**

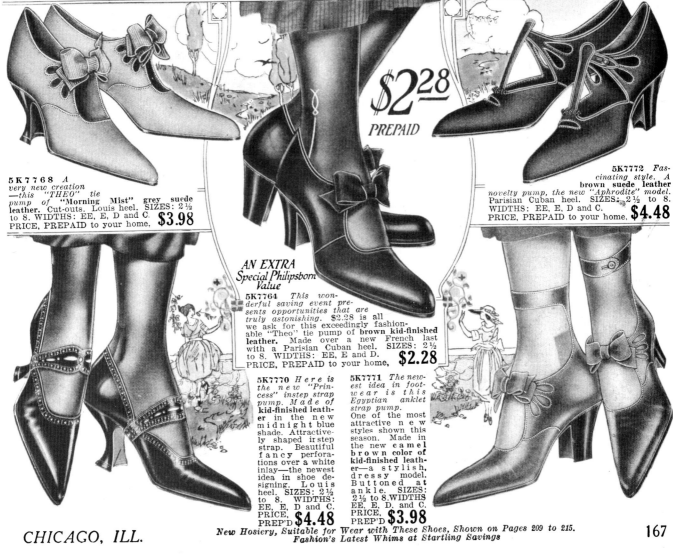

5K7768 *A very new creation* —this "THEO" tie pump of "Morning Mist" grey suede leather. Cut-outs. Louis heel. SIZES: 2½ to 8. WIDTHS: EE, E, D and C. PRICE, PREPAID to your home, **$3.98**

$2²⁸ PREPAID

AN EXTRA Special Philipsborn Value

5K7764 *This wonderful saving event presents opportunities that are truly astonishing.* $2.28 is all we ask for this exceedingly fashionable "Theo" tie pump of **brown kid-finished leather.** Made over a new French last with a Parisian Cuban heel. SIZES: 2½ to 8. WIDTHS: EE, E and D. PRICE, PREPAID to your home, **$2.28**

5K7772 *Fascinating style.* A **brown suede leather** *novelty pump, the new* "Aphrodite" *model.* Parisian Cuban heel. SIZES: 2½ to 8. WIDTHS: EE, E, D and C. PRICE, PREPAID to your home, **$4.48**

5K7770 *Here is the new* "Princess" *instep strap pump.* Made of kid-finished leather in the new midnight blue shade. Attractively shaped instep strap. Beautiful fancy perforations over a white inlay—the newest idea in shoe designing. Louis heel. SIZES: 2½ to 8. WIDTHS: EE, E, D and C. PRICE, PREP'D **$4.48**

5K7771 *The newest idea in footwear is this Egyptian anklet strap pump.* One of the most attractive new styles shown this season. Made in the new camel brown color of kid-finished leather—a stylish, dressy model. Buttoned at ankle. SIZES: 2½ to 8. WIDTHS: EE, E, D and C. PRICE, PREP'D **$3.98**

CHICAGO, ILL.

New Hosiery, Suitable for Wear with These Shoes, Shown on Pages 209 to 215.
Fashion's Latest Whims at Startling Savings

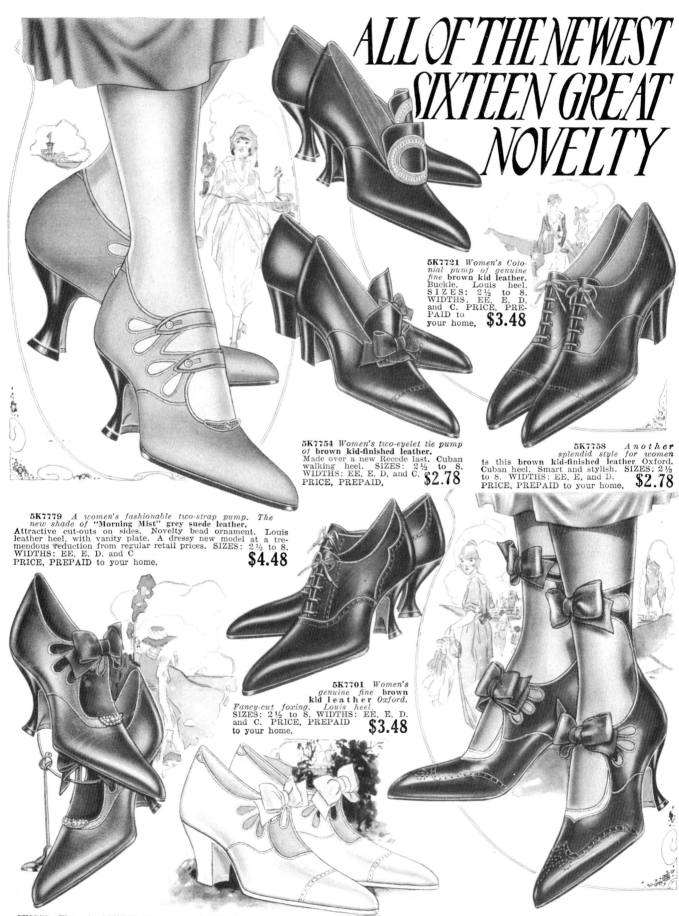

ALL OF THE NEWEST SIXTEEN GREAT NOVELTY

5K7721 *Women's Colonial pump of genuine fine* **brown kid leather.** Buckle. Louis heel. SIZES: 2½ to 8. WIDTHS: EE, E, D, and C. PRICE, PREPAID to your home, **$3.48**

5K7754 *Women's two-eyelet tie pump of* **brown kid-finished leather.** Made over a new Recede last. Cuban walking heel. SIZES: 2½ to 8. WIDTHS: EE, E, D, and C. PRICE, PREPAID, **$2.78**

5K7758 *Another splendid style for women* is this **brown kid-finished leather Oxford.** Cuban heel. Smart and stylish. SIZES: 2½ to 8. WIDTHS: EE, E, and D. PRICE, PREPAID to your home, **$2.78**

5K7779 *A women's fashionable two-strap pump. The new shade of* **"Morning Mist"** *grey suede leather.* Attractive cut-outs on sides. Novelty bead ornament. Louis leather heel, with vanity plate. A dressy new model at a tremendous reduction from regular retail prices. SIZES: 2½ to 8. WIDTHS: EE, E, D, and C. PRICE, PREPAID to your home, **$4.48**

5K7701 *Women's genuine fine* **brown kid leather Oxford.** *Fancy-cut foxing. Louis heel.* SIZES: 2½ to 8. WIDTHS: EE, E, D, and C. PRICE, PREPAID to your home, **$3.48**

5K7757 *Women's* **"THEO"** *tie pump of* **camel brown kid-finished leather.** Novelty bead ornament. Cut-outs. Louis heel. SIZES: 2½ to 8. WIDTHS: EE, E, D, and C. PRICE, PREPAID to your home, **$3.48**

5K7778 *Women's* **white kid-finished leather "THEO"** *tie pump with fashionable cut-outs on sides.* Parisian Cuban heel and leather sole have white enamel finish. Perforated tip. Very economically priced. SIZES: 2½ to 8. WIDTHS: EE, E, D, and C. PRICE, PREPAID to your home, **$3.98**

5K7777 *Women's* Egyptian anklet tie pump made of **kid-finished leather** *in the beautiful Alice blue shade.* White inlay on vamp. Cut-outs on strap and sides. Louis heel. One of the season's most beautiful models. SIZES: 2½ to 8. WIDTHS: EE, E, D, and C. PRICE, PREPAID to your home, **$4.98**

You Must Be Satisfied With Everything You Buy at PHILIPSBORN'S or Your Money Back

PHILIPSBORN'S

DESIGNS and COLORS
SPECIAL VALUES
LOW CUTS

5K7756 Women's two eyelet tie pump of brown kid-finished leather. *Louis heel.* SIZES: 2½ to 8. WIDTHS: EE, E, D, & C. PRICE, PREPAID, **$2.78**

5K7780 One of the most popular pumps of genuine fine brown kid leather for women. Attractively beaded tongue. Cuban walking heel. SIZES: 2½ to 8. WIDTHS: EE, E, D, and C. PRICE, PREPAID to your home, **$3.98**

5K7776 Unexcelled value in a women's genuine fine brown kid leather Colonial pump. Handsome cut steel buckle. Cuban heel. SIZES: 2½ to 8. WIDTHS, EE, E, D, and C. PRICE, PREPAID to your home, **$3.48**

5K7775 These smart, "THEO" tie pumps for women have all the high quality of pumps selling elsewhere at very much higher prices. Made of kid-finished leather in the newest and popular shade of Alice blue. New style cut-outs on sides. Beaded ornament on vamp. Parisian walking heel, with vanity plate. SIZES: 2½ to 8. WIDTHS: EE, E, D, and C. PRICE, PREPAID to your home, **$3.48**

Rubber Heels

5K7700 Extra quality Brogue Oxford of genuine fine brown kid leather. Cuban rubber tipped heel. SIZES: 2½ to 8. WIDTHS: EE, E, D, and C. PRICE, PREPAID, **$3.48**

5K7774 One of the very smartest of the crossed strap pumps at a tremendous reduction in price. Genuine brown kid leather model with novelty cut-outs on straps. Parisian walking heel. Very dressy. SIZES: 2½ to 8. WIDTHS: EE, E, D, and C. PRICE, PREPAID to your home. **$3.78**

5K7744 Here is White footwear that will suit the most particular and fastidious women. Colonial pump of fine quality white kid-finished leather. Novelty metal buckle. Louis heel. SIZES: 2½ to 8. WIDTHS: EE, E, D, and C. PRICE, PREPAID to your home, **$3.98**

5K7760 Here is the popular "THEO" tie pump for women at big reduction. Made of genuine brown kid leather. Bead ornament. Cuban heel. SIZES: 2½ to 8. WIDTHS: EE, E, D, and C. PRICE, PREPAID to your home, **$3.48**

CHICAGO, ILL.

For Index See Page 274 and Remember PHILIPSBORN'S Prepay All Transportation Charges. There Are No Express or Mailing Charges for You to Pay

169

VOGUE'S SMARTEST DESIGNS and COLORS In Women's Distinctive Boots

5K7591 *Women's stunning new 9-inch boots —all the rage with smart dressers.* Beautiful **blue kid-finished** leather. Fancy perforations over a white inlay. Louis heel. SIZES: 2½ to 8. WIDTHS: EE, E. D, and C. PRICE, PREPAID. **$5.98**

5K7592 *Women's 9-inch boot of* **camel brown** kid finished leather. Orange silk stitching. Perforations over a white inlay. Parisian walking heel. SIZES: 2½ to 8. WIDTHS: EE, E, D, and C. PRICE, PREPAID to your home, **$5.98**

5K7590 *A beauty in a woman's 9-inch boot and exceptionally low priced.* Beautiful **blue kid-finished** leather. Perforations over white inlay. Newest Parisian walking heel. SIZES: 2½ to 8. WIDTHS: EE, E, D. C. PRICE. **$5.98**

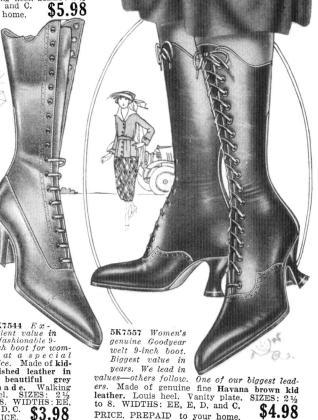

5K7531 *A woman's dressy walking 9-inch boot that will give you every satisfaction.* **Brown kid-finished leather** model. Wing effect tip Cuban leather walking heel. SIZES: 2½ to 8. WIDTHS: EE, E, D, and C. PRICE, PREPAID to your home, **$3.48**
5K7521 Same only high Louis heel. PRICE, PREPAID, **$3.48**

5K7552 *Here is a smart 9-inch walking boot for women. Cannot be equaled.* **Brown kid-finished leather.** Medium rubber-tipped walking heel. SIZES: 2½ to 8. WIDTHS: EE, E, D, and C. PRICE, PREP'D, **$3.98**

5K7544 *Excellent value in a fashionable 9-inch boot for women at a special price.* Made of kid-finished leather in a beautiful **grey shade.** Walking heel. SIZES: 2½ to 8. WIDTHS: EE, E, D, C. PRICE, **$3.98**

5K7557 *Women's genuine Goodyear welt 9-inch boot. Biggest value in years. We lead in values—others follow. One of our biggest leaders.* Made of genuine fine **Havana brown kid leather.** Louis heel. Vanity plate. SIZES: 2½ to 8. WIDTHS: EE, E, D, and C. PRICE, PREPAID to your home, **$4.98**

WOMEN'S DOUBLE WEAR SERVICE SHOES
6 Months Wear Guaranteed

$3.48 Prepaid
BROWN OR BLACK

WHITE Fiber Soles

5K8530 A fine value in misses' black gunmetal leather shoes. English nature-tread last. Stitched white fibre-rubber soles. Medium low leather heel. SIZES: 11½ to 2. Wide widths. PRICE, PREPAID to your home, **$2.78**

BROWN OR BLACK

5K8504 Misses' serviceable black gunmetal leather shoes. Oak-tanned leather soles. SIZES: 11½ to 2. Wide widths. PRICE, PREPAID to your home **$2.78**
5K8919 Same in brown leather. PRICE, PREPAID to your home **$3.18**

5K7039 Women's sturdy Blucher style service shoe of chrome black ooze leather. Made over a broad toe last. Strong stitched leather soles. An extraordinary value. SIZES: 2½ to 8. Wide widths. PRICE, PREPAID to your home, **$1.98**

5K7543 Brown.   **5K7037** Black.
Women's double-wear service shoes—guaranteed to wear six months or a new pair free of charge at less than pre-war prices. A value that defies competition. Comes in brown or black chrome tanned elk leather. Heavy double-wear "KROMIDE" leather soles. Solid leather throughout. SIZES: 2½ to 8. Wide widths. PRICE, PREPAID to your home, **$3.48**

Guarantee Certificate. Six months satisfactory wear or return 5 K 7037 and 5 K 7543

5K7040 Women's black gunmetal leather blucher with dull black leather top. At less than cost. Heavy leather extension soles. Medium low leather heel. Broad toe last—ideal for walking. SIZES: 2½ to 8. Wide width. PRICE, PREPAID to your home, **$2.98**

Exquisite Soft Sole Footwear for Infants

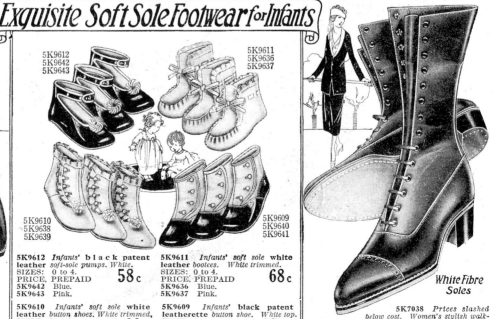

5K9612
5K9642
5K9643

5K9611
5K9636
5K9637

5K9610
5K9638
5K9639

5K9609
5K9640
5K9641

5K9612 Infants' black patent leather soft-sole pumps. White. SIZES: 0 to 4. PRICE, PREPAID **58c**
5K9642 Blue.
5K9643 Pink.

5K9611 Infants' soft sole white leather bootees. White trimmed. SIZES: 0 to 4. PRICE, PREPAID **68c**
5K9636 Blue.
5K9637 Pink.

5K9610 Infants' soft sole white leather button shoes. White trimmed. SIZES: 0 to 4. PRICE, PREPAID **68c**
5K9638 Blue.
5K9639 Pink.

5K9609 Infants' black patent leatherette button shoe. White top. SIZES: 0 to 4. PRICE, PREPAID **68c**
5K9640 Blue top.
5K9641 Pink top.

NEW ENGLISH Walking Last

5K7041 Unsurpassed for quality and service is this new walking boot for women at a pre-war slashed price. An extra special value. Made of black gunmetal leather with dull black leather top. English walking last. Strong oak leather soles. Medium low leather heel. SIZES: 2½ to 8. Wide width. PRICE, PREPAID to your home, **$2.98**

White Fibre Soles

5K7038 Prices slashed below cost. Women's stylish walking shoes at $3.48. Black gunmetal leather tops. White fibre-rubber soles (wear better than leather). Medium leather heel. SIZES: 2½ to 8. Wide width. PRICE, PREPAID to your home, **$3.48**

CHICAGO, ILL.

PHILIPSBORN'S Bargain Prices Include Free Delivery to Your Door. No Extra Charges for Express or Mailing

171

EXTRA
SEASON'S LATEST
Women's 10 inch Novelty
GREAT BARGAINS

$4.48 PREPAID

Rubber Heels

BROWN or BLACK

BROWN or BLACK

5K7585 Brown
5K7093 Black

The fine quality of the leather, the exclusive new style and the high grade workmanship all make this handsome boot a value that cannot be duplicated elsewhere for anywhere near our low price.

We offer you your choice of two very desirable leathers as quoted above, either **brown or black kid-finished leather.** The boot is one of the very new 10-inch models, with wave top and fashionable cut-outs on the sides exactly as pictured. The Parisian Cuban heel shows the newest idea in heels, with Vanity plate. SIZES: 2½ to 8. WIDTHS: EE, E, D and C.
PRICE, PREPAID to your home **$4.48**

5K7584 Brown
5K7085 Black

If you want to save money and still get a very stylish and satisfactory boot, then order this 10-inch model for women. Similar styles are selling elsewhere for about double our price.

You can select this boot in either **brown or black.** It is made of fine quality **kid-finished leather.** The white ivory welting on the extension sole gives a very dressy touch. Further smart style is shown in the wave top and the fancy cut vamp. Parisian Cuban heel is finished with rubber tip. An ideal combination walking and dress boot. SIZES: 2½ to 8. WIDTHS: EE, E, D, and C.
PRICE, PREPAID to your home, **$4.48**

SPECIAL!!!
SENSATIONAL STYLES
Boots all the Big Rage
PREPAID to Your Home

4⁴⁸ PREPAID

BROWN or BLACK

BROWN or BLACK

5K7588 Brown.
5K7095 Black.
Here is a graceful 10-inch boot for street or dress occasions—an unparalleled value at our reduced price.
When you see this boot on your foot you will decide that you have never made a better investment. Women's model made of **fine kid-finished leather in either brown or black**, as listed above. Four stylish cut-outs trim the boot in newest fashion exactly as pictured. Made over a new recede toe last, with wave top, flexible leather sole and Louis heel with vanity heel plate. Perforations. One of our dressiest models at a cash saving. SIZES: 2½ to 8. WIDTHS: EE, E, D and C. PRICE, PREPAID to your home, **$4.48**

5K7589 Brown.
5K7096 Black.
This handsome boot has every appearance of boots that are selling elsewhere from $8.00 to $10.00. Now $4.48.
This is one of the new 10-inch models which women of fashion are choosing this season. Made of **fine selected dull kid-finished leather,** and comes in either **brown or black** as listed above. Especially new features are the scalloped top and the attractively beaded vamp. The boot is made over a modish dress last, with slim toe and Louis heel with vanity heel plate. A most astounding value at the price we ask for this handsomest and most up to date model. SIZES: 2½ to 8. WIDTHS: EE, E, D and C. PRICE, PREPAID to your home, **$4.48**

CHICAGO, ILL.

See Page 274 for Index and Don't Forget When Ordering to State the Color and Size Desired

173

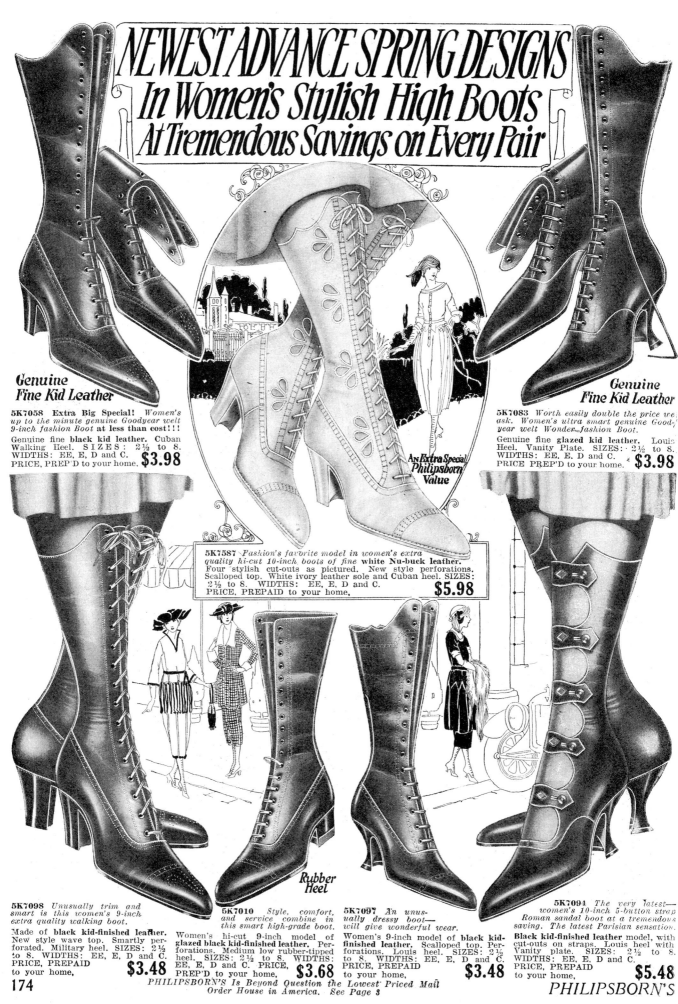

NEWEST ADVANCE SPRING DESIGNS
In Women's Stylish High Boots
At Tremendous Savings on Every Pair

Genuine Fine Kid Leather

5K7058 *Extra Big Special!* Women's up to the minute genuine Goodyear welt 9-inch fashion Boot at less than cost!!! Genuine fine black kid leather. Cuban Walking Heel. SIZES: 2½ to 8. WIDTHS: EE, E, D and C. PRICE, PREP'D to your home, **$3.98**

Genuine Fine Kid Leather

5K7083 *Worth easily double the price we ask.* Women's ultra smart genuine Goodyear welt Wonder fashion Boot. Genuine fine glazed kid leather. Louis Heel. Vanity Plate. SIZES: 2½ to 8. WIDTHS: EE, E, D and C. PRICE PREP'D to your home. **$3.98**

An Extra Special Philipsborn Value

5K7587 *Fashion's favorite model* in women's extra quality hi-cut 10-inch boots of fine white Nu-buck leather. Four stylish cut-outs as pictured. New style perforations. Scalloped top. White ivory leather sole and Cuban heel. SIZES: 2½ to 8. WIDTHS: EE, E, D and C. PRICE, PREPAID to your home, **$5.98**

Rubber Heel

5K7098 *Unusually trim and smart* is this women's 9-inch extra quality walking boot. Made of black kid-finished leather. New style wave top. Smartly perforated. Military heel. SIZES: 2½ to 8. WIDTHS: EE, E, D and C. PRICE, PREPAID to your home, **$3.48**

5K7010 *Style, comfort, and service combine* in this smart high-grade boot. Women's hi-cut 9-inch model of glazed black kid-finished leather. Perforations. Medium low rubber-tipped heel. SIZES: 2½ to 8. WIDTHS: EE, E, D and C. PRICE, PREP'D to your home, **$3.68**

5K7097 *An unusually dressy boot*—will give wonderful wear. Women's 9-inch model of black kid-finished leather. Scalloped top. Louis heel. SIZES: 2½ to 8. WIDTHS: EE, E, D and C. PRICE, PREPAID to your home, **$3.48**

5K7094 *The very latest*—women's 10-inch 5-button strap Roman sandal boot at a tremendous saving. The latest Parisian sensation. Black kid-finished leather model, with cut-outs on straps. Louis heel with Vanity plate. SIZES: 2½ to 8. WIDTHS: EE, E, D and C. PRICE, PREPAID to your home, **$5.48**

PHILIPSBORN'S Is Beyond Question the Lowest Priced Mail Order House in America. See Page 3

PHILIPSBORN'S

WOMEN'S EXTRA QUALITY FLEXO-KID
Combination Comfort-Dress E-Z- Shoes
Lowest Prices-Prepaid To Your Home

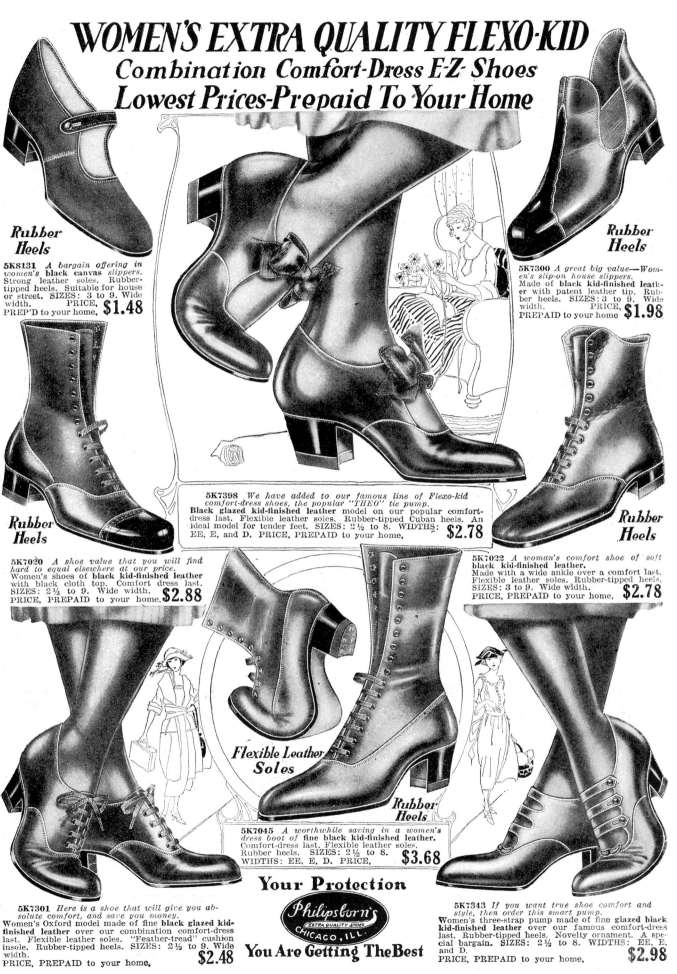

Rubber Heels

5K8131 *A bargain offering in women's* **black canvas** *slippers.* Strong leather soles. Rubber-tipped heels. Suitable for house or street. SIZES: 3 to 9. Wide width.   PRICE, PREP'D to your home, **$1.48**

Rubber Heels

5K7300 *A great big value—Women's slip-on house slippers.* Made of **black kid-finished leather** with patent leather tip. Rubber heels. SIZES: 3 to 9. Wide width.   PRICE, PREPAID to your home **$1.98**

Rubber Heels

5K7020 *A shoe value that you will find hard to equal elsewhere at our price.* Women's shoes of **black kid-finished leather** with black cloth top. Comfort dress last. SIZES: 2½ to 9. Wide width. PRICE, PREPAID to your home, **$2.88**

5K7398 *We have added to our famous line of Flexo-kid comfort-dress shoes, the popular "THEO" tie pump.* **Black glazed kid-finished leather** model on our popular comfort-dress last. Flexible leather soles. Rubber-tipped Cuban heels. An ideal model for tender feet. SIZES: 2½ to 8. WIDTHS: EE, E, and D. PRICE, PREPAID to your home, **$2.78**

Rubber Heels

5K7022 *A woman's comfort shoe of soft* **black kid-finished leather.** Made with a wide ankle over a comfort last. Flexible leather soles. Rubber-tipped heels. SIZES: 3 to 9. Wide width. PRICE, PREPAID to your home, **$2.78**

Flexible Leather Soles

Rubber Heels

5K7045 *A worthwhile saving in a women's dress boot of* **fine black kid-finished leather.** Comfort-dress last. Flexible leather soles. Rubber heels. SIZES: 2½ to 8. WIDTHS: EE, E, D. PRICE, **$3.68**

5K7301 *Here is a shoe that will give you absolute comfort, and save you money.* Women's Oxford model made of **fine black glazed kid-finished leather** over our combination comfort-dress last. Flexible leather soles. "Feather-tread" cushion insole. Rubber-tipped heels. SIZES: 2½ to 9. Wide width. PRICE, PREPAID to your home, **$2.48**

Your Protection

Philipsborn's
EXTRA QUALITY SHOES
CHICAGO, ILL.

You Are Getting The Best

5K7343 *If you want true shoe comfort and style, then order this smart pump.* Women's three-strap pump made of **fine glazed black kid-finished leather** over our famous comfort-dress last. Rubber-tipped heels. Novelty ornament. A special bargain. SIZES: 2½ to 8. WIDTHS: EE, E, and D. PRICE, PREPAID to your home, **$2.98**

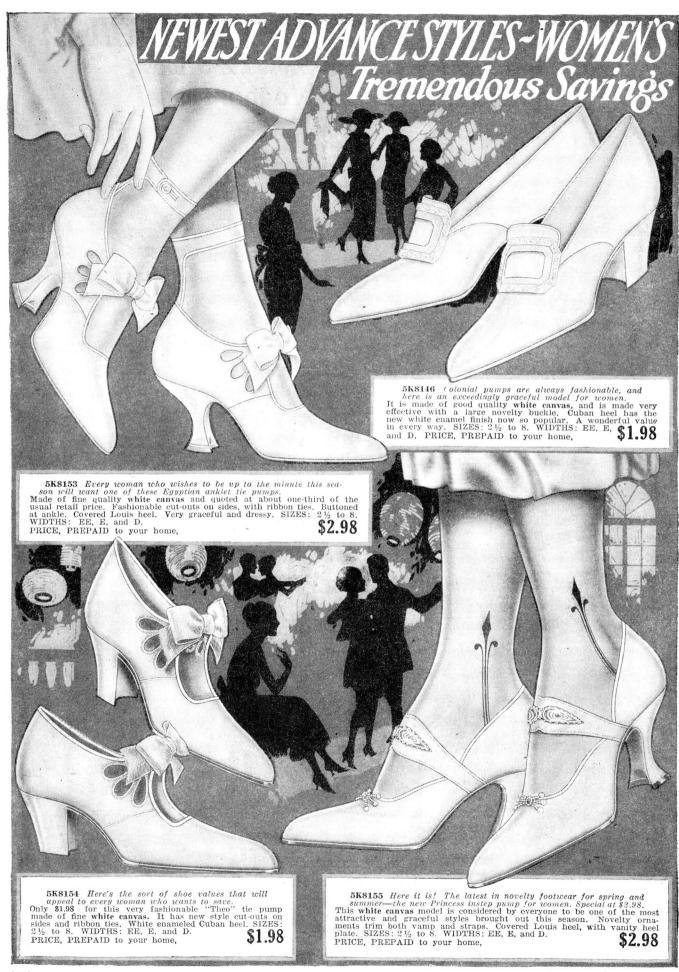

NEWEST ADVANCE STYLES~WOMEN'S
Tremendous Savings

5K8146 *Colonial pumps are always fashionable, and here is an exceedingly graceful model for women.* It is made of good quality **white canvas**, and is made very effective with a large novelty buckle. Cuban heel has the new white enamel finish now so popular. A wonderful value in every way. SIZES: 2½ to 8. WIDTHS: EE, E, and D. PRICE, PREPAID to your home, **$1.98**

5K8153 *Every woman who wishes to be up to the minute this season will want one of these Egyptian anklet tie pumps.* Made of fine quality **white canvas** and quoted at about one-third of the usual retail price. Fashionable cut-outs on sides, with ribbon ties. Buttoned at ankle. Covered Louis heel. Very graceful and dressy. SIZES: 2½ to 8. WIDTHS: EE, E, and D. **$2.98** PRICE, PREPAID to your home,

5K8154 *Here's the sort of shoe values that will appeal to every woman who wants to save.* Only $1.98 for this very fashionable "Theo" tie pump made of fine **white canvas**. It has new style cut-outs on sides and ribbon ties. White enameled Cuban heel. SIZES: 2½ to 8. WIDTHS: EE, E, and D. PRICE, PREPAID to your home, **$1.98**

5K8155 *Here it is! The latest in novelty footwear for spring and summer—the new Princess instep pump for women. Special at $2.98.* This **white canvas** model is considered by everyone to be one of the most attractive and graceful styles brought out this season. Novelty ornaments trim both vamp and straps. Covered Louis heel, with vanity heel plate. SIZES: 2½ to 8. WIDTHS: EE, E, and D. PRICE, PREPAID to your home, **$2.98**

Order at Our Risk. Your Money Back if You Are Not Satisfied

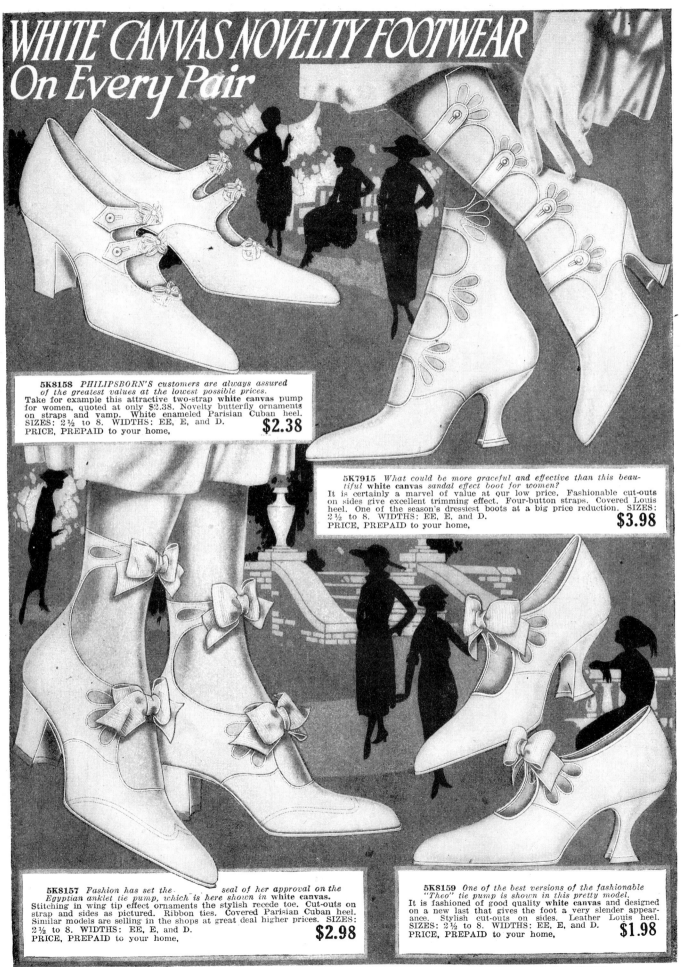

WHITE CANVAS NOVELTY FOOTWEAR
On Every Pair

5K8158 *PHILIPSBORN'S customers are always assured of the greatest values at the lowest possible prices.* Take for example this attractive two-strap **white canvas** pump for women, quoted at only $2.38. Novelty butterfly ornaments on straps and vamp. White enameled Parisian Cuban heel. SIZES: 2½ to 8. WIDTHS: EE, E, and D. PRICE, PREPAID to your home, **$2.38**

5K7915 *What could be more graceful and effective than this beautiful* **white canvas** *sandal effect boot for women?* It is certainly a marvel of value at our low price. Fashionable cut-outs on sides give excellent trimming effect. Four-button straps. Covered Louis heel. One of the season's dressiest boots at a big price reduction. SIZES: 2½ to 8. WIDTHS: EE, E, and D. PRICE, PREPAID to your home, **$3.98**

5K8157 *Fashion has set the____ seal of her approval on the Egyptian anklet tie pump, which is here shown in* **white canvas.** Stitching in wing tip effect ornaments the stylish recede toe. Cut-outs on strap and sides as pictured. Ribbon ties. Covered Parisian Cuban heel. Similar models are selling in the shops at great deal higher prices. SIZES: 2½ to 8. WIDTHS: EE, E, and D. PRICE, PREPAID to your home, **$2.98**

5K8159 *One of the best versions of the fashionable "Theo" tie pump is shown in this pretty model.* It is fashioned of good quality **white canvas** and designed on a new last that gives the foot a very slender appearance. Stylish cut-outs on sides. Leather Louis heel. SIZES: 2½ to 8. WIDTHS: EE, E, and D. PRICE, PREPAID to your home, **$1.98**

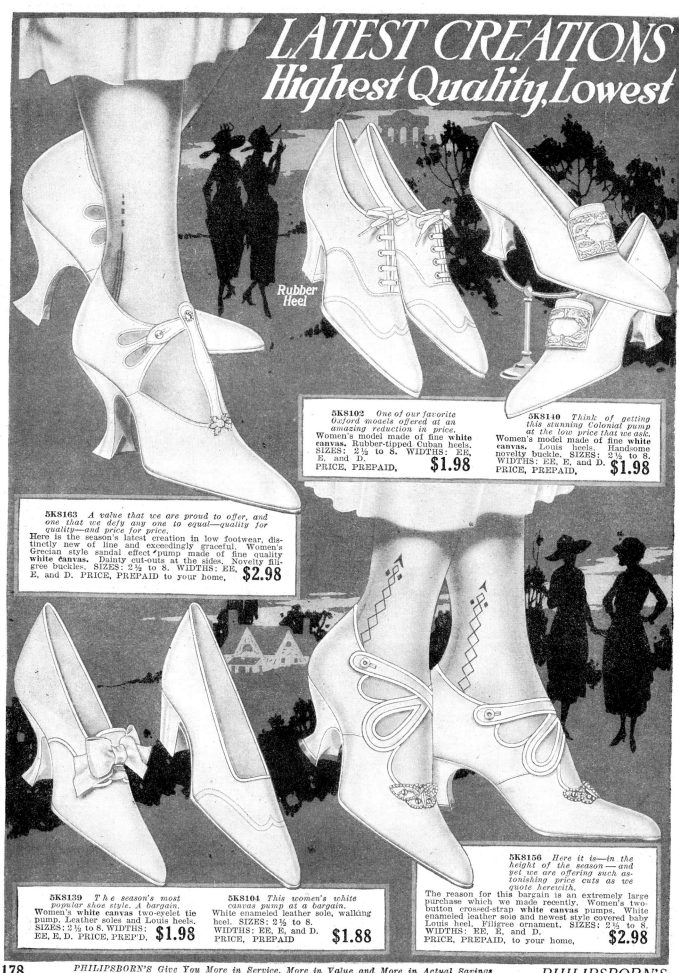

LATEST CREATIONS
Highest Quality, Lowest

Rubber Heel

5K8102 *One of our favorite Oxford models offered at an amazing reduction in price.* Women's model made of fine **white canvas**. Rubber-tipped Cuban heels. SIZES: 2½ to 8. WIDTHS: EE, E, and D. PRICE, PREPAID, **$1.98**

5K8140 *Think of getting this stunning Colonial pump at the low price that we ask.* Women's model made of fine **white canvas**. Louis heels. Handsome novelty buckle. SIZES: 2½ to 8. WIDTHS: EE, E, and D. PRICE, PREPAID, **$1.98**

5K8163 *A value that we are proud to offer, and one that we defy any one to equal—quality for quality—and price for price.* Here is the season's latest creation in low footwear, distinctly new of line and exceedingly graceful. Women's Grecian style sandal effect pump made of fine quality **white canvas**. Dainty cut-outs at the sides. Novelty filigree buckles. SIZES: 2½ to 8. WIDTHS: EE, E, and D. PRICE, PREPAID to your home, **$2.98**

5K8156 *Here it is—in the height of the season—and yet we are offering such astonishing price cuts as we quote herewith.* The reason for this bargain is an extremely large purchase which we made recently. Women's two-button crossed-strap **white canvas** pumps. White enameled leather sole and newest style covered baby Louis heel. Filigree ornament. SIZES: 2½ to 8. WIDTHS: EE, E, and D. PRICE, PREPAID, to your home, **$2.98**

5K8139 *The season's most popular shoe style. A bargain.* Women's **white canvas** two-eyelet tie pump. Leather soles and Louis heels. SIZES: 2½ to 8. WIDTHS: EE, E, D. PRICE, PREP'D, **$1.98**

5K8104 *This women's white canvas pump at a bargain.* White enameled leather sole, walking heel. SIZES: 2½ to 8. WIDTHS: EE, E, and D. PRICE, PREPAID **$1.88**

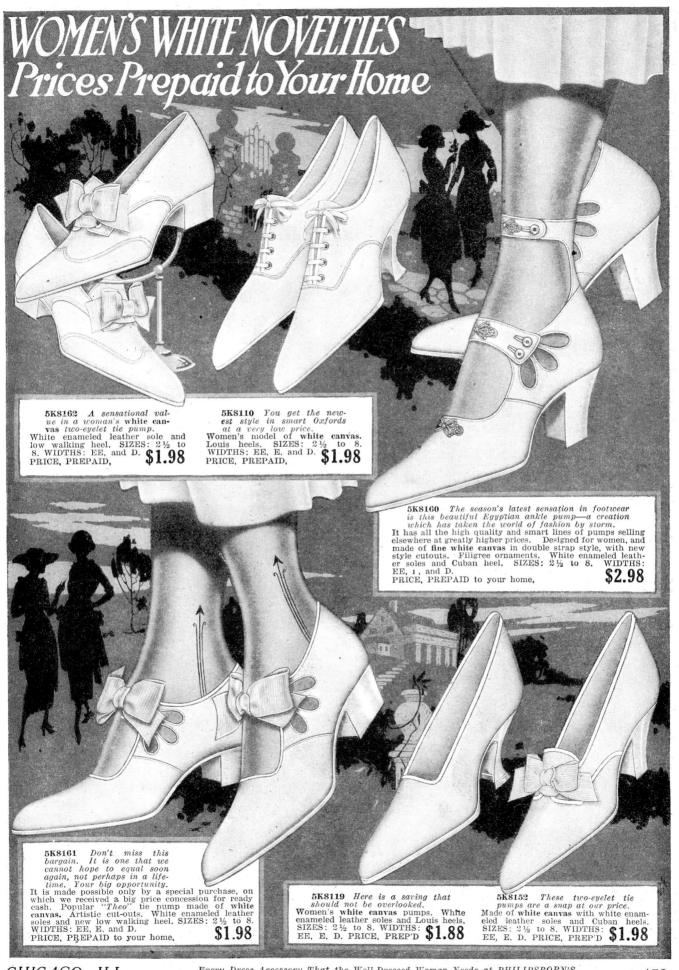

WOMEN'S WHITE NOVELTIES
Prices Prepaid to Your Home

5K8162 *A sensational value in a woman's* **white canvas** *two-eyelet tie pump.*
White enameled leather sole and low walking heel. SIZES: 2½ to 8. WIDTHS: EE, E, and D. PRICE, PREPAID, **$1.98**

5K8110 *You get the newest style in smart Oxfords at a very low price.*
Women's model of **white canvas.** Louis heels. SIZES: 2½ to 8. WIDTHS: EE, E, and D. PRICE, PREPAID, **$1.98**

5K8160 *The season's latest sensation in footwear is this beautiful Egyptian ankle pump—a creation which has taken the world of fashion by storm.*
It has all the high quality and smart lines of pumps selling elsewhere at greatly higher prices. Designed for women, and made of **fine white canvas** in double strap style, with new style cutouts. Filigree ornaments. White enameled leather soles and Cuban heel. SIZES: 2½ to 8. WIDTHS: EE, 1, and D.
PRICE, PREPAID to your home, **$2.98**

5K8161 *Don't miss this bargain. It is one that we cannot hope to equal soon again, not perhaps in a lifetime. Your big opportunity.*
It is made possible only by a special purchase, on which we received a big price concession for ready cash. Popular "Theo" tie pump made of **white canvas.** Artistic cut-outs. White enameled leather soles and new low walking heel. SIZES: 2½ to 8. WIDTHS: EE, E, and D. PRICE, PREPAID to your home, **$1.98**

5K8119 *Here is a saving that should not be overlooked.*
Women's **white canvas** pumps. White enameled leather soles and Louis heels. SIZES: 2½ to 8. WIDTHS: EE, E, D. PRICE, PREP'D **$1.88**

5K8152 *These two-eyelet tie pumps are a snap at our price.*
Made of **white canvas** with white enameled leather soles and Cuban heels. SIZES: 2½ to 8. WIDTHS: EE, E, D. PRICE, PREP'D **$1.98**

WOMEN'S EXTRA QUALITY-LATEST
Lowest Prices~

5K8167 *Simply unbeatable value in this* **white canvas** *Russia leather trimmed sport Oxford for women.* Leather sole and heel. Perforations. A wonderful bargain. SIZES: 2½ to 8. WIDTHS: EE, E, and D. PRICE, PREPAID to your home, **$2.48**

5K8120 *These values speak for themselves.* $2.48 *for women's* **fine white canvas** *pumps.* Made over a new last with modish covered walking heel. Beautiful cut steel ornament. SIZES: 2½ to 8. WIDTHS: EE, E, and D. PRICE, PREPAID **$2.48**

5K8168 *When it comes to a combination of good style, excellent quality, and lowest prices,* PHILIPSBORN'S *leads them all. Extraordinary value.* Here is a stunning new strap pump on which we quote an exceptionally low price. It is designed for women and is made of fine quality **white canvas** in two-button strap style. Strap is attractively slashed. White enamel finished leather sole. Covered Louis heel. An exquisite new model. SIZES: 2½ to 8. WIDTHS: EE, E, and D. PRICE, PREPAID to your home, **$2.78**

Leather Sole and Heel

5K7925 *Woman's stylish 9-inch boot of fine quality* **white canvas** *at a big reduction.* Our very low price offers you a tremendous saving. Leather sole and medium low walking heel. SIZES: 2½ to 8. WIDTHS: EE, E, and D. PRICE, PREPAID to your home, **$1.98**

5K7902 *One of our biggest shoe values—women's 9-inch* **white canvas** *dress boot.* White enameled leather sole and Louis heel. Our money-saving price actually below cost. SIZES: 2½ to 8. WIDTHS: EE, E, and D. PRICE, PREPAID to your home, **$1.98**

5K7943 *An exclusive* PHILIPSBORN'S *creation in a women's 9-inch* **white canvas** *boot.* New style cut-outs on sides. White enameled leather sole and Cuban heel. A splendid value. SIZES: 2½ to 8. WIDTHS: EE, E, and D. PRICE, PREPAID to your home, **$3.48**

PHILIPSBORN'S

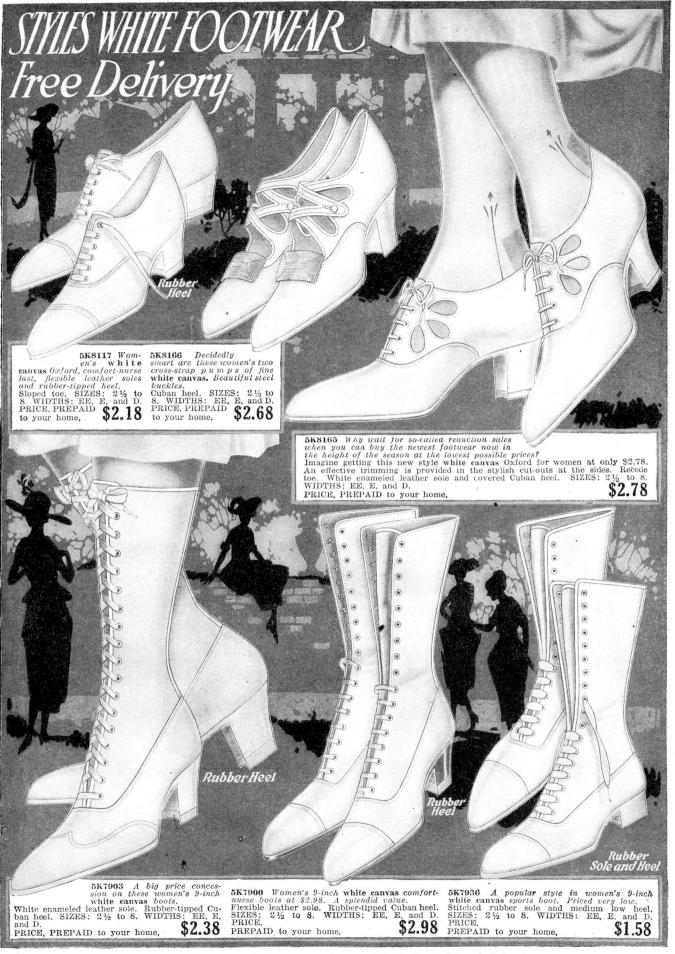

STYLES WHITE FOOTWEAR
Free Delivery

5K8117 Women's **white canvas** Oxford, comfort-nurse last, flexible leather soles and rubber-tipped heel. Sloped toe. SIZES: 2½ to 8. WIDTHS: EE, E, and D. PRICE, PREPAID to your home, **$2.18**

5K8166 Decidedly smart are these women's two cross-strap **p u m p s** of fine **white canvas**. Beautiful steel buckles. Cuban heel. SIZES: 2½ to 8. WIDTHS: EE, E, and D. PRICE, PREPAID to your home, **$2.68**

5K8165 Why wait for so-called reduction sales when you can buy the newest footwear now in the height of the season at the lowest possible prices? Imagine getting this new style **white canvas** Oxford for women at only $2.78. An effective trimming is provided in the stylish cut-outs at the sides. Recede toe. White enameled leather sole and covered Cuban heel. SIZES: 2½ to 8. WIDTHS: EE, E, and D. PRICE, PREPAID to your home, **$2.78**

5K7903 A big price concession on these women's 9-inch **white canvas boots.** White enameled leather sole. Rubber-tipped Cuban heel. SIZES: 2½ to 8. WIDTHS: EE, E, and D. PRICE, PREPAID to your home, **$2.38**

5K7900 Women's 9-inch **white canvas** comfort-nurse boots at $2.98. A splendid value. Flexible leather sole. Rubber-tipped Cuban heel. SIZES: 2½ to 8. WIDTHS: EE, E, and D. PRICE, PREPAID to your home, **$2.98**

5K7936 A popular style in women's 9-inch **white canvas** sports boot. Priced very low. Stitched rubber sole and medium low heel. SIZES: 2½ to 8. WIDTHS: EE, E, and D. PRICE, PREPAID to your home, **$1.58**

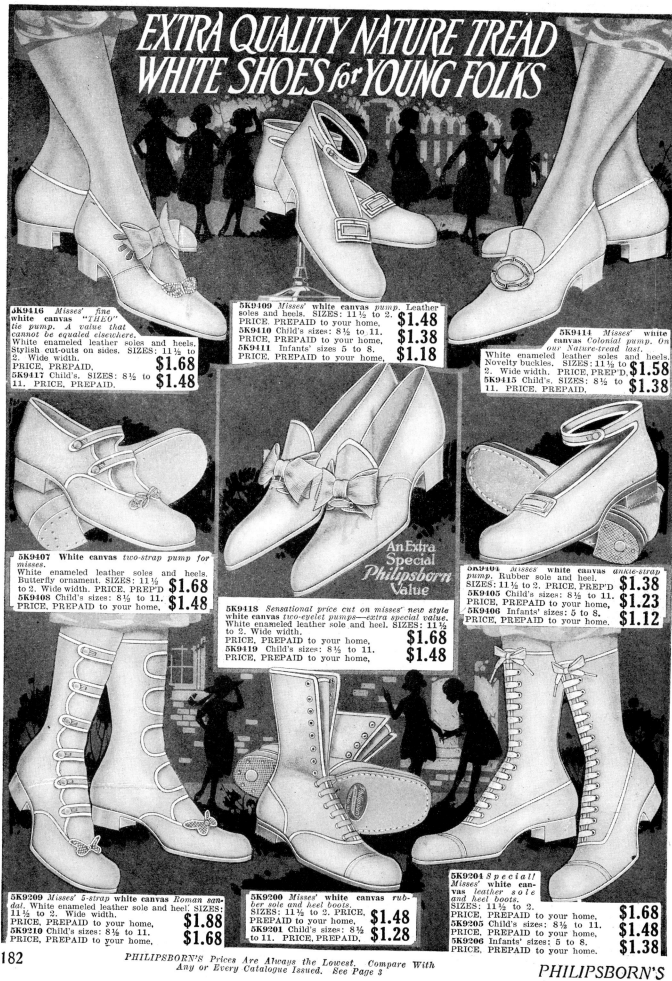

EXTRA QUALITY NATURE TREAD
WHITE SHOES for YOUNG FOLKS

5K9416 *Misses' fine white canvas "THEO" tie pump. A value that cannot be equaled elsewhere.* White enameled leather soles and heels. Stylish cut-outs on sides. SIZES: 11½ to 2. Wide width.
PRICE, PREPAID, **$1.68**
5K9417 Child's. SIZES: 8½ to 11. PRICE, PREPAID. **$1.48**

5K9409 *Misses' white canvas pump.* Leather soles and heels. SIZES: 11½ to 2.
PRICE. PREPAID to your home, **$1.48**
5K9410 Child's sizes: 8½ to 11.
PRICE, PREPAID to your home, **$1.38**
5K9411 Infants' sizes 5 to 8.
PRICE. PREPAID to your home, **$1.18**

5K9414 *Misses' white canvas Colonial pump. On our Nature-tread last.* White enameled leather soles and heels. Novelty buckles. SIZES: 11½ to 2. Wide width. PRICE, PREP'D **$1.58**
5K9415 Child's. SIZES: 8½ to 11. PRICE, PREPAID. **$1.38**

5K9407 *White canvas two-strap pump for misses.* White enameled leather soles and heels. Butterfly ornament. SIZES: 11½ to 2. Wide width. PRICE, PREP'D **$1.68**
5K9408 Child's sizes: 8½ to 11. PRICE, PREPAID to your home, **$1.48**

An Extra Special Philipsborn Value

5K9418 *Sensational price cut on misses' new style white canvas two-eyelet pumps—extra special value.* White enameled leather sole and heel. SIZES: 11½ to 2. Wide width.
PRICE, PREPAID to your home, **$1.68**
5K9419 Child's sizes: 8½ to 11. PRICE, PREPAID to your home, **$1.48**

5K9404 *Misses' white canvas ankle-strap pump.* Rubber sole and heel. SIZES: 11½ to 2. PRICE, PREP'D **$1.38**
5K9405 Child's sizes: 8½ to 11. PRICE, PREPAID to your home, **$1.23**
5K9406 Infants' sizes: 5 to 8. PRICE, PREPAID to your home, **$1.12**

5K9209 *Misses' 5-strap white canvas Roman sandal.* White enameled leather sole and heel. SIZES: 11½ to 2. Wide width.
PRICE, PREPAID to your home, **$1.88**
5K9210 Child's sizes: 8½ to 11. PRICE, PREPAID to your home, **$1.68**

5K9200 *Misses' white canvas rubber sole and heel boots.* SIZES: 11½ to 2. PRICE, PREPAID to your home, **$1.48**
5K9201 Child's sizes 8½ to 11. PRICE, PREPAID, **$1.28**

5K9204 *Special! Misses' white canvas leather sole and heel boots.* SIZES: 11½ to 2. PRICE, PREPAID to your home, **$1.68**
5K9205 Child's sizes: 8½ to 11. PRICE, PREPAID to your home, **$1.48**
5K9206 Infants' sizes: 5 to 8. PRICE, PREPAID to your home. **$1.38**

182

PHILIPSBORN'S Prices Are Always the Lowest. Compare With Any or Every Catalogue Issued. See Page 3

PHILIPSBORN'S

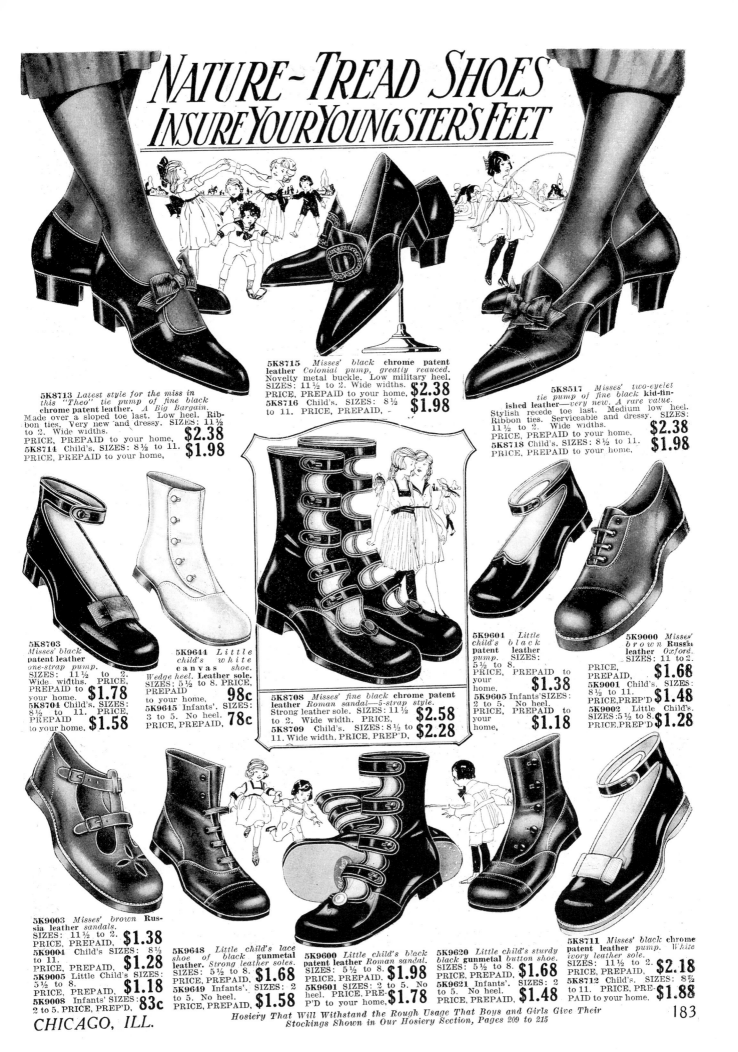

NATURE-TREAD SHOES
INSURE YOUR YOUNGSTER'S FEET

5K8713 *Latest style for the miss in this "Theo" tie pump of fine black* **chrome patent leather.** *A Big Bargain.* Made over a sloped toe last. Low heel. Ribbon ties. Very new and dressy. SIZES: 11½ to 2. Wide widths.
PRICE, PREPAID to your home, **$2.38**
5K8714 Child's. SIZES: 8½ to 11.
PRICE, PREPAID to your home, **$1.98**

5K8715 *Misses' black* **chrome patent leather** *Colonial pump, greatly reduced.* Novelty metal buckle. Low military heel. SIZES: 11½ to 2. Wide widths.
PRICE, PREPAID to your home, **$2.38**
5K8716 Child's. SIZES: 8½ to 11. PRICE, PREPAID, **$1.98**

5K8517 *Misses' two-eyelet tie pump of fine black* **kid-finished leather**—*very new. A rare value.* Stylish recede toe last. Medium low heel. Ribbon ties. Serviceable and dressy. SIZES: 11½ to 2. Wide widths.
PRICE, PREPAID to your home, **$2.38**
5K8518 Child's. SIZES: 8½ to 11. PRICE, PREPAID to your home, **$1.98**

5K8703 *Misses' black* patent leather one-strap pump. SIZES: 11½ to 2. Wide widths. PRICE, PREPAID to your home, **$1.78**
5K8704 Child's. SIZES: 8½ to 11. PRICE, PREPAID to your home, **$1.58**

5K9644 *Little child's* **white canvas shoe.** *Wedge heel.* Leather sole. SIZES: 5½ to 8. PRICE, PREPAID to your home, **98c**
5K9645 Infants'. SIZES: 3 to 5. No heel. PRICE, PREPAID, **78c**

5K8708 *Misses' fine black* **chrome patent leather** *Roman sandal—5-strap style.* Strong leather sole. SIZES: 11½ to 2. Wide width. PRICE, **$2.58**
5K8709 Child's. SIZES: 8½ to 11. Wide width. PRICE, PREP'D, **$2.28**

5K9604 *Little child's black* patent leather pump. SIZES: 5½ to 8. PRICE, PREPAID to your home, **$1.38**
5K9605 Infants' SIZES: 2 to 5. No heel. PRICE, PREPAID to your home, **$1.18**

5K9000 *Misses' brown* **Russia leather** *Oxford.* SIZES: 11 to 2. PRICE, PREPAID, **$1.68**
5K9001 Child's. SIZES: 8½ to 11. PRICE, PREP'D **$1.48**
5K9002 Little Child's. SIZES: 5½ to 8. PRICE, PREP'D **$1.28**

5K9003 *Misses' brown* **Russia leather** *sandals.* SIZES: 11½ to 2. PRICE, PREPAID, **$1.38**
5K9004 Child's SIZES: 8½ to 11. PRICE, PREPAID, **$1.28**
5K9005 Little Child's SIZES: 5½ to 8. PRICE, PREPAID, **$1.18**
5K9008 Infants'. SIZES: 2 to 5. PRICE, PREP'D, **83c**

5K9648 *Little child's lace shoe of black* **gunmetal leather.** *Strong leather soles.* SIZES: 5½ to 8. PRICE, PREPAID, **$1.68**
5K9649 Infants'. SIZES: 2 to 5. No heel. PRICE, PREPAID, **$1.58**

5K9600 *Little child's black* patent leather *Roman sandal.* SIZES: 5½ to 8. PRICE, PREPAID, **$1.98**
5K9601 SIZES: 2 to 5. No heel. PRICE, PREP'D to your home, **$1.78**

5K9620 *Little child's sturdy black* **gunmetal** *button shoe.* SIZES: 5½ to 8. PRICE, PREPAID, **$1.68**
5K9621 Infants'. SIZES: 2 to 5. No heel. PRICE, PREPAID, **$1.48**

5K8711 *Misses' black* **chrome patent leather** *pump. White ivory leather sole.* SIZES: 11½ to 2. PRICE, PREPAID, **$2.18**
5K8712 Child's. SIZES: 8½ to 11. PRICE, PREPAID to your home, **$1.88**

CHICAGO, ILL.

Hosiery That Will Withstand the Rough Usage That Boys and Girls Give Their Stockings Shown in Our Hosiery Section, Pages 209 to 215

MEN'S EXTRA QUALITY
Lowest Prices. Pre-

$2 78 Prepaid

$2 68 Prepaid

Brown or Black

RUBBER HEEL

Brown or Black

5K7825 Brown.   **5K7826 Black.**
Don't miss this tremendous money-saving offering in a powerfully constructed work shoe for men. It gives you comfort and absolute satisfaction at a price that simply can't be beat. If you buy PHILIPSBORN'S extra quality Shoes—you buy the best.

It is made of *tough, sturdy* **brown or black chrome ooze leather**, and is strongly stitched throughout. Double-wear wing tip. Double-wear "KROMIDE" leather soles. SIZES: 6 to 12. Wide widths.
PRICE, PREPAID to your home, **$2.78**

5K7809 Brown.   **5K7810 Black.**
Here is a wonderful example of shoe values that you get at PHILIPSBORN'S. Men's extra quality outing shoe of **brown or black chrome ooze leather** *at a sensational saving on every pair. Ideal shoe for hard wear and maximum comfort.*
Made over the Munson army last, fibre-rubber soles, clinch nailed and stitched. Rubber heel. SIZES: 6 to 12, Wide widths.
PRICE, PREPAID to your home, **$2.68**

$2 88 Prepaid

$2 98 Prepaid

Brown or Black

Black Only

5K7803 Brown.   **5K7804 Black.**
You save real money on this splendid work shoe for men, which we quote at a phenomenally low price,—a shoe that can be depended upon for the hardest kind of wear. None better made for the money.

Made of sturdy **brown or black leather** with bellows tongue (excludes the dirt). Heavy strong double-wear "KROMIDE" leather soles, clinch nailed and stitched. Munson army last. Low broad leather heels. SIZES: 6 to 12. Wide widths. PRICE, PREPAID to your home, **$2.88**

5K7821 Black only.
At less than pre-war prices to give our customers the benefit of every possible saving. Here is a splendid selection in a plain toe blucher for the man with tender feet, who must have maximum service at the lowest price.
Made of soft, pliable but sturdy black **"NUKROME" leather** over the Munson army last. Double-wear heavy "KROMIDE" leather soles. Strongly clinch nailed and stitched. For comfort and service this shoe has no equal at the price we name. SIZES: 6 to 12. Wide widths.
PRICE, PREPAID to your home, **$2.98**

Men's and Boys' Clothing—A Complete Assortment of High Grade Merchandise at Notable Price Reductions. See Pages 256 to 273.

PHILIPSBORN'S

DOUBLE-WEAR SERVICE SHOES
Paid To Your Home

Soft Chrome Leather
$3 28 prepaid

Brown or Smoked Pearl

5K7817 Brown.   **5K7818 Smoked Pearl.**
Don't judge the quality of this shoe for men by the remarkably low price that we quote. It is a value made possible only by our tremendous buying power.
Men's outing shoe made of **brown or smoked pearl chrome tanned elk leather.** Munson army last. Double-wear "KROMIDE" leather soles. Low broad leather heels. Clinch nailed and stitched. SIZES: 6 to 12. Wide widths.
PRICE, PREPAID to your home,   **$3.28**

$3 48 Brown Only

5K7837 Brown only. *Reduced to $3.48 and certainly the rarest of bargains at that price—Men's double-wear hi-cut 8-inch service boots.*
Powerfully made of **sturdy brown leather,** specially tanned to resist barnyard acids. Double-wear "KROMIDE" leather soles. Low broad leather heels. Clinch nailed and stitched. SIZES: 6 to 12. Wide widths.
PRICE, PREPAID to your home,   **$3.48**

RUBBER HEEL
$3 48 Brown Only

5K7822 Brown only. *This shoe is designed especially for the man who has tender feet and still must have an unusually strong and serviceable shoe.*
We have priced it at only $3.48 which is very much under prevailing market prices. Made of **combination tanned brown "NUKROME" leather.** Bellows tongue (keeps dirt out). Fibre-rubber soles which wear better than leather. Clinch nailed and stitched. Rubber heel. An all-around service shoe. SIZES: 6 to 12. Wide widths.
PRICE, PREPAID to your home;   **$3.48**

$3 48 prepaid

Brown or Smoked Pearl

5K7811 Brown.   **5K7819 Smoked Pearl.**
Here is a wonderfully, soft, pliable shoe for the man with tender, sensitive feet. Greatly underpriced at $3.48.
Made of high grade **chrome tanned brown or smoked pearl elk leather.** Bellows tongue. Oak-tanned flexible leather outsole. Clinch nailed and stitched.
SIZES: 6 to 12. Wide width.
PRICE, PREPAID to your home,   **$3.48**

PHILIPSBORN'S MEN'S FAMOUS "CONSERVATOR" Double-Wear SERVICE SHOES

EXTRA QUALITY

Brown or Black

$3.48 PREPAID

EXTRA-EXTRA!!! MEN'S CONSERVATOR Double-Wear Model

At a price that defies all Competition

$2.78 PREPAID

Your Choice of Brown or Black

Brown or Black

Men's Famous "KROMIDE"
ALL LEATHER SERVICE SHOES

6 Month's Wear GUARANTEED
$4.48 Prepaid

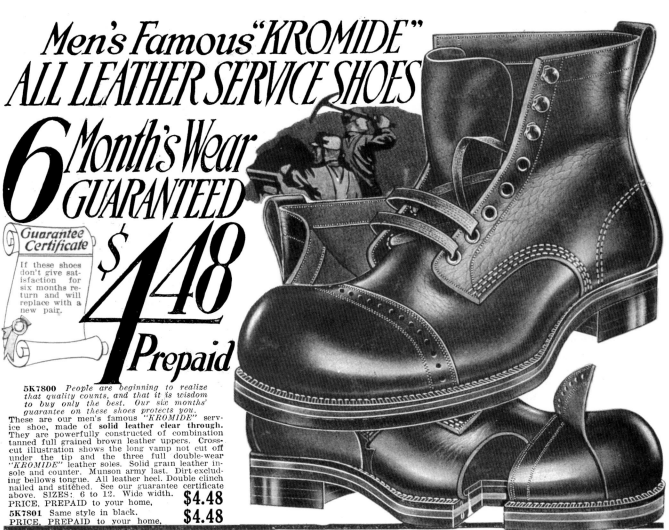

Guarantee Certificate

If these shoes don't give satisfaction for six months return and will replace with a new pair.

5K7800 *People are beginning to realize that quality counts, and that it is wisdom to buy only the best. Our six months' guarantee on these shoes protects you.*
These are our men's famous "KROMIDE" service shoe, made of **solid leather clear through**. They are powerfully constructed of combination tanned full grained brown leather uppers. Cross-cut illustration shows the long vamp not cut off under the tip and the three full double-wear "KROMIDE" leather soles. Solid grain leather insole and counter. Munson army last. Dirt excluding bellows tongue. All leather heel. Double clinch nailed and stitched. See our guarantee certificate above. SIZES: 6 to 12. Wide width.
PRICE, PREPAID to your home, **$4.48**
5K7801 Same style in black.
PRICE, PREPAID to your home, **$4.48**

MEN'S DeLux DRESS SHOES
6 Month's Wear Guaranteed
Your Choice $5.98 Prepaid

5K7898 *All past season's records for shoe values have been eclipsed in this offer of ours. A splendid style in men's "DE LUX" shoes.* Every pair fully guaranteed for six months. This offers you a wonderfully good selection in a dress shoe made of fine **mahogany Russia leather**. Over a new broad toe last. Two heavy oak tanned leather soles clear through to the heel. Genuine Goodyear welt. SIZES: 6 to 12. A wonderful value. WIDTHS: EE, E and D.
PRICE, PREPAID to your home, **$5.98**
5K7879 Same style as above in fine **black gunmetal leather**.
PRICE, PREPAID to your home, **$5.98**

5K7884 *Once you have shopped at PHILIPSBORN'S you will be convinced that we have the best values to offer of any Mail Order House. Take for example these "DE LUX" dress shoes for men.* They are made of fine **mahogany Russia leather** over the new Strand last, and are guaranteed to give six months' wear or your money refunded. Two full oak-tanned leather soles. Genuine Goodyear welt. Every pair a big bargain. SIZES: 6 to 12. WIDTHS: EE, E, and D.
PRICE, PREPAID to your home, **$5.98**
5K7885 Same as above but made of **black gunmetal leather**.
PRICE, PREPAID to your home, **$5.98**

CHICAGO, ILL.

Our Bargain Prices Include Free Delivery to Your Door.
No Extra Charges for Express or Mailing

De LUX
Extra Quality Shoes for Men

Brown or Black

Brown or Black

$3.98 Prepaid

5K7863 *Values that bring our customers back season after season to PHILIPSBORN'S.* Men's ultra smart "DE LUX" dress oxfords of **brown Russia leather** made over an English Last. Solid oak tanned leather outsole. Leather insole. Rubber-tipped heel. SIZES: 6 to 12. WIDTHS: EE, E, and D. PRICE, PREPAID to your home, **$3.98**

5K7864 Same style and sizes as above in black gunmetal leather. PRICE, PREPAID to your home, **$3.68**

5K7848 *This amazing bargain is one of the sensations of the season. Wonderful value.* Oxfords of **brown Russia leather**, one of the newest of our "DE LUX" dress shoes for men. Latest English last. White fibre rubber sole and heel, wear better than leather. SIZES: 6 to 12. WIDTHS: EE, E, D. PRICE, PREPAID to your home, **$3.98**

5K7849 Same as above in black gun metal leather. PRICE, PREPAID to your home, **$3.68**

5K7865 *Blucher Oxford* of **brown Russia leather**. *Hi-toe last. Heavy extension leather sole. Rubber tipped heel.* SIZES: 6 to 12. WIDTHS: EE, E, and D. PRICE, PREPAID to your home, **$3.98**

5K7866 Same style and sizes as above in black gunmetal leather. PRICE, PREPAID, **$3.68**

$3.98 Prepaid

5K7859 *Men's dressy shoe of mahogany* **Russia leather**. *Specially priced.* Latest English walking last. Strong leather sole. Rubber tipped heel. SIZES: 6 to 12. WIDTHS: EE, E and D. PREPAID, **$3.98**

5K7860 Same style and sizes in black gunmetal leather PRICE, PREPAID, **$3.68**

5K7852 *Men's mahogany* **Russia leather** *shoe with stitched white fibre rubber sole and heel.* SIZES: 6 to 12. WIDTHS: EE, E and D. PRICE, PREPAID to your home, **$3.98**

5K7853 Same style and sizes as above in black gunmetal leather. PRICE, PREPAID, **$3.68**

5K7861 *Drastic reductions on men's* **dark brown Russia leather** *Bluchers.* Made with solid leather extension sole. Rubber-tipped heels. SIZES: 6 to 12. WIDTHS: EE, E and D. PRICE, PREPAID to your home, **$3.98**

5K7862 Same style and sizes in black gunmetal leather. PRICE, PREPAID, **$3.68**

188

We Guarantee to Please You. Your Money Cheerfully Refunded in Case We Don't

PHILIPSBORN'S

Men's "CONSERVATOR" Dress Shoes

Lowest Prices-Biggest Savings
Prepaid To Your Home

Your Choice $3.48 Brown or Black

Per Pair

BROWN or BLACK

BROWN or BLACK

5K7831 Brown   **5K7832 Black**

Designed for the man who wants a shoe that is full of style and snap and will stand all kinds of hard wear is this "Conservator" shoe.
Blucher model made of **brown Russia leather** or **black gunmetal leather** over a broad toe last. One of the greatest shoe values ever offered. Buy a pair and be convinced of their wonderful quality and their extraordinary value. SIZES: 6 to 12. Wide widths.
PRICE, PREPAID to your home,   **$3.48**

5K7833 Brown   **5K7834 Black**

Stylish, serviceable, and extremely good-looking describes these "Conservator" dress shoes for men—special at $3.48.
English Bal model made of either **brown Russia leather** or **black gunmetal leather.** Heavy oak-tanned leather soles. A shoe that cannot be duplicated elsewhere at anywhere near this special price. SIZES: 6 to 12. Wide widths.
PRICE, PREPAID to your home,   **$3.48**

Men's "Feather Tread" Dress Shoes
For Men With Tender Feet
Made of Fine Genuine Black Glazed Kid Leather
YOUR CHOICE EITHER STYLE

$4.48 Prepaid

5K7854 High Shoe   **5K7899 Oxford**

Men with tender, sensitive feet will appreciate the comfort of these wonderful "Feathertread" dress shoes at less than pre-war prices.
They are made of genuine fine glazed **black kid leather** and are so very soft and pliable that they do not have to be broken in. They may be had in either high Blucher style or Oxford style. Made over our famous Pershing last. Heavy, flexible leather soles. Live, springy rubber heels. SIZES: 6 to 12. Wide widths.
PRICE, PREPAID to your home,   **$4.48**

Hi-Shoe or Oxford

CHICAGO, ILL.

For Stormy Weather You Will Want PHILIPSBORN'S Good Quality Rubbers.
Refer to Page 192

189

MEN'S EXTRA QUALITY
Lowest Prices ALL Pre-

Genuine Goodyear Welt

$4.98
PREPAID

Genuine Goodyear Welt

Rubber Heels

Rubber Heels

BROWN OR BLACK	5K7894 Brown Russia leather 5K7895 Black gunmetal leather *The man who knows values will appreciate this extraordinary opportunity to secure a very handsome dress shoe at decidedly less than pre-war prices.* Made of fine chrome tanned leather in

brown or black. Stylish English last. Oak leather soles. Rubber-tipped heels. Genuine Goodyear welt. SIZES: 6 to 12. WIDTHS: EE, E and D.
5K7894 PRICE, PREPAID, **$4.98**
5K7895 PRICE, PREPAID to your home. **$4.78**

5K7844 Genuine Goodyear welt.
A splendid value in a man's high grade **brown Russia leather** *Oxford.* English last. Oak leather soles. Rubber-tipped heels. SIZES: 6 to 12. WIDTHS: EE, E and D. PRICE, PREPAID to your home, **$4.78**
5K7845 Same style in black. PRICE, PREP'D to your home, **$4.58**

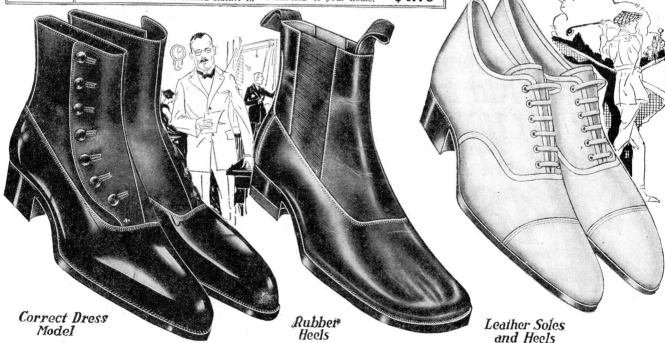

Correct Dress Model

Rubber Heels

Leather Soles and Heels

5K7857 *For formal dress occasions every man should have a pair of these dress shoes.* Correct dress model of fine **black chrome patent leather** with harmonizing black cloth top. Button style. Smart new last. Genuine Goodyear welt. SIZES: 6 to 12. Widths: EE, E and D. PRICE, PREPAID to your home, **$4.98**

5K7856 *Exceedingly comfortable shoe for the man with tender feet.* Made of soft **black genuine kid leather,** with elastic side gores. Made over a wide, roomy last with plain toe. SIZES: 6 to 12. Wide width. PRICE, PREP'D to your home, **$4.48**

5K9852 *Special bargain!* Men's **white canvas** *Oxford.* White finished leather sole and low broad heel. Will give wonderful satisfaction. A big value. SIZES: 6 to 12. Wide width. PRICE, PREPAID, **$1.98**

190   *PHILIPSBORN'S Give Away Over $500,000. See Page 3 for This and Other Interesting Facts*   **PHILIPSBORN'S**

DeLUX DRESS SHOES
PAID TO YOUR HOME

Latest Brogue Model
$3.98
PREPAID

Rubber Heels

Rubber Heels

5K7846 *Men's stylish,* **brown Russia leather,** *Scotch brogue Oxford.* SIZES: 6 to 12. WIDTHS: EE, E, and D. PRICE, PREPAID to your home, **$3.98**
5K7847 Same style in black. PRICE, PREPAID, **$3.68**

5K7896 *The man who wants to dress stylishly will recognize in this De Luxe dress shoe a bargain of bargains. It is offered at a clear saving of $3.00.* It is made of a fine quality **brown Russia leather** in the newest brogue model. Heavy over-weight leather extension soles. Low, broad rubber-tipped heels. SIZES: 6 to 12. WIDTHS: EE, E and D. PRICE, PREPAID to your home, **$3.98**
5K7897 Same style in black. PRICE, to your home, **$3.68**

BROWN OR BLACK

Brown

Orthopedic Rubber Heel

Rubber Heels

Rubber Heels

5K7827 *Men's ventilated Oxfords of* **brown Russia leather,** *greatly reduced.* Made by the genuine stitchdown process. Orthopedic rubber heel. SIZES: 6 to 12. Wide widths. PRICE, PREPAID to your home, **$2.98**

5K7855 *Comfort and serviceability at a sensationally low price.* Men's plain toe shoe of fine genuine soft, **black kid leather.** Strong leather soles. Low, rubber-tipped heel. SIZES: 6 to 12. Wide widths. PRICE, PREPAID, **$4.48**

5K7867 *A favored style in a man's button shoe. A saving on every pair.* De Luxe dress model of **black gunmetal leather** with stylish perforations. Heavy leather soles. SIZES: 6 to 12. WIDTHS: EE, E, and D. PRICE, PREPAID, **$4.28**

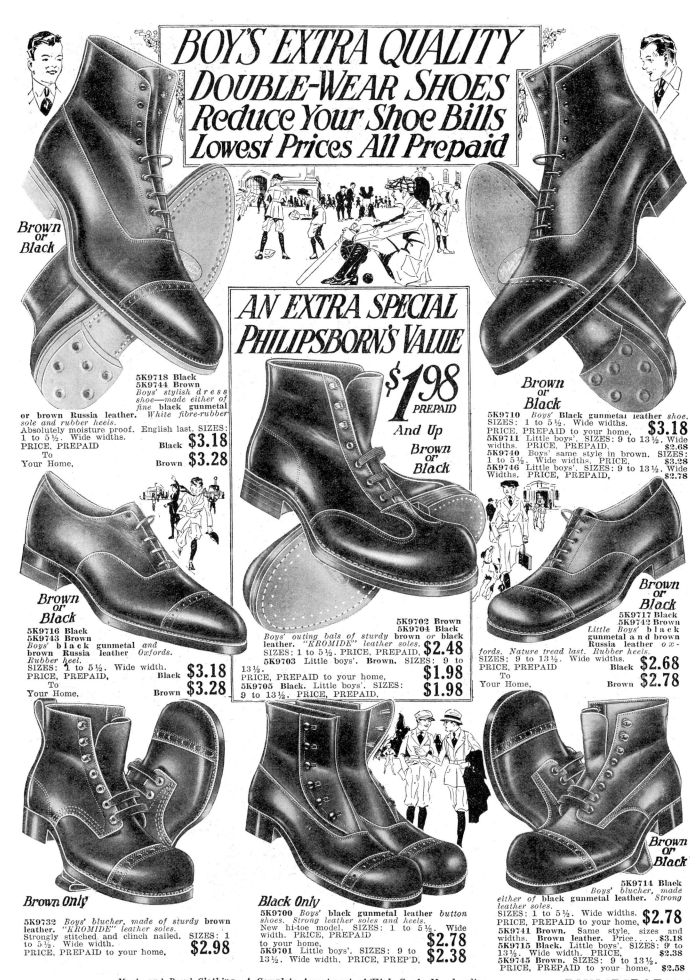

BOY'S EXTRA QUALITY
DOUBLE-WEAR SHOES
Reduce Your Shoe Bills
Lowest Prices All Prepaid

AN EXTRA SPECIAL PHILIPSBORN'S VALUE

$1.98 PREPAID
And Up
Brown or Black

Brown or Black

5K9718 Black
5K9744 Brown
Boys' stylish dress shoe—made either of fine black gunmetal or brown Russia leather. White fibre-rubber sole and rubber heels. Absolutely moisture proof. English last. SIZES: 1 to 5½. Wide widths.
PRICE, PREPAID To Your Home, Black **$3.18**
Brown **$3.28**

Brown or Black

5K9710 *Boys'* Black gunmetal leather shoe. SIZES: 1 to 5½. Wide widths. PRICE, PREPAID to your home, **$3.18**
5K9711 Little boys'. SIZES: 9 to 13½. Wide widths. PRICE, PREPAID, **$2.68**
5K9740 Boys' same style in brown. SIZES: 1 to 5½. Wide widths. PRICE, **$3.28**
5K9746 Little boys'. SIZES: 9 to 13½. Wide Widths. PRICE, PREPAID, **$2.78**

Brown or Black

5K9716 Black
5K9743 Brown
Boys' black gunmetal and brown Russia leather Oxfords. Rubber heel. SIZES: 1 to 5½. Wide width.
PRICE, PREPAID, To Your Home, Black **$3.18**
Brown **$3.28**

5K9702 Brown
5K9704 Black
Boys' outing bals of sturdy brown or black leather. "KROMIDE" leather soles. SIZES: 1 to 5½. PRICE, PREPAID, **$2.48**
5K9703 Little boys'. Brown. SIZES: 9 to 13½.
PRICE, PREPAID to your home, **$1.98**
5K9705 Black. Little boys'. SIZES: 9 to 13½. PRICE, PREPAID, **$1.98**

Brown or Black

5K9717 Black
5K9742 Brown
Little Boys' black gunmetal and brown Russia leather oxfords. Nature tread last. Rubber heels. SIZES: 9 to 13½. Wide widths.
PRICE, PREPAID To Your Home, Black **$2.68**
Brown **$2.78**

Brown Only

5K9732 *Boys' blucher, made of sturdy brown leather. "KROMIDE" leather soles. Strongly stitched and clinch nailed.* SIZES: 1 to 5½. Wide width.
PRICE, PREPAID to your home, **$2.98**

Black Only

5K9700 *Boys' black gunmetal leather button shoes. Strong leather soles and heels. New hi-toe model.* SIZES: 1 to 5½. Wide width. PRICE, PREPAID to your home, **$2.78**
5K9701 Little boys'. SIZES: 9 to 13½. Wide width. PRICE, PREP'D, **$2.38**

Brown or Black

5K9714 Black
Boys' blucher, made either of black gunmetal leather. Strong leather soles. SIZES: 1 to 5½. Wide widths. PRICE, PREPAID to your home, **$2.78**
5K9741 Brown. Same style, sizes and widths. Brown leather. Price.....**$3.18**
5K9715 Black. Little boys'. SIZES: 9 to 13½. Wide width. PRICE, **$2.38**
5K9745 Brown. SIZES: 9 to 13½. PRICE, PREPAID to your home, **$2.58**

Men's and Boys' Clothing—A Complete Assortment of High Grade Merchandise—at Notable Price Reductions. See Pages 256 to 273

PHILIPSBORN'S

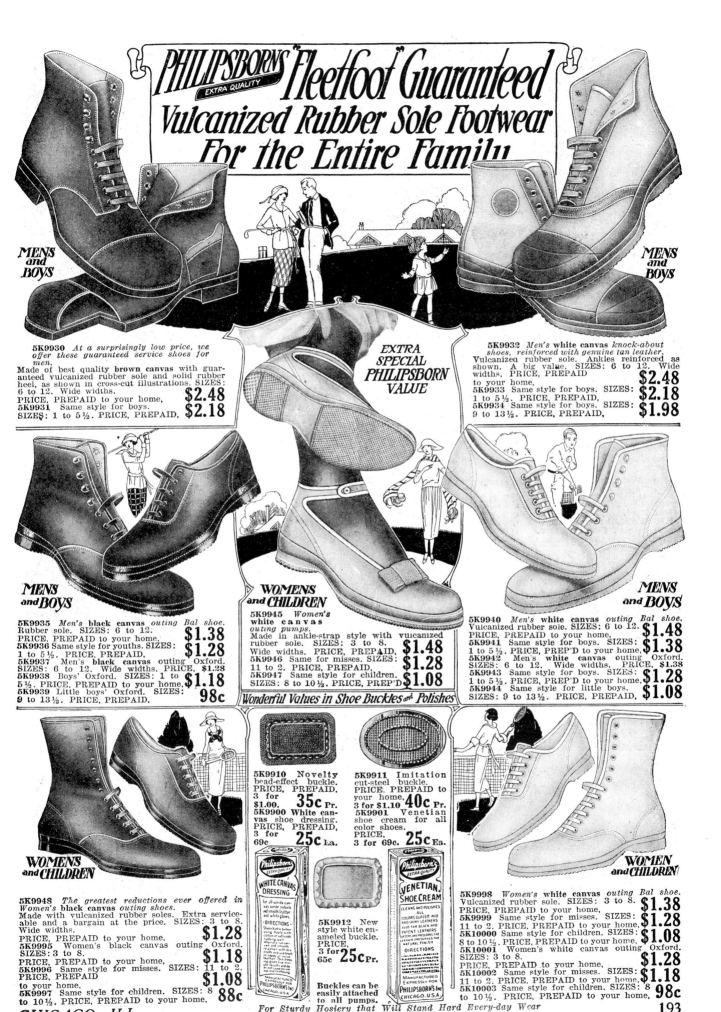

PHILIPSBORNS *EXTRA QUALITY* "Fleetfoot" Guaranteed Vulcanized Rubber Sole Footwear For the Entire Family

MENS and BOYS

5K9930 *At a surprisingly low price, we offer these guaranteed service shoes for men.* Made of best quality **brown canvas** with guaranteed vulcanized rubber sole and solid rubber heel, as shown in cross-cut illustrations. SIZES: 6 to 12. Wide widths. PRICE, PREPAID to your home, **$2.48**
5K9931 Same style for boys. SIZES: 1 to 5½. PRICE, PREPAID, **$2.18**

EXTRA SPECIAL PHILIPSBORN VALUE

MENS and BOYS

5K9932 *Men's white canvas knock-about shoes, reinforced with genuine tan leather.* Vulcanized rubber sole. Ankles reinforced as shown. A big value. SIZES: 6 to 12. Wide widths. PRICE, PREPAID to your home, **$2.48**
5K9933 Same style for boys. SIZES: 1 to 5½. PRICE, PREPAID, **$2.18**
5K9934 Same style for boys. SIZES: 9 to 13½. PRICE, PREPAID, **$1.98**

MENS and BOYS

5K9935 *Men's black canvas outing Bal shoe.* Rubber sole. SIZES: 6 to 12. PRICE, PREPAID to your home, **$1.38**
5K9936 Same style for youths. SIZES: 1 to 5½. PRICE, PREPAID, **$1.28**
5K9937 Men's black canvas outing Oxford. SIZES: 6 to 12. Wide widths. PRICE, **$1.28**
5K9938 Boys' Oxford. SIZES: 1 to 5½. PRICE, PREPAID to your home, **$1.18**
5K9939 Little boys' Oxford. SIZES: 9 to 13½. PRICE, PREPAID, **98c**

WOMENS and CHILDREN

5K9945 *Women's white canvas outing pumps.* Made in ankle-strap style with vulcanized rubber sole. SIZES: 3 to 8. Wide widths. PRICE, PREPAID, **$1.48**
5K9946 Same for misses. SIZES: 11 to 2. PRICE, PREPAID, **$1.28**
5K9947 Same style for children. SIZES: 8 to 10½. PRICE, PREP'D **$1.08**

MENS and BOYS

5K9940 *Men's white canvas outing Bal shoe.* Vulcanized rubber sole. SIZES: 6 to 12. PRICE, PREPAID to your home, **$1.48**
5K9941 Same style for boys. SIZES: 1 to 5½. PRICE, PREP'D to your home, **$1.38**
5K9942 Men's white canvas outing Oxford. SIZES: 6 to 12. Wide widths. PRICE, **$1.38**
5K9943 Same style for boys. SIZES: 1 to 5½. PRICE, PREP'D to your home, **$1.28**
5K9944 Same style for little boys. SIZES: 9 to 13½. PRICE, PREPAID, **$1.08**

Wonderful Values in Shoe Buckles and Polishes

5K9910 Novelty bead-effect buckle. PRICE, PREPAID. 3 for $1.00. **35c** Pr.
5K9900 White canvas shoe dressing. PRICE, PREPAID. 3 for 69c **25c** La.

5K9911 Imitation cut-steel buckle. PRICE. PREPAID to your home, 3 for $1.10 **40c** Pr.
5K9901 Venetian shoe cream for all color shoes. PRICE, 3 for 69c. **25c** Ea.

Philipsborns *EXTRA QUALITY* WHITE CANVAS DRESSING
DIRECTIONS
MANUFACTURED EXPRESSLY FOR PHILIPSBORN'S Inc. CHICAGO, U.S.A.

5K9912 New style white enameled buckle. PRICE, 3 for 65c **25c** Pr.

Philipsborn's *EXTRA QUALITY* VENETIAN SHOE CREAM
CLEANS AND POLISHES ALL COLORS GLAZED KID AND SHINY LEATHERS ALSO TAN BLACK AND PATENT LEATHERS SOFTENS AND PRESERVES THE LEATHER, PRESERVES THE NATURAL FINISH
DIRECTIONS
MANUFACTURED EXPRESSLY FOR PHILIPSBORN'S Inc CHICAGO, U.S.A.

Buckles can be easily attached to all pumps.

WOMENS and CHILDREN

5K9948 *The greatest reductions ever offered in Women's black canvas outing shoes.* Made with vulcanized rubber soles. Extra serviceable and a bargain at the price. SIZES: 3 to 8. Wide widths. PRICE, PREPAID to your home, **$1.28**
5K9995 Women's black canvas outing Oxford. SIZES: 3 to 8. PRICE, PREPAID to your home, **$1.18**
5K9996 Same for misses. SIZES: 11 to 2. PRICE, PREPAID to your home, **$1.08**
5K9997 Same style for children. SIZES: 8 to 10½. PRICE, PREPAID to your home, **88c**

WOMEN and CHILDREN

5K9998 *Women's white canvas outing Bal shoe.* Vulcanized rubber sole. SIZES: 3 to 8. PRICE, PREPAID to your home, **$1.38**
5K9999 Same style for misses. SIZES: 11 to 2. PRICE, PREPAID to your home, **$1.28**
5K10000 Same style for children. SIZES: 8 to 10½. PRICE, PREPAID to your home, **$1.08**
5K10001 Women's white canvas outing Oxford. SIZES: 3 to 8. PRICE, PREPAID to your home, **$1.28**
5K10002 Same style for misses. SIZES: 11 to 2. PRICE, PREPAID to your home, **$1.18**
5K10003 Same style for children. SIZES: 8 to 10½. PRICE, PREPAID to your home, **98c**

CHICAGO, ILL.

For Sturdy Hosiery that Will Stand Hard Every-day Wear Consult Pages 209 to 215 and Save Money

FIRST QUALITY "WATERTYTE"
Guaranteed Rubber Footwear
For the Entire Family

Men's and Boys'

5K9963 Men's first quality Watertyte storm rubbers. SIZES: 6 to 12. PRICE, PREPAID to your home, **$1.18**
5K9964 Boys'. Sizes: 2½ to 6. PRICE, PREPAID, 98c
5K9965 Youths'. SIZES: 11 to 2. PRICE, PREPAID, 78c

Men's and Boys'

5K9950 Men's half hip length first quality Watertyte black rubber storm boots. SIZES: 6 to 12. (Order one size larger than shoes.) PRICE, PREPAID, **$3.98**
5K9951 Boys'. SIZES: 3 to 6. PRICE, PREPAID to your home, **$3.18**
5K9952 Youths'. SIZES: 11 to 2. PRICE, PREPAID to your home, **$2.38**

An Extra Special PHILIPSBORN VALUE

Men's and Boys'

5K9953 Men's first quality Watertyte knee-length boots of dull black rubber. Friction lined. SIZES: 6 to 12. (Order one size larger than shoes.) PRICE, PREPAID, **$3.48**
5K9954 Boys'. SIZES: 3 to 6. PRICE, PREPAID to your home, **$2.58**
5K9955 Youths'. SIZES: 11 to 2. PRICE, PREPAID to your home, **$1.88**

Men's and Boys'

5K9966 Men's Jersey lined Watertyte storm rubbers. SIZES: 6 to 12. (Order one-half size larger than shoes.) PRICE, **$1.08**
5K9967 Boys'. SIZES: 2½ to 6. PRICE, PREPAID to your home, **88c**

Women's and Childrens

Fleece Lined

5K9974 First quality Watertyte black rubber boots. Fleece lined. Moire effect on leg. Women's. SIZES: 2½ to 8. PRICE, **$2.18**
5K9975 Misses'. SIZES: 11 to 2, 1.78
5K9976 Children's. SIZES: 6 to 10½. 1.58

Men's and Boys'

5K9971 Men's Jersey lined Watertyte rubbers. SIZES: 6 to 12. (Order one-half size larger than shoes.) PRICE, PREPAID, **$1.08**
5K9972 Boys'. SIZES: 2½ to 6. PRICE, PREPAID to your home, **88c**

Women's only

5K9986 Women's first quality Watertyte dress rubbers at a low price. Jersey cloth. Lined. SIZES: 2½ to 8. (Order one-half size larger than shoes.) PRICE, PREPAID, to your home, **73c**

Women's only

5K9984 Women's first quality Watertyte dress rubbers with Louis heel. Specially priced. SIZES: 2½ to 8. (Order one-half size larger than shoes.) PRICE, PREPAID, to your home, **73c**

Women's only

5K9983 Women's sandal foot holds of first quality Watertyte rubber. Will fit any height heel. SIZES: 2½ to 8. (Order same size as your shoe.) PRICE, PREPAID to your home, **58c**

Women's and Children's

5K9988 First quality Watertyte storm rubbers Women's. Jersey cloth lined. SIZES: 2½ to 8. PRICE, PREPAID, **73c**
5K9989 Misses', 11 to 2. PRICE, **68c**
5K9990 Children's. 6 to 10½. PRICE, **58c**

Women's only

5K9985 Women's first quality Watertyte storm rubbers at a cash saving. SIZES: 2½ to 8. (Order one-half size larger than shoes.) PRICE, PREPAID, to your home, **73c**

194

PHILIPSBORN'S Give You More in Service, More in Value and More in Actual Savings Than You Can Get Any Where Else. See Page 3

PHILIPSBORN'S

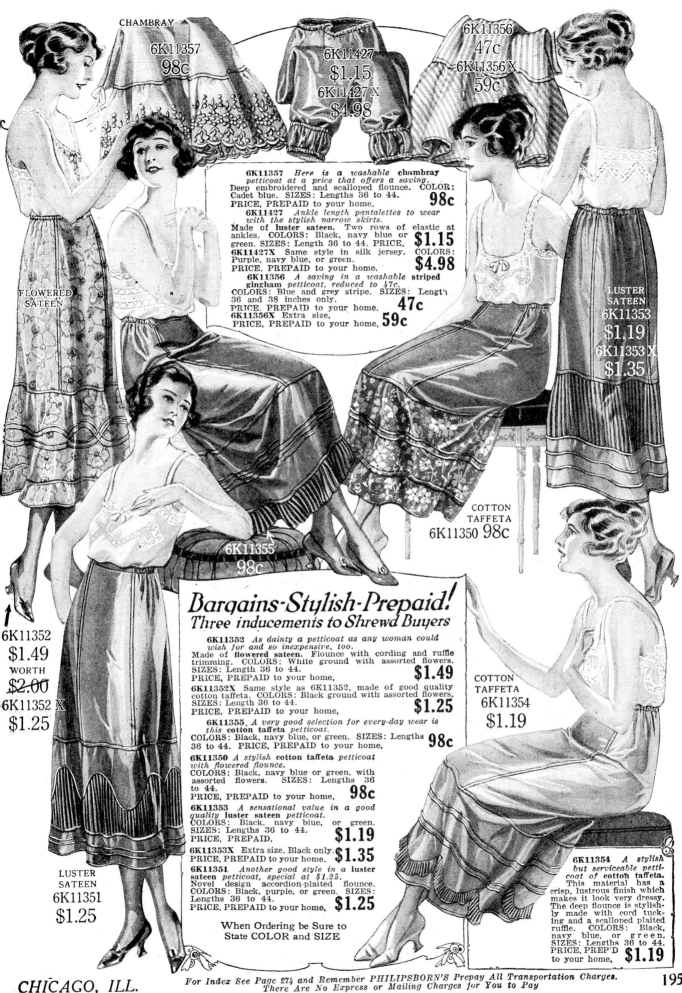

CHAMBRAY
6K11357
98c

6K11427
$1.15
6K11427 X
$4.98

6K11356
47c
6K11356 X
59c

FLOWERED
SATEEN

LUSTER
SATEEN
6K11353
$1.19
6K11353 X
$1.35

6K11357 *Here is a washable* chambray *petticoat at a price that offers a saving.*
Deep embroidered and scalloped flounce. COLOR:
Cadet blue. SIZES: Lengths 36 to 44.
PRICE, PREPAID to your home, **98c**
6K11427 *Ankle length pantalettes to wear with the stylish narrow skirts.*
Made of **luster sateen.** Two rows of elastic at ankles. COLORS: Black, navy blue or green. SIZES: Length 36 to 44. PRICE, **$1.15**
6K11427X Same style in silk jersey. COLORS:
Purple, navy blue, or green.
PRICE, PREPAID to your home, **$4.98**
6K11356 *A saving in a washable* striped gingham *petticoat, reduced to 47c.*
COLORS: Blue and grey stripe. SIZES: Length 36 and 38 inches only.
PRICE, PREPAID to your home, **47c**
6K11356X Extra size,
PRICE, PREPAID to your home, **59c**

6K11355
98c

COTTON
TAFFETA
6K11350 98c

6K11352
$1.49
WORTH
$2.00
6K11352 X
$1.25

COTTON
TAFFETA
6K11354
$1.19

Bargains-Stylish-Prepaid!
Three inducements to Shrewd Buyers

6K11352 *As dainty a petticoat as any woman could wish for and so inexpensive, too.*
Made of **flowered sateen.** Flounce with cording and ruffle trimming. COLORS: White ground with assorted flowers. SIZES: Length 36 to 44.
PRICE, PREPAID to your home, **$1.49**
6K11352X Same style as 6K11352, made of good quality cotton taffeta. COLORS: Black ground with assorted flowers. SIZES: Length 36 to 44.
PRICE, PREPAID to your home, **$1.25**
6K11355 *A very good selection for every-day wear is this cotton taffeta petticoat.*
COLORS: Black, navy blue, or green. SIZES: Lengths 36 to 44. PRICE, PREPAID to your home, **98c**
6K11350 *A stylish* **cotton taffeta** *petticoat with flowered flounce.*
COLORS: Black, navy blue or green, with assorted flowers. SIZES: Lengths 36 to 44.
PRICE, PREPAID to your home, **98c**
6K11353 *A sensational value in a good quality* **luster sateen** *petticoat.*
COLORS: Black, navy blue, or green. SIZES: Lengths 36 to 44.
PRICE, PREPAID, **$1.19**
6K11353X Extra size. Black only. **$1.35**
PRICE, PREPAID to your home,
6K11351 *Another good style in a* luster sateen *petticoat, special at $1.25.*
Novel design accordion-plaited flounce.
COLORS: Black, purple, or green. SIZES: Lengths 36 to 44.
PRICE, PREPAID to your home, **$1.25**

When Ordering be Sure to
State COLOR and SIZE

LUSTER
SATEEN
6K11351
$1.25

6K11354 *A stylish but serviceable petticoat of* cotton taffeta. This material has a crisp, lustrous finish which makes it look very dressy. The deep flounce is stylishly made with cord tucking and a scalloped plaited ruffle. COLORS: Black, navy blue, or green. SIZES: Lengths 36 to 44. PRICE, PREP'D to your home, **$1.19**

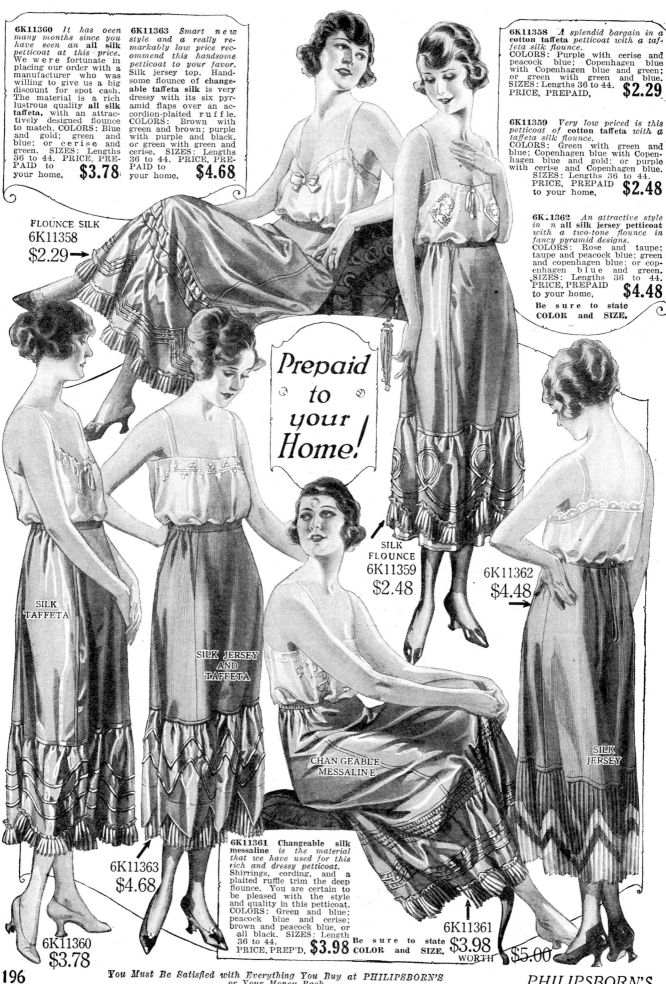

6K11360 It has been many months since you have seen an all silk petticoat at this price. We were fortunate in placing our order with a manufacturer who was willing to give us a big discount for spot cash. The material is a rich lustrous quality **all silk taffeta,** with an attractively designed flounce to match. COLORS: Blue and gold; green and blue; or cerise and green. SIZES: Lengths 36 to 44. PRICE, PREPAID to your home, **$3.78**

6K11363 Smart new style and a really remarkably low price recommend this handsome petticoat to your favor. Silk jersey top. Handsome flounce of **changeable taffeta silk** is very dressy with its six pyramid flaps over an accordion-plaited ruffle. COLORS: Brown with green and brown; purple with purple and black, or green with green and cerise. SIZES: Lengths 36 to 44. PRICE, PREPAID to your home, **$4.68**

6K11358 A splendid bargain in a **cotton taffeta** petticoat with a taffeta-silk flounce. COLORS: Purple with cerise and peacock blue; Copenhagen blue with Copenhagen blue and green; or green with green and blue. SIZES: Lengths 36 to 44. PRICE, PREPAID, **$2.29**

6K11359 Very low priced is this petticoat of **cotton taffeta** with a taffeta silk flounce. COLORS: Green with green and blue; Copenhagen blue with Copenhagen blue and gold; or purple with cerise and Copenhagen blue. SIZES: Lengths 36 to 44. PRICE, PREPAID to your home, **$2.48**

6K11362 An attractive style in n all silk jersey petticoat with a two-tone flounce in fancy pyramid designs. COLORS: Rose and taupe; taupe and peacock blue; green and copenhagen blue; or copenhagen blue and green. SIZES: Lengths 36 to 44. PRICE, PREPAID to your home, **$4.48**

Be sure to state COLOR and SIZE.

FLOUNCE SILK
6K11358
$2.29 →

Prepaid to your Home!

SILK TAFFETA

SILK JERSEY AND TAFFETA

← SILK FLOUNCE
6K11359
$2.48

6K11362
$4.48 →

SILK JERSEY

CHANGEABLE MESSALINE

6K11361 Changeable silk messaline is the material that we have used for this rich and dressy petticoat. Shirrings, cording, and a plaited ruffle trim the deep flounce. You are certain to be pleased with the style and quality in this petticoat. COLORS: Green and blue; peacock blue and cerise; brown and peacock blue, or all black. SIZES: Length 36 to 44. PRICE, PREP'D, **$3.98**

Be sure to state COLOR and SIZE.

6K11363
$4.68

6K11360
$3.78

6K11361
$3.98 WORTH $5.00

You Must Be Satisfied with Everything You Buy at PHILIPSBORN'S or Your Money Back

6K11366 *Seco silk top— silk taffeta flounce petticoat.* An immense bargain. COLORS: Green with green and cerise; Copenhagen blue with Copenhagen blue and gold; or purple with blue and red. SIZES: Lengths 36 to 44. PRICE, PREPAID to your home, **$2.38**

6K11364 *Tussah silk top, silk taffeta flounce petticoat.* COLORS: Copenhagen blue with gold and Copenhagen blue; green with cerise and green; or purple with blue and red. SIZES: Lengths 36 to 44. PRICE, PREPAID to your home, **$1.88**

6K11365 *Cotton taffeta top— silk taffeta flounce petticoat.* A big value. COLORS: Purple with blue and cerise; navy blue with green and cerise; or green with green and blue. SIZES: Lengths, 36 to 44. PRICE, PREPAID **$1.98**

6K11398 *An attractive style in a silk-mixed crepe dressing jacket.* Contrasting embroidery stitching on collar and sleeves. COLORS: Lavender, pink, light blue or yellow. SIZES: 32 to 44. PRICE, PREPAID, **$2.48**

6K11368 *Our well-known policy of keeping up quality and keeping down prices is conclusively shown here.* Think of getting this beautiful petticoat for only $3.88. It is made with a silk jersey top and a silk taffeta flounce. Fancy double cross cording on flounce. COLORS: French blue with copper and Copenhagen blue; green with green and blue; or purple with purple and black. SIZES: Length 36 to 44. PRICE. **$3.88**

6K11369 *Here are petticoat values that will create a sensation among women who are interested in saving.* At retail this petticoat would cost you not less than $7.00. Beautifully made of excellent grade silk jersey. Accordion plaited flounce has set-in diamond shaped panels of contrasting color. COLORS: Purple with gold; Copenhagen blue with rose; or taupe with rose. SIZES: Length 36 to 44. PRICE, PREPAID, **$3.98**

6K 11364 $1.88 WORTH $2.50
← SILK FLOUNCE

CREPE 6 K 11398 $2.48

6 K 11366 $2.38

SILK TAFFETA FLOUNCE →

The Best! at Low Prices!

6 K 11399 $1.59

SERPENTINE CREPE →

6 K 11365 $1.98 WORTH $2.50 ↓

WORTH $5.00

SILK JERSEY TOP SILK TAFFETA FLOUNCE 6 K 11368 $3.88

ALL SILK TAFFETA 6 K 11367 $3.75

Special Style Offerings

6K11399 *Serpentine crepe kimono jacket. Very special.* Embroidery. COLORS: Rose, Copenhagen blue or lavender. SIZES: 32 to 44. PRICE. **$1.59**

6K11367 *All silk taffeta petticoat.* COLORS: Blue and green; green and cerise; or rose and gold. SIZES: Lengths 36 to 44. PRICE. **$3.75**

ALL SILK JERSEY

6 K 11369 $3.98 WORTH $5.00

PHILIPSBORN'S "Everdainty" Undergarments Are Especially Designed for You Who Delight in Dainty Lingerie of New Style and High Quality. See Pages 216 to 241

STRIPED
GINGHAM
6 K 11372
$1.78

← CHAMBRAY
6 K 11373
$1.88

FLOWERED
VOILE
6 K 11371
$1.78

CHAMBRAY
6 K 11374
$2.68

CHECKED
GINGHAM
6 K 11376
$2.98

For Descriptions
See Page 199

Biggest Values
Latest Styles
Prepaid to your door

FLOWERED
VOILE
6 K 11375
$2.48

PLAID
GINGHAM
6 K 11370
$1.49

WORTH $2.00

"A Thing or Two to Remember" and Some Other Interesting
Facts to Be Found on Page 3

Descriptions of Garments on page 198

6K11370 We quote a very low price on this **plaid gingham** house dress. Real bargain value. Similar quality and style are selling in the shops at 50 to 75 cents more. Smartly shaped chambray collar. Poplin tie. Checked trimming. COLORS: Blue or rose plaid. SIZES: 32 to 44 bust. PRICE, PREPAID, **$1.49**

6K11372 Any woman would delight in wearing this dress apron. A pretty, high grade garment of good quality **striped gingham**. Chambray collar, attractively embroidered. COLORS: Lavender, Copenhagen blue, or grey. SIZES: 32 to 44 bust. PRICE, PREPAID to your home, **$1.78**

6K11374 It would be hard to find a more serviceable or attractive dress than this house or porch apron. The price is especially low for this quality **chambray**, the material that makes the garment. Embroidered collar and vestee. Fancy pockets. COLORS: Blue and white or pink and white. SIZES: 32 to 44 bust. PRICE, PREPAID to your home, **$2.68**

6K11375 The newest style in a house or porch dress is herewith offered you at a 25% reduction in price. Made of a pretty pattern **flowered voile**. Dressy enough for street wear. Large organdie collar, vestee, and cuffs. Patch pockets. COLORS: Lavender, Copenhagen blue, or rose. SIZES: 32 to 44 bust. PRICE, PREPAID, **$2.48**

6K11376 There is nothing more serviceable or better wearing than **checked gingham** which makes this dress. Although listed with our house dresses, this model is suitable for porch or street wear. Organdie collar. Organdie ruching as pictured. Self-material sash. COLORS: Pink or blue check. SIZES: 32 to 44 bust. PRICE, PREPAID to your home, **$2.98**

Be sure to state color and size desired.

6K11371 This house and porch dress of a pretty pattern **flowered voile** is very serviceable. With its embroidery shawl collar and wide sash, this model is dressy enough for street wear. COLORS: Copenhagen blue, lavender, or rose. SIZES: 32 to 44 bust. PRICE, PREPAID, **$1.78**

6K11373 Made in an entirely new style is this slip-over apron. Made of **plaid gingham and chambray**. Large round chambray collar. Rickrack trimming. COLORS: Blue plaid with blue or pink plaid with pink. SIZES: 32 to 44 bust. PRICE, PREPAID to your home, **$1.88**

STRIPED GINGHAM
6K11377
$1.69
WORTH $2.00

CHAMBRAY
6K11378
$2.98
WORTH $3.50

DOTTED VOILE
6K11379
$3.78
WORTH $4.50

Very! Special!

3 Stout-Special Values!

6K11377 It is so easy to save here when you practically have the money handed to you. Take for example this splendid style in a **striped gingham** house dress for stout women. Ordinarily, you would not be able to buy a dress of this quality for less than $2.00. Our special price is only $1.69. Note the becoming style of the new shaped lapel collar. Chambray and pearl button trimming. Patch pockets. A big value. COLORS: Blue or grey stripe. SIZES: 39 to 53 bust. PRICE, PREPAID to your home, **$1.69**

6K11378 The slump in prices which we predicted has taken place—prices reduced accordingly. When the crash came, we with our usual foresight were not overstocked, and were prepared to replenish our various lines at rock-bottom prices. Here is a remarkable value in a **chambray** house or porch dress for stout women. New style contrasting embroidery trims both collar and cornucopia-shaped patch pockets. Front yoke with soft plaits. COLORS: Lavender or blue. SIZES: 39 to 53 bust. PRICE, PREP'D, **$2.98**

6K11379 We believe in giving values that will make you come back to us season after season. Our prices are always very low, even though we make only a modest profit on each order. The price we ask for this stylish house or porch dress for stout women is actually little more than the material would cost you at retail. Fashioned of **dotted voile** and made in a style that makes it especially becoming to full figures. COLORS: Navy blue, lavender or black. SIZES 39 to 53 bust. PRICE, PREPAID, **$3.78**

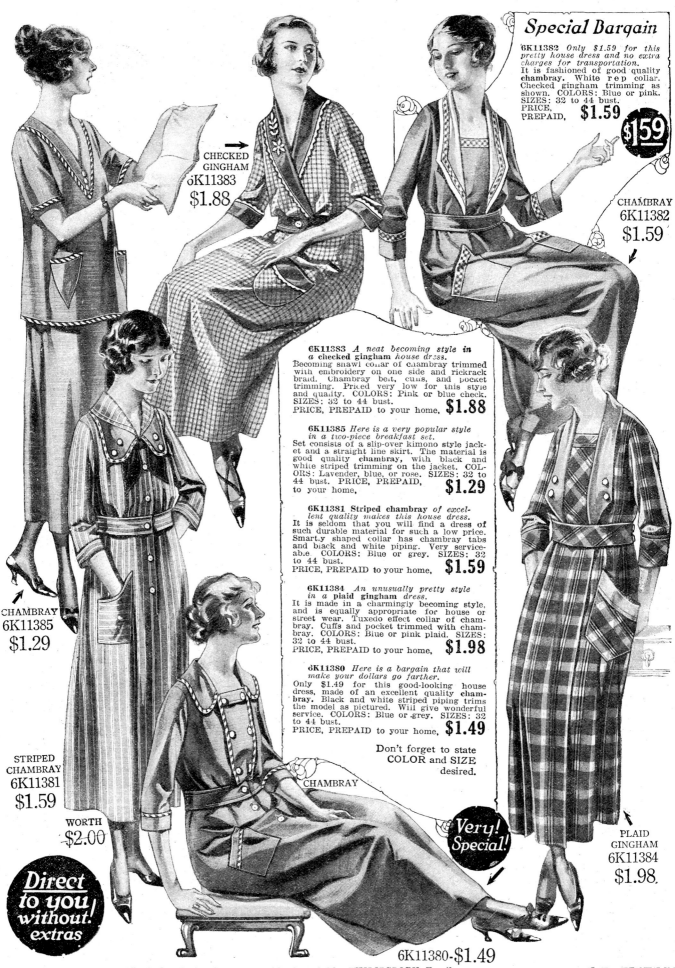

200
"Goods by the Yard." A New Member of The PHILIPSBORN Family. See Pages 250 to 255

PHILIPSBORN'S

6K11391 *An unusual value in a porch or house dress.* When you see how pretty this model is, you will decide that you have never made a better investment. It is fashioned of good quality **striped voile.** Organdie ruching forms fetching little frills on the large, becoming collar, vestee, and sleeves. Belt with sash ends. A bargain at the price. COLORS: Lavender or light blue. SIZES: 32 to 44 bust. PRICE, PREPAID to your home, **$1.98**

VOILE
6K11391
$1.98

6K11387
$1.69
WORTH ~~$2.00~~

GINGHAM

GINGHAM AND CHAMBRAY
6K11388
$1.98

Here they are! All Bargains!

6K11387 *You will make no mistake if you select this house dress.* The material is a durable **striped gingham.** Large, attractive collar. Chambray trimming. Rick-rack braid. COLORS: Cadet blue and white or grey and white stripe. SIZES: 32 to 44 bust. PRICE, PREPAID to your home, **$1.69**

6K11386 *The biggest bargain offering that you will find this year.* This attractive house or porch dress of good quality **chambray,** special at $1.98. Organdie ruching as shown. COLORS: Light blue or pink. SIZES: 32 to 44 bust. PRICE, PREPAID to your home, **$1.98**

6K11388 *Here is a very individual style in a house or porch dress.* **Checked gingham** model with chambray skirt and trimming. COLORS: Cadet blue skirt with blue check or pink skirt with pink check. SIZES: 32 to 44 bust. PRICE, PREPAID to your home, **$1.98**

6K11389 *As comfortable as it is attractive is this* **chambray dress.** It is intended for either house or porch wear, and is prettily trimmed with fancy cord braiding. Made in one piece and loosely belted. COLORS: Pink or cadet blue. SIZES: 32 to 44 bust. PRICE, PREPAID to your home, **$2.48**

6K11390 *Any woman will delight in wearing this house or porch dress.* It is a **checked gingham** model, made very becoming with a large Tuxedo collar of rep. Rep cuffs. Single sash end. Patch pocket. COLORS: Light blue or lavender check. SIZES: 32 to 44 bust. PRICE, PREPAID to your home, **$2.48**

Always be Sure to State COLOR and SIZE Desired

6K11390
$2.48

CHAMBRAY
6K11389
$2.48

CHAMBRAY

Bargain Prices
6K11386
$1.98

GINGHAM

CHICAGO, ILL.

For Comfortable House Slippers and Shoes, See Our Shoe Section, Pages 157 to 194

Dresses with Style and Charm

6K11392 *Your big chance to save money. A bargain.* The only thing that this house or porch dress has in common with house dresses is the very moderate price. It is made of **figured box voile** and charming enough for indoor or outdoor wear. Large crossover collar terminates in sash ends. Organdie ruching. COLORS: Pink, blue or lavender. SIZES: 32 to 44 bust. PRICE, PREP'D to your home, **$2.98**

6K11394 *A very youthful style house dress. Priced extremely low.* One of our most becoming house or porch dresses, made of **plaid voile** and designed with basque front, sash and tunic over a full gathered skirt. Embroidered organdie collar and cuffs. Piping. A money-saving opportunity. COLORS: Combination plaid of blue, rose and green. SIZES: 32 to 44 bust. PRICE, PREPAID, **$2.98**

6K11396 *Extremely effective and very reasonably priced. Real big value.* This house or porch dress is so very pretty that it really belongs among our regular wash dresses. It is a **plaid gingham** model made very smart and becoming with a Tuxedo effect collar and vestee. Both collar and vestee have embroidery and hemstitching in harmonizing color. Set-in flared pockets. Sash belt. COLORS: Blue or pink plaid. SIZES: 32 to 44 bust. PRICE, PREPAID to your home, **$3.75**

6K11395 *Undoubtedly one of our most becoming styles.* This charming two-piece house or porch dress is made of excellent quality **washable pongee**, a new and favored material of beautiful silky texture. Organdie vestee and collar. Set-in pockets. Sash belt. COLORS: Blue or pink. SIZES: 32 to 44 bust. PRICE, PREPAID to your home, **$3.75**

Be Sure to Always State Color and Size

VOILE

6K11395
$3.75

6K11396
$3.75

PLAID GINGHAM

PLAID GINGHAM
6K11394
$2.98
WORTH
$3.75

WASHABLE PONGEE

6K11392
$2.98

Be Sure to Always State Color and Size

6K11393 *Here is a distinctive house or porch dress priced very low.* It is a dress that any woman would delight in wearing, and is quoted at a special price reduction. The material is a good quality **linene**. The style a new long waisted model which slips over head. Contrasting embroidery and stitching. Linene vestee and collar. Part-way button fastening. COLORS: Light blue or pink. SIZES: 32 to 44 bust. PRICE, PREPAID, **$2.88**

6K11397 *If you want real value you will not overlook this amazing offer.* We have eclipsed all previous efforts in this offer. House or porch dress of **novelty figured voile** in the very newest design, yet the price is only $3.69. Separate bolero blouse opening over organdie vestee. Skirt has wide piped folds, button trimming. COLORS: Blue or rose. SIZES: 32 to 44 bust. PRICE, PREPAID to your home, **$3.69**

6K11393
$2.88

Big! Value! **$3.69** 6K11397
VOILE

PHILIPSBORN'S

Bought Right and Sold Right!

6K11404 *An exceedingly attractive Japanese Kimono.* **Japanese cotton crepe** with all-over floral embroidery makes this garment an unusually fine value at the low price that we quote. Wide, flowing sleeves in real Japanese style add extreme gracefulness. Sash belt. You will be delighted with the beauty and grace of this kimono. COLORS: Lavender, cadet blue, or rose. SIZES: One size only. Full cut. PRICE, PREPAID to your home, **$2.98**

6K11402 *We underbuy and we undersell as these prices show.* Where but at PHILIPSBORN'S would you hope to find a kimono of this style and quality for only $1.88. Made of good quality **serpentine crepe.** Inch-wide Persian banding trims the wide, smartly-shaped sleeves, the neck and front of garment. Shirrings. Tassels and button trimming. COLORS: Rose, light blue, or lavender. SIZES: 32 to 44 bust. PRICE, PREPAID to your home, **$1.88**

6K11401 *Every woman should have one of these pretty embroidered kimonos.* We have priced this garment at only $1.98,—a very reasonable figure as you will agree when you see the excellent quality **serpentine crepe** of which it is made. Harmonizing silk floss embroidery. Ribbon bows at front fastening. Single pocket. COLORS: Copenhagen blue or rose. SIZES: 32 to 44 bust. PRICE, PREPAID to your home, **$1.98**

6K11403 *One of the most charming of the new slip-over kimonos.* This pretty garment is made of good quality **serpentine crepe,** with hand embroidery buttonholing around neck, sleeves, and sash openings. Sides gracefully draped and finished with tassels. COLORS: Copenhagen blue or rose. SIZES: 32 to 44 bust. PRICE, PREPAID, **$2.28**

Always be Sure to State COLOR and SIZE Desired

JAPANESE CREPE
6K11404
$2.98

SERPENTINE CREPE
6K11402
$1.88

WORTH
$3.75

6K11403
$2.28
CREPE

CHALLIS
6K11400
$1.98

SERPENTINE CREPE
6K11401
$1.98

SERPENTINE CREPE
6K11405
$2.98

6K11400 *An inexpensive selection in a pretty new kimono.* The low price, too, is an added attraction—only $1.98 for an exceptionally good grade of **flowered challis.** Solid color crepe is used for the large Dutch collar and cuffs, both edged with silk cord. Elastic waistband. Silk bow. COLORS: Copenhagen blue with navy blue and rose flower, or rose with blue flower. SIZES: 32 to 44 bust. PRICE, PREPAID to your home, **$1.98**

6K11405 *A most attractive style in a serpentine crepe kimono.* We have not shown a prettier style or a greater value in many seasons than this kimono, specially priced at $2.98. New features are the butterfly sleeves and the cone-shaped patch pockets. Satin trimming around collar, sleeves, and pockets. Elastic waistband. Ribbon bow. COLORS: Copenhagen blue, rose or purple. SIZES: 32 to 44 bust. PRICE, PREPAID to your home, **$2.98**

Latest Style **Big Bargain** $1.98

CHICAGO, ILL.

For Index See Page 274 and Remember PHILIPSBORN'S Prepay All Transportation Charges. There Are No Express or Mailing Charges for You to Pay

203

Novel and Stylish

6K11406 *Jacket-effect kimono* of **silk and cotton crepe.** Embroidered designs both front and back. Embroidered sash opening for ribbon sash. COLORS: Copenhagen blue or rose. SIZES: 32 to 44 bust. PRICE, PREPAID to your home. **$3.98**

CREPE
6K11406
$3.98
WORTH
$5.00

SERPENTINE CREPE
6K11411
$2.98

COATEE EFFECT

SECO SILK

6K11409
$3.48

6K11408 We are able to offer you the lowest possible prices because we buy right.
On this attractive kimono we are giving you the advantage of every saving that we have been able to make. It is a **flowered serpentine crepe** model, designed with coatee-effect overblouse that is very new and becoming. Ribbon ruching adds dressiness as pictured. COLORS: Lavender, Copenhagen blue or rose. SIZES: 32 to 44 bust. PRICE, PREP'D. **$3.98**

FANCY SERPENTINE CREPE
6K11408
$3.98
WORTH $5.00

SERPENTINE CREPE
6K11407
$3.48

SERPENTINE CREPE
6K11410
$3.68

Last Minute Styles
Imported Adaptations

6K11407 *Slip-over kimonos at an extremely low price.* **Serpentine crepe** of extra good quality makes the model. Contrasting and self-color embroidery forms an elaborate design both front and back. Narrow satin puffings outline the neck, the part-way opening and the kimono sleeves. Ribbon sash. Lavender, rose, or Copenhagen blue. SIZES: 32 to 44 bust. PRICE, PREPAID, **$3.48**

6K11410 *Here is an exceptionally dressy style in a new kimono model.* The material is a good quality **serpentine crepe,** and the smart design features graceful Mandarin sleeves. Richly embroidered both front and back. Ribbon sash and ruchings. Embroidered sash openings. Full length front opening. COLORS: Copenhagen blue, rose or lavender. SIZES: 32 to 44 bust. PRICE, PREPAID to your home, **$3.68**

6K11411 *A new style kimono—at a bargain price.* It is fashioned of **serpentine crepe,** and is made very attractive with a large self-material cape collar. Self-tone embroidery through center of collar. Embroidery scalloping on edge of collar and cuffs. Elastic waistband. Patch pockets. COLORS: Rose or Copenhagen blue. SIZES: 32 to 44 bust. PRICE PREPAID to your home **$2.98**

6K11409 *One of our prettiest slip-over kimonos—dainty and priced low.* **Dotted seco silk** of excellent quality makes the model. Shirrings at the front and back hold the garment to graceful lines. Satin ribbon banding at square neckline and kimono sleeves. Satin ribbon bows at each side of shirrings. COLORS: Lavender, rose, or Copenhagen blue. SIZES: 32 to 44 bust. PRICE, PREPAID to your home, **$3.48**

A New Department—"Goods by the Yard." You Cannot Equal These Values Any Where. See Pages 250 to 255

PHILIPSBORN'S

PERCALE
6K11414
$1.69

PERCALE
6K11417
$1.48

7
Bargains

MERCERIZED
RAMIE
6K11413
$1.69

WORTH
$2.00

GINGHAM
6K11418
$1.39

PERCALE

CHAMBRAY

PERCALE

47c
6K11412

Priced to Give the Greatest Value

6K11418 *A neat serviceable style in a coverall house dress or apron.* Made of **striped gingham** with chambray collar, cuffs, vestee and pocket trimming. COLORS: Cadet blue or grey stripe. SIZES: Small, medium or large. PRICE, PREPAID to your home, **$1.39**

6K11412 *Offered at a special price saving is this tea apron of* **figured percale.** Just what you will want to slip over your best dresses. It will pay you to order a few of these. Patch pockets. Ruffle trimming. COLORS: White with assorted figures. Cut large. PRICE, PREPAID, **47c**

6K11413 *As pretty a style as you could want, and very moderately priced.* Coverall house dress or apron of **mercerized ramie.** Embroidered rickrack braid and rep trimming. COLORS: Pink or cadet blue. SIZES: Small, medium or large. PRICE, PREPAID to your home, **$1.69**

6K11416 *A money-saving opportunity in this coverall house dress or apron.* Made of good quality **chambray.** Plaid percale trimming. Smartly shaped yoke. Rickrack braid trimming. COLORS: Blue or pink. SIZES: Small, medium or large. PRICE, PREPAID, **$1.37**

When ordering state Color and Sizes desired.

6K11414 *A novel style in a plaid percale house dress or apron.* Sash belt. COLORS: Pink or blue plaid. SIZES: Small, medium or large. PRICE, PREPAID, **$1.69**

6K11417 Plaid percale *coverall house dress or apron at a cash saving.* Chambray trimming. Fancy rickrack braid. COLORS: Pink or blue plaid. SIZES: Small, medium or large. PRICE, PREPAID to your home, **$1.48**

6K11415 *Great serviceability at a low price—coverall house dress or apron, only $1.48.* Made of **striped percale** with solid color chambray trimming. COLORS: Pink, blue or lavender. SIZES: small, medium or large. PRICE, PREPAID to your home, **$1.48**

6K11416-$1.37 6K11415-$1.48

CHICAGO, ILL.

There Is Genuine Economy in PHILIPSBORN'S Hosiery.
Consult Pages 209 to 215 and Save Money

205

6K11420 49c

Serviceable & Economical!
All Big Values!

6K11423 A splendid economy for you in this coverall house dress or apron. Made of **striped percale**. Neat piping. COLORS: White ground with contrasting stripes of blue, lavender, pink and grey. SIZES: small, medium or large. PRICE, PREPAID to your home, **$1.29**

6K11420 A bib apron is really a necessity with one's good dresses. **Novelty figured percale** with contrasting piping. Patch pocket. COLORS: White with assorted figure. SIZES: cut large. PRICE, PREPAID to your home, **49c**

6K11419 One of the most practical aprons made is this water-proof garment. Material is a **rubberized checked fabric**. Bib style. COLORS: Black and white check or navy blue and white check. SIZES: cut large. PRICE, PREPAID to your home, **59c**

6K11425 Many women prefer an apron that does not show soil readily. The neat coverall apron is of **indigo material**. Kimono sleeves. All around belt. Patch pocket. COLOR: Indigo blue. SIZES: Small, medium or large. PRICE, PREP'D to your home, **$1.25**

6K11424 Special! **Striped gingham** coverall dress or apron. Rick-rack braid. Patch pocket. COLOR: Blue and grey stripe. SIZES: Small, medium or large. PRICE, PREPAID to your home **$1.19**

STRIPED PERCALE

PERCALE

6K11419 59c

INDIGO CLOTH

6K11425 $1.25

RUBBERIZED

GINGHAM
6K11424
$1.19
←

↑
6K11423
$1.29

PERCALE
6K11426
$1.25

Bargain!

6K11426 You'll rarely find an apron of such good material at so low a price. Made of solid color **percale** with striped piping. Rep vestee. Rep-trimmed patch pocket. Striped piping as pictured. Can be worn as a house dress. COLORS: Blue or pink. SIZES: Small, medium or large. PRICE, PREP'D, **$1.25**

LINENE

6K11422 A neat, becoming style in a coverall house dress or apron at a big price cut. Made of **linene** with contrasting piping. COLORS: Light blue or pink. SIZES: Small, medium or large. PRICE, PREPAID to your home, **99c**

6K11421 For the woman who prefers an unbelted style we offer this coverall or apron. Made of **checked gingham** and neatly piped. COLORS: Navy blue and white check or black and white check. SIZES: Small, medium or large. PRICE, PREPAID to your home, **78c**

6K 11422
99c

GINGHAM WORTH $1.00

6K11421   78c

First Quality Triple Switch

This is a very satisfactory switch and a wonderful economy at our low price. It is easy to dress in any desired style.

3K30000 18 inches. Wt. 1¼ oz. PRICE. **$1.10**
3K30001 20 inches. Wt. 1½ oz. PRICE. **$1.49**
3K30002 22 inches. Wt. 1¾ oz. PRICE. **$1.69**
3K30003 24 inches. Weight, 2 oz. PRICE, PREPAID to your home. **$1.98**
3K30004 26 inches. Wt. 2½ oz. PRICE. **$2.39**
3K30005 28 inches. Wt. 3 oz. PRICE. **$2.98**

Be sure to send sample of your hair cut close to the roots.

Castle Bob-Newest Craze!

3K30016 The "Castle Bob"—the very latest style in hair dressing. Made of first quality human hair, and furnished in all colors except grey. Easy to arrange. PRICE, PREPAID to your home. **$3.98**

Castle Swirl Comb Free!

3K30018 The "Castle" swirl or puff—with beautiful Spanish comb free.
The puff is made of first quality wavy human hair, and can be supplied in all regular shades. No grey. PRICE, PREPAID to your home, **$3.69**

Castle Psyche Knot on Comb

Here is the "Castle" Psyche knot—comb foundation, Made of naturally wavy human hair.
3K30021 Regular shades. PRICE, PREPAID to your home, **$2.49**
3K30022 Grey to white. PRICE, PREPAID to your home, **$3.98**

Castle Ear Puffs

3K30017 A charming youthful style—"Castl" ear puffs of first quality human hair. Beautifully waved and easy to pin in place. Regular shades. No grey. PRICE, PREPAID to your home, **$1.79**

Extra Superfine Quality Triple Switch

A special offering in an extra superfine quality triple switch. Made of specially refined human hair with beautiful natural wave. All colors except grey and white.
3K30006 18 inches. Weight, 1¼ oz. PRICE, **$1.78**
3K30007 20 inches. Weight, 1½ oz. PRICE, **$2.59**
3K30008 22 inches. Weight, 1¾ oz. PRICE, **$2.98**
3K30009 24 inches. Weight, 2 oz. PRICE, PREPAID, **$3.98**
3K30010 26 inches. Weight, 2½ oz. PRICE **$4.98**
3K30011 28 inches. Weight, 3 oz. PRICE, **$5.98**

Be sure to send sample of your own hair cut close to the roots.

Castle Ear Puffs with Curls

3K30020 A bewitching style—"Castle" ear puffs with curls at side. Made of first quality human hair with beautiful natural wave. Regular shades. No grey. Send sample of own hair cut close to roots. PRICE, PREPAID to your home, **$2.78**

Genuine French Convent First Quality Triple Switch

One of our finest switches at a bargain price.
Made of first quality genuine French convent hair. Can be had in all colors except grey and white.
3K30012 18 inches. Weight 1¼ oz. PRICE PREP'D **$3.98**
3K30013 20 inches. Wt. 1½ oz. PRICE, PREP'D **$4.98**
3K30014 22 inches. Wt. 1¾ oz. PRICE, PREP'D **$6.98**
3K30015 24 inches. Wt. 2 oz. PRICE, PREP'D **$8.98**

Be sure to send sample of your own hair cut close to the roots.

Transformations

You can dress your hair in the most becoming styles with this beautiful transformation of medium quality human hair. Beautifully waved. All regular shades.

	Regular shades.	
3K30023 Fine medium.	22-inch band	$1.98
3K30025 Fine medium.	14-inch band	1.59
3K30027 Extra superfine.	22-inch band	2.69
3K30029 Extra superfine.	14-inch band	1.98
3K30031 French 1st quality.	22-inch band	4.98

	Grey to white.	
3K30024 Fine medium.	22-inch band	2.98
3K30026 Fine medium.	14-inch band	2.69
3K30028 Extra superfine.	22-inch band	4.98
3K30030 Extra superfine.	14-inch band	2.98
3K30032 French 1st quality.	22-inch band	6.98

Be sure to send sample of your own hair cut close to the roots.

La Veda
Kleinerts
Invisible!
Garment Shield

9K1766 *Kleinert's garment shield with front and back sections of* **pink or white scrim** *net. Rubberized shields. State bust measure.* SIZES: 3, 4 and 5. PRICE, PREPAID, **95c**

Marvel *Shields*
Dress *Made by Kleinert* *Shields*

9K1767 *Kleinert's marvel dress shield. White nainsook. Rubber interlining.* PRICE PREPAID to your home. Size 2, 15c; Size 3, 17c; Size 4, 19c; Size 5, 21c.

Rubber Sheeting!

9K1780 *Rubber sheeting for infants' bed sheets, mattress protectors, etc.* Comes in different widths and grades. ¾ single face sheeting. PRICE, PREPAID to your home, **49c**
9K1781 *4/4 single face sheeting.* PRICE, PREPAID to your home, **79c**
9K1782 *4/4 double face sheeting.* PRICE, PREPAID to your home, **89c**
9K1783 *6/4 double face sheeting* (1½ yards). PRICE, PREPAID to your home. **$2.19**

Kleinerts

Curity Curad's **6** Pad Continuous Roll Sanitary Napkins

Sanitary Napkins

9K1751 *Absorbent Sanitary napkins.*
Price Prepaid to Your Home — Pkg. of 6 for **19c** — Pkg. of 12 for **36c**

9K1752 *Sanitary napkins. Six in roll. Curad's.* PRICE, PREPAID to your home, Package of 6 for **35c**

Kleinerts "Jiffy" Pants

9K1755 *Infants' rubber drawers.* Large, medium or small. PRICE, **39c**

Pure Gum Rubber!

Kleinerts "Snookums"

9K1756 *Infants' drawers.* SIZES: Small, medium or large. PRICE, PREPAID. **49c**

4-Ply

Birdseye Napkins

9K1785 *4-ply birdseye sanitary napkins, removable rubber protector.* PRICE, PREP'D to your home, **39c**

"Hickory" Waist with Garters for Boys or Girls

9K1778 *Made of white sateen with garters attached.* SIZES: 2 to 14. PRICE, PREP'D. **89c**

Hose Supporters Childrens

9K1779 *Children's elastic garters. White or black.* SIZES: 2, 3, 4. PRICE, PREPD. **15c**

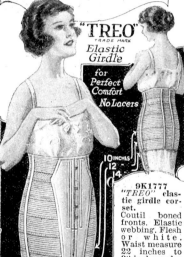

"TREO"
TRADE MARK
Elastic Girdle
for Perfect Comfort No Lacers

10 INCHS 12 14

9K1777 *"TREO" elastic girdle corset.* Coutil boned fronts. Elastic webbing. Flesh or white. Waist measure 22 inches to 30 inches; also 32 inches. PRICE, P'P'D
10 inch **$2.88**
12 inch **3.38**
14 inch **3.68**

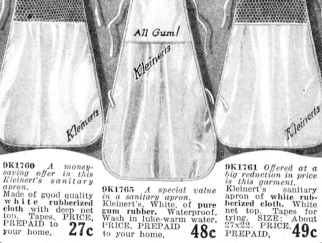

All Gum! Kleinerts Kleinerts Kleinerts

9K1760 *A money-saving offer in this Kleinert's sanitary apron.* Made of good quality **white rubberized** cloth with deep net top. Tapes. PRICE, PREPAID to your home. **27c**

9K1765 *A special value in a sanitary apron.* Kleinert's, White, of **pure gum rubber.** Waterproof. Wash in luke-warm water. PRICE, PREPAID to your home, **48c**

9K1761 *Offered at a big reduction in price is this garment.* Kleinert's sanitary apron of white rubberized cloth. White net top. Tapes for tying. SIZE: About 27x22. PRICE, PREPAID, **49c**

Womens Girdle Hose Supporters

9K1776 *Women's girdle hose supporters.* Mercerized elastic waistband in back. Four combination hose supporters attached full length. SIZES: Small, medium or large. PRICE, PREPAID to your home, **69c**

Sew on Hose Supporters

9K1775 *Women's white elastic garters. Ready to sew on corsets.* PRICE, **19c**

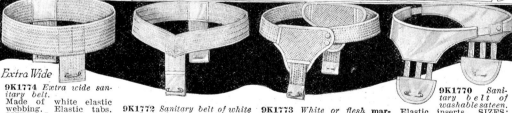

Extra Wide
9K1774 *Extra wide sanitary belt.* Made of white elastic webbing. Elastic tabs. SIZES: Small, medium or large. PRICE, PREPAID, **39c**

9K1772 *Sanitary belt of white or flesh elastic webbing.* Small, medium or large. PRICE, PREP'D **37c**

9K1773 *White or flesh marquisette sanitary belt.* Small, medium or large. PRICE, PREP'D **69c**

9K1770 *Sanitary belt of washable sateen.* Elastic inserts. SIZES: Small, medium or large. PRICE, PREP'D to your home, **29c**

9K1759 *Sanitary belt of white or flesh elastic.* SIZES: Small, medium or large. PRICE, **27c**

First Quality Rubber Goods

9K1769 Red rubber *fountain syringe.* Three hard rubber attachments: infant, rectal and curved vaginal. Guaranteed one year. PREP. **98c**
9K1787 *Same.* Best quality syringe. Guaranteed two years. Full set parts. PREPAID, **$1.75**

9K1764 *Hot water bag of* **good live rubber.** PRICE, PRPD. **98c**
9K1789 Combination parts for water bag and syringe. PRICE, PRPD. **69c**
9K1790 Hot water bottle and syringe attachment. PRICE, **$1.59**

9K1791 *Hot water bag of good rubber.* Guaranteed two years. PREPAID, **$1.45**
9K1792 Combination parts to fit 9K1791 consisting of syringe attachments. Prepaid, **69c**
9K1793 Combination hot water bottle and syringe Prepaid, **$1.98**

Douche

9K1753 *Vaginal douche with whirling spray. Hard rubber tube.* PRICE, PREPAID **98c**

Rubber Gloves U.S.

9K1786 *Seamless rubber gloves.* Order one size larger than ordinary glove—sizes: 7 to 10. PRICE, PREP'D to your home **45c**

PHILIPSBORN'S
Hosiery Bargains for the Family!

3 for $1.00 Guaranteed!
10K94

10K94 At our very latest reduced price these socks for men represent the best value it is possible to give. We guarantee three pairs of these socks to wear three months or new pairs free, if holes appear within that time. Knit from an excellent grade of **combed cotton.** Elastic ribbed tops. Reinforced footing. COLORS: Black, cordovan, or navy blue. SIZES: 9½ to 11½. PRICE, PREPAID to your home, 3 pairs for **$1.00**

3 for 69c Guaranteed!

10K12 Important savings on boys' or girls' guaranteed stockings—the greatest hosiery bargain that your money will buy. Three pairs guaranteed to wear three months or new pairs free. These extra durable stockings are knit from good quality **cotton** in wide, heavy rib. A special feature is the reinforced double knee which insures extra wear. The footing is knit in extra fine rib and is double knit at the heels and toes. Don't miss this splendid chance to secure these guaranteed stockings at a price that is no more than you would pay for stockings without a guarantee. Three pairs guaranteed three months or new pairs free if holes appear within that time. COLOR: Black only. SIZES: 5½ to 9½. PRICE, PREPAID to your home, 3 pairs for **69c**

10K12

3 for $1.45 Guaranteed!
10K46

10K46 A thrift message of importance for women who like to economize—3 pairs of stockings guaranteed to wear three months, or new pairs will be sent free. The price, too, has been specially reduced. Owing to the recent lull in business, we were fortunate in obtaining unusual price cuts from the manufacturers of these stockings, and we are passing this extra saving along to you. The stockings are made from **mercerized lisle,** are nicely proportioned with narrowed ankle and widened calf and have a seam up the back. The two-ply footing insures extra reinforcement where the wear comes. Double garter tops. These stockings have a very dressy appearance, and are among the most satisfactory of our moderately-priced hosiery. Remember our guarantee of wear—three pairs for three months, or new pairs free. COLORS: Black, white, brown, or grey. SIZES: 8½ to 10. PRICE, PREPAID to your home, 3 pairs for **$1.45**

CHICAGO, ILL.

Remember, There Are No Extra Charges for Express and Mailing When You Shop Here. We Prepay All Transportation Charges

209

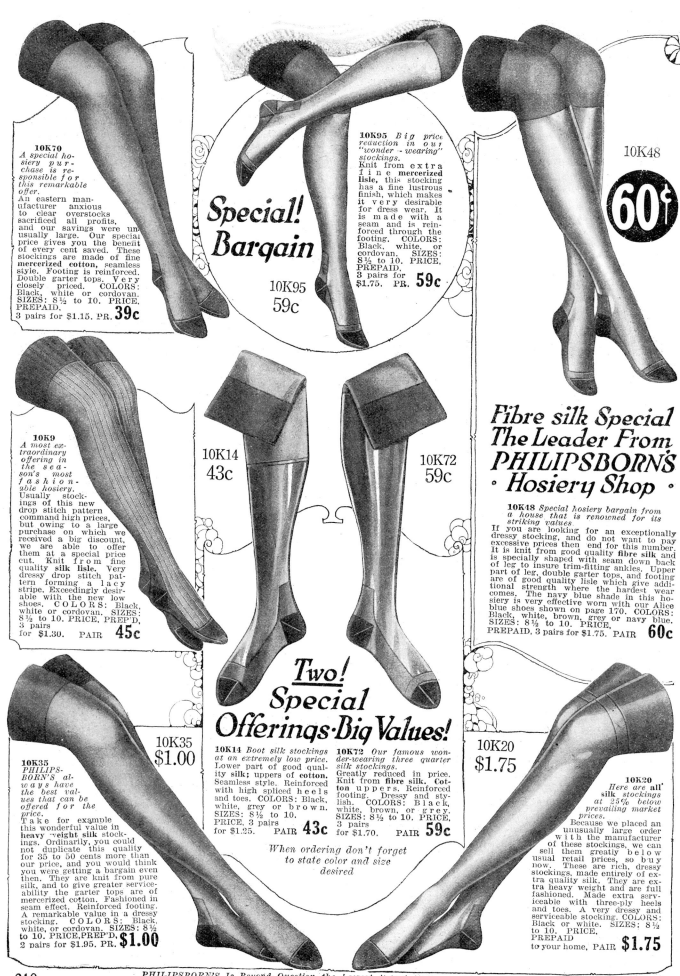

10K70
A special hosiery purchase is responsible for this remarkable offer.
An eastern manufacturer anxious to clear overstocks sacrificed all profits, and our savings were unusually large. Our special price gives you the benefit of every cent saved. These stockings are made of fine mercerized cotton, seamless style. Footing is reinforced. Double garter tops. Very closely priced. COLORS: Black, white or cordovan. SIZES: 8½ to 10. PRICE, PREPAID. 3 pairs for $1.15. PR. **39c**

Special! Bargain
10K95
59c

10K95 Big price reduction in our "wonder-wearing" stockings.
Knit from extra fine mercerized lisle, this stocking has a fine lustrous finish, which makes it very desirable for dress wear. It is made with a seam and is reinforced through the footing. COLORS: Black, white, or cordovan. SIZES: 8½ to 10. PRICE, PREPAID. 3 pairs for $1.75. PR. **59c**

10K48
60c

10K9
A most extraordinary offering in the season's most fashionable hosiery.
Usually stockings of this new drop stitch pattern command high prices, but owing to a large purchase on which we received a big discount, we are able to offer them at a special price cut. Knit from fine quality silk lisle. Very dressy drop stitch pattern forming a lacy stripe. Exceedingly desirable with the new low shoes. COLORS: Black, white or cordovan. SIZES: 8½ to 10. PRICE, PREP'D. 3 pairs for $1.30. PAIR **45c**

10K14
43c

10K72
59c

Fibre silk Special The Leader From PHILIPSBORN'S Hosiery Shop

10K48 Special hosiery bargain from a house that is renowned for its striking values.
If you are looking for an exceptionally dressy stocking, and do not want to pay excessive prices then end for this number. It is knit from good quality fibre silk and is specially shaped with seam down back of leg to insure trim-fitting ankles. Upper part of leg, double garter tops, and footing are of good quality lisle which give additional strength where the hardest wear comes. The navy blue shade in this hosiery is very effective worn with our Alice blue shoes shown on page 170. COLORS: Black, white, brown, grey or navy blue. SIZES: 8½ to 10. PRICE, PREPAID, 3 pairs for $1.75. PAIR **60c**

Two! Special Offerings·Big Values!

10K14 Boot silk stockings at an extremely low price. Lower part of good quality silk; uppers of cotton. Seamless style. Reinforced with high spliced heels and toes. COLORS: Black, white, grey or brown. SIZES: 8½ to 10. PRICE, 3 pairs for $1.25. PAIR **43c**

10K72 Our famous wonder-wearing three quarter silk stockings.
Greatly reduced in price. Knit from fibre silk. Cotton uppers. Reinforced footing. Dressy and stylish. COLORS: Black, white, brown, or grey. SIZES: 8½ to 10. PRICE, 3 pairs for $1.70. PAIR **59c**

When ordering don't forget to state color and size desired

10K35
$1.00

10K35
PHILIPSBORN'S always have the best values that can be offered for the price.
Take for example this wonderful value in heavy-weight silk stockings. Ordinarily, you could not duplicate this quality for 35 to 50 cents more than our price, and you would think you were getting a bargain even then. They are knit from pure silk, and to give greater serviceability the garter tops are of mercerized cotton. Fashioned in seam effect. Reinforced footing. A remarkable value in a dressy stocking. COLORS: Black, white, or cordovan. SIZES: 8½ to 10. PRICE, PREP'D. 2 pairs for $1.95. PR. **$1.00**

10K20
$1.75

10K20
Here are all silk stockings at 25% below prevailing market prices.
Because we placed an unusually large order with the manufacturer of these stockings, we can sell them greatly below usual retail prices, so buy now. These are rich, dressy stockings, made entirely of extra quality silk. They are extra heavy weight and are full fashioned. Made extra serviceable with three-ply heels and toes. A very dressy and serviceable stocking. COLORS: Black or white. SIZES: 8½ to 10. PRICE, PREPAID to your home, PAIR **$1.75**

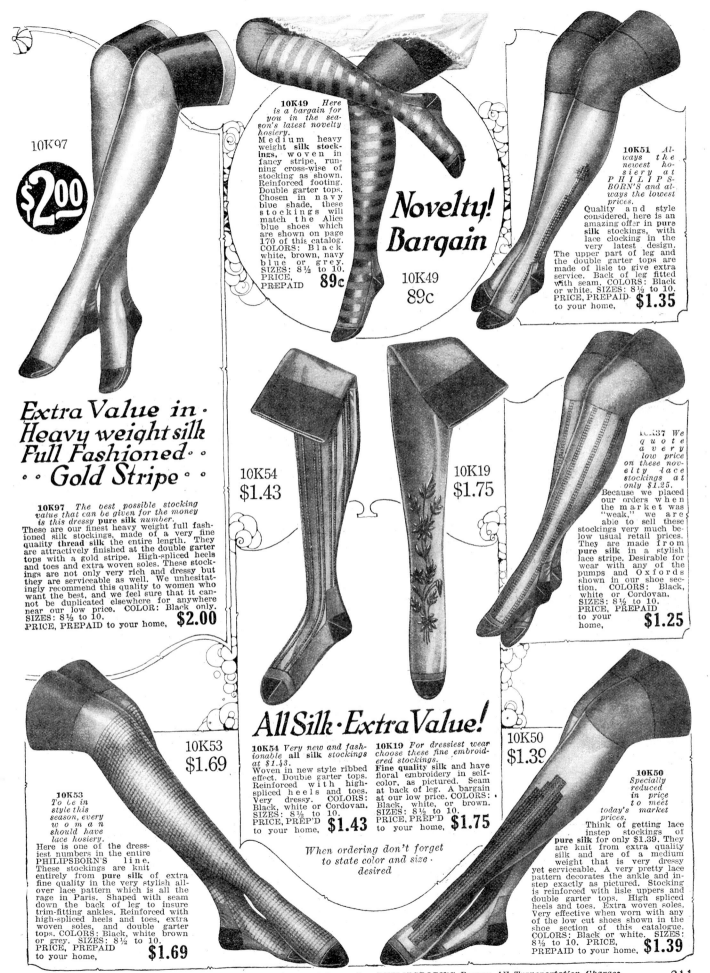

10K97

$2.00

Extra Value in Heavy weight silk Full Fashioned Gold Stripe

10K97 *The best possible stocking value that can be given for the money is this dressy* **pure silk** *number.*
These are our finest heavy weight full fashioned silk stockings, made of a very fine quality **thread silk** the entire length. They are attractively finished at the double garter tops with a gold stripe. High-spliced heels and toes and extra woven soles. These stockings are not only very rich and dressy but they are serviceable as well. We unhesitatingly recommend this quality to women who want the best, and we feel sure that it cannot be duplicated elsewhere for anywhere near our low price. COLOR: Black only. SIZES: 8½ to 10.
PRICE, PREPAID to your home, **$2.00**

10K49 *Here is a bargain for you in the season's latest novelty hosiery.*
Medium heavy weight **silk stockings**, woven in fancy stripe, running cross-wise of stocking as shown. Reinforced footing. Double garter tops. Chosen in navy blue shade, these stockings will match the Alice blue shoes which are shown on page 170 of this catalog. COLORS: Black, white, brown, navy blue or grey. SIZES: 8½ to 10. PRICE, PREPAID **89c**

Novelty! Bargain

10K49
89c

10K51 *Always the newest hosiery at* PHILIPSBORN'S *and always the lowest prices.*
Quality and style considered, here is an amazing offer in **pure silk** stockings, with lace clocking in the very latest design. The upper part of leg and the double garter tops are made of lisle to give extra service. Back of leg fitted with seam. COLORS: Black or white. SIZES: 8½ to 10. PRICE, PREPAID to your home, **$1.35**

10K54
$1.43

10K19
$1.75

10K37 *We quote a very low price on these novelty lace stockings at only $1.25.*
Because we placed our orders when the market was "weak," we are able to sell these stockings very much below usual retail prices. They are made from **pure silk** in a stylish lace stripe. Desirable for wear with any of the pumps and Oxfords shown in our shoe section. COLORS: Black, white or Cordovan. SIZES: 8½ to 10. PRICE, PREPAID to your home, **$1.25**

All Silk·Extra Value!

10K53
$1.69

10K54 *Very new and fashionable* **all silk** *stockings at $1.43.*
Woven in new style ribbed effect. Double garter tops. Reinforced with high-spliced heels and toes. Very dressy. COLORS: Black, white or Cordovan. SIZES: 8½ to 10. PRICE, PREP'D to your home, **$1.43**

10K19 *For dressiest wear choose these fine embroidered stockings.*
Fine quality silk and have floral embroidery in self-color, as pictured. Seam at back of leg. A bargain at our low price. COLORS: Black, white, or brown. SIZES: 8½ to 10. PRICE, PREP'D to your home, **$1.75**

When ordering don't forget to state color and size desired

10K50
$1.39

10K53 *To be in style this season, every woman should have* lace *hosiery.*
Here is one of the dressiest numbers in the entire PHILIPSBORN'S line. These stockings are knit entirely from **pure silk** of extra fine quality in the very stylish all-over lace pattern which is all the rage in Paris. Shaped with seam down the back of leg to insure trim-fitting ankles. Reinforced with high-spliced heels and toes, extra woven soles, and double garter tops. COLORS: Black, white brown or grey. SIZES: 8½ to 10. PRICE, PREPAID to your home, **$1.69**

10K50 *Specially reduced in price to meet today's market prices.*
Think of getting lace instep stockings of **pure silk** for only $1.39. They are knit from extra quality silk and are of a medium weight that is very dressy yet serviceable. A very pretty lace pattern decorates the ankle and instep exactly as pictured. Stocking is reinforced with lisle uppers and double garter tops. High spliced heels and toes. Extra woven soles. Very effective when worn with any of the low cut shoes shown in the shoe section of this catalogue. COLORS: Black or white. SIZES: 8½ to 10. PRICE, PREPAID to your home, **$1.39**

CHICAGO, ILL.

For Index See Page 274 and Remember PHILIPSBORN'S Prepay All Transportation Charges. There Are No Express or Mailing Charges for You to Pay

211

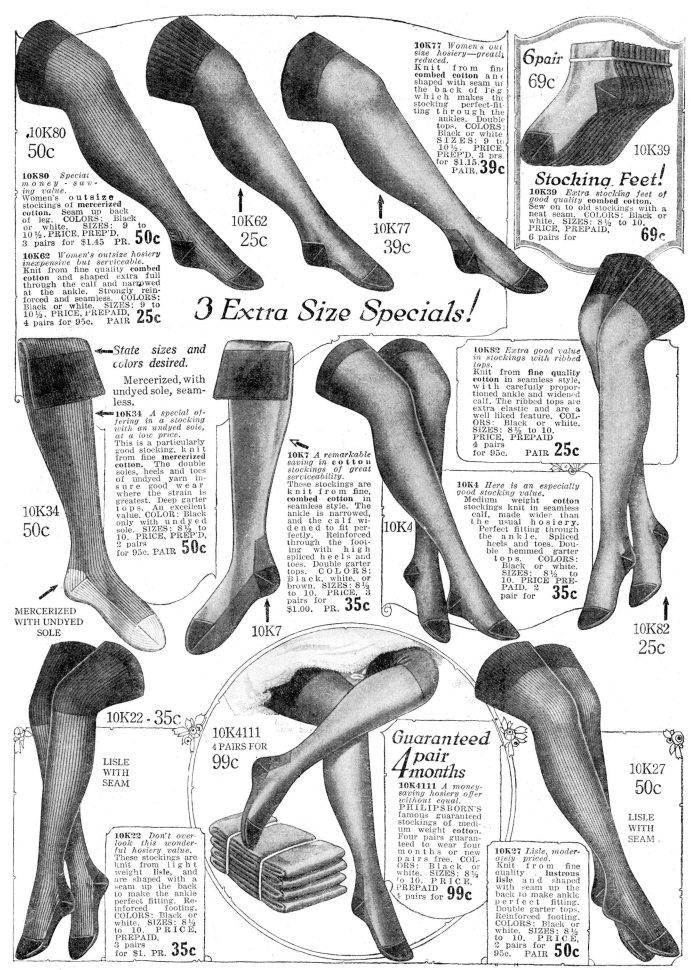

10K80
50c

10K80 *Special money - saving value.* Women's outsize stockings of **mercerized cotton.** Seam up back of leg. COLORS: Black or white. SIZES: 9 to 10½. PRICE, PREP'D. 3 pairs for $1.45 PR. **50c**

10K62 *Women's outsize hosiery inexpensive but serviceable.* Knit from fine quality **combed cotton** and shaped extra full through the calf and narrowed at the ankle. Strongly reinforced and seamless. COLORS: Black or white. SIZES: 9 to 10½. PRICE, PREPAID, 4 pairs for 95c. PAIR **25c**

10K62
25c

10K77
39c

10K77 *Women's outsize hosiery—greatly reduced.* Knit from fine **combed cotton** and shaped with seam up the back of leg which makes the stocking perfect-fitting through the ankles. Double tops. COLORS: Black or white SIZES: 9 to 10½. PRICE, PREP'D. 3 prs. for $1.15. PAIR, **39c**

6pair
69c

10K39

Stocking Feet!

10K39 *Extra stocking feet of good quality* **combed cotton.** Sew on to old stockings with a neat seam. COLORS: Black or white. SIZES: 8½ to 10. PRICE, PREPAID, 6 pairs for **69c**

3 Extra Size Specials!

← *State sizes and colors desired.*

Mercerized, with undyed sole, seamless.

← **10K34** *A special offering in a stocking with an undyed sole, at a low price.* This is a particularly good stocking, knit from fine **mercerized cotton.** The double soles, heels and toes of undyed yarn insure good wear where the strain is greatest. Deep garter tops. An excellent value. COLOR: Black only with undyed sole. SIZES: 8½ to 10. PRICE, PREP'D, 2 pairs for 95c. PAIR **50c**

10K34
50c

MERCERIZED
WITH UNDYED
SOLE

10K7 *A remarkable saving in cotton stockings of great serviceability.* These stockings are knit from fine, **combed cotton** in seamless style. The ankle is narrowed, and the calf widened to fit perfectly. Reinforced through the footing with high spliced heels and toes. Double garter tops. COLORS: Black, white, or brown. SIZES: 8½ to 10. PRICE, 3 pairs for $1.00. PR. **35c**

10K7

10K82 *Extra good value in stockings with ribbed tops.* Knit from **fine quality cotton** in seamless style, with carefully proportioned ankle and widened calf. The ribbed tops are extra elastic and are a well liked feature. COLORS: Black or white. SIZES: 8½ to 10. PRICE, PREPAID 4 pairs for 95c. PAIR **25c**

10K4 *Here is an especially good stocking value.* Medium weight **cotton** stockings knit in seamless calf, made wider than the usual hosiery. Perfect fitting through the ankle. Spliced heels and toes. Double hemmed garter tops. COLORS: Black or white. SIZES: 8½ to 10. PRICE PREPAID, 2 pair for **35c**

10K4

10K82
25c

10K22 · 35c

LISLE
WITH
SEAM

10K22 *Don't overlook this wonderful hosiery value.* These stockings are knit from light weight lisle, and are shaped with a seam up the back to make the ankle perfect fitting. Reinforced footing. COLORS: Black or white. SIZES: 8½ to 10. PRICE, PREPAID, 3 pairs for $1. PR. **35c**

10K4111
4 PAIRS FOR
99c

Guaranteed
4 pair
months

10K4111 *A money-saving hosiery offer without equal.* PHILIPSBORN'S famous guaranteed stockings of medium weight **cotton.** Four pairs guaranteed to wear four months or new pairs free. COLORS: Black or white. SIZES: 8½ to 10. PRICE, PREPAID **99c** 4 pairs for

10K27
50c

LISLE
WITH
SEAM

10K27 *Lisle, moderately priced.* Knit from fine quality **lustrous lisle** and shaped with seam up the back to make ankle perfect fitting. Double garter tops. Reinforced footing. COLORS: Black or white. SIZES: 8½ to 10. PRICE, 2 pairs for 95c. PAIR **50c**

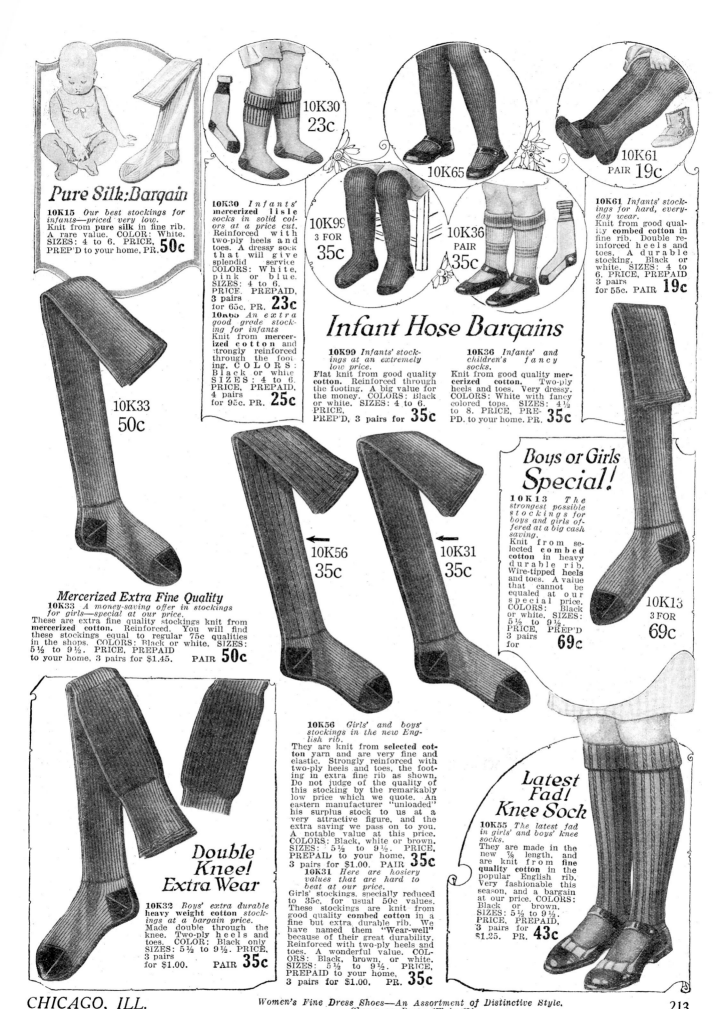

Pure Silk Bargain

10K15 *Our best stockings for infants—priced very low.* Knit from **pure silk** in fine rib. A rare value. COLOR: White. SIZES: 4 to 6. PRICE, PREP'D to your home, PR. **50c**

10K33 **50c**

Mercerized Extra Fine Quality
10K33 *A money-saving offer in stockings for girls—special at our price.* These are extra fine quality stockings knit from **mercerized cotton**. Reinforced. You will find these stockings equal to regular 75c qualities in the shops. COLORS: Black or white. SIZES: 5½ to 9½. PRICE, PREPAID to your home, 3 pairs for $1.45. PAIR **50c**

Double Knee! Extra Wear
10K32 *Boys' extra durable heavy weight cotton stockings at a bargain price.* Made double through the knee. Two-ply heels and toes. COLOR: Black only. SIZES: 5½ to 9½. PRICE, 3 pairs for $1.00. PAIR **35c**

10K30 **23c**

10K99 **3 FOR 35c**

10K56 **35c**

10K31 **35c**

10K30 *Infants' mercerized lisle socks in solid colors at a price cut.* Reinforced with two-ply heels and toes. A dressy sock that will give splendid service. COLORS: White, pink or blue. SIZES: 4 to 6. PRICE, PREPAID, 3 pairs for 65c. PR. **23c**

10K65 *An extra good grade stocking for infants.* Knit from mercerized cotton and strongly reinforced through the footing. COLORS: Black or white. SIZES: 4 to 6. PRICE, PREPAID, 4 pairs for 95c. PR. **25c**

Infant Hose Bargains

10K99 *Infants' stockings at an extremely low price.* Flat knit from good quality cotton. Reinforced through the footing. A big value for the money. COLORS: Black or white. SIZES: 4 to 6. PRICE, PREP'D, 3 pairs for **35c**

10K36 *Infants' and children's fancy socks.* Knit from good quality **mercerized cotton**. Two-ply heels and toes. Very dressy. COLORS: White with fancy colored tops. SIZES: 4½ to 8. PRICE, PREPD. to your home. PR. **35c**

10K65

10K36 **PAIR 35c**

10K61 PAIR 19c

10K61 *Infants' stockings for hard, everyday wear.* Knit from good quality **combed cotton** in fine rib. Double reinforced heels and toes. A durable stocking. Black or white. SIZES: 4 to 6. PRICE, PREPAID 3 pairs for 55c. PAIR **19c**

Boys or Girls Special!
10K13 *The strongest possible stockings for boys and girls offered at a big cash saving.* Knit from selected **combed cotton** in heavy durable rib. Wire-tipped heels and toes. A value that cannot be equaled at our special price. COLORS: Black or white. SIZES: 5½ to 9½. PRICE, PREP'D 3 pairs for **69c**

10K13 **3 FOR 69c**

10K56 *Girls' and boys' stockings in the new English rib.* They are knit from **selected cotton** yarn and are very fine and elastic. Strongly reinforced with two-ply heels and toes, the footing in extra fine rib as shown. Do not judge of the quality of this stocking by the remarkably low price which we quote. An eastern manufacturer "unloaded" his surplus stock to us at a very attractive figure, and the extra saving we pass on to you. A notable value at this price. COLORS: Black, white or brown. SIZES: 5½ to 9½. PRICE, PREPAID to your home, 3 pairs for $1.00. PAIR **35c**

10K31 *Here are hosiery values that are hard to beat at our price.* Girls' stockings, specially reduced to 35c, for usual 50c values. These stockings are knit from good quality **combed cotton** in a fine but extra durable rib. We have named them "Wear-well" because of their great durability. Reinforced with two-ply heels and toes. A wonderful value. COLORS: Black, brown, or white. SIZES: 5½ to 9½. PRICE, PREPAID to your home, 3 pairs for $1.00. PR. **35c**

Latest Fad! Knee Sock
10K55 *The latest fad in girls' and boys' knee socks.* They are made in the new ⅞ length, and are knit from **fine quality cotton** in the popular English rib. Very fashionable this season, and a bargain at our price. COLORS: Black or brown. SIZES: 5½ to 9½. PRICE, PREPAID, 3 pairs for $1.25. PR. **43c**

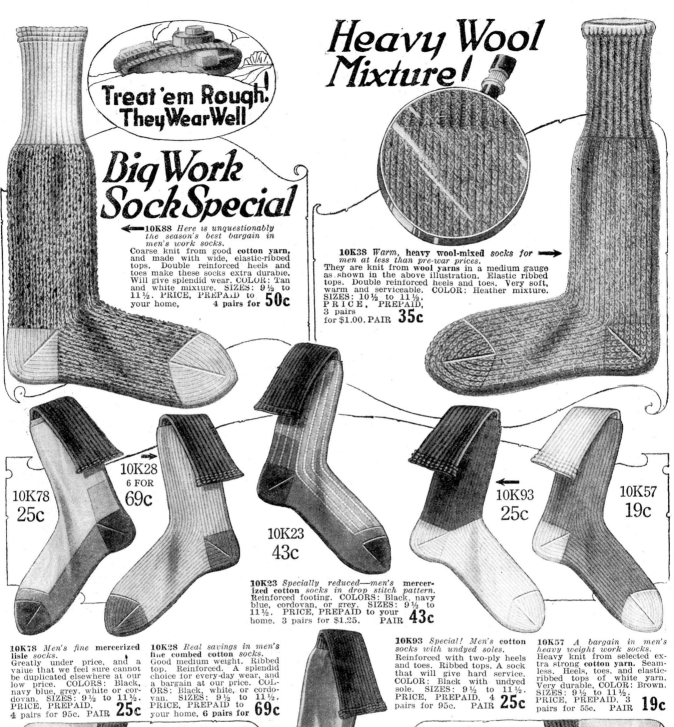

Treat 'em Rough! They Wear Well

Big Work Sock Special

10K88 *Here is unquestionably the season's best bargain in men's work socks.* Coarse knit from good **cotton** yarn, and made with wide, elastic-ribbed tops. Double reinforced heels and toes make these socks extra durable. Will give splendid wear. COLOR: Tan and white mixture. SIZES: 9½ to 11½. PRICE, PREPAID to your home, **4 pairs for 50c**

Heavy Wool Mixture!

10K38 *Warm, heavy wool-mixed socks for men at less than pre-war prices.* They are knit from **wool** yarns in a medium gauge as shown in the above illustration. Elastic ribbed tops. Double reinforced heels and toes. Very soft, warm and serviceable. COLOR: Heather mixture. SIZES: 10½ to 11½. PRICE, PREPAID, 3 pairs for $1.00. PAIR **35c**

10K78 **25c**

10K28 6 FOR **69c**

10K23 **43c**

10K93 **25c**

10K57 **19c**

10K23 *Specially reduced—men's mercerized cotton socks in drop stitch pattern.* Reinforced footing. COLORS: Black, navy blue, cordovan, or grey. SIZES: 9½ to 11½. PRICE, PREPAID to your home. 3 pairs for $1.25. PAIR **43c**

10K78 *Men's fine* **mercerized lisle** *socks.* Greatly under price, and a value that we feel sure cannot be duplicated elsewhere at our low price. COLORS: Black, navy blue, grey, white or cordovan. SIZES: 9½ to 11½. PRICE, PREPAID, 4 pairs for 95c. PAIR **25c**

10K28 *Real savings in men's fine* **combed cotton** *socks.* Good medium weight. Ribbed top. Reinforced. A splendid choice for every-day wear, and a bargain at our price. COLORS: Black, white, or cordovan. SIZES: 9½ to 11½. PRICE, PREPAID to your home, 6 pairs for **69c**

10K93 *Special! Men's* **cotton** *socks with undyed soles.* Reinforced with two-ply heels and toes. Ribbed tops. A sock that will give hard service. COLOR: Black with undyed sole. SIZES: 9½ to 11½. PRICE, PREPAID, 4 pairs for 95c. PAIR **25c**

10K57 *A bargain in men's heavy weight work socks.* Heavy knit from selected extra strong **cotton** yarn. Seamless. Heels, toes, and elastic-ribbed tops of white yarn. Very durable. COLOR: Brown. SIZES: 9½ to 11½. PRICE, PREPAID, 3 pairs for 55c. PAIR **19c**

Artificial Silk Mercerized Top!

10K89 *Men's fine quality plated* **fibre silk** *socks at a 25% reduction.* These socks are knit in fine, elastic rib, and can scarcely be told from all silk. The ribbed tops have mercerized finish. Footing is specially reinforced. A very dressy sock for very little money. COLORS: Black, white or brown. SIZES: 9½ to 11½. PRICE, PREPAID, 2 pairs for $1.35. PAIR **69c**

Pure Silk Special

10K96 *Our finest socks for men quoted at a big reduction.* Knit entirely of **fine quality pure silk**, and strongly reinforced through the footing. Elastic rib tops. A fine dressy sock at a saving. COLORS: Black or cordovan. SIZES: 9 to 11½. PRICE, PREPAID, 2 pairs for $1.45. PAIR **75c**

Guaranteed 6 for $1.00

10K67 *Men's guaranteed socks specially reduced.* Knit from a very fine quality **combed cotton**. Reinforced heels and toes. Ribbed tops. A big bargain. COLORS: Black, white, grey, or brown. SIZES: 9½ to 11½. PRICE, PREP'D, 6 pairs for $1.00. PR. **19c**

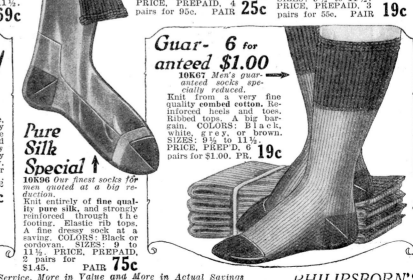

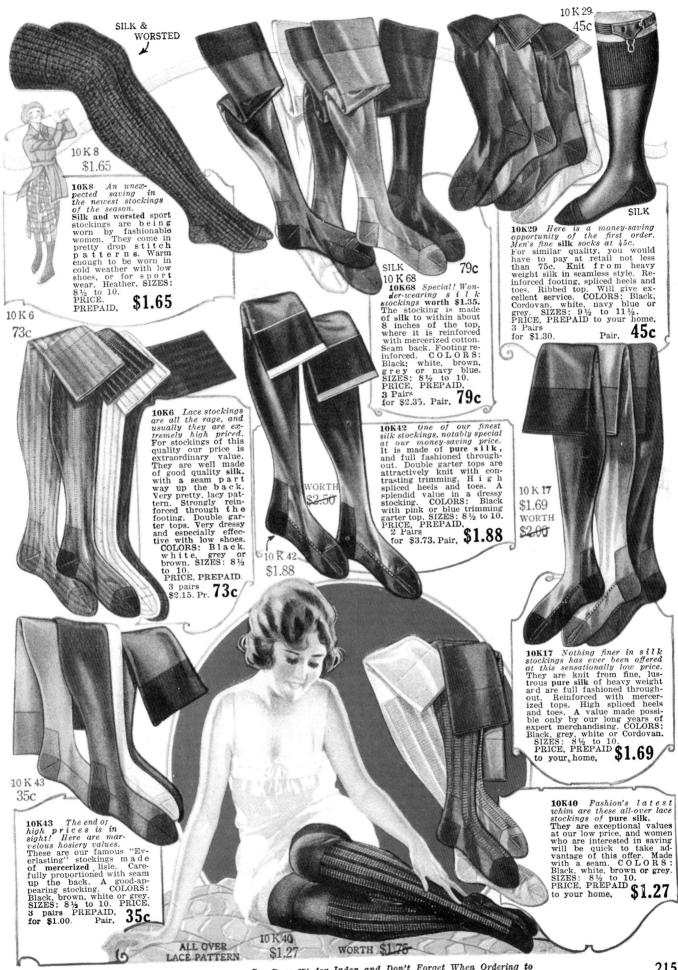

SILK & WORSTED

10K8 $1.65

10K8 An unexpected saving in the newest stockings of the season. **Silk and worsted** sport stockings are being worn by fashionable women. They come in pretty drop stitch patterns. Warm enough to be worn in cold weather with low shoes, or for sport wear. Heather. SIZES: 8½ to 10. PRICE, PREPAID, **$1.65**

SILK 79c
10K68

10K68 Special! Wonder-wearing silk stockings worth $1.35. The stocking is made of silk to within about 8 inches of the top, where it is reinforced with mercerized cotton. Seam back. Footing reinforced. COLORS: Black; white, brown, grey or navy blue. SIZES: 8½ to 10. PRICE, PREPAID, 3 Pairs for $2.35. Pair, **79c**

10 K 29 45c

10K29 Here is a money-saving opportunity of the first order. Men's fine silk socks at 45c. For similar quality, you would have to pay at retail not less than 75c. Knit from heavy weight silk in seamless style. Reinforced footing, spliced heels and toes. Ribbed top. Will give excellent service. COLORS: Black, Cordovan, white, navy blue or grey. SIZES: 9½ to 11½. PRICE, PREPAID to your home, 3 Pairs for $1.30. Pair, **45c**

SILK

10 K 6 73c

10K6 Lace stockings are all the rage, and usually they are extremely high priced. For stockings of this quality our price is extraordinary value. They are well made of good quality silk, with a seam part way up the back. Very pretty, lacy pattern. Strongly reinforced through the footing. Double garter tops. Very dressy and especially effective with low shoes. COLORS: Black, white, grey or brown. SIZES: 8½ to 10. PRICE, PREPAID, 3 pairs $2.15. Pr. **73c**

WORTH $2.50

10 K 42 $1.88

10K42 One of our finest silk stockings, notably special at our money-saving price. It is made of **pure silk**, and full fashioned throughout. Double garter tops are attractively knit with contrasting trimming. High spliced heels and toes. A splendid value in a dressy stocking. COLORS: Black with pink or blue trimming garter top. SIZES: 8½ to 10. PRICE, PREPAID, 2 Pairs for $3.73. Pair, **$1.88**

10 K 17 $1.69 WORTH $2.00

10K17 Nothing finer in silk stockings has ever been offered at this sensationally low price. They are knit from fine, lustrous **pure silk** of heavy weight and are full fashioned throughout. Reinforced with mercerized tops. High spliced heels and toes. A value made possible only by our long years of expert merchandising. COLORS: Black, grey, white or Cordovan. SIZES: 8½ to 10. PRICE, PREPAID to your home, **$1.69**

10 K 43 35c

10K43 The end of high prices is in sight! Here are marvelous hosiery values. These are our famous "Everlasting" stockings made of **mercerized** lisle. Carefully proportioned with seam up the back. A good-appearing stocking. COLORS: Black, brown, white or grey. SIZES: 8½ to 10. PRICE, 3 pairs PREPAID, for $1.00. Pair, **35c**

10K40 Fashion's latest whim are these all-over lace stockings of **pure silk**. They are exceptional values at our low price, and women who are interested in saving will be quick to take advantage of this offer. Made with a seam. COLORS: Black, white, brown or grey. SIZES: 8½ to 10. PRICE, PREPAID to your home, **$1.27**

ALL OVER LACE PATTERN

10 K 40 $1.27 WORTH $1.75

CHICAGO, ILL.

See Page 274 for Index and Don't Forget When Ordering to State the Color and Size Desired

SILK CREPE DE CHINE
4 K 213
$3.98

2 Specials!

4K213 The luxury of silk underwear at bargain prices. "EVERDAINTY" nightgown of good quality silk crepe de chine. Shadow lace top, front and back alike. COLOR: Pink. SIZES: 15-16-17 or 32 to 44 bust. PRICE, **$3.98**

4K1031 Unheard-of values in finest silk underwear. "EVERDAINTY" envelope chemise of excellent quality silk crepe de chine. Shadow lace trimming in attractive design. COLOR: Pink. SIZES: 32 to 44 bust. PRICE, **$1.98**

SILK CREPE DE CHINE
4 K 1031
$1.98

BATISTE
4 K 1011
93c

IRENE CASTLE DESIGN
4 K 1042
$1.89
WORTH $2.75

4K207 Worth every cent of $3.00. Attractive new design in "EVERDAINTY" two-piece pajamas of nainsook. COLOR: Pink or white with colored trimming. SIZES: 15-16-17 or 32 to 44 bust. PRICE, PREPAID to your home, **$1.75**

4 K 207
$1.75

2 PIECE PAJAMA

4K1011 Here is one of the prettiest envelope chemises ever sold. "EVERDAINTY" batiste model. Pointed design at bottom. COLOR: Pink with blue trimming. SIZES: 32 to 44 bust. PRICE, **93c**

4K223 Prices such as these are a direct challenge to profiteers. We offer this "EVERDAINTY" nightgown of flowered batiste at a big reduction in price. Colored shirrings and stitchings as shown. COLOR: Pink. SIZES: 15-16-17 or 32 to 44 bust. PRICE, PREPAID, **$1.69**

4K2002 Satin and lace boudoir cap. PRICE, PREPAID, **69c**

CAP
4 K 2002
69c

4 K 223
$1.69

IRENE CASTLE DESIGN
4 K 1041
$1.98
WORTH $2.75

2 Original designs by Irene Castle

4K1041 A new "EVERDAINTY" envelope chemise, designed by IRENE CASTLE. Made of fine quality batiste and elaborately trimmed with princess pattern lace. A wonder value. COLOR: Pink. SIZES: 32 to 44 bust. PRICE, PREPAID, to your home, **$1.98**

4K1042 Another IRENE CASTLE'S exquisite creations is this "EVERDAINTY" combination. Fashioned of batiste. Lace trimmed. COLOR: Pink or white. SIZES: 32 to 44 bust. PRICE, PREPAID to your home, **$1.89**

SILK CREPE DE CHINE
4K450
$2.98

4K1100
$1.45

4K710
89c

Dainty Lace Petticoat!

4K450 For party wear what could be prettier than this "EVER-DAINTY" petticoat? Fashioned of silk crepe de chine, and one of the prettiest styles. Shadow lace flounce with shadow lace insertion. Ribbon trimming. COLOR: Pink. SIZES: 36 to 42 length. PRICE, PREP'D, **$2.98**

CAP 4K2000
59c

4K453
$2.25

4K210
$2.25

4K1004
$1.50

ONE PIECE PAJAMA

"Everdainty" in Sets or in Separate Pieces

4K1100 Unequalled at our low price are these "EVERDAINTY" bloomers of figured silk Jacquard. Filet pattern lace. COLOR: Pink. SIZES: 23 to 29 side length. PRICE, PREPAID. **$1.45**

4K453 A wonderfully attractive style in an "EVERDAINTY" silk Jacquard mull petticoat; specially priced. Lace-trimmed flounce. COLOR: Pink. SIZES: 36 to 44 length. PRICE, PREPAID, **$2.25**

4K710 Here is your chance to save money on an "EVERDAINTY" camisole of silk Jacquard. Filet pattern lace. COLOR: Pink. SIZES: 32 to 44 bust. PRICE, PREPAID to your home, **89c**

4K1004 A very attractive "EVERDAINTY" envelope chemise, of silk Jacquard at $1.50. Filet pattern lace. COLOR: Pink. SIZES: 32 to 44 bust. PRICE, PREPAID, **$1.50** The above numbers including the nightgown 4K210 and 4K2000 may be had in perfectly matching sets, or may be had separately as listed above. PRICE, for complete set, **$8.85**

4K1014 $1.39

BATISTE WORTH $2.00

$1.39

Very Special

4K1014 Here is the new Poiret chemise—a new style combination with drawers. Special at this price. Good quality batiste, trimmed with wide contrasting batiste bands. Hand embroidery in colors. COLOR: White with pink trimming. SIZES: 32 to 44 bust. PRICE, PREPAID, **$1.39**

4K202 Here is value for you at only $1.29. "EVERDAINTY" one-piece pajamas of good quality nainsook. Trimmed with colored binding. Pocket. COLOR: Pink or white. SIZES: 32 to 44 bust or 14 to 17. PRICE, PREP'D, **$1.29**

4K210 "EVERDAINTY" nightgown of pink Jacquard silk and filet lace. Pink. SIZES: 14 to 17 or 32 to 44 bust. **$2.25** PRICE, PREP'D. **4K2000** Satin and lace boudoir cap. Dutch style. COLOR: Pink or blue trimming. PRICE, PREPAID, **59c**

4K 202
$1.29

The Best-dressed Women Everywhere Wear PHILIPSBORN'S Clothes—Prices Always the Lowest, Quality Always the Highest

4K461 *"EVERDAINTY" muslin petticoat—VERY SPECIAL.* Handsome embroidery flounce. Embroidery beading. Ribbon threading. White. SIZES: 36 to 44 length. PRICE, **$1.89**

4K749 *"EVERDAINTY"* nainsook corset cover. Lace trimmed. White. SIZES: 32 to 44 bust. PRICE, PREPAID, **49c**

4K513 *"EVERDAINTY" muslin petticoat.* Deep flounce of eyelet embroidery. COLOR: White. SIZES: 36 to 44 length. PRICE, **$1.75**

4K719 *"EVERDAINTY"* nainsook corset cover. COLOR: White. SIZES: 32 to 44 bust. PRICE, PREPAID, **65c**

4K462 *"EVERDAINTY" petticoat,* white muslin top batiste flounce. Lace trimmed. SIZES: 36 to 44 length. PRICE, **$1.79**

4K725 *"EVERDAINTY"* bust confiner of cluny lace and mercerized brocade. Pink. SIZES: 34 to 48 bust. PRICE, **59c**

Biggest Value! Ever Offered

4K749 49c

4K719 65c

4K513 $1.75 WORTH $2.50

4K725 59c

4K461 $1.89

4K462 $1.79

"Everdainty" Petticoats at unheard-of Bargain Prices!

4K464 *Worth $3.50 and a special bargain at the price we ask.* A very handsome selection in an *"EVERDAINTY"* muslin petticoat. Duchess pattern lace flounce. White. SIZES: 36 to 44 length. PRICE, PREPAID, **$2.59**

4K752 Camisole of satin and Georgette. Pink. SIZES: 32 to 44 bust. PRICE, PREPAID, **99c**

4K458 *An especially good bargain in an "EVERDAINTY" muslin petticoat.* Deep flounce of handsome embroidery. Embroidered beading. Ribbon threading. White. SIZES: 36 to 44 length. PRICE, PREPAID, **$1.85**

4K726 *"EVERDAINTY"* satin and filet pattern lace camisole. Pink. SIZES: 32 to 44 bust. PRICE, PREPAID, **96c**

4K752 99c

4K726 96c WORTH $1.25

4K464 $2.59

4K458 $1.85

Don't forget Philipsborn's prepay!

4K455 $1.19

4K472 93c

4K705 43c

4K465 $1.39

4K516 75c

4K831 88c

4K749 49c

4K455 *Our bargains in "EVERDAINTY" underwear will interest you.* This season our prices are from 25% to 33-1/3% lower than those charged by other houses. As for example, this beautiful muslin petticoat at only $1.19. Finished with an embroidery trimmed flounce with ribbon threading COLOR: White SIZES 36 to 44 length. PRICE, **$1.19**

4K516 *Nowhere will you find such real, honest-to-goodness values as we offer.*
Very often we secure amazing price concessions from manufacturers, and the saving we pass on to you. We quote this "EVERDAINTY" muslin petticoat at a special reduction. Embroidery flounce. A tremendous value. COLOR: White. SIZES: 36 to 44 length. PRICE, PREPAID. **75c**

4K472 *PHILIPSBORN'S bargains are greater than ever.* This is a wonderful bargain in an "EVERDAINTY" muslin petticoat. Flounce of embroidery as pictured. COLOR: White. SIZES: 36 to 44 length. PRICE, PREPAID, **93c**

4K524 *Big special! This low price will appeal to the thrifty woman.* "EVERDAINTY" muslin model with fine eyelet embroidery flounce and insertion. COLOR: White. SIZES: 36 to 44. PRICE, PREPAID, **$1.39**

4K831 "EVERDAINTY" satin camisole. Upper part of blue satin; lower part of pink satin. SIZES: 32 to 44 bust. PRICE, PREPAID, **88c**

Cambric non-transparent

4K467 $1.00

4K493 $1.00

4K524 $1.39 **Big! Special**

4K705 "EVERDAINTY" bust confiner of heavy corset material. Lace trimming. COLOR: Pink. SIZES: 34 to 46 bust. PRICE, PREPAID, **43c**

4K465 *Reduced prices such as these show how you can save money and still secure good materials.* "EVERDAINTY" muslin petticoat. Lace-trimmed flounce. COLOR: White. SIZES: 36 to 44 length. PRICE, PREPAID, **$1.39**

4K467 *A special saving is offered in this "EVERDAINTY" nontransparent cambric petticoat.* Made with a double panel front, which takes the place of two petticoats. COLOR: White. SIZES: 36 to 44 length. PRICE, PREPAID, **$1.00**

4K493 *If you paid double the price, you could not secure better material or a prettier style than we offer you in this petticoat.* "EVERDAINTY" muslin model with handsome embroidery flounce and insertion. A bargain value. COLOR: White. SIZES: 36 to 44 length. PRICE, PREPAID, **$1.00**

4K523 - $1.15

4K523 *This "EVERDAINTY" muslin petticoat only $1.15.* Hemstitching and a wide band of lace insertion trims the flounce as pictured. White. SIZES: 36 to 44 length. PRICE, **$1.15**

4K749 "EVERDAINTY" nainsook corset cover. Trimmed both front and back with filet pattern lace and embroidered batiste. COLOR: White. SIZES: 32 to 44 bust. PRICE, PREPAID to your home, **49c**

CHICAGO, ILL.

For Index See Page 274 and Remember PHILIPSBORN'S Prepay All Transportation Charges. There Are No Express or Mailing Charges for You to Pay

219

4K506 85c

4K506X $1.19

4K468 The downward trend of prices is seen in this "EVERDAINTY" petticoat. Made of muslin and finished with a deep embroidery flounce. COLOR: White. SIZES: 36 to 44 length. PRICE, PREPAID, **$1.89**

4K717 "EVERDAINTY" satin camisole. Hand embroidery and hemstitching. COLOR: Pink. SIZES: 32 to 44 bust. PRICE, **98c**

4K451 93c

4K717 98c

4K468 $1.89

4K459 $1.43

4K720 $1.59

Save! Buy Here

4K718 $1.39

4K469-$1.59

Style! and Value! at Low! Prices

4K473 $1.39

4K457 $1.10

4K452 95c

4K506 Here is an "EVERDAINTY" muslin petticoat which you would consider a bargain at $1.50. Eyelet embroidery flounce. COLOR: White. SIZES: 36 to 44 length. PRICE, PREPAID, **85c**
4K506X Same style in Extra Sizes. PRICE, PREPAID, **$1.19**
4K469 These great reductions will save you money. "EVERDAINTY" muslin petticoat. Embroidery flounce. COLOR: White. SIZES: 36 to 44. PRICE, PREPAID, **$1.59**
4K718 "EVERDAINTY" satin camisole. Rich Cluny lace. COLOR: Pink. SIZES: 32 to 44 bust. PRICE, PREPAID, **$1.39**
4K459 An exceedingly handsome "EVERDAINTY" petticoat is here offered you at a very special reduction. It is fashioned of good-wearing muslin. Eyelet embroidery forms the deep flounce. Embroidery insertion. COLOR: White. SIZES: 36 to 44 length, PRICE, PREPAID to your home, **$1.43**

4K451 Here is an example in value-giving which we defy competitors to equal at our very low price. "EVERDAINTY" muslin petticoat neatly finished with cluster tucking and embroidery flouncing. COLOR: White. SIZES: 36 to 44 length. PRICE, PREPAID, **93c**

4K473 Another splendid offering is this "EVERDAINTY" muslin petticoat—a wonderful value.
Positively one of the prettiest petticoats ever sold for so little money. Deep embroidery flounce. COLOR: White. SIZES: 36 to 44 length. PRICE, PREPAID, **$1.39**

4K720 Here are savings opportunities that are truly astonishing. Absolutely unheard-of reduced prices. Only $1.59 for this "EVERDAINTY" camisole of flowered satin ribbon and satin. Ribbon straps. Very dressy. COLOR: Pink. SIZES: 32 to 44 bust. PRICE, PREPAID, **$1.59**

4K457 You will find nothing in the shops to compare with this petticoat unless you pay higher prices. It is another of our "EVERDAINTY" muslin and finished with a deep embroidery insertion. COLOR: White. SIZES: 36 to 44 length. PRICE, PREPAID, **$1.10**

4K452 Just imagine getting an "EVERDAINTY" petticoat of this quality and attractive style at this price. The material is good quality muslin, the flounce prettily trimmed with filet pattern lace insertion and lace edging. Offered at a mere fraction of its actual worth. COLOR: White. SIZES: 36 to 44 length. PRICE, **95c**

Six Bargains!
Prepaid to your door!

4K1022 You would have to pay from 25 to 50 cents more for this envelope chemise if you bought it anywhere else. "EVERDAINTY" model made of good-wearing **nainsook**. Eyelet embroidery forms the V-shaped front yoke, which is attractively run with ribbon. A bargain offering. COLOR: White. SIZES: 32 to 44 bust.
PRICE, PREPAID to your home, **69c**

Special
$1.29

← 4K1033

4K1039
$1.15

4K1022
69c

4K1035
$1.69

4K1039 Here is the new "step-in" envelope chemise, another of our popular "EVERDAINTY" models.
The material, a dainty **batiste**, is made very attractive with shirrings and colored embroidery. Sides are slashed and made extra wide for sanitary purposes. To put the garment on, step into it as shown in miniature and draw up over shoulders. Worth at least $1.50. COLOR: White or pink. SIZES: 32 to 44 bust. PRICE PREPAID to your home, **$1.15**

3 in 1 Novelty Model

4K1034-$1.49

4K1035 A new style in an "EVERDAINTY" step-in chemise.

4K1036
$1.35

4K1034 The latest thing in French combinations.
"EVERDAINTY" three-in-one garment. It combines the features of a chemise, bloomer drawers, and a skirt in one garment. Made of fine quality **nainsook** and trimmed with fancy colored stitching. Open style drawers. COLOR: Pink or white. SIZES: 32 to 44 bust. PRICE, PREP'D to your home, **$1.49**

4K1033 Sensational value in this offer—worth $1.75.
French **voile** with a mercerized stripe for this "EVERDAINTY" envelope chemise. Shadow lace bands the camisole top and forms the shoulder straps. Colored shirrings. One of the prettiest garments ever offered at this price. COLOR: Pink. SIZES: 32 to 44 bust. PRICE, PREP'D to your home, **$1.29**

4K1036 A bargain that will interest thrifty buyers.
This "EVERDAINTY" envelope chemise is made of a fine quality **nainsook**. A bargain at the price we quote. Elaborately trimmed with filet pattern and Val lace. Panel style front. Camisole top. Worth $2.00. COLOR: White. SIZES: 32 to 44 bust. PRICE, PREP'D to your home, **$1.35**

4K1035 A new style in an "EVERDAINTY" step-in chemise.
Here is your chance to secure one of these popular new garments at a price that is no more than you would pay for ordinary designs. The model is made of good quality **nainsook**. A special feature is provided in the circular-cut lower section. Shadow lace and Val lace trimming. COLOR: White. SIZES: 32 to 44 bust. PRICE, PREP'D to your home, **$1.69**

4K1010 An extremely pretty style in an "EVERDAINTY" step-in chemise of fine batiste. Camisole top trimmed with washable satin, with hand embroidery and shirrings. A marvelous offering. COLOR: Pink, blue trimming. SIZES: 32 to 44 bust. PRICE, PREPAID, $1.69

4K1028 Every woman will be interested in this astounding value in an envelope chemise. "EVERDAINTY" model made of fine nainsook. Colored embroidery and stitching. COLOR: White. SIZES: 32 to 44 bust. PRICE, PREPAID, 65c

4K1002 We bought these "EVER-DAINTY" envelope chemise when the first big slump in prices occurred. The style and quality equal any $2.00 garment on the market. Made of batiste, and daintily trimmed with shadow lace. Back is lace trimmed. COLOR: White. SIZES: 32 to 44 bust. PRICE, PREPAID to your home. $1.29

4K1028
65c

BATISTE
BLUE SATIN
TRIMMING

HAND
EMBR'D

4K1010
$1.69

SPECIAL

4K1002
$1.29

4K1006
79c

"Everdainty" Envelope Chemise Bargains

4K1001 Special! Worth $1.50 and an exceptional bargain at our price. The "BILLIE BURKE" combination here pictured is one of our most popular models. Made of nainsook, the camisole top banded with wide filet pattern lace. Bloomer style drawers. Elastic bands at knees. Colored stitching. COLORS: White or pink. SIZES: 32 to 44 bust. PRICE, 95c

4K1006 Don't overlook this chance to secure an "EVER-DAINTY" envelope chemise. The material is a fine quality batiste, one of the daintiest and most desirable of underwear fabrics. Shadow lace forms the camisole top. Colored shirrings trim the front in attractive style. Colored rolled edging at bottom. COLOR: Pink. SIZES: 32 to 44 bust. PRICE, PREP'D, to your home, 79c

4K1023 You need not do without pretty underwear when you can buy things so reasonable. Here is an "EVERDAINTY" nainsook envelope chemise which really should sell for 50 cents more, but owing to an extra large purchase we are able to offer it to you at an immense reduction. Filet pattern lace at the camisole top. Crochet edging at bottom. A value extraordinary. COLOR: Pink or white. SIZES: 32 to 44 bust. PRICE, PREPAID, 50c

4K1023
50c

4K1001 95c

A Bargain! of Bargains

4K355 You will always get the highest quality at the lowest price when you trade here. At only $1.59 this "*EVERDAINTY*" muslin princess slip is a bargain. Embroidery yoke and flounce. Ribbon trimming. COLOR: White. SIZES: 32 to 44 bust. PRICE, **$1.59**

4K374 The camisole top of this "*EVERDAINTY*" muslin princess slip is a new and well-liked feature usually found only on high priced garments, yet $1.65 is all we ask. Filet pattern lace and insertion make a very rich and effective trimming. Ribbon threading. Front closing. Priced way below what others are asking for similar styles. COLOR: White. SIZES: 32 to 44 bust. PRICE, PREP'D to your home, **$1.65**

4K350 Here is an exceedingly good style in an "*EVERDAINTY*" princess slip offered at a price saving that will astonish even our regular customers. The material is good-wearing **muslin**, with an eyelet embroidery flounce and yoke. An exceptional value at our price. COLOR: White. SIZES: 32 to 44 bust. $1.69 PRICE, PREPAID to your home, **$1.69**

4K384 Prices have come back to normal. What you have been waiting for has happened. Everything has gone down in price. When the first break in the market occurred, we were ready with thousands of dollars to snap up bargains such as this "*EVERDAINTY*" muslin princess slip. Embroidery flounce and yoke. COLOR: White. SIZES: 32 to 44 bust. PRICE, PREPAID, **$1.79**

4K355
$1.59
WORTH
~~$2.00~~

4K374
$1.65

4K353X-$2.25
4K353
$1.98

4K350
$1.69

SPECIAL
4K384
$1.79

Every one! is an "Everdainty" and a Real! Bargain!

4K353 When the big slump in prices took place, we bought at the new revised prices. Only $1.98 for this "*EVERDAINTY*" nainsook princess slip. Camisole top and flounce richly trimmed with dainty laces and embroidery insertion. COLOR: White. SIZES: 32 to 44 bust. PRICE, PREPAID, **$1.98**

4K353X SIZES: 46-48-50 bust. PRICE, PREPAID, **$2.25**

CHICAGO, ILL.

See Page 274 for Index and Don't Forget When Ordering to State the Color and Size Desired

223

4K211 $1.48

4K215 $1.19

4K206 $1.15

PINK BATISTE

CAP 4K2007 49c

4K270 $1.29

4K211 *"EVERDAINTY" batiste nightgown at a special reduction.* It is positively worth $2.00 and more. Filet pattern lace and embroidered batiste give a rich trimming. COLOR: Pink. SIZES: 32 to 44 bust or sizes: 14 to 17. PRICE, PREPAID, **$1.48**

4K270 *Compare our prices with others, and you will always trade with us.* Here is an out-of-the ordinary value in an *"EVERDAINTY"* nainsook nightgown. Front yoke is trimmed with Val lace and embroidered batiste bands. Colored shirrings. COLOR: White. SIZES: 32 to 44 bust or sizes: 14 to 17. PRICE, PREPAID, **$1.29**

4K1037 *Hand-embroidered underwear from the Philippine Islands is now in great demand.* This envelope chemise is all hand made even to the hems and is a wonderful value at our low price. The garment is made of finest **nainsook**, sheer but durable, and is exquisitely embroidered by hand. COLOR: White. SIZES: 32 to 44 bust. PRICE, PREPAID, **$2.98**

4K206 *"EVERDAINTY" nightgown of good quality* **nainsook.** Deep front yoke of alternating rows of filet lace and embroidered batiste insertion. A money-saving value. COLOR: White. SIZES: 32 to 44 bust, or sizes: 14 to 17. PRICE, PREPAID, **$1.15**

4K215 *A neat, practical "EVERDAINTY"* **nainsook** *nightgown.* Square, hemstitched neck and kimono sleeves. Colored stitching. A tremendous value. COLOR: White. SIZES: 32 to 44 bust or sizes: 14 to 17. PRICE, PREPAID, **$1.19**

4K2007 *Boudoir cap of white dotted Swiss.* PRICE, **49c**

4K212 *One of our most popular numbers—"BILLIE BURKE" two-piece pajamas.* The material is flowered **nainsook** of an unusually dainty pattern. Hemstitching and colored shirrings trim the jacket. Single patch pocket. Full length, trousers have elastic at ankles. COLORS: Blue or pink. SIZES: 32 to 44 bust or sizes: 14 to 17. PRICE, PREPAID, **$1.98**

WORTH $5.00

Philippine Hand Embr'd

4K225 $2.98

2 PIECE BILLIE BURKE PAJAMA

Very! Special

4K225 *Philippine embroidered nightgown.* The material is **nainsook** of the very best quality. Hand embroidery of exquisite quality. Hand made throughout. COLOR: White. SIZES: 32 to 44 bust or sizes: 14 to 17. PRICE, **$2.98**

4K1037—$2.98

WORTH $5.00

4K212

$1.98

"Goods by the Yard." A New Member of The PHILIPSBORN Family See Pages 250 to 255

PHILIPSBORN'S

2 Big Specials

4K203
93c

4K203X
$1.29

← **4K245**
$1.15

4K205
$1.09

4K203 *Special offering in an "EVERDAINTY" batiste nightgown.*
Attractively trimmed with colored shirrings, stitchings, and an embroidery spray. COLOR: White or pink. SIZES: 32 to 44 or 14 to 17. PRICE. **93c**

4K203X Same style in extra sizes: 46, 48, 50 bust. White only. PRICE, PREPAID. **$1.29**

4K228 *"EVERDAINTY" one-piece pajamas.*
Flowered batiste. Colored shirrings and stitchings enhance the beauty of the garment. Full length front opening. Single pocket. COLOR: Pink or blue. SIZES: 14 to 17 or 32 to 44 bust. PRICE, PREPAID. **$1.79**

4K226 *Another of our well-liked "EVERDAINTY" models.*
The material is good-wearing nainsook. Eyelet embroidery front yoke and edging. COLOR: White. SIZES: 32 to 44 bust; or 14 to 17. PRICE, PREPAID, **98c**

4K227 *A very fine quality "EVERDAINTY" nainsook nightgown.*
With V neck and long sleeves. Embroidery insertion with cluster tucking forms the front yoke. White. SIZES: 32 to 44 bust, or sizes 14 to 17. PRICE, PREPAID, **$1.88**

4K245 *An unusual chance to effect a saving on a V-necked, long-sleeved nightgown.*
This is an *"EVERDAINTY"* model of good quality muslin. Embroidery trimming. COLOR: White. SIZES: 14 to 17 or 32 to 44 bust. PRICE, PREPAID, **$1.15**

4K205 *A neat, practical style in an "EVERDAINTY" nightgown at a bargain.*
The material is good quality nainsook. Hand embroidery in dainty colors. Colored stitching and shirrings. COLOR: White or pink. SIZES: 14 to 17 or 32 to 44 bust. PRICE, PREPAID. **$1.09**

4K229 *A new style sleeveless nainsook nightgown. "EVERDAINTY" model.*
New style top is designed in camisole effect, with wide bands of filet lace and embroidered batiste. COLOR: White. SIZES: 32 to 44 bust, or 14 to 17. PRICE, PREPAID **95c**

4K222 *A big bargain in a beautiful "EVERDAINTY" nightgown of nainsook.*
Lace and embroidered batiste trimming. Slip-over. White. SIZES: 32 to 44 bust, sizes 14 to 17. PRICE, PREPAID, **$1.50**

4K2008 Novelty boudoir cap of satin and lace. Pink or blue trimming. PRICE, PREPAID, **59c**

4K229
95c

4K228
$1.79

4K226
98c

4K227
$1.88

Big Bargains

CAP
4K2008
59c

4K222
$1.50

Save Money Worth **$2.25**

CHICAGO, ILL.

PHILIPSBORN'S Skirts—Wonderfully Smart and Perfectly Tailored.
Prices Lowest in America. See Pages 66 to 82

225

4K827 *You couldn't buy the materials themselves for the price.* "EVERDAINTY" **nainsook corset cover.**
The deep front yoke is made very elaborate and dressy with princess pattern lace and embroidered batiste bands. Dainty lace edging. Invisible front closing. COLOR: White. SIZES: 32 to 44 bust.
PRICE, PREPAID, **39c**

4K703 *Special!* **Worth 75c,** *and certainly a bargain, as you will readily admit when you see this attractive* "EVERDAINTY" *camisole.*
The lower half of the camisole is made of good quality washable **Jap satin**; the upper half of **filet pattern lace.** Filet pattern shoulder straps. Slip-over model. COLOR: Pink. SIZES: 32 to 44 bust.
PRICE, PREPAID, **43c**

4K813 *The woman who prefers a sleeve-style corset cover will be glad to find this* "EVERDAINTY" *model. Priced right.*
Shadow lace in deep pointed design forms the deep front yoke, which is run with ribbon as pictured. Sleeves of shadow lace to correspond. Front closing. COLOR: White. SIZES: 32 to 44 bust. PRICE, PREPAID to your home, **98c**

4K716 *Did you ever see a more charming style in a camisole than this* "EVERDAINTY" *model? A real economy. Worth $1.00.*
Fully two-thirds of the garment is made of **filet pattern lace**; the rest of good quality washable *crepe de chine.* Model fastens invisibly at front. COLOR: Pink. SIZES: 32 to 44 bust.
PRICE, PREPAID to your home, **55c**

4K706 *A sensational value in an* "EVERDAINTY" *batiste and filet lace camisole—very special. A bargain.*
Lace designed in points. COLOR: Pink. SIZES: 32 to 44 bust. PRICE, PREPAID **59c**

4K717 Satin and hand embroidery *make this* "EVERDAINTY" *camisole a very desirable selection and real value.*
Quoted at a 25% reduction. COLOR: Pink. SIZES: 32 to 44 bust. PRICE, PREPAID, **98c**

4K718 *That you can get the prettiest styles of the season here at a low price is convincingly shown in this camisole.*
"EVERDAINTY" model is made of washable **satin.** Very handsome Cluny lace in attractive new design trims front, forms shoulder straps, and bands top. An unheard-of bargain at this price. COLOR: Pink. SIZES: 32 to 44 bust. PRICE, PREPAID, **$1.39**

4K722 *Our prices are lower than ever this year, and our styles more attractive.*
Here is an "EVERDAINTY" slip-over corset cover that every woman will adore. Fashioned of **washable satin** and inset with puffings of Georgette crepe. Hand embroidery and Val lace as shown. COLOR: Pink. SIZES: 32 to 44 bust. PRICE, PREPAID, **$1.69**

4K829 *A favored style in an* "EVERDAINTY" *corset cover, of alternating rows of* **Val lace** *and* **embroidery.**
Back to correspond. A bargain offering. COLOR: White. SIZES: 32 to 44 bust. PRICE, PREPAID, **95c**

4K751 *A big price cut in an* "EVERDAINTY" *camisole of* **satin,** *elaborately trimmed with* **fine filet lace.**
Ribbon threading and ribbon rosebuds. COLOR: Pink. SIZES: 32 to 44 bust. PRICE, PREPAID, **93c**

PHILIPSBORN'S Values are the Best Ever!! Prepaid also!

4K763 *At a lowered price—*"EVERDAINTY" *batiste camisole, attractively hand embroidered and shirred.*
A very pretty and thoroughly practical style. COLOR: Pink. SIZES: 32 to 44 bust. PRICE, PREP'D, **55c**

4K704 *Specially reduced. A neat style in* "EVERDAINTY" *corset cover. Good quality nainsook.*
Eyelet embroidery fashions the front yoke. Neat, durable lace edging. COLOR: White. SIZES: 32 to 44 bust. PRICE, PREPAID, **39c**

4K721 *An unusual opportunity to secure one of the new dark-colored camisoles which are so much worn nowadays by women of fashion with dark blouses.*
The "EVERDAINTY" model pictured above is especially handsome, fashioned of **navy blue satin** and richly embroidered in contrasting color. Navy blue. SIZES: 32 to 44 bust. PRICE, PREPAID, **$1.88**

4K715 *High prices are a thing of the past. Here is an* "EVERDAINTY" *corset cover of* **cross-bar lawn.**
Filet lace trimming. A special price reduction. COLOR: Pink. SIZES: 32 to 44 bust. PRICE, PREPAID, **59c**

4K720 *Smash go prices! An unusual value in an* "EVERDAINTY" *camisole of* **flowered ribbon and satin.**
Ribbon shoulder straps. COLOR: Pink and blue combination. SIZES: 32 to 44 bust. PRICE, **$1.59**

4K724 *No woman who knows values will overlook this chance to effect a worthwhile saving on a brassiere.* "EVERDAINTY" model made of good quality **muslin.** Eyelet embroidery forms the front and back yoke and trims the front of garment. COLOR: White. SIZES: 34 to 48 bust. PRICE PREPAID to your home, **59c**

4K733 *Here is a bargain extraordinary in a good-fitting* "EVERDAINTY" *muslin brassiere, quoted at a reduced price.*
There is a front and back yoke of eyelet embroidery. Neat braid finish. At this special price, it will pay you to buy now for future needs. COLOR: White. SIZES: 34 to 46 bust. PRICE, PREPAID, to your home, **29c**

4K723 *One of the most useful and practical of garments is this* "EVERDAINTY" *brassiere with rubber shields.*
The material is good quality muslin and the shields are washable. Every woman should have at least one of these brassieres. COLOR: White. SIZES: 34 to 48 bust. PRICE, **59c** PREPAID to your home,

4K705 *You have no idea how much better your blouses will look if worn over a perfect-fitting bust confiner.*
You can buy this "EVERDAINTY" model at a big cash saving. Made of a **very strong material** sometimes used to fashion corsets. Lace-trimmed front. Back closing. COLOR: Pink. SIZES: 34 to 48 bust. PRICE, PREPAID to your home, **43c**

4K724 59c

4K733 29c
WORTH 50c

4K791 $1.59

4K723 59c

4K705
←43c

4K747 59c

SATIN HAND EMBR'D

4K752 99c

SATIN AND GEORGETTE

4K727 $1.39

4K791 *A rich looking* "EVERDAINTY" *brassiere of Cluny lace and* **mercerized silk brocade.** The equal of any $2.50 brassiere. COLOR: Pink. SIZES: 34 to 48 bust. PRICE, PREPAID, **$1.59**
4K749 *A big cash saving is offered you in the purchase of this* "EVERDAINTY" **nainsook corset cover.** Lace and embroidered batiste trimming. COLOR: White. SIZES: 32 to 44 bust. PRICE, PREPAID to your home. **49c**

4K727 *Here is one of the most sensational bargains it has been our good fortune to offer.* Where but at PHILIPSBORN'S could you hope to find as pretty a camisole as this for only $1.39? "EVERDAINTY" model made of **satin,** richly trimmed with fine filet pattern lace. Ribbon straps. Pink. SIZES: 32 to 44 bust. PRICE, **$1.39**

Prices Smashed! in this Sale of White that's Right!

4K752 *Our prices are always the lowest; our styles always the prettiest; and our quality always the very best.* There is convincing proof of these statements in the "EVERDAINTY" camisole herewith shown. The material is satin with an inset of embroidered Georgette across front. Filet pattern lace. COLOR: Pink. SIZES: 32 to 44 bust. PRICE, PREPAID, **99c**

4K747 *A splendid number and a big value in a n* "EVERDAINTY" *muslin brassiere.* Quoted at less than cost. Richly trimmed with fine Cluny lace. COLOR: White. SIZES: 34 to 48 bust. PRICE, PREPAID, **59c**
4K719 "EVERDAINTY" *corset cover of* **nainsook.** Hand embroidered design. Handkerchief points over shoulders. COLOR: White. SIZES: 32 to 44 bust. PRICE, PREPAID, **65c**

4K749 49c

4K831 88c

SATIN
4K709 95c

4K726 96c

SATIN

4K719 65c

WORTH $1.25

4K725 59c

4K744 85c

WORTH $1.25

4K831 *The season's latest novelty in a two-color camisole is shown in this* "EVERDAINTY" *model.* COLOR: Upper part of blue satin, bottom of pink. SIZES: 32 to 44 bust. PRICE, PREPAID, **88c**
4K725 *One of our most beautiful styles in an* "EVERDAINTY" *bust confiner at a bargain.* **Mercerized brocade** and **Cluny lace.** COLOR: Pink. SIZES: 34 to 48 bust. PRICE, PREPAID. **59c**

4K709 *You will have to admit that we have smashed prices to the limit when you see such values as this* "EVERDAINTY" *navy blue satin camisole.* The very latest thing in camisoles. Satin straps. Hemstitching. For wear with dark blouses. COLOR: Navy blue. SIZES: 32 to 44 bust. PRICE, PREPAID, **95c**

4K726 *Greatly underpriced and a lovely style in this* "EVERDAINTY" *satin and filet lace camisole.* Specially shaped lace straps. COLOR: White. SIZES: 32 to 44 bust. PRICE, PREPAID, **96c**
4K744 *An attractive bust confiner at a price within every woman's reach. Excellent value.* "EVERDAINTY" *model.* Made entirely of handsome Cluny lace. COLOR: White. SIZES: 34 to 48 bust. PRICE, PREPAID, **85c**

CHICAGO, ILL.

For Index See Page 274 and Remember PHILIPSBORN'S Prepay All Transportation Charges. There Are No Express or Mailing Charges for You to Pay

227

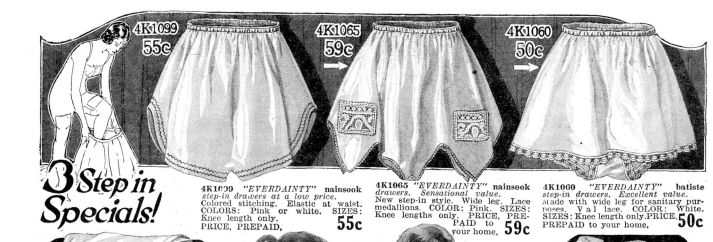

3 Step-in Specials!

4K1099 "EVERDAINTY" nainsook step-in drawers at a low price. Colored stitching. Elastic at waist. COLORS: Pink or white. SIZES: Knee length only. PRICE, PREPAID, **55c**

4K1065 "EVERDAINTY" nainsook drawers. Sensational value. New step-in style. Wide leg. Lace medallions. COLOR: Pink. SIZES: Knee lengths only. PRICE, PREPAID to your home, **59c**

4K1060 "EVERDAINTY" batiste step-in drawers. Excellent value. Made with wide leg for sanitary purposes. Val lace. COLOR: White. SIZES: Knee length only. PRICE, PREPAID to your home, **50c**

4K1079 An extraordinary price concession on these "EVERDAINTY" muslin drawers. Embroidery flounces. Open style. White. SIZES: 23 to 29 side length. PRICE, PREP'D to your home, **59c**
4K1080 Same as above in closed style. PRICE, PREPAID to your home, **59c**

4K1063 "EVERDAINTY" muslin drawers. Embroidery flounces. Open style. White. SIZES: 23 to 29 side length. PRICE, PREP'D to your home, **69c**
4K1064 Same as above in closed style. PRICE, PREPAID to your home, **69c**

Everdainty Bargains! for thrifty Buyers!!

4K1040 "EVERDAINTY" nainsook short chemise with genuine hand embroidery. Camisole style top. COLOR: Pink or white. SIZES: 32 to 44 bust. PRICE, PREPAID, **95c**

4K1059 A 25% reduction on "EVERDAINTY" satin bloomers. Reinforced. COLOR: Pink. SIZES: 23 to 29 side length. PRICE, PREPAID, **$2.98**

4K1038 Bodice style in an "EVERDAINTY" nainsook short chemise. COLOR: Pink or white. SIZES: 34 to 44 bust. PRICE, PREPAID to your home, **59c**

4K1056 "EVERDAINTY" step-in drawers of flowered nainsook with dainty lace trimming. Pocket. COLOR: Pink or blue. SIZES: Knee length only. PRICE, PREPAID, **89c**

4K1079
4K1080
59c

4K1063
4K1064
69c

4K1038 59c

GENUINE HAND EMBR'D. **4K1040 95c**

SATIN

4K1059 $2.98

4K1056 89c

4K1073 50c

4K1066 65c

4K1057 59c

4K1054 A new style in "EVERDAINTY" bloomer drawers. Of nainsook in open style. Colored shirrings. Elastic waistband. COLOR: Pink. SIZES: 23 to 29 side length. PRICE, PREPAID, **85c**

4K1096 A wonderful value at our price and worth at least 30c more than we ask are these "EVERDAINTY" bloomers. Made of nainsook. Elastic bands at waist and knees. COLOR: Pink or white. SIZES: 23 to 29 side length. PRICE, PREPAID, **59c**

4K1073 "EVERDAINTY" nainsook bloomers. Elastic bands at waist and knees. COLOR: Pink. SIZES: 23 to 29 side length. PRICE, **50c**

4K1066 "EVERDAINTY" mercerized cotton crepe de chine bloomers. Ruffles with colored stitching. COLOR: Pink. SIZES: 23 to 29 side length. PRICE, PREP'D, **65c**

4K1057 A bargain in "EVERDAINTY" bloomers of nainsook. Lace-trimmed. Elastic bands. COLOR: Pink or white. SIZES: 23 to 29 side length. PRICE, **59c**

4K1054 85c

4K1096 59c

For Misses and Children
"Everdainty" Bargains

4K2053 Prices such as these show you how to save money. Only $1.00 for this "EVERDAINTY" princess slip for misses. Made of **nainsook** with embroidery trimming. A tremendous value. COLOR: White. SIZES: 14-16-18 years. PRICE, PREPAID, **$1.00**

4K2052 A bargain at the price. Girls' princess slip. "EVERDAINTY" model of good quality **nainsook**. Fine filet lace trimming. Hemstitching. White. SIZES: 6 to 14 yrs. PRICE, PREPAID, **95c**

4K2058 A 25% reduction on this princess slip for misses. "EVERDAINTY" **nainsook** model. Eyelet embroidery front yoke. Flounce, and trimming across front. COLOR: White. SIZES: 14 to 18 years. PRICE. **$1.10**

4K2059 Here is an attractive style, greatly underpriced. Girls' "EVERDAINTY" princess slip of good quality **nainsook**. Camisole top banded with embroidery. Embroidery flounce. Shirrings. Ribbon straps COLOR: White. SIZES: 6 to 14 years. PRICE, PREPAID to your home, **93c**

4K2053 **$1.00**

4K2059 **93c**

4K2058 **$1.10**

4K2052 **95c**

4K2057 Refuse to pay high prices. Big cash savings. Misses' "EVERDAINTY" **nainsook** princess slip made with camisole top. Filet pattern lace. COLOR: White. SIZES: 14 to 18 years. PRICE, PREPAID, **98c**

4K2123 A bargain that appeals to every mother. "EVERDAINTY" princess slip. Made of good quality **nainsook**. COLOR: White. SIZES: 6 to 14 years. PRICE, PREPAID, **65c**

4K2095 Bargains such as these are not offered daily. "EVERDAINTY" princess slip for girls. Made of **nainsook**. COLOR: White. SIZES: 2 to 14 years. PRICE, PREPAID, **79c**

4K2099 Special! At a big reduction in price. Girls' "EVERDAINTY" princess slip, good quality **nainsook**. Embroidery flouncing and edging. White. SIZES: 6 to 14 years. PRICE, PREPAID, **85c**

4K2057 **98c** WORTH **$1.25**

4K2123 **65c**

4K2095 **79c**

4K2099 85c

CHICAGO, ILL.

Hosiery That Will Withstand the Rough Usage That Boys and Girls Give Their Stockings. Shown in Our Hosiery Section, Pages 209 to 215

229

4K2060—$1.19

4K2060 *Girls' "EVER-DAINTY" white* muslin *nightgown, V-necked.* 4 to 14 years. PRICE, PREP'D. **$1.19**
4K2054 *Girls' "EVER-DAINTY" white* nainsook *bloomers.* 4 to 12 years. PRICE, PREP'D. **45c**
4K2054X *Same for Misses.* 14 to 18 years. PRICE, PREP'D. **55c**

4K2054 45c
4K2054X 55c

4K2116 *Special. Girls' "EVERDAINTY" white* nainsook *bloomers.* SIZES: 2 to 12 yrs. PRICE, PREP'D. **35c**

4K2116 35c

For Boys or Girls

4K2089 79c

4K2104 59c

4K2105 75c

4K2090 88c

4K2061 95c

4K2051—59c
4K2051X—79c

4K2051 *"EVERDAINTY" night-gowns for children and girls. Great big bargain.* For this gown we have used good-wearing **nainsook** and trimmed it very daintily with colored shirrings and stitchings. COLOR: White. SIZES: 4 to 14 yrs. PRICE, **59c**
4K2051X SIZES: 14 to 18 years. PRICE, **79c**

Childrens Underwear at Real Low Bargain Prices!

4K2061 *Money-saving value in girls' one-piece pajamas.* Made of **batiste** in sleeveless style. COLOR: Pink. SIZES: 8 to 12 yrs. PRICE, **95c**

4K2104 *"EVER-DAINTY" nain-sook sleeping gar-ment for boys or girls. White only.* 2 to 6 years. PRICE, **59c**
4K2105 SIZES: 8 to 10 years. PRICE, **75c**

4K2089 *"EVER-DAINTY" white nain-sook underwaist and drawers.* 2 to 6 years. PRICE, **79c**
4K2090 SIZES: 8 to 14 years. PRICE, **88c**

4K2092 50c

4K2091—45c

4K2114 39c

4K2091 *Offered at a big price saving—misses' "EV-ERDAINTY" muslin draw-ers.* Embroidery flouncing. Sensational value. COLOR: White. SIZES: 14 to 18 years. PRICE, **45c**
4K2114 *A 25% reduction on girls' "EVERDAINTY" muslin drawers. Buy now and save. Real bargain.* COLOR: White. SIZES: 4 to 12 years. PRICE, PREPAID, **39c**
4K2092 SIZES: 14 to 18 years. PRICE, **50c**

4K2085—21c   **4K2086—35c**

Boys or Girls Under Waist

4K2085 *"EVERDAIN-TY" cambric underwaist for boys or girls. Front closing. Splendid value.* Taped buttons and eye-lets. COLOR: White. SIZES: 2 to 12 years. PRICE, **21c**
4K2086 *"EVERDAIN-TY" muslin underwaist. Boys or girls. Back clos-ing. Extra reinforce-ments.* White. SIZES: 2 to 12 years. PRICE, PREP'D. **35c**

4K2056 59c

4K2063 35c

4K2062 50c

4K2102 45c

4K2056 *You can always "do bet-ter" at PHILIPSBORN'S.* Here is a girls' **muslin** petticoat for which you would pay considerably more else-where. Embroidery trimming. COLOR: White. SIZES: 6 to 14 years. PRICE, PREPAID to your home, **59c**
4K2062 *It is foolish to pay big prices, save money—trade here.* We quote a very low price on this *"EVER-DAINTY"* muslin underwaist and drawers for children. Drop seat. COLOR: White. SIZES: 2 to 6 years. PRICE, PREPAID to your home, **50c**

4K2063 *Save your money, compare our prices with others.* An unusual value, indeed, is offered you in these *"EVERDAINTY"* muslin drawers for children. Embroidery trimming. COL-OR: White. SIZES: 6 to 12 years. PRICE, PREPAID to your home, **35c**
4K2102 *When you consider the quality these prices are very low.* Children's *"EVERDAINTY"* underwaist and skirt made of fine quality muslin. Embroidery trimming. COLOR: White. SIZES: 2 to 6 years. PRICE, PREPAID to your home, **45c**

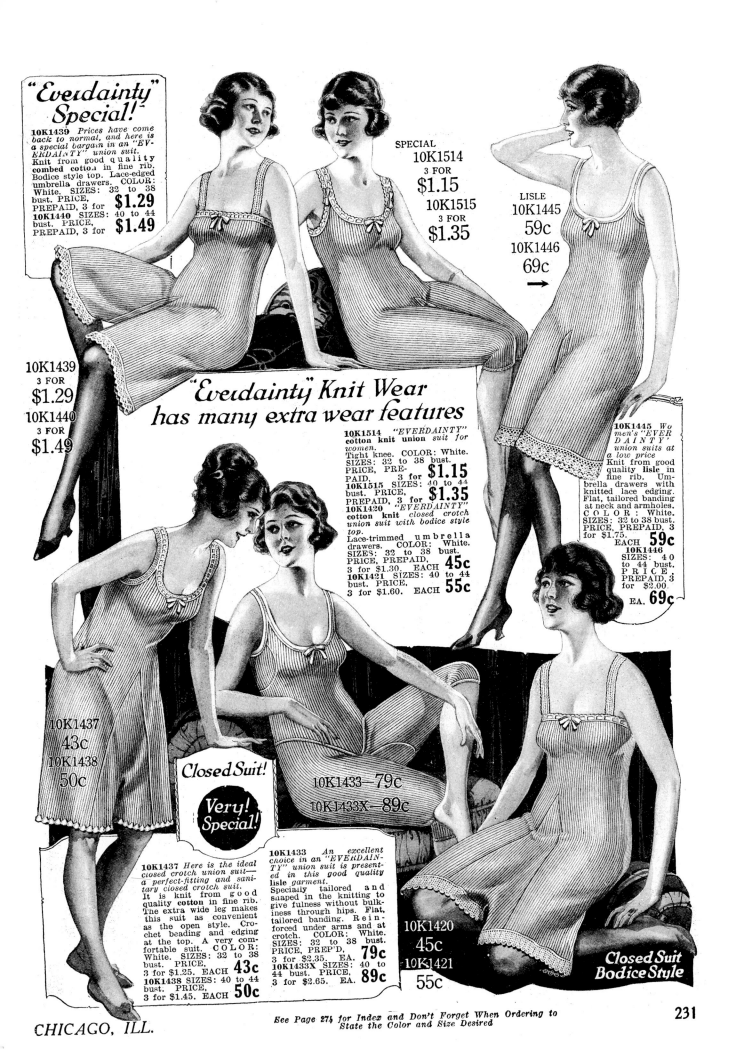

"Everdainty" Special!

10K1439 *Prices have come back to normal, and here is a special bargain in an "EVERDAINTY" union suit.* Knit from good quality combed cotton in fine rib. Bodice style top. Lace-edged umbrella drawers. COLOR: White. SIZES: 32 to 38 bust. PRICE, PREPAID, 3 for **$1.29**
10K1440 SIZES: 40 to 44 bust. PRICE, PREPAID, 3 for **$1.49**

SPECIAL
10K1514
3 FOR
$1.15
10K1515
3 FOR
$1.35

LISLE
10K1445
59c
10K1446
69c
→

10K1439
3 FOR
$1.29
10K1440
3 FOR
$1.49

"Everdainty" Knit Wear has many extra wear features

10K1514 *"EVERDAINTY" cotton knit union suit for women.* Tight knee. COLOR: White. SIZES: 32 to 38 bust. PRICE, PREPAID, 3 for **$1.15**
10K1515 SIZES: 40 to 44 bust. PRICE, PREPAID, 3 for **$1.35**
10K1420 *"EVERDAINTY" cotton knit closed crotch union suit with bodice style top.* Lace-trimmed umbrella drawers. COLOR: White. SIZES: 32 to 38 bust. PRICE, PREPAID, 3 for $1.30. EACH **45c**
10K1421 SIZES: 40 to 44 bust. PRICE, 3 for $1.60. EACH **55c**

10K1445 *Women's "EVERDAINTY" union suits at a low price.* Knit from good quality lisle in fine rib. Umbrella drawers with knitted lace edging. Flat, tailored banding at neck and armholes. COLOR: White. SIZES: 32 to 38 bust. PRICE, PREPAID, 3 for $1.75. EACH **59c**
10K1446 SIZES: 40 to 44 bust. PRICE, PREPAID, 3 for $2.00. EA. **69c**

10K1437
43c
10K1438
50c

Closed Suit!
Very! Special!

10K1433 — 79c
10K1433X — 89c

10K1437 *Here is the ideal closed crotch union suit—a perfect-fitting and sanitary closed crotch suit.* It is knit from good quality cotton in fine rib. The extra wide leg makes this suit as convenient as the open style. Crochet beading and edging at the top. A very comfortable suit. COLOR: White. SIZES: 32 to 38 bust. PRICE, 3 for $1.25. EACH **43c**
10K1438 SIZES: 40 to 44 bust. PRICE, 3 for $1.45. EACH **50c**

10K1433 *An excellent choice in an "EVERDAINTY" union suit is presented in this good quality lisle garment.* Specially tailored and shaped in the knitting to give fulness without bulkiness through hips. Flat, tailored banding. Reinforced under arms and at crotch. COLOR: White. SIZES: 32 to 38 bust. PRICE, PREP'D, 3 for $2.35. EA. **79c**
10K1433X SIZES: 40 to 44 bust. PRICE, 3 for $2.65. EA. **89c**

10K1420
45c
10K1421
55c

Closed Suit Bodice Style

CHICAGO, ILL.

See Page 274 for Index and Don't Forget When Ordering to State the Color and Size Desired

Bargains! that we recommend to you

BARGAIN

10K1495
50c
10K1495X
60c

10K1490
3 FOR
$1.19

10K1491-3 FOR
$1.29

10K1494
49c
10K1494X
59c

CLOSED STYLE

10K1496-48c
10K1497-58c

10K1504
59c
10K1505
69c

10K1441
55c
10K1442
65c

10K1490 *Important savings in women's* **fine cotton** *knit union suits.* Lace-edged unbrella drawers. Crochet beading at top. COLOR: White. SIZES: 32 to 38 bust. PRICE, PREPAID to your home, 3 for **$1.19**
10K1491 Same style. SIZES: 40 to 44 bust. PRICE, PREPAID, 3 for **1.29**
10K1495 *You always find the biggest* **underwear** *bargains at PHILIPSBORN'S.* Women's **cotton** knit union suit with lace front yoke. COLOR: White. SIZES: 32 to 38 bust. PRICE, PREPAID to your home, 3 for $1.45. EACH **50c**
10K1495X Same style. SIZES: 40 to 44 bust. PRICE, PREPAID to your home, 3 for $1.75. EACH **60c**
10K1494 *Many women prefer the closed* **crotch** *union suit which we show here.* Knit from good quality in elastic rib. Extra wide, lace trimmed unbrella drawers. Won't-slip top. COLOR: White. SIZES: 32 to 38 bust. PRICE, PREP'D, 3 for $1.35. EA. **49c**
10K1494X Same style. SIZES: 40 to 44 bust. PRICE, PREPAID to your home, 3 for $1.75. EACH **59c**
10K1441 *A worthwhile saving in a woman's bodice top* **cotton** *knit union suit.* Knitted shoulder straps. Crochet-edged umbrella drawers. COLOR: Pink. SIZES: 32 to 38 bust. PRICE, PREP'D, 3 for $1.60. **55c**
10K1442 Same style. SIZES: 40 to 44 bust. PRICE, 3 for $1.90. EACH **65c**

10K1504 *The most value for your money at PHILIPSBORN'S.* Bodice top **cotton** knit union suit. Tight knee. COLOR: White. SIZES: 32 to 38 bust. PRICE, 3 for $1.75. EA. **59c**
10K1505 SIZES: 40 to 44 bust. PRICE, PREPAID, 3 for $2.00. EACH **69c**
10K1496 *Complete revision of all prices to meet today's conditions.* A big reduction on women's fine **cotton** knit union suits. Finished with tailored band top. Tight knee. COLOR: White. SIZES: 32 to 38 bust. PRICE, 3 for $1.40. EACH **48c**
10K1497 SIZES: 40 to 44 bust. PRICE, PREPAID, 3 for $1.70. EACH **58c**

232

Our Bargain Prices Include Free Delivery to Your Door. No Extra Charges for Express or Mailing

PHILIPSBORN'S

10K1506 *We offer a 25% reduction on this closed crotch union suit for women.* Knit from fine **combed cotton**. Extra wide umbrella drawers. COLOR: White. SIZES: 32 to 38 bust. PRICE, PREPAID to your home, 3 for $1.90.   EACH **65c**

10K1506X SIZES: 40 to 44 bust. PRICE, PREPAID, 3 for $2.20.   EACH **75c**

10K1400 *An extraordinary offering in women's open mesh* **cotton** *knit union suits.* Delightfully cool and comfortable. Umbrella drawers. Lace edging. COLOR: White. SIZES: 32 to 38 bust. PRICE, PREPAID to your home,   **89c**

10K1400X SIZES: 40 to 44 bust. PRICE, PREPAID to your home,   **99c**

10K1443 *The best bargain we have ever offered in underwear for women.* Double extra size light weight union suit of good quality **combed cotton**, knit in fine elastic rib. Umbrella drawers. Lace edging. Crochet beading at neck. COLOR: White. SIZES: 46 to 52 bust. PRICE, PREPAID to your home, 3 for $2.35.   EACH **79c**

10K1405 *A wonderful economy in a double extra size union suit for stout women.* Knit from fine **combed cotton** in medium rib. Made with tight knee drawers. Crochet beading and edging at neck and armholes. COLOR: White. SIZES: 46 to 52 bust. PRICE, PREPAID, 3 for $2.20.   EACH **75c**

CLOSED STYLE

Prepaid to your Door!

10K1400
89c
10K1400X
99c

MESH

10K1506
65c
10K1506X
75c

DOUBLE EXTRA SIZE

10K1405
75c

DOUBLE EXTRA SIZE

10K1443
79c

10K1401 $1.69
10K1402 $1.69

10K1401 *An underwear bargain that will interest all women.* Fine **combed cotton** union suit made with glove silk top. Tight knee. Tailored band top. COLOR: Pink. SIZES: 32 to 38 bust. PRICE, PREPAID to your home,   **$1.69**

10K1402 SIZES: 40 to 44 bust. PRICE, PREPAID to your home,   **$1.69**

10K1432 *Special bargain in a women's* **glove silk** *union suit.* An excellent suit that will give you splendid returns for your money. Wide knee. Tailored band top. COLOR: Pink or white. SIZES: 32 to 44 bust. PRICE, PREPAID to your home,   **$3.98**

GLOVE SILK

10K1432—$3.98

CHICAGO, ILL.

{*Important—Be Sure to State COLOR and SIZES When Ordering—Important*

233

10K1458 *Because we bought the materials below regular market prices, we are able to quote a specially reduced price on these athletic suits. A most popular style for women. Made of checked nainsook. Provided with a knitted waistband across the back. Button fastening. If you want one of the most comfortable suits you have ever worn, then order one of these models. COLOR: White. SIZES: 32 to 44.* PRICE, PREPAID, **88c**

10K1412 *For the woman who likes the slip-over styles, we have provided this new model athletic suit, pictured at the left. It is made of fine quality Batiste, and is just as dainty a garment as any woman could desire. Reinforced with a knitted waistband as shown in the miniature panel. Hemstitching. A bargain offering in an especially fine suit. COLOR: Pink or white. SIZES: 32 to 44.* PRICE, PREPAID, **95c**

10K1412
95c
WORTH
$1.25

10K1458
88c

10K1455
89c

"Everdainty" Priced low for Savings!

10K1455 *We offer this athletic style union suit at a saving which we feel confident you could not equal at any other mail order house in the country. The material is checked nainsook, made in the popular slip-over style. Camisole top. A special reduction on a suit that ordinarily sells for considerably more. COLOR: White.* SIZES: 32 to 44. PRICE. **89c**

10K1431 *We anticipated the large demand which these athletic union suits would have, and bought plentifully while prices were at their lowest. Good quality nainsook makes the model. It features the favored camisole style top and full length button opening. Colored hemstitching adds a dainty trimming. COLOR: White or pink. SIZES: 32 to 44.* PRICE, PREPAID, **$1.25**

10K1413 *An extraordinary offering in the popular athletic style union suit—usually found in this quality at high prices. Our special price is only $1.15. Fashioned of nainsook, the garment features the well-liked camisole top. Colored hemstitching. Slip-over model. Knitted waistband. COLOR: White. SIZES: 34 to 44.* PRICE, PREPAID, **$1.15**

10K1431
$1.25

10K1417
$1.19

10K1417 *A well-known manufacturer cut his prices to us on this lot of athletic union suits, otherwise we could not offer garments of this quality for less than $2.00.*
The comfort of these athletic style union suits has made them prime favorites with PHILIPS-BORN'S customers. The model pictured above is fashioned of good quality nainsook. Colored hemstitching adds a dainty touch. A knitted band across the back relieves any strain when stooping or bending. Full length button fastening. COLOR: White or pink. SIZES: 32 to 44. PRICE, PREPAID to your home, **$1.19**

10K1413
$1.15

234

Big Special Value!

10K1434 Women are beginning to realize that quality counts, and that it is wisdom to buy the best they can afford.

Here is a chance for the wise shopper to secure an "EVERDAINTY" glove silk undervest without paying big prices. Full, liberal sizes. Tailored band top. Reinforced. COLORS: Pink or white. SIZES: 32 to 44 bust. PRICE, PREPAID to your home, **$2.35**

Embroidered Glove Silk Bargain!

WORTH $3.75

10K1435 Every woman enjoys the luxury of silk underwear, and this is especially low priced. "EVERDAINTY" glove silk undervest, beautifully embroidered as pictured. This is a finely woven silk that will give excellent service. COLORS: pink or white. SIZES: 32 to 44 bust. PRICE, PREP'D to your home, **$2.88**

Stout Sizes

10K1406 A special price cut on a stout woman's undervest. Double extra size garment knit from fine combed cotton. Extra wide armholes. Finished with crochet beading. COLOR: White. SIZES: 46 to 52 bust. PRICE, PREPAID, 3 for $1.45. EACH **50c**

Stout

10K1602
$3.50

10K1600
$3.99

ENVELOPE SUIT

10K1603 If you like a bodice top undervest, send for this model. It is an "EVERDAINTY" garment made of fine quality glove silk which will give extremely satisfactory wear. Reinforced under arms. COLOR: Pink or white. SIZES: 32 to 44 bust, PRICE, PREPAID to your home, **$1.98**

10K1407
50c

10K1436
$2.79

10K1528
45c
10K1529
55c

10K1546
50c
10K1546X
59c

Everdainty Glove Silk Union suits!

10K1602 Greatly under priced for this excellent quality—"EVERDAINTY" envelope chemise, $3.50. Of fine glove silk, fronts beautifully embroidered in self. Ribbon shoulder straps. COLORS: Pink or white. SIZES: 32 to 44 bust. PRICE, PREPAID to your home, **$3.50**

10K1407 A splendid bargain for the stout woman in double extra size drawers, only 50c. Knit from good quality cotton in fine rib. Wide umbrella bottoms trimmed with knitted lace. COLOR: White. SIZES: 46 to 52 bust. PRICE, PREPAID, 3 for $1.45. EACH **50c**

10K1436 Think of getting these "EVERDAINTY" glove silk bloomers for only $2.79. Made with elastic bands at the waist and knees. Crotch is reinforced. COLORS: Pink or white. SIZES: Side length 23 to 29. PRICE, PREPAID to your home, **$2.79**

10K1600 An unparalleled offer in an "EVERDAINTY" glove silk union suit—a third under price. A style that every woman likes—bodice top and athletic style drawers. Reinforced crotch. COLOR: Pink or white. SIZES: 32 to 44 bust. PRICE, PREPAID to your home, **$3.99**

10K1528 A money-saving bargain in "EVERDAINTY" cotton knit umbrella style drawers. Knitted lace edge. COLOR: White. SIZES: 32 to 38 bust. PRICE, PREPAID, 3 for $1.35. EACH **45c**

10K1529 SIZES: 40 to 44 bust. PRICE, PREPAID 3 for $1.60. EACH **55c**

10K1546 Fine cotton knit light weight "EVERDAINTY" bloomers. Elastic waistband and knees. COLOR: Pink. SIZES: 4, 5 and 6. PRICE, PREPAID, 2 for 95c. EACH **50c**

10K1546X SIZES: For large women, 7, 8 and 9. PRICE 2 for $1.15. EACH **59c**

CHICAGO, ILL.

For Index See Page 274 and Remember PHILIPSBORN'S Prepay All Transportation Charges. There Are No Express or Mailing Charges for You to Pay

235

FINE COTTON

COTTON KNIT

FLESH COLOR

COTTON KNIT

A Big! Extra Value

Bodice Top

10K1508 *For the woman who wants to save.* This is a favorite style for wear with sheer blouses and evening dresses. Knit from good quality **cotton** in fine Swiss rib. At the price we quote it is a decided economy for you to buy this vest here. COLOR: White. SIZES: 32 to 38 bust. PRICE, 3 for 55c. **19c**

10K1508X SIZES: 40 to 44 bust. PRICE, 3 for 65c. EA. **23c**

10K1522 Flat knit vest. COLOR: White. SIZES: 32 to 38 bust. PRICE, 3 for 55c. EACH **19c**
10K1523 SIZES: 40 to 44 bust. PRICE, 3 for 69c. EACH **25c**

10K1507 Cotton knit vest. Flesh. SIZES 32 to 38 bust. PRICE 3 for 73c. EACH **25c**
10K1507X SIZES: 40 to 44 bust. PRICE, 3 for 95c. EACH **33c**

10K1520 Bodice style vest. COLOR: White. SIZES: 32 to 38 bust. PRICE, 3 for 43c. EACH **15c**
10K1520X SIZES: 40 to 44 bust. PR., PREP'D, 3 for 60c. EACH **21c**

SPECIAL COTTON KNIT

ALL AROUND LACE YOKE

10K1410 Bodice style. COLOR: Pink. SIZES: 32 to 38 bust. PRICE, PREP'D 3 for 73c. **25c**
10K1410X SIZES: 40 to 44 bust. PRICE. 3 for $1.00. **35c**

10K1526 Lace yoke. COLOR: White. SIZES: 32 to 38 bust. PRICE, PREP'D 3 for 73c. **25c**
10K1526X SIZES: 40 to 44 bust. PRICE, 3 for $1.00. EA. **35c**

10K1521 Cotton knit vest. "Wont-slip" shoulders. COLOR: White. SIZES: 32 to 38 bust. PRICE, 3 for 65c. EACH **23c**
10K1521X SIZES: 40 to 44 bust. PRICE, PREP'D 3 for 85c. EACH **29c**

10K1447 Bodice style vest. Knit from fine combed cotton. COLOR: White. SIZES: 32 to 38 bust. PRICE, 3 for $1.00. EACH **35c**
10K1448 SIZES: 40 to 44 bust. PRICE, PREP'D 3 for $1.25. EACH **43c**

10K1492 3 for 39c

Extra fine Swiss Ribbed Bargain!

10K1519 *For the woman who wants a light weight summer vest with short sleeves, here is an excellent value.* It is knit from good quality **cotton** in extra fine Swiss rib, with low neck and **short** sleeves. Crochet beading at neck is run with tape. **The short sleeves are a well-liked feature, as they absorb perspiration and take the place of shields.** COLOR: White. SIZES: 32 to 38 bust. PRICE, 3 for 55c. EA. **19c**
10K1527 SIZES: 40 to 44 bust. PRICE, PREPAID. EACH **23c**

10K1524 *Worthwhile reductions on women's undervests.* Knit from fine quality **cotton** in Swiss rib. Finished with French banding at top and arm holes. "Won't-slip" shoulders. COLOR: White. SIZES: 32 to 38 bust. PRICE, PREP'D 3 for 65c. **23c**
10K1525 SIZES: 40-44 bust. PRICE, 3 for 85c. EACH **29c**

3 for 39c
49c

10K1492 PHILIPSBORN'S prices are always bargain prices. Fine **cotton** knit vests. "Won't-slip" shoulders. Crochet beading and edging. COLOR: White. SIZES: 32 to 38 bust. PRICE, PREP'D, 3 for **39c**
10K1493 SIZES: 40 to 44 bust. PRICE, PREPAID, 3 for **49c**

10K1493 3 for 49c

236

"Goods by the Yard." A New Member of The PHILIPSBORN Family. See Pages 250 to 255

PHILIPSBORN'S

10K1449 *Lowered prices on an underwaist for boys or girls.* Knit from good quality **cotton.** Taped buttons for fastening outer garments. Garter eyelets. COLOR: White. SIZES: 2 to 13 years. PRICE, PREP'D, 3 for 55c. EA. **19c**

10K1444 *A remarkable value in a child's* **cotton** *knit undervest.* Because we bought a large supply of these vests we received a special price concession which we pass on to you at this low price. COLOR: White. SIZES: 2 to 12 years. PRICE, PREPAID, 3 for 43c. EACH **15c**

Very Special Bargain!

10K1484 *A value that will appeal to thrifty women.* Infants' knitted **cotton** wrappers made with crossover style fronts which give double warmth. Buttoned straps at back. Cream white. SIZES: 0 to 6,— for child up to 2 years. PRICE, 3 for $1.00. EA. **35c**

10K1533 *Special! Girls' waist union suit knit from good quality* **cotton.** Extra buttons. Drop seat. Knitted straps. COLOR: White. SIZES: 2 to 13 years. PRICE, PREPAID, 3 for $1.35. EA. **49c**

10K1640 *Two garments in one— girls' underwaist and bloomer drawers of* **checked nainsook.** Reinforced straps. Taped buttons for attaching outer garments. Elastic at knees. COLOR: White. SIZES: 2 to 12 years. PRICE, PREPAID 3 for $1.60. EA. **55c**

10K1641 *A brand new offering in a girls' bloomer waist union suit.* Upper part of garment is made of **checked nainsook,** lower part of dark blue **plain nainsook.** COLOR: as described. SIZES: 2 to 12 years. PRICE, PREPAID, 3 for $2.00. EACH **69c**

Knit Union Suits at Big Savings!

10K1532 *The biggest Bargain ever in a girls'* **cotton** *knit union suit.* Made with umbrella drawers and drop seat. COLOR: White. SIZES: 2 to 16 years. PRICE, PREPAID, 3 for $1.30. Each **45c**

10K1584 *Here is a sensational value in girls'* **cotton** *knit* **bloomers.** Elastic bands at waist and knees. COLOR: Black or white. SIZES: 2 to 6 years. PRICE, **39c**

Made for the Kiddies. Cut to fit them Right!

10K1411 *A splendid selection in a girl's* **cotton** *knit closed crotch union suit.* Wide umbrella drawers are finished with knitted lace. Crochet beading at top. A big value. COLOR: White. SIZES: 6 to 16 years. PRICE, PREP'D, 3 for $1.25. EACH **43c**

10K1646 *Boys' or girls' skeleton waist.* Made of **strong** webbing, with elastic garters. Taped buttons for attaching outer garments. COLOR: White. SIZES: 2 to 12 years. PRICE, PREPAID, **29c**

CHICAGO, ILL.

Every Dress Accessory That the Well-dressed Woman Needs at PHILIPSBORN'S— *Stylish Neckwear Shown on Pages 103 and 104*

237

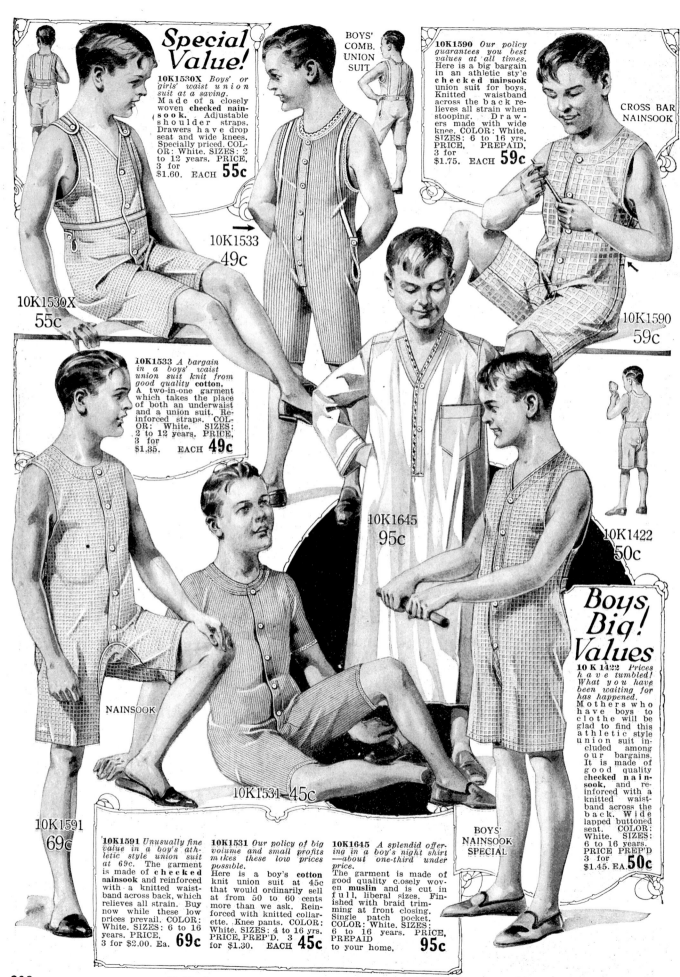

Special Value!

10K1530X *Boys' or girls' waist union suit at a saving.* Made of a closely woven **checked nainsook.** Adjustable shoulder straps. Drawers have drop seat and wide knees. Specially priced. COLOR: White. SIZES: 2 to 12 years. PRICE, 3 for $1.60. **EACH 55c**

BOYS' COMB. UNION SUIT

10K1590 *Our policy guarantees you best values at all times.* Here is a big bargain in an athletic sty'e **checked nainsook** union suit for boys. Knitted waistband across the back relieves all strain when stooping. Drawers made with wide knee. COLOR: White. SIZES: 6 to 16 yrs. PRICE, PREPAID, 3 for $1.75. **EACH 59c**

CROSS BAR NAINSOOK

10K1530X 55c

10K1533 49c

10K1590 59c

10K1533 *A bargain in a boys' waist union suit knit from good quality cotton.* A two-in-one garment which takes the place of both an underwaist and a union suit. Reinforced straps. COLOR: White. SIZES: 2 to 12 years. PRICE, 3 for $1.35. **EACH 49c**

10K1645 95c

10K1422 50c

NAINSOOK

Boys Big! Values

10 K 1422 *Prices have tumbled! What you have been waiting for has happened.* Mothers who have boys to clothe will be glad to find this athletic style union suit included among our bargains. It is made of good quality **checked nainsook,** and reinforced with a knitted waistband across the back. Wide lapped buttoned seat. COLOR: White. SIZES: 6 to 16 years. PRICE PREP'D 3 for $1.45. EA. **50c**

10K1531 45c

10K1591 69c

BOYS' NAINSOOK SPECIAL

10K1591 *Unusually fine value in a boy's athletic style union suit at 69c.* The garment is made of **checked nainsook** and reinforced with a knitted waistband across back, which relieves all strain. Buy now while these low prices prevail. COLOR: White. SIZES: 6 to 16 years. PRICE, 3 for $2.00. Ea. **69c**

10K1531 *Our policy of big volume and small profits makes these low prices possible.* Here is a boy's **cotton** knit union suit at 45c that would ordinarily sell at from 50 to 60 cents more than we ask. Reinforced with knitted collarette. Knee pants. COLOR: White. SIZES: 4 to 16 yrs. PRICE, PREP'D, 3 for $1.30. **EACH 45c**

10K1645 *A splendid offering in a boy's night shirt—about one-third under price.* The garment is made of good quality closely woven **muslin** and is cut in full, liberal sizes. Finished with braid trimming at front closing. Single patch pocket. COLOR: White. SIZES: 6 to 16 years. PRICE, PREPAID to your home, **95c**

Men's Underwear Bargains!

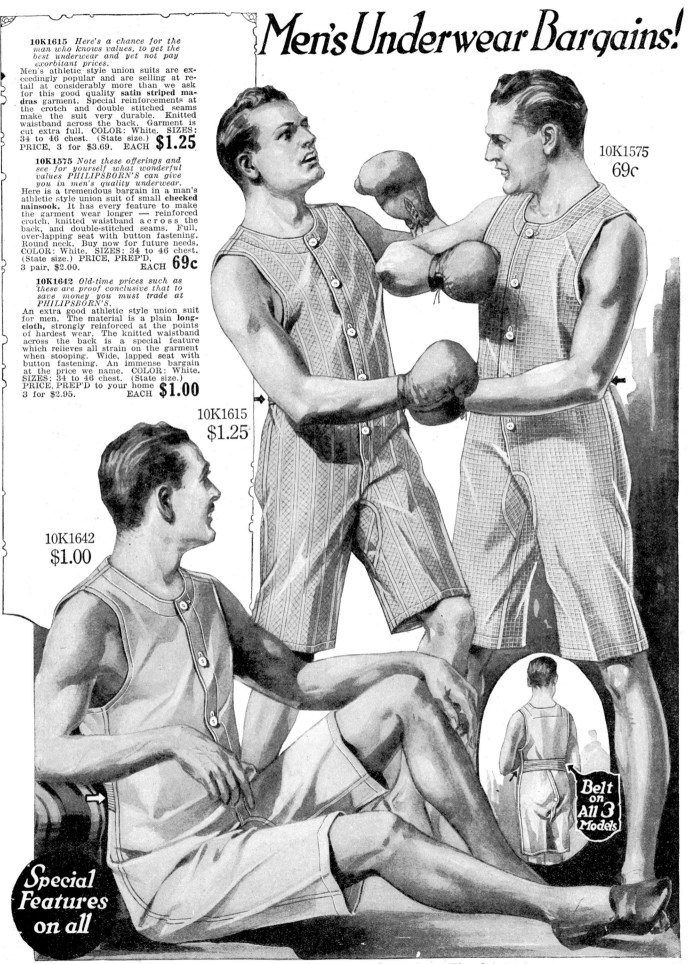

10K1615 *Here's a chance for the man who knows values, to get the best underwear and yet not pay exorbitant prices.*
Men's athletic style union suits are exceedingly popular and are selling at retail at considerably more than we ask for this good quality **satin striped madras** garment. Special reinforcements at the crotch and double stitched seams make the suit very durable. Knitted waistband across the back. Garment is cut extra full. COLOR: White. SIZES: 34 to 46 chest. (State size.) PRICE, 3 for $3.69. EACH **$1.25**

10K1575 *Note these offerings and see for yourself what wonderful values PHILIPSBORN'S can give you in men's quality underwear.*
Here is a tremendous bargain in a man's athletic style union suit of small **checked nainsook**. It has every feature to make the garment wear longer — reinforced crotch, knitted waistband across the back, and double-stitched seams. Full, over-lapping seat with button fastening. Round neck. Buy now for future needs. COLOR: White. SIZES: 34 to 46 chest. (State size.) PRICE, PREP'D, 3 pair, $2.00. EACH **69c**

10K1642 *Old-time prices such as these are proof conclusive that to save money you must trade at PHILIPSBORN'S.*
An extra good athletic style union suit for men. The material is a plain **longcloth**, strongly reinforced at the points of hardest wear. The knitted waistband across the back is a special feature which relieves all strain on the garment when stooping. Wide, lapped seat with button fastening. An immense bargain at the price we name. COLOR: White. SIZES: 34 to 46 chest. (State size.) PRICE, PREP'D to your home 3 for $2.95. EACH **$1.00**

10K1575
69c

10K1615
$1.25

10K1642
$1.00

Belt on All 3 Models

Special Features on all

CHICAGO, ILL.

See Page 274 for Index and Don't Forget When Ordering to State the Color and Size Desired

239

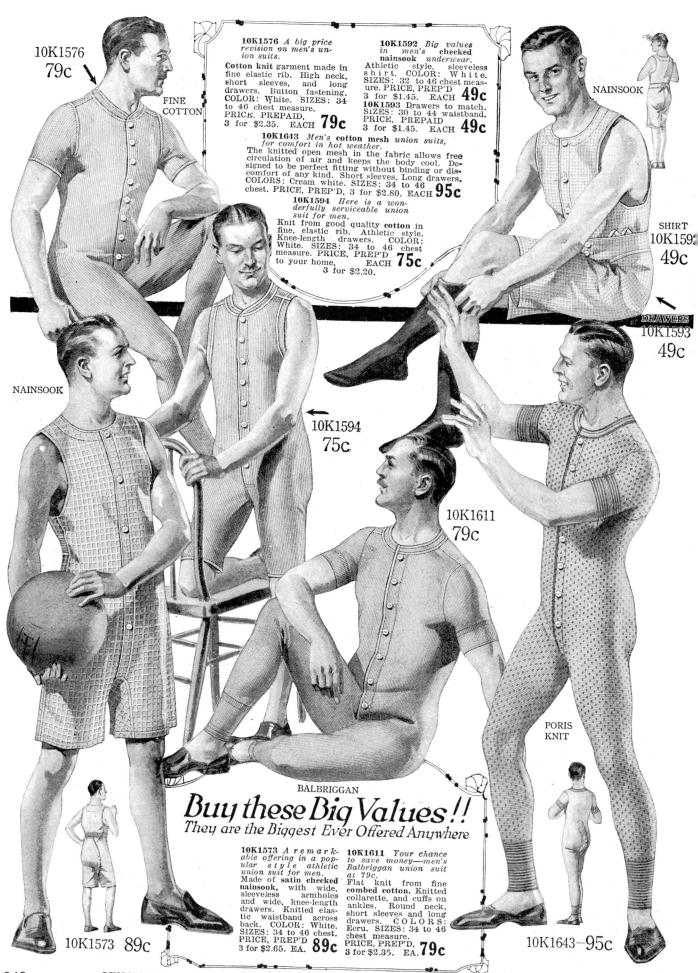

10K1576
79c

FINE
COTTON

10K1576 *A big price revision on men's union suits.*
Cotton knit garment made in fine elastic rib. High neck, short sleeves, and long drawers. Button fastening. COLOR: White. SIZES: 34 to 46 chest measure. PRICE, PREPAID, 3 for $2.35. EACH **79c**

10K1592 *Big values in men's* **checked** *nainsook underwear.* Athletic style, sleeveless shirt. COLOR: White. SIZES: 32 to 46 chest measure. PRICE, PREP'D 3 for $1.45. EACH **49c**
10K1593 Drawers to match. SIZES: 30 to 44 waistband. PRICE, PREPAID 3 for $1.45. EACH **49c**

10K1643 *Men's* **cotton mesh** *union suits, for comfort in hot weather.*
The knitted open mesh in the fabric allows free circulation of air and keeps the body cool. Designed to be perfect fitting without binding or discomfort of any kind. Short sleeves. Long drawers. COLORS: Cream white. SIZES: 34 to 46 chest. PRICE, PREP'D 3 for $2.80. EACH **95c**

10K1594 *Here is a wonderfully serviceable union suit for men.*
Knit from good quality **cotton** in fine, elastic rib. Athletic style. Knee-length drawers. COLOR: White. SIZES: 34 to 46 chest measure. PRICE, PREP'D to your home, EACH **75c** 3 for $2.20.

NAINSOOK

SHIRT
10K1592
49c

DRAWERS
10K1593
49c

NAINSOOK

10K1594
75c

10K1611
79c

PORIS
KNIT

BALBRIGGAN

Buy these Big Values!!
They are the Biggest Ever Offered Anywhere

10K1573 *A remarkable offering in a popular style athletic union suit for men.*
Made of **satin checked nainsook**, with wide, sleeveless armholes and wide, knee-length drawers. Knitted elastic waistband across back. COLOR: White. SIZES: 34 to 46 chest. PRICE, PREP'D 3 for $2.65. EA. **89c**

10K1611 *Your chance to save money—men's Balbriggan union suit at 79c.*
Flat knit from fine **combed cotton**. Knitted collarette, and cuffs on ankles. Round neck, short sleeves and long drawers. COLORS: Ecru. SIZES: 34 to 46 chest measure. PRICE, PREP'D, 3 for $2.35. EA. **79c**

10K1573   89c

10K1643—95c

PHILIPSBORN'S

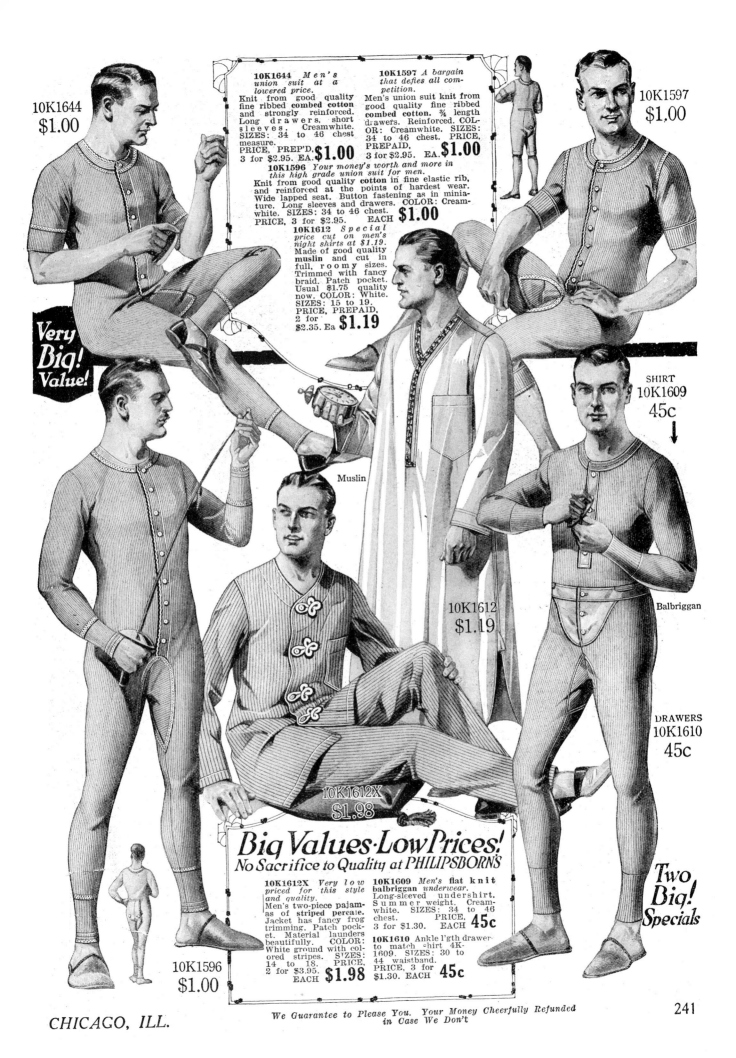

10K1644
$1.00

Very Big! Value!

10K1644 *Men's union suit at a lowered price.* Knit from good quality fine ribbed **combed cotton** and strongly reinforced. Long drawers, short sleeves. Creamwhite. SIZES: 34 to 46 chest measure. PRICE, PREP'D, 3 for $2.95. EA. **$1.00**

10K1597 *A bargain that defies all competition.* Men's union suit knit from good quality fine ribbed **combed cotton**. ¾ length drawers. Reinforced. COLOR: Creamwhite. SIZES: 34 to 46 chest. PRICE, PREPAID, 3 for $2.95. EA. **$1.00**

10K1596 *Your money's worth and more in this high grade union suit for men.* Knit from good quality **cotton** in fine elastic rib, and reinforced at the points of hardest wear. Wide lapped seat. Button fastening as in miniature. Long sleeves and drawers. COLOR: Creamwhite. SIZES: 34 to 46 chest. PRICE, 3 for $2.95. EACH **$1.00**

10K1612 *Special price cut on men's night shirts at $1.19.* Made of good quality **muslin** and cut in full, roomy sizes. Trimmed with fancy braid. Patch pocket. Usual $1.75 quality now. COLOR: White. SIZES: 15 to 19. PRICE, PREPAID, 2 for $2.35. Ea **$1.19**

10K1597
$1.00

SHIRT
10K1609
45c
↓

Muslin

10K1612
$1.19

Balbriggan

10K1612X
$1.98

DRAWERS
10K1610
45c

10K1596
$1.00

Big Values·Low Prices!
No Sacrifice to Quality at PHILIPSBORN'S

10K1612X *Very low priced for this style and quality.* Men's two-piece pajamas of striped percale. Jacket has fancy frog trimming. Patch pocket. Material launders beautifully. COLOR: White ground with colored stripes. SIZES: 14 to 18. PRICE, 2 for $3.95. EACH **$1.98**

10K1609 Men's flat knit *balbriggan underwear.* Long-sleeved undershirt. Summer weight. Creamwhite. SIZES: 34 to 46 chest. PRICE, 3 for $1.30. EACH **45c**

10K1610 Ankle l'gth drawers to match shirt 4K1609. SIZES: 30 to 44 waistband. PRICE, 3 for $1.30. EACH **45c**

Two Big! Specials

CHICAGO, ILL.

PHILIPSBORN'S
Corsets have extra Service · Features

A Specially shaped at the hip line to confine the flesh of the thighs.

B Elastic insert at back holds corset securely to figure when standing, and allows for comfortable expansion when sitting.

C Elastic inserts at bust line prevent corset from cutting into flesh and does away with unsightly corset ridges.

4K1207 *The selection of a corset is of first importance in a woman's wardrobe. With the right corset, the simplest suit or dress gains added charm.*
Here is a new PHILIPSBORN'S corset, specially designed to bring out the grace of the average figure. It is made of pink **brocade** in front lacing style. The free, unboned hip is a particularly desirable feature. Elastic inserts at the low bustline and at lower center back (See miniature). COLOR: Pink. SIZES: 20 to 30. (Order one inch smaller than regular waist measure taken over dress.)
PRICE, PREPAID to your home, **$2.98**

4K1238 *One of our specials—special in quality and extremely low priced is this PHILIPSBORN'S corset which is offered at less than regular retail prices.*
It is a back-lacing model, fashioned of rich pink **silk brocade**, and is intended for average figures. Boning is so placed as to leave the sensitive hip-bone free, and to give the flat hip and back of fashion's demands. Elastic inserts at low bustline. A value without equal. COLOR: Pink. SIZES: 20 to 30. (Order two inches smaller than regular waist measure taken over dress.)
PRICE, PREPAID to your home, **$2.49**

SPECIAL
4K1207
$2.98

SILK BROCADE
4K1238
$2.49

PHILIPSBORN'S

5 Wonderful Reducing Models

4K1235 *A coutil model for the woman who requires special reducing features.*
PHILIPSBORN'S reducing model. A wide elastic band confines the too prominent abdomen and fleshy thighs to graceful lines. COLOR: White. SIZES: 22 to 36. (Order two inches smaller than regular waist measure taken over dress.)
PRICE, PREPAID to your home, **$3.50**

4K1227 *You have no idea how comfortable a reducing corset can be until you try this model.*
For the stout woman with large, fleshy hips and thighs. The material is coutil. Elastic inserts. Lacings at hips. White. SIZES: 22 to 36. (Order two inches smaller than regular waist measure taken over dress.)
PRICE, PREPAID to your home, **$4.45**

4K1219
$3.75

4K1235
$3.50

WORTH
$4.00

4K1215
$2.98

4K1220
$4.88

4K1227
$4.45

Very Special

4K1220 *The stout woman more than any other needs to be particular about the corset she wears, for the corset can make or mar her appearance.*
The special reducing features of this PHILIPSBORN'S coutil corset will transform your figure as though by magic—making a difference of from two to three inches in your hips and abdomen, almost immediately. Note the specially shaped sections at the sides and front, which hold the flesh firmly in place. The elastic bands are an extra reducing feature which confines prominent abdomens without, however, unhealthful restraint. Boning is close set and substantial. No woman who needs a reducing corset should hesitate about an investment of this sort. COLOR: White. SIZES: 23 to 36. (Order two inches smaller than regular waist measure taken over dress.)
PRICE, PREPAID to your home, **$4.88**

4K1219 *Graceful lines for the short waisted heavy woman have been skilfully embodied in this PHILIPSBORN'S corset of coutil.*
Heavy boning close set to support the figure properly. Specially reinforced across the front—a feature that gives straight lines across the abdomen. Elastic inserts at the medium low bustline allow the flesh to fall comfortably within the corset. High at back. Elastic gussets at the hip line. White. SIZES: 22 to 36. (Order two inches smaller than regular waist measure taken over dress.)
PRICE, PREPAID, **$3.75**

4K1215 *Here is an exceptional opportunity to effect a saving in our famous reducing corset, a scientifically designed model.*
Made of extra quality coutil. Elastic belt extends all around and interlaces through the corset, holding the model snugly to the figure and reducing the abdomen. The medium high bustline is shaped higher at the back to confine the shoulder blades. (See miniature.) COLOR: White. SIZES: 23 to 36. (Order two inches smaller than regular waist measure taken over dress.)
PRICE, PREPAID, **$2.98**

Style, Savings and Comfort

4K1258 *One of the most satisfactory corsets ever designed for the tall, medium figure, yet priced remarkably low.* We have used good quality coutil for the model, and have placed the boning so that it does not touch the sensitive hipbones. Elastic inserts, low bust. A corset of ideal proportions. COLOR: White. SIZES: 20 to 30. (Order one inch smaller than regular waist measure taken over dress.) PRICE, PREPAID, **$2.29**

4K1202 *At PHILIPSBORN'S you get the best values for your money. Extraordinary low prices for corsets of this quality.* PHILIPSBORN'S model of brocaded coutil. It is designed for average figures, and features the new flat hip and flat back of fashion's demands. Medium bust. COLOR: Pink. SIZES: 20 to 30. (Order one inch smaller than waist measure taken over dress.) PRICE, PREP'D **$2.48**

4K1258→ $2.29

4K1202 $2.48

4K1200→ $2.00 WORTH $3.00

←4K1212 $1.95

4K1257 $2.45

4K1212 *PHILIPSBORN'S corset for slight figures. Splendid value.* Made of a dainty flesh-colored coutil, and identical in quality with models selling elsewhere at high prices. Light boning. COLOR: Pink. SIZES: 20 to 30. (Order one inch smaller than regular waist measure taken over dress.) PRICE, PREPAID to your home, **$1.95**

4K1200 *The large woman need not pay prohibitive prices for her corsets, providing she shops at PHILIPSBORN'S.* At our low price, this coutil model is a wonder value. Medium bust. Long over hips and back. COLOR: White. SIZES: 20 to 30. (Order one inch smaller than regular waist measure taken over dress.) PRICE, PREPAID to your home, **$2.00**

4K1257 *A correctly fitting corset is of the utmost importance from the standpoint of appearance, health and comfort.* Here is a new style coutil corset, specially designed for the average woman. It has a medium bust (about 4½ inches above the waistline) which takes care of surplus flesh about the shoulders. Embroidered batiste top. COLOR: White. SIZES: 20 to 30. (Order one inch smaller than regular waist measure taken over dress.) PRICE, PREPAID to your home, **$2.45**

PHILIPSBORN'S Petticoats in a Variety of Splendid Fabrics, Very Economically Priced. See Pages 195, 196, and 197

PHILIPSBORN'S

Special Models for Special Figures

4K1205 *Here is a new style corset which we have added to the PHILIPSBORN'S line this season, and for which we ask a remarkably low price.* It is designed for the large, full-formed woman, and is made of good quality coutil. Closely but flexibly boned. Graduated front clasp which "anchors" corset to the figure. Specially tailored and reinforced. COLOR: White. SIZES: 20 to 30. (Order two inches smaller than regular waist measure.) PRICE, PREPAID, **$1.88**

4K1213 *The woman who wishes to safeguard her own health cannot be too careful in the selection of her maternity corset.* This special PHILIPSBORN'S maternity model is of coutil, with special flexible boning and lacings. COLOR: White. SIZES: 23 to 36. (Order two inches smaller than regular waist measure.) PRICE, PREPAID, **$2.88**

4K1214 Same style as above without nursing flaps. PRICE, PREPAID to your home, **$2.88**

4K1221
$1.67

4K1213
4K1214
$2.88

4K1205
$1.88

4K1203
$2.25
WORTH
$3.50

4K1261—$4.75

4K1261 *Here is a corset that is a triumph of designing,—offering as it does ideal proportions for the full, heavy figure with large hips.* Extra good quality coutil, specially tailored and boned. Elastic belt under front of model extends from the sides as shown,—a reducing feature that decreases the size of the hips very noticeably. COLOR: White. SIZES: 22 to 36. (Order two inches smaller than regular waist measure taken over dress.) PRICE, PREPAID to your home, **$4.75**

4K1203 *The stout woman need not envy her more slender sister if she makes the right selection in a corset.* This PHILIPSBORN'S coutil corset has special reducing features which give height and slenderness to the full figure. Adjustable straps at the sides confine the hips and abdomen to graceful lines. COLOR: White. SIZES: 20 to 36. (Order two inches smaller than regular waist measure.) PRICE, PREPAID to your home, **$2.25**

4K1221 *If you know what the shops are asking for corsets, you will appreciate what an amazing value we offer here.* At a dollar more this PHILIPSBORN'S coutil corset would be a big bargain, and it certainly is a wonderful value for our price. Very durably boned. Designed for the stout woman of average height. COLOR: White. SIZES: 20 to 36. (Order two inches smaller than regular waist measure.) PRICE, PREPAID to your home, **$1.67**

CHICAGO, ILL.

See Page 274 for Index and Don't Forget When Ordering to State the Color and Size Desired

245

4K1260 Before buying your new clothes be sure that you get the right corset which is equivalent to saying that it should be a PHILIPSBORN'S model.
Here is a front-lacing **coutil** corset, specially designed to give grace to tall, medium figures. Elastic inserts at low bustline. COLOR: White. SIZES: 20 to 30. (Order one inch smaller than regular waist measure taken over dress.)
PRICE, PREPAID to your home, **$2.45**

4K1242 There is nothing that gives that "well-groomed" look which every woman wants so surely as a well-fitting PHILIPSBORN'S corset.
Silk brocade is the material which fashions the front-lacing model shown below. Low bust. For average figures. COLOR: Pink. SIZES: 20 to 30. (Order one inch smaller than regular waist measure taken over dress.)
PRICE, PREPAID to your home, **$3.45**

"All Philipsborns" Corsets Prepaid to your home

4K1216 The woman who does not like the ordinary corset will revel in the freedom of this PHILIPSBORN'S model.
Made of good quality coutil with wide inserts of elastic down the sides. The bustline is extremely low, making the model ideal for athletic purposes. An ideal model for the woman who is active. COLOR: White. SIZES: 20 to 30. (Order one inch smaller than regular waist measure taken over dress.)
PRICE, PREPAID, **$2.75**

4K1260 $2.45

4K1216 $2.75

4K1242 $3.45

4K1241 Here is a bargain in a specially designed athletic corset, intended for the growing girl's first corset or for the slender woman.
It is made of good quality **coutil** and reinforced across the back as shown in miniature. Very light boning. A splendid model. COLOR: White. SIZES: 20 to 28. (Order one inch smaller than regular waist measure taken over dress.)
PRICE, PREPAID to your home, **$1.59**

4K1248 Comfort on hot, summer days is assured if you invest in one of these new style ventilated corsets, a special PHILIPSBORN'S design.
The model is made of **coutil**, with open mesh material at the sides. Elastic inserts at the medium low bustline. Front lacing. COLOR: White. SIZES: 20 to 30. (Order one inch smaller than regular waist measure taken over dress.)
PRICE, PREPAID to your home, **$1.98**

4K1241 $1.59

4K1248 $1.98

WORTH $2.25

Here's the Last Word in Corsets

4K1206 *You would never dream that a corset could be so comfortable until you have tried this.* We have designed this corset to take care of average figures that do not require a heavily boned model. The material—a wonderful quality **brocade**—will be certain to please you with its daintiness. Elastic inserts at the very low bustline prevents the corset from cutting into the flesh. COLOR: Pink. SIZES: 20 to 28. (Order two inches smaller than regular waist measure taken over dress.) PRICE, **$1.88**

4K1259 *Never have corset comfort and moderate pricing been so splendidly combined as in this coutil corset—one of our most popular models.* It is specially designed for the short, slender woman and miss. Low bustline. Free unboned hip. COLOR: White. SIZES: 20 to 28. (Order two inches smaller than regular waist measure taken over dress.) PRICE, PREPAID to your home, **$1.89**

4K1218 *The woman and miss engaged in active pursuits, whether for work or athletic will appreciate the comfort of this new "sport" corset.* It is made in the new topless style of good quality **coutil**. Full length elastic inserts. Light boning. COLOR: Pink. SIZES: 20 to 30. (Order two inches smaller than regular waist measure taken over dress.) PRICE, PREPAID to your home, **96c**

4K1206
$1.88
→
WORTH
$2.50

→ 4K1259
$1.89

4K1218
96c

4K1243 $2.98 →

4K1243 *No matter how expensive your dress, it will not have that something we call "style" unless it is worn over the proper corset, one that suits your particular figure.* The woman with large hips and thighs will find her figure wonderfully improved if she selects this **coutil** model. Elastic gussets. COLOR: White. SIZES: 20 to 30. (Order two inches smaller than regular waist measure taken over dress.) PRICE, PREPAID to your home, **$2.98**

4K1209 *We quote a surprisingly low price on this corset, one of the most popular of our topless models. We feel sure that you will not find its equal at our price.* It is made of good quality **coutil**, with full length side inserts of elastic webbing. For the woman and miss who cannot wear a heavily boned corset. COLOR: White. SIZES: 20 to 40. (Order two inches smaller than regular waist measure taken over dress.) PRICE, PREPAID to your home, **$1.88**

4K1209
$1.88

SPECIAL

Priced Low! & Delivered to Your Door!

4K1255 *Special! At a very low price we offer this PHILIPSBORN'S* coutil *corset for average figures. Medium boning.*
COLOR: White. SIZES: 20 to 30. (Order two inches smaller than regular waist measure over dress.)
PRICE, PREPAID to your home, **$1.45**

4K1239 *A corset of unusual flexibility and comfort is this PHILIPSBORN'S* coutil *model. Low bust line with elastic inserts.*
COLOR: White. SIZES: 20 to 28. (Order two inches smaller than regular waist measure taken over dress.) PRICE, PREP'D **$1.79**

4K1204 *A PHILIPSBORN'S* **coutil** *corset for the average figures. Free unboned hip. Elastic top. Low bust line.*
COLOR: Pink. SIZES: 20 to 28. (Order two inches smaller than regular waist measure taken over dress.)
PRICE, PREPAID, **$1.49**

4K1249 *A summer corset for the hot weather is always a good investment, especially at this price.* **Coutil** *model with open mesh material at sides. Low bust line with elastic inserts.* COLOR: White. SIZES: 20 to 30. (Order two inches smaller than regular waist measure over dress.)
PRICE, PREPAID, **$1.79**

4K1210 *PHILIPSBORN'S corset waist for the growing girl—a bargain price.* Made of firm-textured **jean**. Bust pockets. Very flexible. COLOR: White. SIZES: 20 to 28. (Order two inches smaller than regular waist measure taken over dress.)
PRICE, PREP'D, **99c**

4K1211 *Here is a lightly-boned PHILIPSBORN'S* **batiste** *corset. Designed for misses and small women.* White. SIZES: 20 to 28. (Order 2 inches smaller than regular waist measure taken over dress.)
PRICE, PREPAID, **$1.29**

4K1225 *For the medium or large woman.* **Coutil** *very durably boned.* White. SIZES: 20 to 30. (Order two inches smaller than waist measure taken over dress.)
PRICE, PREP'D, **$1.95**

4K1255 $1.45

4K1204 $1.49

4K1239 $1.79

4K1249

4K1210 99c WORTH $1.39

4K1211 $1.29

4K1225 $1.95

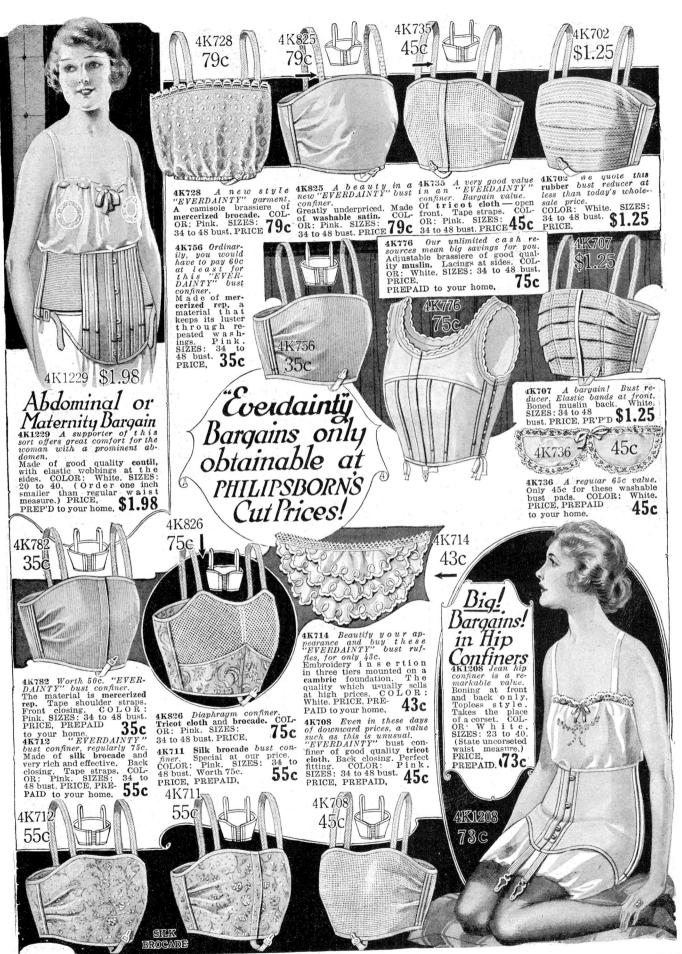

4K728 79c

4K825 79c

4K735 45c

4K702 $1.25

4K728 *A new style* "EVERDAINTY" *garment.* A camisole brassiere of **mercerized brocade.** COLOR: Pink. SIZES: 34 to 48 bust. PRICE **79c**

4K825 *A beauty in a* new "EVERDAINTY" *bust confiner.* Greatly underpriced. Made of **washable satin.** COLOR: Pink. SIZES: 34 to 48 bust. PRICE **79c**

4K735 *A very good value* in an "EVERDAINTY" *confiner. Bargain value.* Of **tricot cloth**—open front. Tape straps. COLOR: Pink. SIZES: 34 to 48 bust. PRICE **45c**

4K702 *we quote this* **rubber** bust reducer at less than today's wholesale price. COLOR: White. SIZES: 34 to 48 bust. PRICE. **$1.25**

4K756 *Ordinarily, you would have to pay 60c at least for this* "EVERDAINTY" *bust confiner.* Made of **mercerized rep,** a material that keeps its luster through repeated washings. Pink. SIZES: 34 to 48 bust. PRICE, **35c**

4K776 *Our unlimited cash resources mean big savings for you.* Adjustable brassiere of good quality **muslin.** Lacings at sides. COLOR: White. SIZES: 34 to 48 bust. PRICE, PREPAID to your home, **75c**

4K707 $1.25

4K756 35c

4K776 75c

4K707 *A bargain! Bust reducer.* Elastic bands at front. Boned muslin back. White. SIZES: 34 to 48 bust. PRICE, PR'P'D **$1.25**

4K736 45c

4K736 *A regular 65c value.* Only 45c for these washable bust pads. COLOR: White. PRICE, PREPAID to your home, **45c**

4K1229 $1.98

Abdominal or Maternity Bargain

4K1229 *A supporter of this sort offers great comfort for the woman with a prominent abdomen.* Made of good quality **contil,** with elastic webbings at the sides. COLOR: White. SIZES: 20 to 40. (Order one inch smaller than regular waist measure.) PRICE, PREP'D to your home, **$1.98**

"Everdainty" Bargains only obtainable at PHILIPSBORN'S Cut Prices!

4K782 35c

4K826 75c

4K714 43c

4K782 *Worth 50c.* "EVERDAINTY" *bust confiner.* The material is **mercerized rep.** Tape shoulder straps. Front closing. COLOR: Pink. SIZES: 34 to 48 bust. PRICE, PREPAID to your home. **35c**

4K712 "EVERDAINTY" *bust confiner, regularly 75c.* Made of **silk brocade** and very rich and effective. Back closing. Tape straps. COLOR: Pink. SIZES: 34 to 48 bust. PRICE, PREPAID to your home. **55c**

4K826 *Diaphragm confiner.* **Tricot cloth** and **brocade.** COLOR: Pink. SIZES: 34 to 48 bust. PRICE, **75c**

4K711 *Silk brocade bust confiner.* Special at our price. COLOR: Pink. SIZES: 34 to 48 bust. Worth 75c. PRICE, PREPAID, **55c**

4K714 *Beautify your appearance and buy these* "EVERDAINTY" *bust ruffles, for only 43c.* Embroidery insertion in three tiers mounted on a **cambric** foundation. The quality which usually sells at high prices. COLOR: White. PRICE, PREPAID to your home, **43c**

4K708 *Even in these days of downward prices, a value such as this is unusual.* "EVERDAINTY" *bust confiner* of good quality **tricot cloth.** Back closing. Perfect fitting. COLOR: Pink. SIZES: 34 to 48 bust. PRICE, PREPAID, **45c**

Big! Bargains! in Hip Confiners

4K1208 *Jean hip confiner is a remarkable value.* Boning at front and back only. Topless style. Takes the place of a corset. COLOR: White. SIZES: 23 to 40. (State uncorseted waist measure.) PRICE, PREPAID. **73c**

4K712 55c

4K711 55c

4K708 45c

4K1208 73c

SILK BROCADE

Organdies · Dainty as Spring!

11K20192 Printed novelty organdies *in a variety of new patterns—very crisp, mercerized finish.* Comes in 38 to 39 inch width makes up to advantage. COLORS: White grounds (morning glory or rose figure), colors rose, copenhagen blue, lavender or maize. Colored grounds (same patterns). Rose, copenhagen blue, maize or lavender.
PRICE, PREPAID to your home, **45c** yd.

Calico!
10 yd. lengths only

Blue B. · Red B. · Black B.

11K20146 *Here is a splendid economy in fast color "WASHWELL" calico—sold in 10-yard lengths only.*
This material comes in a variety of attractively printed patterns—width 24 inches. Ideal for house dresses, aprons, children's dresses, and garments that one uses for everyday wear. COLORS: White ground with blue figure (B); white ground with black figure (B); white ground with red figure (B); in dark grounds, pattern (A); cadet blue, rose, lavender, tan or black.
PRICE, PREPAID to your home, **10 yards only $1.10**

We do NOT send Samples of any dress materials.

Apron Check or Nurses' Stripe Gingham
10 yd. lengths only

11K20150 *Bargain* apron check or nurses' stripe gingham. *Width 26 in.* COLORS: Navy blue and white, black and white, brown and white checks; nurses' stripe. White grounds with blue or grey stripes. Sold only in 10-yard bolts of one color and pattern.
PRICE, PREPAID to your home, 10 yds. only **$1.18**

Plisse Lingere Krinkle

11K20210 *Width about 30 inches.* Plisse lingerie krinkle selected cotton yarn—soft, mercerized finish. Krinkle permanent. Used for nightgowns and underwear. COLOR: White only. PRICE, PREPAID, **23c** yd.

Voiles ····· Special Value!

11K20201 *Most unusual at our low price is this offering in* printed cotton voile. Furnished in artistic new patterns and very fashionable this season for dresses. Widths 37 to 38 inches. Will launder well and give splendid satisfaction. COLORS: Copenhagen blue, rose, black, navy blue or lavender.
PRICE, PREPAID to your home, **19c** yd.

Standard Percales
5 yd. lengths only

11K20145 *Here is an extraordinary value in standard quality* percales *in various patterns.* Width 36 inches. Serviceable grade. COLORS: Solid pink, light blue, lavender, navy blue or cadet blue (style C); White grounds with black, blue or pink figured patterns (style B); Navy or Copenhagen blue grounds with white assorted patterns, styles (A1) (A2) (D1) (D2). Sold only in 5-yard bolts of one color and pattern. PRICE, PREPAID to your home, **5 yards only 79c**

We do NOT send Samples of any dress materials.

Featuring Famous! WASHWELL Fabric Bargains!

SOISETTE
REGISTERED

11K20211 *Through co-operation with the manufacturers we are able to offer this popular fabric at a big discount. Width 31 to 32 inches.*
This is a registered fabric, popularly known as soisette. It is a fine soft lustrous fully mercerized cotton fabric specially desirable for costumes, dresses, shirts, sport skirts, waists, and children's clothing. A very high grade material. COLORS: White, nile green, cream, tan, flesh, helio, navy blue, black or light blue.
PRICE, PREPAID to your home, **39c** yd.

Romper Suitings!

11K20154 *Special sale* romper suitings—*makes durable rompers, children's garments, aprons, etc.* Standard quality, width 32 inches. Fast color. COLORS: (Solid) (No. 1) Cadet blue, pink, navy blue or tan; (Stripes) (No. 2) Cadet blue, navy blue, dark brown; (No. 3) Two-tone stripes, cadet blue and brown, navy blue and red.
PRICE, PREPAID to your home, **25c** yd.

Ginghams Sale!

11K20152 Dress Gingham.
COLORS: (A) Overplaid—white grounds with green, cadet blue, brown or navy blue. (C) Solid cadet blue, rose, pink, tan, green or helio. (B) Checks—white grounds with cadet blue, pink, or navy blue. (D) Black and white shepherd check. Width 26 inches.

15c PREP'D
WORTH **25c** YARD

Chambray
10 yd. lengths only

11K20151 *The low price that we quote on this* chambray *will appeal to shrewd shoppers.* It is woven of medium weight cotton yarn, and is very satisfactory for work shirts, children's or women's clothing. Sold in 10-yard bolts of one color only. A special bargain. COLORS: Light blue, dark blue, tan, brown, grey or pink. Width 26 inches. PRICE, PREPAID to your home, **10 yards only $1.19**

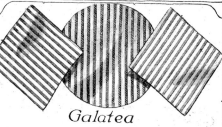

Galatea

11K20155 *Save money — standard quality* galatea cloth *special price. Width 25 to 26 inches.*
This is a closely woven twilled cotton fabric, printed in neat patterns. Excellent for making aprons, dresses, house dresses, children's dresses, rompers and little boys' suits. COLORS: White grounds, cadet blue, tan, pink or navy blue stripe.
PRICE, PREPAID to your home, **19c** yd.

Nainsook
10 yd. lengths only

11K20250 *Good quality* **nainsook.** Combed cotton yarn. Lighter in weight than long cloth, finer. For nightgowns, underwear. Width 36 inches. Snow white. SOLD only in 10-yard bolts. PRICE, PREP'D, 10 yds. for **$1.49**

11K20251 36-inch width. **Our best quality**—sold in 10-yard bolts only. Snow white. PRICE, PREPAID, 10 yds. for **$1.79**

Muslin
Standard Quality
10 yd. lengths Only
2 Grades

We do NOT Send Samples of any yard goods.

11K20240 *Don't miss these bargain values in standard quality muslins.*
Two grades of these muslins the higher priced proportionately finer. Made from a fine grade cotton and carefully finished and bleached. Width 36 inches. Suitable for a countless variety of household garments—women's and children's underwear, infants' wear, etc. Every housekeeper should take advantage of our low money-saving prices on these reliable muslins. Snow white. Sold in 10-yard bolts only.
PRICE, PREPAID to your home, **10 yards for $1.29**

11K20241 **Our better quality,**—36-inch width.
PRICE, PREPAID to your home, **10 yards for $1.49**

Long Cloth
10 yd. lengths only
2 Grades

11K20244 *Splendid values in two grades of* **long cloth.**
This is a plain white cotton fabric resembling muslin but lighter in weight and softer in finish. Sold only in 10-yard bolts. 36-inch width. PREPAID, 10 yds. **$1.39**

11K20245 **Our best quality.** Width 36 inches. PREPAID, 10 yds **$1.65**

Mercerized Pongee Costs Less

11K20212 Mercerized cotton pongee. COLORS: White, cream, pink, lavender, light blue, copenhagen blue, tan, old rose, dark brown, navy blue, black, reseda, myrtle green or pearl grey. Width 25 to 26 inches. PRICE, PREPAID, **19c yd.**

11K20213 A better quality and wider width, 32 inches. Same shades as 11K20212. PRICE, PREPAID, **37c yd.**

Batiste the Ideal Summer Fabric

11K20193 *Soft-finished* mercerized batiste *specially reduced.* Width 30 inches. COLORS: White or flesh. PREP'D to your home, 10 yds. for $1.95. **20c yd.**

11K20194 French batiste. Sheer and crisp. Fine, even weave. COLORS: White, cream, flesh, orchid, maize or light blue. Width 38 to 39 inches. PREPAID to your home, 5 yds. for $1.39. **29c yd.**

Choice Fabrics from WASH WELL the Worlds' Best Looms

11K20190 Organdie. Width 38 to 40 inches. COLORS: White, flesh, bisque, nile green, maize, steel grey, pink, light blue, lavender, copenhagen blue, dark copenhagen blue or rose. PRICE, PREPAID, **25c yd.**

11K20191 Better quality. Width 39 to 40 inches. Colors as 11K20190 and tan, reseda green or navy blue. PRICE, PREPAID, **34c yd.**

Organdies all Shades

VOILES !!
Matchless Values

11K20185 Cotton voile. Width 38 to 39 inches. COLORS: White, light blue, pink, navy blue, lilac, rose, copenhagen blue, tan or black. PRICE, PREPAID to your home, **22c yd.**

Voile Dotted Swiss
11K20161 Voile. Dotted Swiss effect. Big value. Width about 38 inches. COLORS: White ground with copenhagen blue, red or black dots. Light blue ground or pink, copenhagen blue, navy blue, black, brown or rose with white dots or navy blue with cerise dots. PRICE, PREPAID, **69c yd.**

Checks Voiles Stripes

11K20188 *Reduced*—Striped voile of selected twisted mercerized cotton yarn. Suitable for afternoon frocks, dresses and waists. Snow white. Width 35 to 36 inches. PRICE, PREPAID to your home, **33c yd.**

11K20189 Plaid or check voiles of corded hard twisted cotton yarn. Width 35 to 36 inches. Assorted patterns. PRICE, PREPAID to your home, **38c yd.**

11K20186 Fine quality mercerized voile. Width 38 to 40 inches. COLORS: White, cream, maize, pink, light blue, lilac, nile green, steel grey, copenhagen blue, rose, navy blue or black. PRICE, PREPAID to your home, **25c yd.**

11K20187 *Best grade.* Width 40 inches. COLORS: White, maize, nile green, light blue, pink, copenhagen blue, bisque (Tan) steel grey, rose, reseda green, lilac, navy blue or black. PRICE, PREPAID to your home, **35c yd.**

Dimity • Stripes • Checks

11K20181 *Extra quality* dimity. Comes in stripe effects similar to illustration. Light weight cotton fabric woven of selected yarn. Snow white. Width 27 inches. PRICE, PREPAID to your home, **25c yd.**

11K20182 Checked dimity—perfectly bleached snow white. Assorted patterns. Width about 26 inches. PRICE, PREPAID to your home, **25c yd.**

Mercerized Poplin

11K20168 *Saving on* **mercerized poplin**—*good weight. Width 25 to 26 inches.*
COLORS: White, pink, old rose, light blue, copenhagen blue, reseda green, brown, black, navy blue, lavender, grey or tan.
PRICE, PREPAID to your home. **25c** yd.
11K20169 Better quality poplin. Width 35 to 36 inches. Same colors as above.
PRICE, PREPAID to your home. **47c** yd.

Colored Novelty Voile

11K20202 Cotton voile—*neat colored checks. Width 35 to 36 inches.*
COLORS: Pink, nile green, light blue, maize, tan, old rose, copenhagen blue, navy blue, black or light helio.
PREPAID, to your home **39c** yd.
11K20203 Fancy colored voile stripe. Width 35 to 36 inches. COLORS: Pink, light blue, nile green, maize, tan, old rose, copenhagen blue, navy blue, black or light helio.
PRICE, PREPAID to your home, **35c** yd.

Seasons' Newest Dress Fabric Silk Novelty Weave Fibre Tricolette

11K20163 *One of the season's newest and most popular dress materials is this* **fibre silk tricolette.** *Width 35 inches.*
It is a silk-mixed fabric, woven with an effective satin stripe, rich in appearance. Makes up beautifully by itself without trimming of any kind. It is in great demand for dresses, blouses, and the better quality of negligees. A value that you will find difficult to duplicate at our low price. COLORS: Copenhagen blue, cream, pink, light blue, Pekin blue, navy blue, black, corn, helio, tan, reseda green, rose, battleship grey, flesh. PRICE, PREPAID to your home, **79** yd.

We do **NOT** Send Samples of any dress materials.

Pure Silk Shantung!

11K20024 *An exceedingly fashionable material for summer suits and dresses is this* **pure silk** **Shantung,** *an imported all silk pongee.*
This is a well-woven material, which will give splendid service. Also used for draperies. Width 33 inches. Natural color tan only.
PRICE, PREPAID to your home, **89c** yd.

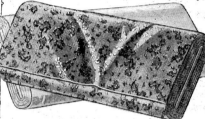

Tussah Silk plain or brocaded

11K20166 *New stylish* **Tussah** *silk, desirable for women's and misses' dresses, waists, children's garments.*
Silk and cotton yarn in solid color. Width 35 inches. COLORS: Ivory white, light blue, pink, lavender, myrtle green, black, taupe, rose or navy blue.
PRICE, PREPAID to your home, **49c** yd.
11K20167 Good quality Tussah silk, brocaded in floral pattern. **Colors as listed above.** Width 35 to 36 inches.
PRICE, PREPAID to your home, **68c** yd.

Novelty Fabrics! ◆WASHWELL◆ Lowest Prices!!

Rep all shades • Kimono Crepe

11K20196 *Exceptional values in* Mercerized rep.
Medium weight fine-ribbed, cuts to advantage. Width 35 to 36 inches. Good-looking fabric for skirts, infants' coats and children's wash suits. COLORS: White, pink, light blue, lavender, medium blue, copenhagen blue, rose, grey or tan.
PRICE, PREPAID to your home, **29c** yd.

11K20209 *Price concession, good quality* kimono crepe.
This is a cotton crepe material which has been specially treated to retain the crinkled appearance. It should not be ironed. Width 29 inches. COLORS: White, cream, pink, lilac, coral (rose), nickel grey, navy blue, black, light blue or copenhagen blue. PRICE, PREPAID to your home, **29c** yd.

Linene

11K20195 French mercerized linene, *strongly woven cotton material, which resembles linen.*
Standard Quality—good weight wonderful durability. Excellent for women's suits, dresses, and children's wear. Width 33 to 34 inches. COLORS: White, pink, light blue, lavender, tan or cadet blue.
PRICE, PREPAID to your home, **22c** yd.

Cotton Gabardine

11K20102 *Dress material that will give excellent service and satisfaction. Reasonable.*
Here is an exceptionally well-made **cotton gabardine,** woven of selected yarns. Width 35 to 36 inches. COLORS: Grey, dark brown, copenhagen blue, myrtle green, wine, navy blue, black, light blue, tan, rose, white or cream.
PRICE, PREPAID, **48c** yd.

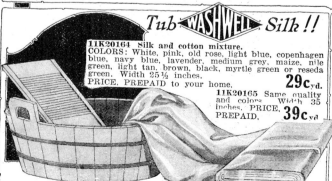

Tub WASHWELL Silk !!

11K20164 Silk and cotton mixture.
COLORS: White, pink, old rose, light blue, copenhagen blue, navy blue, lavender, medium grey, maize, nile green, light tan, brown, black, myrtle green or reseda green. Width 25½ inches.
PRICE, PREPAID to your home. **29c** yd.
11K20165 Same quality and colors. Width 35 inches. PRICE, PREPAID, **39c** yd.

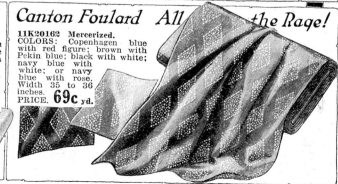

Canton Foulard All the Rage!

11K20162 Mercerized.
COLORS: Copenhagen blue with red figure; brown with Pekin blue; black with white; navy blue with white; or navy blue with rose. Width 35 to 36 inches.
PRICE, **69c** yd.

Poplins! WOOL Two Grades

11K20061 *DUROTEX* all wool poplin. Two grades, the higher priced proportionately finer. This is a finely finished fabric popular for women's suits, coats, skirts and dresses. Width 54 inches. **Every thread all wool.** COLORS: Black, navy blue, plum, dark brown, wine, dark green or taupe grey.
PRICE PREPAID to your home, **$2.29** yd.

11K20062 Durotex all wool poplin—a sturdy fabric. Width about 37 inches. COLORS: Black, navy blue, dark brown, plum, burgundy, Copenhagen blue, or taupe grey.
PRICE, PREPAID to your home, **$1.59** yd.

11K20070 Shepherd checks and plaids *at savings.* Width 35 to 36 inches. Of half worsted yarns for dresses, suits, skirts, or capes, children's wear. (A) medium sized check; (B) small check; (C) popular plaid. PRICE, PREPAID to your home, **49c** yd.
11K20071 Same fabric as 11K20070, 42 inches wide. Order by pattern A, B, or C. PRICE, PREPD to your home. **59c** yd.

Worsted Finish

Serges! WOOL Mixed

11K20110 *Bargain in serviceable* wool-mixed serge. This is a good quality storm serge, about 50% wool. Width 36 inches. Especially desirable for women's dresses and children's dresses and coats. One of the most satisfactory materials you can buy at this low price. COLORS: Black, navy blue, dark green, wine, dark brown, or cream.
PRICE, PREP'D, **69c** yd.
11K20111 A very good grade of French serge—about 50% wool. 35 inches wide. COLORS: Dark Copenhagen blue, black, navy blue, dark brown, myrtle green, taupe grey, plum, tan or wine.
PRICE, PREPAID, **73c** yd.

Famous PHILIPSBORN'S DUROTEX Fabrics · Economy Prices

Cotton

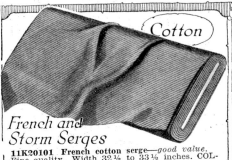

French and Storm Serges

11K20101 French cotton serge—*good value.* Fine quality. Width 32½ to 33½ inches. COLORS: Tan, copenhagen blue, myrtle green, plum, navy blue, black, taupe grey, medium brown, wine, navy blue or black.
PRICE, PREPAID to your home. **39c** yd.
11K20100 Cotton storm serge. Worsted-like finish. Width 33 to 34 inches. COLORS: Cream, copenhagen blue, rose, tan, green, brown, plum, wine, navy blue or black.
PRICE, PREPAID to your home, **30c** yd.

Fine Mohair .... Sicilian

11K20091 Sicilian mohair—*lustrous fabric.* For skirts, dresses, summer suits, or coats. Width 50 inches. COLORS: Cream, medium grey, medium brown, myrtle green, navy blue or black. PRICE, PREPAID to your home, **99c** yd.

Pekin · Percaline

11K20271 Width 36 inches. For interlinings, drop skirts, etc. COLORS: White, pink, tan, grey, navy blue, brown, black, green or light blue.
PRICE, PREPAID. **20c**

"Tico" Sateen

11K20270 *Bargain in STRONGWOVE* "Tico" sateen. Width 36 inches. For linings, petticoats, bloomers, boys' blouses, etc. COLORS: Old rose, white, steel grey, Copenhagen blue, emerald green, navy blue, or black.
PRICE, PREPAID to your home, **31c** yd.

All Wool Panama

11K20059 *DUROTEX* all wool panama—*the best fabric obtainable at the price.* A splendid, firmly woven fabric, finely finished and suitable for women's dresses, skirts, lightweight wraps, and all children's apparel. Width 53 to 54 inches. COLORS: Black, navy blue, wine, taupe, brown or plum.
PRICE, PREPAID to your home **$1.88** yd.

PLAIDS All the Rage Wool Mixed

11K20072 *Season's smartest serviceable* wool-mixed plaid. Woven from wool and cotton yarns. Suitable for sport skirts, dress effects, trimmings, children's wear. Width 36 inches. COLORS: All navy blue grounds with (Tan and black), (Green and Copen and white), (Red, navy and green), (Green, black and Copen), or (Red, green and black) overplaid.
PRICE, PREPAID to your home, **69c** yd.

Wool

Two Grades Tricotines

11K20130 Tricotine. Wool and cotton yarns. COLORS: Black, navy blue, myrtle green, dark wine, dark copenhagen blue, plum or dark brown. Width 36 inches. PRICE, PREP'D to your home, **79c** yd.
11K20135 All wool fine quality tricotine. Width 53 to 54 inches. COLORS: Reindeer, brown, plum, wine, myrtle green, black or navy blue. PR. **$3.75** yd.

All Wool Jersey

11K20136 Width 42 inches. All Wool. COLORS: Navy blue, tan, steel grey, dark brown, myrtle green, black, plum, wine or copenhagen blue.
PREPAID, **$1.98** yd.

STRONGWOVE Fine Twill Messaline

11K20273 Mercerized. Width about 31 inches. COLORS: White, cream, rose, copenhagen blue, navy blue, brown, emerald green, black or grey.
PRICE, PREP'D to your home, **39c** yd.

STRONGWOVE Chevy Chase Messaline

11K20272 *Figured.* Suitable for linings, petticoats, trimmings, etc. Width about 36 inches. COLORS: Floral designs with copenhagen blue, navy blue, grey, black or brown grounds.
PRICE, PREPAID to your home, **35c** yd.

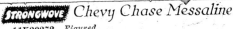

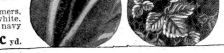

CHICAGO, ILL.

Fashion's Latest Creations in Summer Furs Are Shown on Page 45 of This Catalog. A Choice Assortment of Spring and Summer Dress Accessories

253

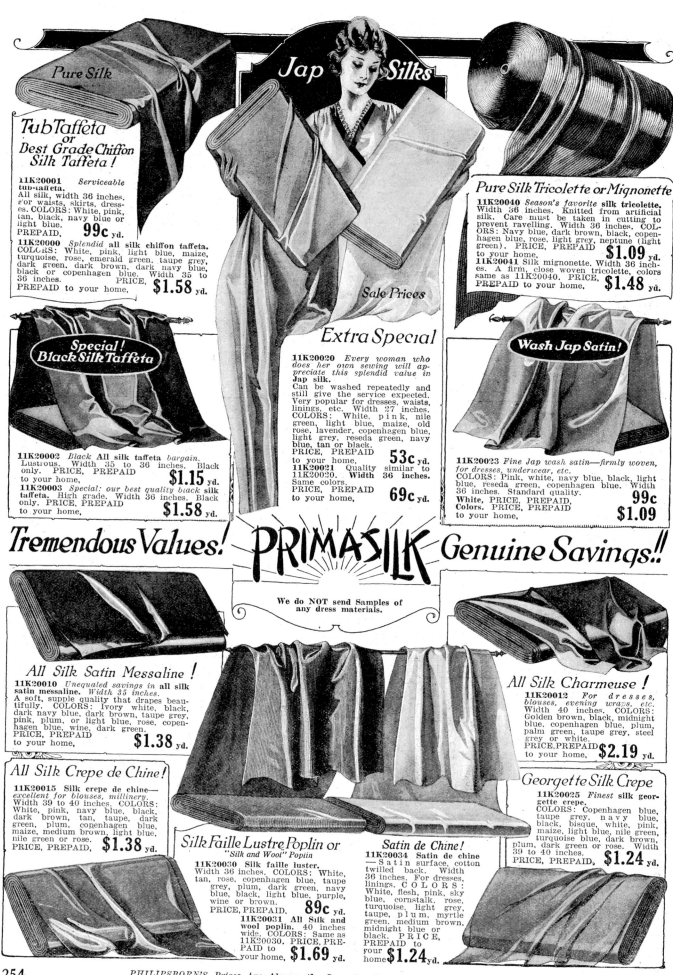

Jap Silks

Pure Silk

Tub Taffeta or Best Grade Chiffon Silk Taffeta!

11K20001 *Serviceable tub-taffeta.* All silk, width 36 inches. For waists, skirts, dresses. COLORS: White, pink, tan, black, navy blue or light blue. PREPAID, **99c** yd.

11K20000 *Splendid all silk chiffon taffeta.* COLORS: White, pink, light blue, maize, turquoise, rose, emerald green, taupe grey, dark green, dark brown, dark navy blue, black or copenhagen blue. Width 35 to 36 inches. PRICE, PREPAID to your home, **$1.58** yd.

Special! Black Silk Taffeta

11K20002 *Black All silk taffeta bargain.* Lustrous. Width 35 to 36 inches. Black only. PRICE, PREPAID to your home, **$1.15** yd.

11K20003 *Special: our best quality black silk taffeta.* High grade. Width 36 inches. Black only. PRICE, PREPAID to your home, **$1.58** yd.

Sale Prices

Extra Special

11K20020 *Every woman who does her own sewing will appreciate this splendid value in Jap silk.* Can be washed repeatedly and still give the service expected. Very popular for dresses, waists, linings, etc. Width 27 inches. COLORS: White, pink, nile green, light blue, maize, old rose, lavender, copenhagen blue, light grey, reseda green, navy blue, tan or black. PRICE, PREPAID to your home, **53c** yd.

11K20021 *Quality* similar to 11K20020. **Width 36 inches.** Same colors. PRICE, PREPAID to your home, **69c** yd.

Pure Silk Tricolette or Mignonette

11K20040 *Season's favorite silk tricolette.* Width 36 inches. Knitted from artificial silk. Care must be taken in cutting to prevent ravelling. Width 36 inches. COLORS: Navy blue, dark brown, black, copenhagen blue, rose, light grey, neptune (light green). PRICE, PREPAID to your home, **$1.09** yd.

11K20041 Silk mignonette. Width 36 inches. A firm, close woven tricolette, colors same as 11K20040. PRICE, PREPAID to your home, **$1.48** yd.

Wash Jap Satin!

11K20023 *Fine Jap wash satin—firmly woven,* for dresses, underwear, etc. COLORS: Pink, white, navy blue, black, light blue, reseda green, copenhagen blue. Width 36 inches. Standard quality. White, PRICE, PREPAID **99c** Colors, PRICE, PREPAID to your home, **$1.09**

Tremendous Values! PRIMASILK Genuine Savings!!

We do NOT send Samples of any dress materials.

All Silk Satin Messaline!

11K20010 *Unequaled savings in all silk satin messaline. Width 35 inches.* A soft, supple quality that drapes beautifully. COLORS: Ivory white, black, dark navy blue, dark brown, taupe grey, pink, plum, or light blue, rose, copenhagen blue, wine, dark green. PRICE, PREPAID to your home, **$1.38** yd.

All Silk Crepe de Chine!

11K20015 *Silk crepe de chine—excellent for blouses, millinery.* Width 39 to 40 inches. COLORS: White, pink, navy blue, black, dark brown, tan, taupe, dark green, plum, copenhagen blue, maize, medium brown, light blue, nile green or rose. PRICE, PREPAID to your home, **$1.38** yd.

Silk Faille Lustre Poplin or "Silk and Wool" Poplin

11K20030 Silk faille luster. Width 36 inches. COLORS: White, tan, rose, copenhagen blue, taupe grey, plum, dark green, navy blue, black, light blue, purple, wine or brown. PRICE, PREPAID, **89c** yd.

11K20031 All Silk and wool poplin. 40 inches wide. COLORS: Same as 11K20030. PRICE, PREPAID to your home, **$1.69** yd.

Satin de Chine!

11K20034 Satin de chine —Satin surface, cotton twilled back. Width 36 inches. For dresses, linings. COLORS: White, flesh, pink, sky blue, cornstalk, rose, turquoise, light grey, taupe, plum, myrtle green, medium brown, midnight blue or black. PRICE, PREPAID to your home **$1.24** yd.

All Silk Charmeuse!

11K20012 *For dresses, blouses, evening wraps, etc.* Width 40 inches. COLORS: Golden brown, black, midnight blue, copenhagen blue, plum, palm green, taupe grey, steel grey or white. PRICE, PREPAID to your home, **$2.19** yd.

Georgette Silk Crepe

11K20025 *Finest silk georgette crepe.* COLORS: Copenhagen blue, taupe grey, navy blue, black, bisque, white, pink, maize, light blue, nile green, turquoise blue, dark brown, plum, dark green or rose. Width 39 to 40 inches. PRICE, PREPAID, **$1.24** yd.

254

PHILIPSBORN'S Prices Are Always the Lowest. Compare With Any or Every Catalogue Issued. See Page 3

PHILIPSBORN'S

"Washwell" Dress Gingham. More Popular than ever.
11K20153 Exceptionally good value in a good quality dress gingham in beautifully selected patterns. Woven of fine cotton yarn in fast colors in close weave. Width 32 inches. Made by one of America's best mills and given a durable finish. Good cutting width. Fashionable for women's and children's dresses. COLORS: Plaids are blue and gold, brown and black, red and black, green and black, blue and red. Solid colors—Tan, green, rose, grey, cadet blue or helio. PRICE, PREPAID, **23c** yd.

11 K 20090 **69c yd.**
"DUROTEX" Dress Poplin.
11K20090 Fashionable dress poplin in a light weight half wool. 32 inches wide. Wanted colors; suitable for dresses and skirts, also children's wear. COLORS: Black, tan, plum, wine, navy blue, cream, taupe grey, copenhagen blue, medium brown, or myrtle green. PRICE, PREPAID, **69c** yd.

"PRIMASILK" Silk Taffeta or Satin Messaline.
11K20004 Standard soft finish all-silk taffeta. Width 35 to 36 inches. Used for skirts, dresses. COLORS: Black, myrtle green, dark brown, navy blue, emerald green, light blue, maize, pink, rose, taupe grey, turquoise blue, white or Copenhagen blue. PRICE, PREP'D, **$1.29** yd.
11K20013 All silk satin messaline. 36 inches. COLORS: Black, dark brown, ivory white, light blue, navy blue, pink, plum, taupe grey, dark green, rose, Copen. blue or wine. PRICE, PREP'D, **$1.29** yd.

11 K 20017 $1.19 yd.

11 K 20026 99c yd.

11 K 20004
11 K 20013
$1.29 yd.

11 K 20153
23c yd.

"PRIMASILK" Silk Crepe de Chine. Spring's Daintiest fabric.
11K20017 Our standard quality all silk crepe de chine. Width 39 to 40 inches. A handsome and fashionable dress material, most desirable shades. A popular material for waists, dresses, lingerie. COLORS: Light blue, nile green, rose, black, copenhagen blue, dark brown, dark green, maize, medium brown, navy blue, pink, plum, bisque, taupe, white or steel grey. PRICE, PREPAID, **$1.19** yd.

"PRIMASILK" Silk Georgette Crepe.
11K20026 One of the season's most fashionable materials, all silk Georgette crepe. Width 39 to 40 inches. Woven of all-silk yarn, distinctive crepe weave—gives satisfactory wear. For waists, dresses, millinery, sleeves, yokes, trimmings. COLORS: Navy blue, rose, taupe grey, black, light blue, copenhagen blue, maize, nile green, pink, bisque, turquoise blue or white, dark brown, plum, dark green. PRICE, PREPAID to your home, **99c** yd.

"DUROTEX" All Wool French Serges.
11K20121 Width 40 inches. For dresses and skirts. COLORS: Black, dark brown, dark copenhagen blue, myrtle green, plum, taupe, wine, tan or navy blue. PRICE, PREPAID, **$1.69** yd.
11K20123 Width about 54 inches. COLORS: Black, dark brown, dark copenhagen blue, myrtle green, plum, taupe, wine, navy blue or tan. PRICE, PREPAID, **$2.59** yd.

11K20160 A splendid offering. Silk and cotton crepe de chine. We recommend this as the best in quality and value. To prevent shrinking when cleaning, stretch material carefully. Width 35 to 36 inches. COLORS: Cream, sky blue, lilac, primrose, wine, flesh, pink, bisque, reseda, navy blue, maize, light grey, copenhagen blue, golden brown or black. PRICE, PREPAID to your home, **55c** yd.

37c yd.
11 K 20200
"Washwell" Voile. Novelty.
11K20200 The season's favorite wash material, novelty figured voile. A very neat figured cotton voile, woven of twisted cotton yarn effective patterns. Widths 39 to 40 inches. Will make very pretty waists and dresses. COLORS: Navy blue, French blue, dark lavender, brown or taupe. PRICE, PREPAID, **37c** yd.

11K20180 The greatest craze of the season—"WASHWELL" dotted swiss in all the new fashionable shades. Width from 35 to 36 inches. Makes very dainty and attractive dresses, waists, negligees and children's dresses. COLORS: Light helio, old rose, maize, black, pink, tan, copenhagen blue, white, light blue, reseda, or navy blue. PRICE, PREPAID to your home, **49c** yd.

"DUROTEX" All Wool Serges.
11K20120 Double warp. Width 36 inches. For dresses, skirts, capes, coats and children's dresses. All wool. COLORS: Navy blue, brown, tan, black, plum, myrtle green, wine, grey or cream. PRICE, PREPAID, **98c** yd.
11K20122 All wool, 50 inches wide. COLORS: Black, myrtle green, grey, brown, plum, wine, tan, navy blue, cream. PRICE, PREPAID, **$1.39** yd.

11 K 20160
55c yd.

11 K 20180 49c yd.

Boys' EXTRA QUALITY WASH SUITS at Lowest Prices
Guaranteed Absolutely
Fast Colors

WORTH $1.35

2K4000 *Boys' middy suit of "peggy" cloth.* Fast color navy blue. SIZES: 3 to 8 yrs. PRICE, PREPAID, **$1.98**
2K3703 Little boys' white duck tam. SIZES: 6⅛ to 7. PRICE, PREPAID, **48c**

2K4001 *This smart little suit is made of Galatea. A real bargain.* It may be had in white with a brown stripe or white with a light blue stripe. Solid color trimming to match stripe. SIZES: 2½ to 8 yrs. PRICE, PREPAID, **$1.98**

An Extra Pair of Navy Blue Pants Free with This Suit
2K4002 *A big bargain—"TEARPROOF" middy suit with extra pair of trousers.* Of firmly woven white jean with navy blue trimming. SIZES: 2½ to 8 yrs. PRICE, PREPAID, **$2.28**
2K3704 White drill middy hat. SIZES: 6⅛ to 7. PRICE, PREPAID to your home, **48c**

2K4003 *Boys' blue chambray suit at a saving.* A good quality firmly woven cloth in a medium blue shade, guaranteed absolutely fast color. White rep collar and trimming. SIZES: 2½ to 8 yrs. PRICE, PREPAID, **$1.48**

2K4004 *Boys' middy suit in two materials.* Blue and white striped galatine or plain white linen-finished cotton. Both styles finished with light blue collar and tie. SIZES: 3 to 8 yrs. PRICE, PREPAID, **98c**

2K3705 *White drill middy hat, blue trimmed. Easily laundered.* SIZES: 6⅛ to 7. PRICE, PREPAID, **48c**

WORTH $2.50

2K4009 *A special bargain in an Oliver Twist suit for boys.* This is one of the most practical "TEARPROOF" suits made for little boys. The material is a finely woven tan **crash** of great durability. Collar and new style belt are made of "Peggy cloth" in a medium blue shade that is absolutely **fast color**. Collar trimmed with braid. Sailor style tie. A great value at our low price and certain to please you. SIZES: 2½ to 8 yrs. PRICE, PREPAID to your home, **$1.98**

2K4008 *Especially good value in this dressy white wash suit for boys.* Comes in white **rep** with a blue collar and belt, or all white. Every one knows the wonderful durability of rep and this is a fine quality. Plaited front. A bargain at this price. SIZES: 2½ to 8 yrs. PRICE, PREPAID to your home, **$1.98**

2K4007 *Without doubt one of the most sensible wash suits ever made.* A splendid "TEARPROOF" model for the small boy, made of a good weight firmly woven **chambray** in a dark grey or blue. Embroidered emblem on front. SIZES: 3 to 8 years. PRICE, PREP'D to your home, **$1.68**

2K4006 *Matchless saving in a "TEARPROOF" suit for the small boy.* This model is a very good style in the material that we have selected—tan **crash** with collar, belt, and tie of blue galatea. One of the most practical of wash suits. SIZES: 3 to 8 yrs. PRICE, PREP'D to your home, **$1.68**

2K4005 *A dressy durable style in an Oliver Twist suit for boys.* Here is one of our prettiest "TEARPROOF" models shown for the small boy. The blouse is made of white **linen-finished cotton** and the trousers are of blue **linene**. New shaped shawl sailor collar is attractively embroidered and piped on the edge with white. Blouse has double-breasted effect button trimming. A saving of at least $1.00. SIZES: 2½ to 8 yrs. PRICE, PREPAID, **$1.98**

256   Order at Our Risk. You Are the Judge. Your Money Back If You Are Not Satisfied   **PHILIPSBORN'S**

Big SAVINGS ON WASH AND PLAY SUITS for the little fellows
All Prepaid to Your Home

2K4010 *A big value in a little boys' wash suit.* Made of a fast color blue woven **chambray.** Collar and belt of white linene. Our low price makes this suit one of the greatest values it is possible to buy. SIZES: 2½ to 8 yrs. PRICE, PREPAID to your home, **98c**

2K4011 *Boys' dressy middy suit offered in two materials.* Made either of white **linene** or plain blue **chambray.** Fast-color navy blue collar and cuffs, or plain blue chambray. Regulation middy style. Considerably underpriced. SIZES: 3 to 8 yrs. PRICE, PREPAID to your home, **$1.48**

2K3411 *At our price this coverall suit cannot be duplicated elsewhere.* Little boys' model made of a fast color **Stifel drill,** navy blue with white stripes. Trimmed collar and pockets. Drop seat. SIZES: 3 to 8 yrs. PRICE, PREPAID to your home, **78c**

2K4012 *Your choice of two materials in this wash suit.* Boys' short sleeved suit made either of white **linene** or plain blue **chambray.** The white suit is trimmed with fast-color blue linene. Blue suit trimmed with white. SIZES: 2½ to 8 yrs. PRICE, PREPAID to your home. **$1.28**

2K4013 *Refuse to pay high prices—this suit only 98c.* This Oliver Twist model can be had in a blue and white stripe galatine or plain white linene blouse with knee pants of plain blue linene. Collar and cuffs of plain blue to match pants. SIZES: 2½ to 8. PRICE, PREPAID, **98c**

2K3400 *PHILIPSBORN'S have knocked the bottom out of high prices with such values as these.* Convincing proof of our values in these "BROWNIE" overalls for small boys. The material is a good weight fast-color blue **double and twist denim.** Style is suitable for either boys or girls. Top of pockets and bib trimmed with turkey red. One of the most durable overalls made. SIZES: 3 to 8 yrs. PRICE, PREPAID to your home, **78c**

2K3412 *Even when prices were highest, PHILIPSBORN'S asked only slight increases on their goods.* And now that we have reduced our prices still further, the savings are simply staggering. Take for instance, this new style coverall for boys or girls. Khaki-colored **drill** of excellent durability. SIZES: 2½ to 8 yrs. PRICE, PREPAID, **78c**

2K4014 *The ever popular Oliver Twist two-piece suit for small boys is here offered at a reduced price.* The quality and workmanship in this suit are superior to suits selling elsewhere at anywhere from 50 to 75 cents more. Blue striped blouse and blue linene trousers which button on to blouse. SIZES: 2½ to 8 yrs. PRICE, PREPAID, **78c**

2K4015 *One of the most durable rompers manufactured and a genuine economy at the low price asked.* This is just another example of PHILIPSBORN'S ability to give you the biggest bargain for the least money. The material is finely woven good weight chambray in a medium blue shade. White piping. Very attractive. SIZES: 2½ to 8 yrs. PRICE, PREPAID, **88c**

2K3413 *One of our special values, a bargain offering that will convince anyone that this is the place to trade.* Here is a coverall suit, one of the best garments of its kind manufactured. It is suitable for boys or girls, and is made of good weight chambray in medium blue shade. Note the new style of the pockets. Collar and pockets are trimmed with fast-color turkey red trimming. All seams double stitched. Drop seat at back. An excellent value in every way. SIZES: 2½ to 8 yrs. PRICE, PREPAID, **98c**

CHICAGO, ILL.

Hosiery That Will Withstand the Rough Usage That Boys and Girls Give Their Stockings— Shown in Our Hosiery Section, Pages 209 to 215

257

Philipsborn's Boys' Famous Onorbilt Overalls

EXTRA QUALITY

A New Pair Free If They Rip

For Special Construction Features See Page 270

← 2K3402 Overalls 2K3403 Coat to match For boys and youths. An extremely good value. These are our famous "ONORBILT" garments, made of a heavy weight double and twist blue denim, all seams triple stitched and guaranteed never to rip. SIZES: 27 to 32 waist; 30 to 36 chest. For boys and youths from 14 to 18 yrs. PRICE, PREPAID,
2K3402 $1.18
2K3403 1.18
Complete Suit $2.30

2K3404 Boys' Indigo blue overalls of Stifel drill with Wabash stripe. Wonderful wear. A new pair free if they rip. SIZES: 6 to 14 yrs. PRICE, PREPAID. **88c**

2K3405 Boys' "ONORBILT" Stifel drill overalls. Our most popular style for boys. Indigo blue with Wabash stripe. Absolutely fast color. SIZES: 14 to 18 yrs. PRICE, PREPAID, **98c**

2K3401 Boys' "ONORBILT" overalls at a saving. Of a good weight double and twist blue denim. Guaranteed not to rip. Fast color. A big value. SIZES: 6 to 14 yrs. PRICE, PREPAID, **98c**

2K3408

2K3407

Lowest Prices
ALL GARMENTS PREPAID TO YOUR HOME

Two Extra Special Philipsborn's Values

EXTRA QUALITY

2K3406 Absolutely no compromise with high prices at PHILIPSBORN'S! Here is an extremely good value in boys' "TEARPROOF" overalls made of a durable blue and white striped drill, known as hickory stripe. All seams strongly stitched. Two pockets in front and one in rear. SIZES: 6 to 14 years. PRICE, PREPAID, **78c**

2K3408 Nothing will please your son better than an outfit of this kind. Cowboy outfit consisting of eight pieces—shirt, trousers, belt, holster, pistol, neck kerchief, hat, and lasso. Made of khaki drill with leatherette trimmings. Greatly underpriced. SIZES: 4 to 14 yrs. Hat SIZES: 6¼ to 7⅛. PRICE, PREPAID to your home, **$2.38**

2K3407 At our low price no boy should be without this boy scout outfit. There are four pieces consisting of a military coat, riding breeches laced at the knee, canvas puttees and hat to match. Made of good quality khaki drill. SIZES: 6 to 16 yrs. Hat SIZES: 6¼ to 7⅛. Be sure to mention size. PRICE, PREPAID to your home, **$2.48**

2K3409 Khaki Drill
2K3410 Blue Chambray
Don't miss this chance to save on the purchase of a splendid-wearing coverall garment for boys or girls. Made either of strong khaki drill or a heavy weight blue chambray. Can be worn over other clothing. SIZES: 2 to 8 yrs. PRICE, PREPAID, **98c**

PHILIPSBORN'S Underwear Is the Best for Style, Service, and Quality. Refer to Pages 216 to 241

PHILIPSBORN'S

Philipsborn's Boys' Tearproof Knickers
Made For Hard Wear

Extra Quality Boys' Raincoats
Guaranteed Absolutely Waterproof

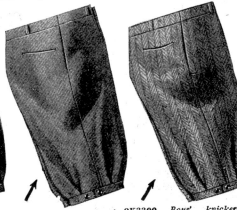

2K3302 *Boys' knicker-bocker trousers of 100% all wool navy blue "TEAR-PROOF" serge.* Full, liberal sizes. Fully lined. A remarkable value at our low price. SIZES: 5 to 17 years. PRICE, PREP'D. **$2.48**

2K3303 *For service, choose these boys' "TEARPROOF" corduroy knickerbockers.* Made of a firmly woven, good weight corduroy in a wide rib. Serviceable drab shade. SIZES: 6 to 16 yrs. PRICE, PREPAID, **$1.28**

2K3304 *Boys' blue serge "TEARPROOF" knicker-bockers at a bargain price.* Made of a wool-mixed serge, and fully lined. Tailored in a first-class manner. SIZES: 6 to 17 years. PRICE, PREP'D to your home, **$1.38**

2K3305 *Buy these boys' knickerbockers and wear out that odd coat.* Made of "TEARPROOF" cassimere in serviceable grey and brown mixtures. Plenty of pockets. SIZES: 6 to 16 yrs. PRICE, PREP'D. **$1.29**

2K3301 *No better boys' knickerbockers made for wear and appearance.* Made of a good weight soft finished blue serge—about one half wool. Big value. SIZES: 6 to 16 years. PRICE, PREP'D to your home, **$1.28**

2K3300 *Boys' knicker-bockers at a bargain price.* Made of wool mixed cassimere in serviceable grey mixture. Don't miss this money saving opportunity. SIZES: 6 to 16 years. PRICE, PREPAID to your home, **98c**

2K4300 Grey **2K4301** Tan *Boys' raincoat, guaranteed absolutely water proof.* Made of Asia cloth. Plaid lined. SIZES: 6 to 18 yrs. PRICE, PREPAID to your home, **$3.98**

2K4302 *Boys' extra quality rubber coat—the best made.* Here is a very good value in a boys' black rubber raincoat. This is a dull-finished rubber, lined with a white sheeting and guaranteed absolutely waterproof. SIZES: 6 to 16 years. PRICE. **$3.88**

2K3700 Grey **2K3701** Tan Rain hat to match above coats. SIZES: 6½ to 7⅛. PRICE, PREPAID to your home, **48c**

2K3702 Rain cap and cape to match coat. SIZES: 6½ to 7⅛. PRICE, **98c**

2K3311 Daytona Cloth **2K3312** Blue Serge For summer wear here is an ideal selection in boys' knee pants. Made of washable Daytona cloth, a firmly woven cotton fabric in a tan shade with a woven stripe. Also of navy blue wool serge. Fully lined. SIZES: 5 to 10 years. **2K3311** PRICE, **68c** **2K3312** PRICE, **$1.48**

2K3308 *The sort of bargain that appeals to every mother.* Boys' knickerbockers of washable crash—ideal washable trousers for summer wear. Made of a firmly woven grey crash of great durability. Will stand any amount of washing, and will always look fresh and clean. SIZES: 7 to 16 years. PRICE, PREP'D to your home, **98c**

2K3306 *No better trousers made for the sturdy red blooded American boy.* "TEARPROOF" knicker-bocker trousers made of a firmly woven wide wale corduroy in a serviceable drab shade. Finished with double seat, which gives double wear. SIZES: 6 to 17 years. PRICE, PREP'D. **$1.78**

2K3307 *Boys' high grade "TEARPROOF" full lined knickerbocker trousers.* Made of a firmly woven, durable cassimere, 100% all wool serge, in shades of grey and brown that will not show the dirt. Will look well with any style of coat. Usual pockets. 6 to 17 yrs. PRICE, PREP'D. **$1.98**

2K3309 Khaki Cloth **2K3310** Tan Beach Cloth Either of these materials will give absolute satisfaction. Big values and low prices. SIZES: 6 to 16 yrs. PRICE, PREPAID, **98c** **2K3310** Same style as above in tan beach cloth. SIZES: 6 to 16 years. PRICE, PREPAID to your home, **98c**

2K3313 Blue Serge **2K3314** Grey mixture Here are little boys' bloomer pants in a choice of two serviceable materials—firmly woven blue serge that contains about one-half wool, or a serviceable grey mixture. Finished with the customary pockets. A splendid money-saving opportunity. SIZES: 5 to 10 years. PRICE, PREPAID to your home, **78c**

CHICAGO, ILL.

For Index See Page 274 and Remember PHILIPSBORN'S Prepay All Transportation Charges. There Are No Express or Mailing Charges for You to Pay

259

BOYS' TEARPROOF SHIRTS and BLOUSES
All Made Full-Roomy Sizes For The Healthy Growing Boy

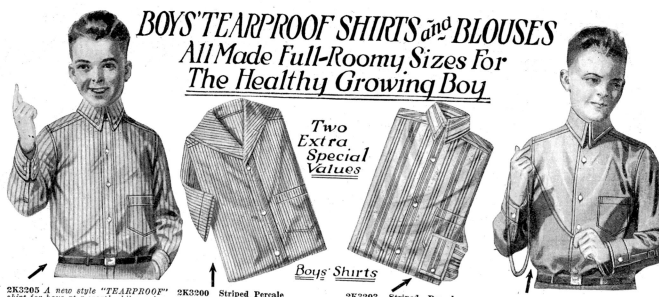

Two Extra Special Values

Boys' Shirts

2K3205 *A new style "TEARPROOF" shirt for boys at a worthwhile saving.* Made of a fine quality **percale** in assorted stripes. SIZES: 12½ to to 14½ neckband. PRICE, PREPAID to your home, **$1.08**

2K3200 Striped Percale
2K3201 White Madras
Boys' shirt, popular style. Your choice in above materials. 12½ to 14½ neckband. PRICE, PREPAID, Your SIZES **98c**

2K3203 Striped Percale
2K3207 Blue Chambray
Boys' shirt. Choice of materials as above. Big values. SIZES: 12½ to 14½ neckband. PRICE, PREPAID to your home. **75c**

2K3204 *Here is an excellent shirt for outing or general wear.* Fine quality **twill** in khaki color. Soft lay-down collar. SIZES 12½ to 14½ neckband. PRICE, PREPAID to your home, **98c**

Blouses

2K3210 Assorted Stripes
2K3217 White Madras
The ever popular sport blouse for little boys is here offered in the above two materials. SIZES: 6 to 16 yrs. PRICE, **78c**

2K3209 *Prices have come down. Here is a wonderful saving in a boys' "TEARPROOF" blouse.* No material will give better satisfaction than the woven striped **gingham** of which this blouse is fashioned. It comes in a neat blue and white stripe—a color that will not show dirt readily. Lay-down collar. SIZES: 6 to 16 yrs. .ICE, PREP'D, **78c**

2K3208 *There is no more popular style in a boy's blouse for general wear than this* **khaki drill** *blouse.* Will launder well and give excellent service. Open cuffs. Yoke back. Will look well with any kind of trousers. SIZES: 6 to 16 yrs. PRICE, PREPAID. **98c**

2K3206 *Here is a bargain in a new style shirt that your boy will want.* This shirt is made of a fine quality **white madras.** The new style buttoned down collar is a feature that will be very popular this season. Finished with turned back cuffs. An ideal selection in a dressy shirt. SIZES: 12½ to 14½ neckband. PRICE, PREPAID, **$1.08**

Shirts

2K3202 *A serviceable blue chambray shirt for boys.* Made of "TEARPROOF" material in popular sports style. Sport collar may be worn high. SIZES: 12½ to 14½ neckband. PRICE, PREPAID to your home, **78c**

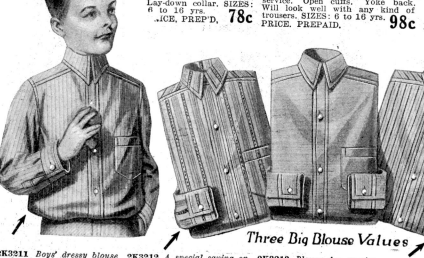

Three Big Blouse Values

2K3211 *Boys' dressy blouse made of fine* **white madras.** Soft collar, open cuffs and yoke back. Will launder well and always look well. SIZES: 6 to 16 yrs. PRICE, PREPAID to your home, **98c**

2K3212 *A special saving on this "TEARPROOF" blouse.* The material is a good quality striped **percale.** It is made with soft collar and open cuffs. SIZES: 6 to 16 yrs. PRICE PREPAID to your home, **79c**

2K3213 *Blouse for service— boys' "TEARPROOF" model.* Of a good quality firmly woven **blue chambray** of great durability. Soft collar and cuffs. SIZES: 6 to 16 yrs. PRICE, PREPAID to your home, **48c**

2K3214—Striped Percale
2K3215 Blue Chambray
Boy's blouse in your choice of the above materials. Open cuffs. Full sizes. SIZES: 6 to 16 yrs. PRICE, PREPAID, **58c**

2K3216 *Here is a handsome blouse for boys. A bargain.* It is made of a fine quality madras in beautiful assorted stripes. Buttoned-down collar. SIZES: 6 to 16 yrs. PRICE, PREPAID to your home, **98c**

The World's Greatest Power—"Public Opinion."
See Page 3

PHILIPSBORN'S

Boys'ExtraBigSpecial

Double Wear
Tearproof Suits
100% ALL WOOL
Serge
or
Cassimere
Double Stitched Throughout
Double Elbows
Double Seats
Double Knees

Your Choice **$8⁷⁵** Prepaid

2K4101 Brown Mixture
2K4102 Greyish Green Mixture
2K4103 Navy Blue Serge

Here at last is a boys' "TEARPROOF" suit that embodies every feature to add to its continued wear. Just the model for the active boy who likes to romp and play and at the same time wants to be well dressed. Made of **all wool** material in serviceable shades of brown and greenish grey mixtures and solid color navy blue serge. The snappy coat has patch pockets, and two lower ones finished with buttoned down flap. Lined with good quality alpaca. The illustrations below show you how carefully tailored and reinforced this suit is,—the invisible double seat, the double knee and double elbow. One of the best suits ever made for boys. SIZES: 8 to 18 years.
PRICE, PREPAID to your home, **$8.75**

2K4104 Brown Mixture
2K4105 Greenish Grey Mixture
2K4106 Navy Blue Serge

If you prefer a Norfolk model for your son, this style should meet with your approval—a smart, "TEARPROOF" suit that is very dressy and very moderately priced. The material is **all wool** mixtures or solid color navy blue serge as quoted above. Regulation Norfolk coat. Note illustrations below to see what extra pains we have taken to make this one of the best suits in the world for the active boy. SIZES: 8 to 18 years.
PRICE, PREPAID to your home, **$8.75**

Philipsborn's Extra Special
Double Wear Tear proof Features

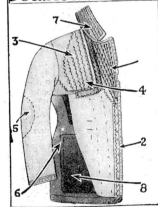
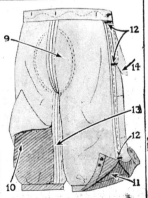

How PHILIPSBORN'S "TEARPROOF" suits are Tailored

1—Best hair cloth front.
2—Edges taped to hold shape.
3—Canvas front shrunk.
4—Felt padding.
5—Invisible double elbow.
6—All pockets bar tacked.
7—Extra stitches to hold shape.
8—Extra strong pocket material.
9—Invisible double seat.
10—Extra durable lining.
11—Invisible double knee.
12—Extra strong bar tacks.
13—All seams taped.
14—Extra strong pocket material.

2K4101
2K4102
2K4103

2K4104
2K4105
2K4106

CHICAGO, ILL.

Order at Our Risk. You Are the Judge. Your Money Back if You Are Not Satisfied

261

CHALLENGE VALUES
Boys' Double Wear

CAP
2K3709

Philipsborn's
*Tearproof Suits
Built Especially
For The Strong
Red Blooded
American Boy.
Buy Them
And Reduce
Your Boy's
Clothing Bills*

Be sure to state color and size desired when ordering.

2K4124

2K4122
2K4123

2K4120
2K4121

An Extra Pair Pants Free With This Suit

2K4120 Brown Mixture
2K4121 Grey Mixture
We sell this stylish suit for boys with an extra pair of trousers—for the one price $7.98.
Every one knows how often a coat outwears a pair of trousers, and as it is not always possible to match the odd coat with another pair, the wisdom of buying a suit with two pairs of trousers will be apparent to any one. This boys' "Tearproof" suit is made of a good quality **wool-mixed cassimere**, specially selected for its good wearing qualities. It comes in the serviceable colors listed above. At our special price you are practically getting a pair of trousers free. The extra trousers will double the life of the suit, and later on you will not have to buy an odd pair to go with the coat. A suit that is sure to please you in every way. SIZES: 8 to 17 yrs. PRICE, PREPAID to your home, **$7.98**

2K4122 Green
2K4123 Brown
You could hardly make a better selection for your son than this natty suit, and the low price makes it a bargain.
It is "TEARPROOF" in every particular and tailored in a smart style. The material is a very strong and durable mixture **100% all wool** and comes in serviceable shades of green and brown. The design shows the popular double-breasted coat with all necessary pockets and an extra cash pocket. Removable belt. Full lined knickerbocker trousers. Great value. SIZES: 8 to 17 yrs. PRICE, PREP'D to your home, **$7.48**

2K3709 Boys' cap of durable material in assorted plaids. Will look well with any style suit. A bargain at 49c. SIZES: 6½ to 7⅛. PRICE, PREPAID to your home, **49c**

2K4127
2K4128

2K4125
2K4126

Washable Norfolk Suits

2K4125 Grey
2K4126 Tan
A challenge value in a boys' "TEARPROOF" washable suit—a top-notch quality at bed-rock prices.
Made of regulation Daytona beach cloth. Nobby coat with yoke. Side plaits and removable belt. Comes in tan and grey. SIZES: 8 to 16 yrs. PRICE, PREPAID to your home, **$3.98**

An Extra Special Philipsborn's Value

2K4124 *A boys' wool-mixed "TEARPROOF" suit at $4.98 is a find.*
This material has been selected from thousands of samples for its great strength and durability. It is a closely woven **cassimere** in serviceable mixture in brown, or green effects. Coat is a neat single breasted model with slanting flap pockets. Full lined knickerbocker trousers. SIZES: 8 to 16 yrs.
PRICE, PREP'D to your home, **$4.98**

2K4127 Tan   **2K4128 Grey**
Dressiness and durability, two important features in boys' clothes, are splendidly combined in this suit.
Junior Norfolk model made of "TEARPROOF" **Crash suiting**, the best-wearing fabric for boys' wash suits. Will look well as long as a piece of the cloth remains. Colors as above. SIZES: 5 to 10 yrs. PRICE, PREPAID, **$3.48**

COLOR and SIZES—Don't Forget to Give This Information When Ordering—COLOR and SIZES   **PHILIPSBORN'S**

DELIVERY PREPAID
Tear-Proof Suits

CAP
2K3708

Philipsborns
EXTRA QUALITY

Boys' Tearproof Suits
Fit Better
Look Better
Wear Better
Cost Less

A Big Saving on Every Suit

2K4109
2K4110

2K4112
2K4113

An Extra Pair Pants Free With this Suit

An Extra Special Philipsborns Value
EXTRA QUALITY

2K4109 Brown   2K4110 Green
An all wool "TEARPROOF" suit at $6.98 is really getting back to pre-war prices.
You will marvel that merchandise of such excellent quality and superior workmanship can be had for such a small amount of money. Model made of a strong "TEARPROOF" 100% all wool cassimere—a dressy suit that will stand a lot of hard wear. Furnished in serviceable shades of green and brown. Very becoming for the average boy, with the new style protected patch pockets. Removable belt. Coat lined with fine quality twill. Full lined knickerbockers. One of the best values quoted at a big price reduction. Colors as listed above. SIZES: 8 to 17 years.
PRICE, PREPAID to your home, **$6.98**

Two Junior Models, Sizes 5 to 10 years

2K4118 Grey   2K4119 Brown
A very becoming suit for the small boy, and just think of getting an all wool suit for only $6.48!
This junior Norfolk model is made of 100% all wool "TEARPROOF" cassimere in dressy durable shades of grey and brown. Coat is style with yoke and side plaits. Full lined knickerbockers. SIZES: 5 to 10 yrs.
PRICE, PREPAID to your home,
$6.48
CHICAGO, ILL.

2K4118
2K4119

2K4116
2K4117

2K4116 Brown   2K4117 Grey
Here is a suit that will give extraordinary service, and the price is at least 25% lower than you would pay elsewhere.
Boys' junior model made of "TEARPROOF" wool-mixed cassimere. Note the becoming style of the single-breasted coat with removable belt, and regulation pockets like dad's. SIZES: 5 to 10 yrs.
PRICE, PREPAID to your home,
$4.78

2K4112 Brown
2K4113 Grey
Boys' "TEARPROOF" suit made of a fine quality all wool cassimere in serviceable shades of grey and brown. Flap pockets. Twill lined. Full lined knickerbockers. SIZES: 8 to 17 yrs.
PRICE, PREP'D. **$7.48**
2K3708 Boys' wool mixture cap. COLORS: Blue, brown or green. SIZES: 6½ to 7⅛.
PRICE, PREPAID, **98c**

2K4114 Green
2K4115 Brown
Free—the extra pair of trousers which we give with this boys' suit practically gives you two suits for the price of one. Made of 100% all wool cassimere in a neat brown or green mixture. Two pair of full-lined knickerbockers. Coat with patch pockets, removable belt. Twill lined. SIZES: 8 to 17 yrs.
PRICE,
PREPAID, **$9.48**

The saving on boys' "TEARPROOF" suits is indeed remarkable, and in ordering same you do not run the slightest risk. We guarantee every garment to be exactly as described, and we will gladly refund the money in cases where the garment does not come up to your expectations.

Our great purchasing power for cash means a great saving, which we turn over to our customers. Order any of these "TEARPROOF" suits feeling sure that you are going to get more than 100 cents for every dollar you spend in style and quality.

See Page 274 for Index and Don't Forget When Ordering to State the Color and Size Desired

263

Boys' Stylish Tearproof Blue Serge Suits
Lowest Prices – All Prepaid To Your Home

CAP →
2K3707
68c

← CAP
2K3710
$1.28

2K4129
2K4130

2K4132

2K4130 *Boys' Tearproof wool-mixed blue serge suit with two pairs of trousers.* Coat with slash pockets and removable belt. Albert twill lining. Full lined knickerbocker trousers. SIZES: 6 to 17 years.
PRICE, PREPAID, **$8.98**
2K4129 Same style suit as above with only one pair of trousers.
PRICE, **$6.98**
2K3707 All wool blue serge cap. SIZES: 6½ to 7½. PRICE, PREPAID, **68c**

2K4131 *Here is one of PHILIPSBORN'S wonderful, value-giving Tearproof suits for boys.*
This is a dress model, made of an absolutely all wool serge of fine smooth finish and great durability,—a suit that will always look well and give unlimited service. The popular single-breasted coat is made with new style slanting flap pockets, removable belt. It is lined with a fine quality Albert twill, and tailored in a first class manner. Full size, full lined knickerbocker trousers. One of the greatest values we have ever offered. SIZES: 8 to 18 years. COLOR: Navy blue.
PRICE, PREPAID to your home, **$8.48**

2K4415 *Youth's Tearproof high school suit of wool-mixed navy blue serge—30% under price.*
Slightly form-fitting single-breasted coat. Collarless vest. Plain or cuff trousers. SIZES: 14 to 19 years; 30 to 35 chest measure; trousers 27 to 32 waistband; and up to 32 inseam.
PRICE, PREPAID to your home, **$13.98**

2K4416 Same style as 2K4415, but made of 100% all wool serge with an alpaca lining.
PRICE, PREPAID to your home, **$17.98**

100% All Wool Serge

2K4132 *A popular style at a popular price—Junior Norfolk suit for the small boy.*
The material is 100% all wool Tearproof serge. If you have shopped for boys' clothing lately we do not need to tell you what an exceptional value an all wool suit at this low price is. Coat has yoke and side plaits to belt. Lined with Albert twill. Full lined knickerbockers. COLOR: Navy blue. SIZES: 5 to 10 years.
PRICE, PREPAID to your home, **$7.78**

2K4418 *The newest style in youth's high school suits—double-breasted model of half-wool "Tearproof" navy blue serge.*
Albert twill lined coat. Collarless vest. Plain or cuff trousers. SIZES: 14 to 19 years; 30 to 35 chest measure; trousers 27 to 32 waist; and from 28 to 32 inseam.
PRICE, PREPAID to your home, **$13.98**
2K4419 Same style as 2K4418 but made of 100% all wool serge, fast color navy blue. High grade alpaca lining.
PRICE, PREPAID to your home, **$17.98**
2K3710 All wool navy blue serge golf cap. SIZES: 6¾ to 7¼.
PRICE, PREPAID to your home, **$1.28**

264

PHILIPSBORN'S Simple One Price to All Policy Is Sweeping the Country. See Page 3

PHILIPSBORN'S

EXTRA!!!—EXTRA!!!

Two Big Reasons Why You Should Wear Philipsborn's Morsnap Clothes

EXTRA QUALITY

Men's and Young Men's 100% All Wool Ultra Smart Fashion Clothes

$18.95

—PREPAID—

2K4406   **Brown Mixture**
2K4407   **Green Mixture**
2K4408   **Navy Blue Serge**

These PHILIPSBORN'S "MORSNAP" suits are the greatest clothing values in the United States, as you will agree when you see the style and the quality of the material.

It is not often that you will find a man's suit 100% all wool at this remarkably low price. The model comes in an **all wool** closely woven **cassimere** in neat brown and green mixtures, specially selected for their good-wearing qualities; also in a firmly woven navy blue **serge**. The illustration shows you the smart lines,—the slightly form-fitting coat with the new style slanting flap pockets, cuff on sleeves, and the new style center vent at the back. The coat is made slightly longer than heretofore in the newest style. Lined in a good quality alpaca and tailored in a first-class manner. Guaranteed to give you the service you would expect from a suit costing $10.00 more. Vest is made in collarless style. Trousers are made with belt loops, two side, two hip, and a watch pocket, and can be had with plain or cuff bottoms. An extraordinary value. SIZES: 34 to 42 chest; 30 to 40 waist measure; 30 and up to 34 inseam.
PRICE, PREPAID
to your home,   **$18.95**

2K4409   **Brown Mixture**
2K4410   **Green Mixture**
2K4411   **Navy Blue Serge**

Here is the very latest "MORSNAP" suit for young men and men who like to dress stylishly. One of the new double-breasted styles, and a wonderful bargain at our price.

We offer you a choice of two materials—either a plain navy blue **serge** or a stylish mixture quoted in the colors above, both every thread **all wool** fabrics. Nobby new double-breasted coat with new long lapels, notch collar, flap pockets, with extra cash pockets and new style derby back as in miniature. Fine quality alpaca lining. SIZES: 34 to 42 chest; 30 to 40 waist measure; 30 and up to 34 inseam.
PRICE, PREPAID
to your home,   **$18.95**

How to Order Suits

Full instructions as to the correct way of taking measurements will be found on page 275 of this catalog.

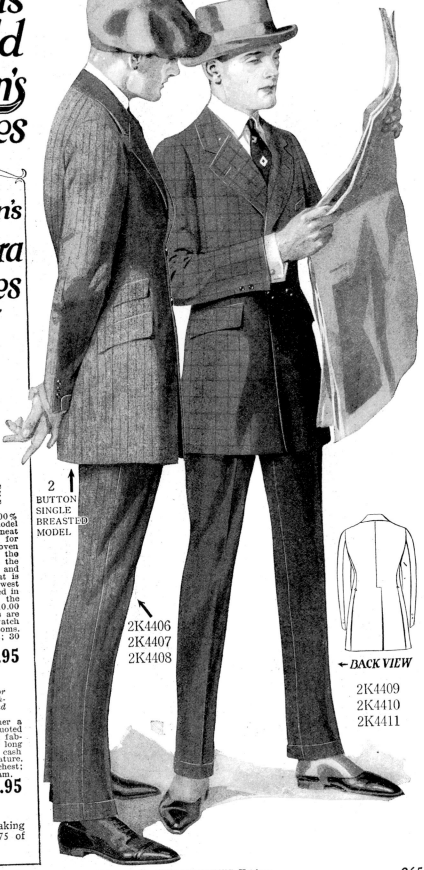

2
BUTTON
SINGLE
BREASTED
MODEL

2K4406
2K4407
2K4408

← BACK VIEW

2K4409
2K4410
2K4411

CHICAGO, ILL.

*There Is Genuine Economy in PHILIPSBORN'S Hosiery.
Consult Pages 209 to 215 and Save Money*

265

Men's and Young Men's Extra
Lowest Reduced Prices

CAP
2K3712
98c

2K4428
2K4429

An Extra Pair Trousers Free With This Suit.

2K4430 *A wonderful value in men's and young men's two-trouser suit.*
At the remarkably low price that we quote on this suit with the two pair of trousers, it is equivalent to getting a pair of trousers free. Made of a firmly woven **100% all wool cassimere** in serviceable shades of brown or green mixture. Double-breasted coat. Collarless vest. Trousers with plain or cuff bottoms. SIZES: 34 to 42 chest; 30 to 42 waist; and 30 to 34 inseam.
PRICE, PREPAID, **$24.98**

2K3712 Men's cap of grey or brown mixed suiting. Will look well with any style of suit. SIZES: 6¾ to 7½.
PRICE, PREPAID. **98c**

2K4428 *A business man's suit at a sensationally low price.*
Here is indeed a wonderful bargain in a man's suit made in a conservative model of a durable **wool-mixed cassimere** in a dark brown or blue mixture. Lined with a fine quality twill. Collarless vest. With four pockets. Trousers may be had in plain or cuff style. Special price $13.98.
SIZES: 34 to 44 chest; 30 to 40 waist; and 30 to 34 inseam. PRICE, **$13.98**
2K4429 Same sizes and style as 2K4428 in a **dark grey worsted**, a wool-mixed material of great durability. A dressy suit that should be good for several seasons' hard wear.
PRICE, PREPAID, **$19.98**

2K4426 *A very special value in a splendid suit for men and young men.*
This conservative model is made of a **wool-mixed serge** that is fast color navy blue. The illustration shows the excellent style of the coat with its flap pockets and soft roll front. Twill lining. Collarless vest. Trousers may be had with plain or cuff bottoms. SIZES: 34 to 44 chest; 30 to 42 waist; and 30 to 34 inseam. PRICE, PREPAID, **$13.98**

2K4427 Same sizes and style as 2K4426 in blue or grey **serge**. Material is a fine quality **100% all wool serge** in a dark navy blue or an Oxford grey.
PRICE, PREPAID, to your home, **$19.98**

Latest Daytona Beach Suits. Tan or Grey

2K4425 *Here is a low-priced durable summer suit that will please you in every way.*
The material is a heavy weight **Daytona beach suiting** in a plain tan or grey with a woven stripe. Will stand any amount of washing and hard wear, and always look fresh and clean. The illustration shows the smart style of the coat which is made unlined and finished with patch pockets. Trousers are made with tunnel loop, five pockets and are finished with cuff bottoms. This is a two-piece suit without a vest. It is made in the best possible manner and will give you all the satisfaction of a high priced suit. SIZES: 34 to 44 chest; 30 to 42 waist; and from 30 to 34 inseam.
PRICE, PREPAID, to your home, **$5.48**

PHILIPSBORN'S

PHILIPSBORN'S Shoes Give Better Service and Satisfaction Than Other Makes—Yet They Are Always Moderately Priced. Refer to Pages 157 to 194.

Quality Morsnap Clothes

Big Saving on Every Suit

Delivered Paid To Your Door

CAP 2K3711

2K4422

Palm Beach
REG. U.S. PAT. OFF.
GENUINE CLOTH
MF'D. BY GOODALL WORSTED CO.

2K4423

2K4400

2K4424

2K4422 *Style, quality and saving in our famous "MOR-SNAP" suits.*

The smart, snappy model pictured above for men and young men is one of our favorite "MORSNAP" suits. It is made of genuine **Palm Beach cloth**, the most popular fabric made for spring and summer wear, and can be furnished in sand, grey, and blue. A suit of this sort is a splendid investment, can be laundered perfectly, and will always retain its fresh, new appearance. The single-breasted two-button coat is finished with three patch pockets,— one outside and one inside pocket. Trousers finished with belt loops, five pockets, and cuff bottoms. SIZES: 34 to 44 chest; 30 to 42 waist; and 30 to 34 inseam. PRICE, PREPAID to your home, **$11.98**
CHICAGO, ILL.

2K4423 *A value without parallel in our finest hand-tailored suit.*

This is an entirely new "MORSNAP" model for men and young men developed in a **fine quality 100% all wool cassimere** in a dark brown or green mixture with an invisible striped effect. Note the illustration for the swagger lines. The coat is designed in the popular two-button single-breasted style with soft roll front. It is slightly form fitting with center vent at back and two side plaits from waist to edge of coat. Collarless vest has **four** pockets. Trousers with plain or cuff bottoms. A suit for style, service, and saving. SIZES: 34 to 42 chest; 30 to 42 waist; and 30 to 34 in eam. PRICE, PREPAID to your home, **$24.95**

2K4400 *A "MORSNAP" suit that combines style, service and saving.*

Designed for men and young men and made of a **100% all wool cassimere** in brown or green mixtures. Single-breasted coat with large patch pockets. Fine quality alpaca lining. Trousers with plain or cuff bottoms. Collarless vest. SIZES: 33 to 42 chest; 30 to 40 waist; and from 30 to 34 inseam. PRICE, PREPAID to your home, **$19.75**
2K3711 Men's golf cap of wool suiting in brown or green mixture. SIZES: 6¾ to 7½. PRICE, PREPAID, **$1.18**

An Extra Pair of Trousers FREE With This Suit

2K4424 *Men's and young men's two-trouser suit at a sensational reduction.*

The material is **100% all wool finely woven cassimere** in grey or brown mixtures. Single-breasted two-button coat with soft front roll. Lined with fine quality alpaca. Collarless vest. Trousers made with plain or cuff bottoms. The extra pair of trousers in this case cost no more than the same suit elsewhere with one pair of trousers. SIZES: 34 to 42 chest; 30 to 40 waist; and from 30 to 34 inseam. PRICE, PREPAID to your home, **$24.95**

For Index See Page 274 and Remember PHILIPSBORN'S Prepay All Transportation Charges.
There Are No Express or Mailing Charges for You to Pay

Men's Extra Quality Raincoats
Guaranteed Absolutely Waterproof

Men's Famous Onorbilt Work Pants
A New Pair Free If they Rip!

2K4600 Grey mixture
2K4601 Tan
Our special price on this men's guaranteed raincoat puts dollars in your pocket.
A big eastern manufacturer who was forced by the recent credit panic to unload an immense stock of overcoats, sold us these coats at 25% below market value. These raincoats are wonderful values at the price we quote, which you can see for yourself when you examine the material, —a durable quality **Asia cloth**. The material is furnished either in a dark grey mixture or a plain tan, with plaid lining with rubber between to make the garment absolutely waterproof. Features that give the model swagger style are the removable belt, and the slash pockets with opening to the clothing underneath. Collar may be buttoned high as shown in the small illustration. Ventilated armholes. A raincoat of this type makes an excellent general service coat, as it is equally appropriate either for rain or sunshine. SIZES: 34 to 46 chest. Average length 48 inches. PRICE, PREPAID to your home, **$6.98**

2K4602 Dark green mixture
2K4603 Dark brown mixture
You haven't seen values like these men's raincoats in five years.
They are extra quality garments, guaranteed absolutely waterproof, and equally suitable for rain or sunshine. Their low price and high quality will interest men who have been paying $15.00 and $20.00 for raincoats. The material is a **Tweed** effect in dark green or dark brown mixtures, with plaid lining and rubber between. Finished with a removable belt and patch pockets with flaps in regulation overcoat style. The appearance of this raincoat is so stylish that it really does not look like a raincoat at all but makes an excellent top coat for general wear—really two coats in one. Collar is convertible to high closing as shown in miniature. An astounding value and an unusually snappy style besides. SIZES: 34 to 46 chest. Average length 46 inches. PRICE, PREPAID to your home, **$10.98**

2K3602 Men's khaki work pants at a bargain price.
Good quality, good weight olive tan khaki, all seams double stitched. SIZES: 30 to 42 waist; 30 to 34 inseam. PRICE, PREPAID to your home. **$1.48**

2K3601 For hard wear—men's grey striped pants cottonade.
Think of getting pants of this quality for only $1.98. SIZES: 30 to 42 waist; 30 to 34 inseam. PRICE, PREPAID to your home, **$1.98**

2K3603 Men's serviceable work pants at a big saving.
Made of a grey striped moleskin. One of the best wearing materials made. SIZES: 30 to 42 waist; 30 to 34 inseam. PRICE PREPAID to your home, **$2.98**

2K3605 A bargain in men's corduroy work pants at $2.98.
A strongly woven wide wale corduroy in serviceable drab color. The right kind for hard wear. SIZES: 30 to 42 waist; 30 to 34 inseam. PRICE, PREPAID to your home. **$2.98**

2K3606 One of the most durable work pants made.
Material is dark grey Kentucky jean, noted for its great durability. All seams double stitched. SIZES: 30 to 42 waist; 30 to 34 inseam. PRICE, PREPAID to your home. **$2.68**

2K3604 Khaki
2K3617 Corduroy
Men's riding breeches.
Comes in either olive drab khaki or thick-set tan corduroy. SIZES: 30 to 42 waist; 30 to 34 inseam.
2K3604 PRICE, PR'PD, **$2.48**
2K3617 PRICE, PR'PD, **$4.98**

PHILIPSBORN'S

Extra Quality Morsnap Dress Trousers For Men and Young Men!
Big Saving on Every Pair!!

2K3607 *One of our greatest values we have ever offered in men's trousers.* Of manipulated blue serge. Plain or cuff bottoms. SIZES: 30 to 42 waist; 30 to 34 inseam. PRICE, PREPAID to your home, **$2.98**

2K3609 *An interesting value in men's stylish trousers at $2.68.* Made of dark grey cotton worsted. Well tailored. SIZES: 30 to 42 waist, 30 to 34 inseam. PRICE, PREP'D to your home. **$2.68**

2K3608 *Think of getting men's all wool blue serge trousers at $3.98.* Fast color navy blue. Fine, dressy texture. Very durable. SIZES: 30 to 42 waist, 30 to 34 inseam. PRICE, PREP'D to your home, **$3.98**

Up To Date Snappy Young Men's Models

2K3612 *Young men's blue serge trousers in high school sizes.* Of fast color navy blue wool-and-cotton-mixed serge—50% wool. Will give splendid satisfaction. A great value. SIZES: 28 to 32 waist and inseam. PRICE, PREPAID. **$2.88**

2K3614 *Grey mixture cassimere trousers for youths and young men.* Firmly woven wool-mixed cassimere in a neat dark grey stripe. Cut over smart young men's models. SIZES: 28 to 32 waist and inseam. PRICE, PREPAID. **$3.48**

2K3613 *Young men's all wool blue serge trousers at a big price cut.* A remarkable saving on trousers that are fast color and 100% all wool. Dressy and durable. SIZES: 28 to 32 waist and inseam. PRICE, PREPAID to your home, **$3.88**

Men's Worsted Trousers

2K3610 Grey worsted
2K3611 Grey striped worsted
2K3610 *Men's worsted trousers offered at a bargain price.* Made of a firmly woven wool-mixed worsted that has been selected for its good wearing qualities. Comes in gray striped. Plain or cuff bottoms. SIZES: 30 to 42 waist; 30 to 34 inseam. PRICE, PREPAID to your home, **$4.98**

2K3611 Men's all wool worsted trousers at about regular wholesale cost. Same style and sizes as 2K3610. Made in a neat dark grey stripe that will look well with any style coat. It will always retain its fine appearance as it is 100% all wool. PRICE, PREPAID to your home, **$6.98**

Young Men's Worsted Trousers

2K3615 Dark grey cotton worsted
2K3616 Dark grey striped wool-mixed worsted
2K3615 *Young men's trousers at a price that cannot be equalled.* A firmly woven worsted-finished cloth in a neat dark grey stripe. SIZES: 28 to 32 waist and inseam. PRICE, PREPAID to your home, **$2.48**
2K3616 Young men's high grade wool-mixed worsted trousers in same style and sizes as above. Dark grey stripe. PRICE, PREPAID to your home, **$3.98**

How to Order Men's Trousers

In ordering men's trousers be sure to state size of waist and inseam; also if whether plain or cuff bottoms are desired and whether you wear suspenders or a belt.

For Men's Gloves, Handkerchiefs, and Other Dress Accessories Refer to Index, Page 274

CHICAGO, ILL.

BACK VIEW

Philipsborns Famous Onorbilt
EXTRA QUALITY
A New Pair

BACK VIEW

TRIPLE STITCHED SEAMS

RIVETED NON-RUST BUTTONS

RIP-PROOF BUTTON HOLES

CONTINUOUS SEAMS

Double Front

Philipsborn's Extra Special Guaranteed Non-Rip Features.

Philipsborn's
Onorbilt Work Clothes
GUARANTEED TO GIVE ABSOLUTE SATISFACTION
WELL FITTING FULL ROOMY SIZES
STRONGLY LOCKED STITCHED
A NEW GARMENT *FREE* IF THEY RIP.
PHILIPSBORN'S, Inc.,   CHICAGO

Lot 3801   Size 42

*A Fac-simile of our
Guarantee Label
Your Protection
That You Are
Getting the Best*

2K3807
2K3808
2K3809

2K3805
2K3806

2K3801
2K3810

SIZES FOR ALL GARMENTS ON THIS PAGE ARE AS FOLLOWS:
Overalls 30 to 44 Waist, 30 to 36 Inseam.
Jackets 36 to 46 Chest.

2K3807 Suspender Back Overall
2K3808 High Back Overall
Bargain in men's "ONORBILT" overalls of heavy white-backed denim, the best wearing cloth made.
Two swinging pockets, two back pockets, rule pocket, watch and pencil pocket.
PRICE, PREPAID to your home,   **$1.78**
2K3809 Coat to match above overalls. Four patch pockets. Removable buttons.
PRICE, PREPAID to your home,   **$1.78**
Complete suit consisting of overalls and coat to match.
PRICE, PREPAID to your home,   **$3.50**

2K3805 Blue Denim
2K3806 Khaki
Here is one of the most practical and satisfactory of "ONORBILT" coverall suits at $2.48.
None better made.   The material is a heavy weight **double** and **twist blue denim** or **tan khaki drill.** One of the best union suits made—suitable for mechanics or any man who has to do his own work. Completely covers and protects your regular clothing. Men who know values will appreciate the quality in these suits.
PRICE, PREPAID to your home, EACH **$2.48**

2K3801 High Back
2K3810 Suspender Back
The double reinforced fronts with which these men's "ONORBILT" overalls are made insure extra service.
They are offered at a special reduction in price, the result of big cuts which manufacturers have made to us, and we in turn are cutting the price to you. Made of a heavy weight **double** and **twist denim** with full double fronts below the knee to give double wear. Two swinging pockets, back pockets, and rule pocket.
PRICE, PREPAID to your home, EACH **$1.78**

*PHILIPSBORN'S Underwear for Men Costs Less and Wears Better Than Ordinary Makes.
See Our Underwear Section, Pages 239, 240, 241*
PHILIPSBORN'S

Guaranteed Work Clothes.
If They Rip.

2K3814 *The non-rip features of these "ONORBILT" waist-band pants overalls insure longer wear and help you to economize—a new pair if they rip.*

These pants overalls are preferred by many men and are made of heavy weight **double and twist denim**. Reinforced with double front. Five pockets. One of the best-wearing overalls made. Don't forget we give you a new pair if they rip. **PRICE,** PREPAID to your home, **$1.68**

2K3811
2K3812

2K3800
2K3813

2K3803
2K3804

SIZES FOR ALL GARMENTS ON THIS PAGE ARE AS FOLLOWS:
Overalls 30 to 44 Waist, 30 to 36 Inseam.
Jackets 36 to 46 Chest.

Special

2K3802 *For good hard wear —"ONORBILT" work jacket.* Made of heavy **double** and **twist** blue **denim**, and strongly reinforced and guaranteed not to rip. Four patch pockets. Strongly reinforced and guaranteed not to rip. Will match overalls 2K3800 and 2K3813 on this page, also 2K3810 and 2K 3410 on page 270. Upper left hand pocket, combination watch and pencil pocket. **PRICE,** PREPAID to your home, **$1.38**
CHICAGO, ILL.

2K3811 High Back Overalls
2K3812 Jacket to Match
Men's "ONORBILT" work clothes at a 25% reduction from regular prices.
Made of heavy **Stifel drill** in a blue and white Wabash stripe. Two swinging pockets, rule pockets, and two patch pockets in rear. Bib has combination watch and pencil pocket. **PRICE,** PREPAID to your home, **$1.18**
2K3812 "ONORBILT" work jacket to match overalls. Three patch pockets. PRICE, **$1.18**
PREPAID to your home, **$1.18**
Complete Suit, PRICE, PREPAID to your home, **$2.25**

2K3800 High Back
2K3813 Suspender Back
Astounding price cuts in men's "ONORBILT" overalls. Worth every cent of $2.00.
These overalls are made of a heavy weight **double** and **twist denim**, noted for its good-wearing qualities. Finished with two swinging pockets at front, two patch pockets in rear, and rule pocket. Bib has combination watch and pencil pocket. Here is a value that you will find hard to equal at our low price. Remember our guarantee—a new pair if they rip. **PRICE,** PREPAID to your home, **$1.38**

2K3803 Overalls
2K3804 Jacket to Match
Men's "ONORBILT" overalls and jacket of hickory striped drill.
This material will stand any amount of wear, and will wash perfectly. Overalls finished with five pockets, and jacket finished with four pockets. Riveted buttons. **PRICE,** PREPAID to your home, **98c**
2K3804 Jacket to match above overalls.
PRICE, PREPAID to your home, **98c**
Complete Suit. PRICE, PREPAID to your home, **$1.90**

See Page 274 for Index and Don't Forget When Ordering to State the Color and Size Desired

Men's Famous Onorbilt Double-Wear Work Shirts

Blue or Grey Chambray
Built on   Honor
Extra Heavy Chambray

THE STRONGEST WORK SHIRT THAT IT IS POSSIBLE TO MAKE

2K3500 Light blue.   **2K3502** Grey.
Men's double-wear chambray work shirts at an unequaled low price.
Material is firmly woven and absolutely fast color. Full liberal sizes; Lay-down collar. SIZES: 14 to 17, neckband. (Half sizes.)
PRICE, PREPAID to your home, **78c**

2K3501 *One of the best men's work shirts made. Will outwear any two ordinary work shirts, all seams triple stitched. A bargain.*
Made of a heavy weight smooth-finished **navy blue chambray.** Double back. (See miniature.) Watch and pencil pockets. SIZES: 14 to 17 neckband. (Half sizes.)
PRICE. PREPAID to your home, **$1.28**

2K3504 Dark blue. **2K3510** Blue stripe.
Men's two good work shirts of extra heavy weight chambray in above patterns. Plain solid blue or blue with light stripe. Strong, double stitched seams. SIZES: 14 to 17 neckband. Also in half sizes.
PRICE, PREPAID to your home, **88c**

Blue Chambray   Khaki Twill

Sizes of all Shirts on This Page are 14 to 17

Blue Chambray   Stiffel Drill or Black Sateen

2K3508 *Men's blue* chambray *sport shirt.* Made of a firmly woven chambray in a light blue shade. Collar buttons high if desired. Short sleeves. SIZES: 14 to 17 neckband. (Half sizes.)
PRICE, PREPAID. **98c**

2K3507 *A very popular number in a man's shirt.* Made of firmly woven fast color khaki twill. Will stand any amount of washing. SIZES: 14 to 17 neckband. (Also half sizes.)
PRICE, PREPAID. **$1.18**

2K3503 *A favorite style work shirt for men.* Made of a firmly woven light blue chambray that will wear and wash excellently. Link buttons. SIZES: 14 to 17 neckband. (Half sizes.)
PRICE, PREP'D, **$1.39**

2K3506 Blue Stifel
2K3511 Black Sateen
Men's work shirts either in blue Stifel with polka dot or black sateen. SIZES: 14 to 17 neckband.
2K3506 PRICE, PREPAID. **98c**
2K3511 PRICE, PREPAID, **98c**

Double Front Extra Strong

Extra Double Back and Elbows

100% ALL WOOL JERSEY

2K3509 *For the man who wants an extra durable shirt, we recommend this number. Will outwear two ordinary shirts.*
Man's work shirt made of heavy blue chambray with double yoke and back. Double armholes and double elbows to give double service. An excellent value. SIZES: 14 to 17 neckband (also in half sizes). PRICE, PREPAID, **$1.28**

2K3901 *A splendid sweater for athletics and general wear—100% all wool Jersey offered at a big price reduction.*
Comes in your choice of navy blue and red, black and orange, maroon and white. A garment that can be depended upon for good hard service. A challenge value in every respect. SIZES: 34 to 46 chest. PRICE, PREPAID, **$2.98**

2K3505 *Here is an extra strong work shirt, which is reinforced with double fronts from shoulders to pockets.*
The material is a heavy weight smooth-finished blue chambray of great durability. Designed for the man who wishes an extra serviceable shirt. Sure to please you and to save you money at our low price. SIZES: 14 to 17 neckband (also in half sizes). PRICE, PREPAID. **$1.08**

"A Thing or Two to Remember" and Some Other Interesting Facts to Be Found on Page 3

PHILIPSBORN'S

Philipsborn's Men's DeLuxe Dress Shirts

EXTRA QUALITY

Fit Better   Look Better   Wear Better   Cost Less

An Extra Special Philipsborn's EXTRA QUALITY Value

A Collar Free With

This Shirt

2K3551 *Here is a De Luxe dress shirt for men at a bargain price. Sold elsewhere at great deal higher prices.*
The material is a fine count **percale** in a white ground with assorted colored stripes, guaranteed fast color. A bargain that will be hard to duplicate at our money-saving price. Here is the sort of shirt that will appeal to the man who wants something extra good for best wear. Made with open turned-back cuffs. SIZES: 14 to 17 neckband. (Made in half sizes.) PRICE, PREPAID to your home, **98c**

2K3553 *One of our most popular De Luxe dress shirts for men—an excellent style that is sure to please.* Made of a fine quality **percale** in white ground with assorted colored stripes. Collar to match is free with shirt. Will look equally well with a white collar. SIZES: 14 to 17 neckband. (Made in half sizes.) PRICE, PREPAID to your home, **$1.48**

2K3556 *Shirts of fine quality at an unusually attractive price—a fact that you will recognize when you see them.*
This is a fine **woven madras** shirt, and as everybody knows there is no material that will give better satisfaction. The rich appearance of the beautiful assorted colored stripes that are guaranteed fast color makes it a popular style with the average man. Guaranteed fast color. SIZES: 14 to 17 neckband. (Made in half sizes.) PRICE, PREPAID to your home, **$1.48**

All Shirts Shown on This Page Come in Sizes 14, 14½, 15, 15½, 16, 16½ and 17 neckband

A Collar Free With this Shirt

Extra Quality Fibre Silk

2K3552 *Men's sport shirt of striped percale.* White ground with colored stripes, short sleeves and convertible collar. SIZES: 14 to 17 neckband. PRICE, PREPAID, **$1.28**

2K3554 *Men's shirt of linen-finished cotton.* Collar to match. Very dressy. COLORS: Blue, pink, or lavender. SIZES: 14 to 17 neckband. PRICE, PREPAID, **$1.98**

2K3557 *Men's high grade fibre silk shirt.* Beautiful assorted colored stripes on a white ground. Looks like pure silk. SIZES: 14 to 17 neckband. PRICE, PREP'D to your home, **$3.48**

2K3555 *The ideal sport shirt for men.* Made of fine white **Oxford cloth** with buttoned-down collar. A big value. SIZES: 14 to 17 neckband. PRICE, PREPAID, **$1.88**

2K3550 *A value that is impossible to duplicate. Men's shirt with attached collar—very special at our price of 96c.*
The material is fast color firmly woven **percale**, with attached lay-down collar. Open turnback cuffs. You have only to compare our prices with those charged in your local shops to realize the wonderful saving that we are offering you in this shirt. SIZES: 14 to 17 neckband. Assorted stripe. (Half sizes.) PRICE, PREPAID to your home, **96c**

CHICAGO, ILL.

3 Colors—Navy—Maroon—or Grey

2K3900 *Here is a sweater that in price and quality is sure to please you.*
Jumbo knit model, made of good quality wool-mixed yarns. Comfortable fit. Finely finished and will give unlimited amount of service. COLORS: Navy blue, maroon or grey. SIZES: 34 to 46 chest. PRICE, PREPAID, **$3.98**

2K3558 *An excellent style for men who like a shirt with the collar attached, and one of our biggest bargains.*
It is made of a fine quality white corded **madras** that will wear well and always look well. It is finished with open, buttoned cuffs and soft, attached collar. This is indeed a fine value, and one that you will find hard to equal at our remarkably low price. SIZES: 14 to 17 neckband. (Half sizes.) PRICE, PREP'D. **$1.28**

INDEX

EXCLUSIVE DESIGNS BY IRENE CASTLE INDICATED IN BLACK FACE TYPE

How to Return Goods

Should it be necessary to return merchandise, please follow these instructions:

All tags MUST be left attached to articles you are returning.

Be sure to write your full name and address on the outside of the package, on the upper left hand corner.

Write us a letter, stating your reasons for returning goods, and tell us what you wish in exchange. In addition, be sure to state the following:

1.—Your full name and address.
2.—Style number and price of each item returned.
3.—Date order was sent, amount of money sent and from what postoffice.
4.—Style numbers, colors, sizes and prices of merchandise wanted in exchange.

Place a two-cent stamp on your letter of instruction and paste the letter securely to the package you are returning. Remember, it is a violation of the Postal Laws to enclose letters or any written matter whatsoever in packages. Your letter should be placed on the OUTSIDE of the package and not mailed separately.

Bear in mind please that the 2c postage is only for the letter. The package too, requires postage in amount according to its weight.

Secure a receipt for your package from the postmaster or rural carrier. This receipt will cost you 1c extra, and must be enclosed with your letter of instruction. We cannot adjust claims without this receipt, so be sure to enclose it with your letter.

Goods on which you desire an exchange or a refund must be returned within ten days after you receive them. We positively will not accept either for exchange or refund goods not returned within this ten-day limit.

Canadian and other foreign customers must ask for necessary affidavits to secure a refund of duty before returning goods.

Use This Blank for Ordering

PHILIPSBORN'S
CHICAGO

I send you this order with the understanding that if I am not completely satisfied, I can return the goods and you will exchange them for other merchandise or refund my money.

If a married woman, write "Mrs." and Husband's first name and middle initial.

1 Is this your first order to us? Please answer YES or NO. _____

2 If we are sending our catalog to more than one member of your family, please give here the names

we should remove from our mailing list _____

3 Please give here the name of the head of your household. This will help us in keeping records.

Name of head of household _____

Mrs., Miss or Mr.	FIRST NAME	Middle Initial	LAST NAME

POST OFFICE _____

STATE _____

R. F. D. No. _____ Box No. _____

STREET and No. _____

CHANGE OF ADDRESS should be brought to our notice so that we may serve you to best advantage. If you have moved recently or any change of post-office address has been made, kindly write the old address here.

PREVIOUS ADDRESS _____

BE SURE TO LIST REMITTANCE HERE

Enclosed please find	Dollars	Cts.
Draft or Check		
P. O. Money Order		
Exp. Money Order		
Credit Check		
Currency		
Postage Stamps		
Have we any money belong'ng to you? How much?		

Total Amount _____

Remit either by Post Office, Express Office Money Order, Bank Draft, Currency or Check. Stamps are not acceptable for order over **50 cents**. Please send **5** and **10**-cent stamps only.

C. O. D. Orders. If desired we will accept C. O. D. orders and ship same subject to examination on your part. You can remit part payment or we will ship total amount of order C. O. D. Of course all C. O. D. orders are subject to shipping and collection charges.

Canada. We do not solicit business from Canada.

Goods in possession of our customers longer than 10 days cannot be returned for exchange or credit.

Do not write in this space

 ## BE VERY SURE TO GIVE
COLORS and SIZES

Delivery Charges are PREPAID by us on Every Article Shown in This Catalogue

The LUXURY TAX is also paid for by us and the prices quoted are the total cost to you. There are no extra charges of any kind at PHILIPSBORN'S

Page	Cat. No. of Article	Quantity	ARTICLE	COLOR	BUST	Waist Band	HIP	Front Length of Skirt	Shoes, Hosiery or Gloves Size	Width	Corset Size	Waist Size	Side Length of Draw's	AGE	Height	Dollars	Cts.

In Giving Corset Measurements State Whether it is Your Actual Corset Size or Waist Measurement — For Corsets. *For Girl's Boy's and Children's Garments.* TOTAL PRICE

For Men's and Young Men's Clothing Please Refer to and Fill Out Diagram on the Reverse Side of This Blank

IMPORTANT NOTICE — If any of the above goods are out of stock, may we substitute a similar style of equal or better value? State Yes or No .... **TOTAL**

It Is Easy to Be Fitted at Philipsborn's

Just Follow Rules Below for Taking Measurements

A CORRECT TAPE MEASURE FURNISHED FREE—ASK FOR IT

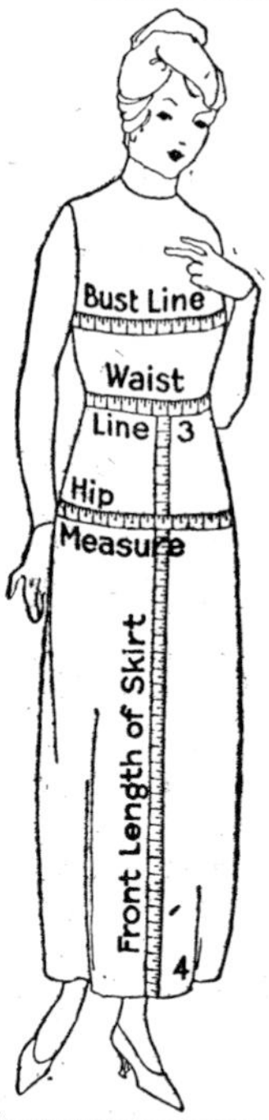

Ladies' and Misses' Garments

How to Find Your Size:

It is very easy to get perfect-fitting garments at **PHILIPSBORN'S**. All you need to do is to have your measurements taken exactly as we describe and picture here and then write them carefully on the other side of this blank.

There is just one proper way to learn your correct size—that is by actually having your measurements taken—not guessing at it.

Therefore, please have your measurements taken according to the diagram shown here, and be sure to use an accurate tape measure.

PHILIPSBORN'S garments are shaped so perfectly and made so carefully that we need to know only a few simple measurements to insure your getting a perfect-fitting garment.

Bust Measure—(Take measurement over shirt-waist or over your dress.) Pass tape measure entirely around the body over the fullest part of the bust, well up under the arms. Do not take this measurement too tight and do not allow tape measure to slip down in back. Make no allowance whatever.

Waist Measure—Take this measurement around smallest part of waist over your skirt.

Hip Measure—Take measurement around hips over skirt, seven inches below waistline, not too tight. Do not allow tape measure to slip up or down.

Length of Skirt or Petticoat—Measure from top of waistband in front (3) to length desired (4). This measurement should be taken from the natural waistline.

Our suits or overcoats for young men are tailored to fit any build or shape. It makes no difference whether you are of regular build or tall or short, thin or stout, we can fit you, or your money back.

First, select model by catalog number. State color desired and then give the measurements required below.

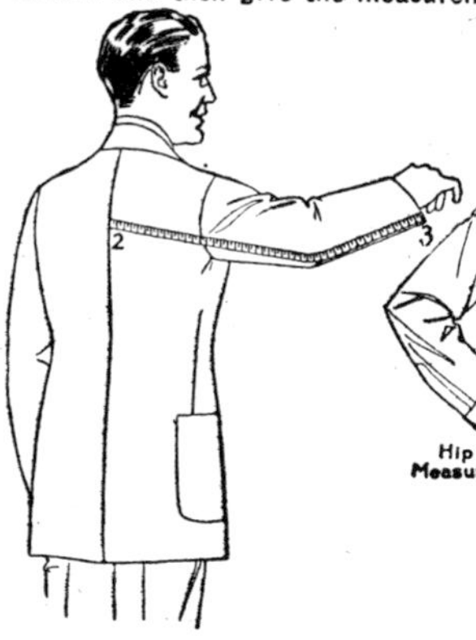

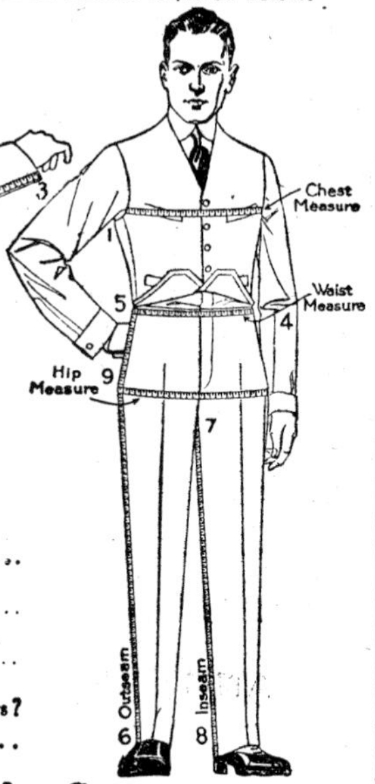

Height ....

Weight ....

Age ....

Do You Wear Belt or Suspenders?

....

How to Order Suits:

Inches

Remove all bulky articles from your pockets

Sleeve Measure—With coat on, measure sleeve length taken from center-back seam (2 on diagram) over elbow to wrist joint (3) as illustrated ....

Coat Measure—With your coat off, take your chest measure over vest (at figure 1). Pass tape measure entirely around body, close up under arms, not too tight ....

Vest Measure—Pass tape measure around body close up under arms (at figure 1) ....

Trousers Measure—Turn up vest at bottom as pictured. Pass tape measure around body at waist over trousers (at figure 4) ....

Hip Measure—Pass tape measure all around body at hips over largest part of seat (at figure 9) ....

Inside Seam—Measure from close up in crotch at (7 on diagram) to heel of shoe (8). Take measurement always to the heel. We will make necessary allowance if cuff bottoms are desired ....

Outside Seam—Measure from top of waistband of trousers (5 on diagram) to heel of shoe (6). Take measurement always to the heel. We will make necessary allowance if cuff bottoms are desired ....

How to Order Top Coats:

Overcoats

Chest Measure—With your coat off, take your chest measure over vest (see 1 on diagram) the same as for a suit coat. Pass tape measure entirely around body, close up under arms, not too tight. We will send you a coat that will fit you perfectly ....

Be sure to give height, weight and age when ordering.

Below are Measurements Required

Be Sure to State All Sizes Carefully

Boys' Clothing—Give age required. State chest measure, height and weight. See suggestions below.

Children's Dresses—Coats—Give age, also if large, small or average size for age.

Clothing, Men's and Young Men's—State all detail measurements required on chart.

Coats, Ladies', Misses' and Juniors'—Give bust measure.

Corsets—To find your correct corset size, follow directions as stated in our descriptions. Be sure to state whether the size given is your corset or waist measurement.

Dresses—Ladies', Misses' and Juniors'—Give bust and waist measure and the length of skirt in front.

Dresses—House—Give bust measure only.

Gloves—See diagram below.

Hosiery—See schedule of sizes as given below.

Kimonos—Give bust measure only.

Petticoats—Give waist measure and front length.

Shoes—See instructions below.

Skirts—Give waist and hip measure, also length in front. (See diagram.)

Suits—Ladies' or Misses'—Give bust, waist and hip measure, also length of skirt in front. (See diagram.)

Underwear—For Gowns, Corset Covers, Brassieres, Princess Slips, Combinations, Knit Vests and Union Suits, give bust measure only. Drawers, give side length. State whether open or closed style. For Petticoats, give front length. For Men's underwear give chest and waist measure.

Waists—Give bust measure (if you want your waist full and blousy, order one or two sizes larger than your actual measure).

How to Order Gloves:

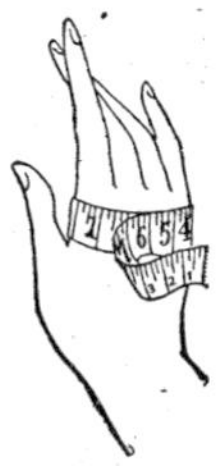

Measure the hand over the knuckles. Draw the tape measure close but not tight. The number of inches your hand measures is the size glove you wear. Never order gloves too small. If your hand measures a little larger than a regular size, order the next larger size. For instance: If your hand measures 6⅜ inches order size 6½. **And in ordering be sure to state size and color desired.**

Children's and Girls' Garments:

If the child is of average size, simply order by age. If you cannot tell size required, give age, chest measure and length desired and we will send the correct size. Unless otherwise stated in the description of the articles, Children's Coats and Dresses are carried in sizes from 2 to 6 years; Girls' Coats from 8 to 14 years; Girls' Dresses from 6 to 14 years.

How to Order Hosiery

If you know what size you wear, order that size. If you do not know, order the size corresponding to the size shoe you wear, following this schedule.

Women's			
Size of Shoe	1½ to 2½	3 to 4½	5 to 6
Size of Hosiery	8½	9	9½
Size of Shoe		6½ to 7	7½ to 8
Size of Hosiery		10	10½

Men's			
Size Shoe	5½–6	6½–7	7½–8
Size Socks	9½	10	10½
Size Shoe		8½–9½	10–11
Size Socks		10½	11

Infants' and Children's						
Size Shoe	1	2	3	4–5	6–7	8–9
Size Stocking	4	4½	5	5½	6	6½

Boys' and Girls'						
Size Shoe	3	4–5	6–7	8–9	10–11	12–13
Size Stocking	5	5½	6	6½	7	7½
Size Shoe	1–2	3	4	5–6	7–8	
Size Stocking	8	8½	9	9½	10	

How to Order Hats and Caps for Men and Boys

Head Measurement in Inches	Hat Sizes	Head Measurement in Inches	Hat Sizes
19⅜	6⅛	22¼	7
19¾	6¼	22½	7⅛
20¼	6⅜	23	7¼
20¾	6½	23⅜	7⅜
21	6⅝	23¾	7½
21½	6¾	24	7⅝
21⅝	6⅞	24½	7¾

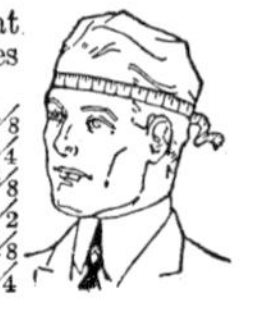

Boys' sizes run from 6 to 7.

Men's sizes run from 6⅝ to 7¾.

If you know what size hat or cap you wear, order by that size. If you don't know your correct size, have your measurement taken as we show you here. Order the hat size which most nearly agrees with your measurement.

How to Order Shoes:

If possible, give the exact marks in your old shoes. If you are unable to do this, then take your measurement according to the **"Easy Measure Chart"** which you will find in the **Shoe Section** of our large catalogue. You will find this a simple, convenient and unfailing way to tell your correct size. We guarantee to fit you if instructions are carefully followed.

How to Order Boys' Clothing:

Some boys, aged 8, require a 10 year old suit or blouse or pants. In ordering your boys' clothing **BE SURE to state the age he requires** — not his actual age—and allow for him to grow a bit. Chest measure, weight and height will help us send you a perfect fitting outfit.

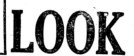

LOOK

Before you mail this order make certain you have given the SIZE and COLOR. We cannot fill your order without this.

Sensational Savings!!!
Boys' Morsnap and Tearproof Suits

CAP
2K3706

2K4412 *Students' Flannel Suit. Very Special at our price $14.98 —a bargain that will be hard to duplicate at our low price.* One of our popular "MOR-SNAP" models, made of a fine smooth-finished **flannel** about 50% wool. Double-breasted, slightly form-fitting coat. Collarless vest. Cuff bottom trousers. COLORS: Green, navy blue, or brown. SIZES: 30 to 35 chest; 27 to 32 waist; and up to 32 inseam. Suitable for boys 15 to 19 yrs. PRICE, PREPAID, **$14.98**

2K4107 *We quote a sensationally low price on this all wool knickerbocker suit for boys— unequaled for service.* It is made of **all wool cassimere**, every thread wool, and is designed in popular Norfolk style. Plaited back. Removable belt. Lined with Albert twill. Full-lined trousers. COLORS: Brown or grey mixtures. SIZES: 8 to 17 years. PRICE, PREPAID, **$7.48**

2K4107
$7.48

Extra Pair Trousers Free With This Suit

2K4413 *A snappy all wool two trouser suit for only $22.75—a real bargain.* It is made of 100% all wool **smooth-finished cassimere** in the popular herringbone effect in grey or brown mixtures. "MORSNAP" model with two-buttoned single-breasted coat, lined with a fine quality alpaca. Collarless vest. Cuff trousers. SIZES 30 to 35 chest; 27 to 32 waist; and up to 32 inseam. Suitable for boys 15 to 19 yrs. PRICE, PREP'D, **$22.75**

2K3706 Boys' and young men's cap made of fine quality woolen suiting. To be worn with suit 2K4413. Unlined. Grey or brown mixture. SIZES: 6⅝ to 7¼. PRICE, PREP'D **98c**

SUIT
2K4108
CAP
2K3707

2K4414 *Here is an entirely new model in a students suit, and one of the most durable. Very Special at our price, $17.48.* "MORSNAP" two-button single-breasted model of 100% all wool **cassimere** in brown or green mixtures. Coat with lower patch pocket and welt pocket at top. Center vent at back and two side plaits from waist down. SIZES: 30 to 35 chest; 27 to 32 waist and up to 32 inseam. Suitable for boys 15 to 19 years. PRICE, PREPAID to your home, **$17.48**

2K4108 *Spectacular sale of boys' flannel suits—a dressy, but at the same time a very durable model.* The material is a smooth-finished **flannel** about 50% wool in blue, brown or green. Alpaca lined coat. Full-lined knickerbocker trousers. SIZES: 8 to 17 years. PRICE, PREPAID to your home, **$7.98**

2K3707 Boys' all wool blue serge cap. SIZES: 6½ to 7⅛. PRICE, PREPAID, **68c**

277

PHILIPSBORN'S, CHICAGO, ILL.

Tremendous Values!!!
Young Men's *Morsnap* Style Suits
100% All Wool

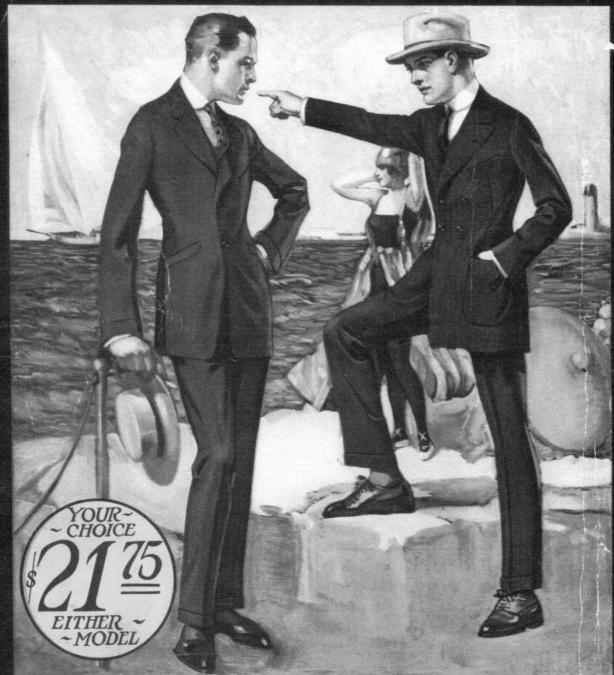

YOUR CHOICE $21.75 EITHER MODEL